About the Author

As a Chartered Mechanical Engineer and member of the Institute of Mechanical Engineers, Almeric was trained to solve presented engineering problems. As Chief Engineer and in other executive roles he was predominantly required to solve organisational problems.

Although a member of the Chartered Management Institute, he read for a Master's degree in Organisational Analysis and Development, at the University of Bath, focusing on the psychology of individual and group decision-making behaviour. Within his studies he examined the socio-technical needs that surfaced through the introduction of new technologies.

Almeric would consider himself to be an organisational problem-solving journeyman who constantly strives to improve his own and others' performance. He works with an applied assumption that all leaders and managers in organisations share the same intent.

Almeric is the founder of The Centre for Organisational Management. This focuses on improving the quality of leaders' and managers' decision-making to enable individuals, teams and the whole organisation to succeed. Executive coaching programmes are designed to enable the individual and their teams to directly transfer the developed competencies into the performance of their organisation.

This book is dedicated to my dear and beloved sister Ann.

Almeric Johnson
MSc. (Bath), C.Eng., M.I.Mech.E., M.C.M.I., C.H.P.C.

LEADERSHIP AND ORGANISATIONAL PROBLEM SOLVING: LEARNING TO LEAD AND MANAGE THE ORGANISATIONAL MAZE

AUSTIN MACAULEY
PUBLISHERS LTD.

A CIP catalogue record for this title is available from the British Library.

ISBN 9781785546624 (Paperback)
ISBN 9781785546631 (Hardback)
ISBN 9781785546648 (E-Book)

www.austinmacauley.com

First Published (2016)
Austin Macauley Publishers Ltd.
25 Canada Square
Canary Wharf
London
E14 5LQ

*Developing the Necessary Organisational Leadership and
Management Competencies to Enable You and Your Organisation
to Thrive in Today's Business Environment*

"We are all redundant if we have yesterday's skills."

A. Toffler

CONTENTS

PRELUDE 14

NOTE OF TERMS USED 18

LIST OF FIGURES 19

LIST OF TABLES 19

ACKNOWLEDGMENTS 21

INTRODUCTION 22

SECTION ONE
BACKGROUND, UNDERSTANDING AND DEVELOPED
ORGANISATIONAL THINKING 30

PART ONE: Dysfunctional Organisational Behaviour 31

CHAPTER ONE
Identifying the Problem 32

CHAPTER TWO
Why Organisations Become Dysfunctional (A Systems Perspective) 45

CHAPTER THREE
The Enemy Within and Why Change Fails (A Behavioural Perspective)   64

PART TWO: Developing a Theory in Practice 95
Goals and Introduction 96

CHAPTER FOUR
Developing A Theory In Practice (Part One)
(Understanding what is being led and managed) 98

CHAPTER FIVE
Developing A Theory In Practice (Part Two)
(The inter-related behaviour of the individual, the group, the organisation and
its environment) 123

SECTION TWO
APPLICATION OF AN ORGANISATIONAL APPROACH 151

PART THREE: Leading Transition for Change 152

CHAPTER SIX
Leading Transition For Change 155

CHAPTER SEVEN
Adaptive Organisational Leadership 177

CHAPTER EIGHT
Workgroups: Leadership Positioning In Workgroups 208

PART FOUR: Technology Change and Managing the Consequences 239
Goals and Introduction 240

CHAPTER NINE
Technology Change And Managing The Consequences 242

CHAPTER TEN
Outsourcing And Contractual Practices
Decision Making and Implementation 272

CHAPTER ELEVEN
Remuneration And Motivation 298

CHAPTER TWELVE
Training, Development and Recruitment 330

PART FIVE: Case Studies 360
Goals and Introduction 361

CASE STUDY ONE
INDUSTRIAL TRANSITION
Influencing Strategic Decision-Making 366

CASE STUDY TWO
AVONMOUTH
Wet Processing, Packaging and Distribution Site 385

CASE STUDY THREE
GREENFIELD BREWING DEVELOPMENT PROJECT 410

CASE STUDY FOUR
ULLAGE, CO_2 AND "AS IF" ORGANISATIONS 421

THE NATIONAL HEALTH SERVICE 429

CASE STUDY FIVE
DISTRICT WORKS LEADING TRANSITION FOR CHANGE 430

CASE STUDY SIX
OPERATING THEATRE RESOLUTION OF CONFLICT
Brook Hospital 445

CASE STUDY SEVEN
GREENWICH DISTRICT HOSPITAL 450

CASE STUDY EIGHT
TRANSITIONAL NURSING CARE
The Solution Equals the Problem 467

Appendix to NHS Case Studies 487

TECHNOLOGY & CHANGE 492

CASE STUDY NINE
FINANCIAL SECTOR ASSURANCE 493

CASE STUDY TEN
THE MILLENNIUM DOME 501

CASE STUDY ELEVEN
CANARY WHARF TECHNOLOGY AND CHANGE 522

REFERENCES 526

PRELUDE

The title *Leadership and Organisational Problem Solving: Learning to Lead and Manage the Organisational Maze* stems from my experience of using an organisational approach for identifying sustainable solutions to presented problems. This approach enlists that all-important leadership competency (E)-Factoring, the capacity to (E)nable people and organisations to succeed.

My motivation for writing this book was to share my passion, experience and developed approach for successfully improving the performance of individuals, workgroups, teams and the overall organisation. To demonstrate that the use of out of date management practices, along with the lack of understanding of what is being led and managed in organisational terms, compromises decision-making that collectively leads to the creation of further unwanted dysfunctional organisational practices. My desire is to persuade leaders and managers to change their current decision-making, along with the use of out-of-date management practices, to solve today's organisational problems. I firmly believe that these observable displaced practices, and the failure to lead and manage an organisation, significantly decrease our ability to compete effectively in today's competitive global markets. Corporate United Kingdom is unable to compete on cost but we are able to compete on high-end quality product, intellectual property and services.

The developed approach is to *think organisationally* and to focus all the activities, including the *management technologies*, to create effective high performance organisations. To achieve this I wanted to share how an organisational thinker develops their intellectual capacity for successfully improving decision-making and directly translating that into the organisation's overall performance. This involves an essential competency, as all leaders are finally judged on their ability to successfully implement the decisions they make.

Working in a variety of organisational situations I found it difficult to keep reworking the same problems in different guises and failed to understand why executives and managers were apparently content recycling the same presented problems. Having an insatiable curiosity, along with a desire to improve the situation, I began a long journey of instituting performance improvement initiatives that, in part, succeeded although at times they were vehemently challenged. It was these sets of behavioural practices that came into play, particularly when a programme was becoming accepted and more expansive, that were being used consciously or unconsciously to aggressively resist change. The nub of the problem was individuals and associated power cabals protecting their created defensive mechanisms that were being used as defences against anxiety at the expense of their organisation's performance.

These induced displaced decision-making practices which consistently created other common organisational problems. These problems manifest in communication, workgroups' (teams') performance, interdepartmental collaboration, conflict management, and individuals becoming disaffected through not being able to influence the decision-making processes, which could be consistently traced to the induced dysfunctional decision-making practices.

Following my passion to improve the situation and develop sustainable solutions it became obvious that the common denominator in any organisation is the organisation. It became evident that when leading and managing major organisational *transition for change* I was acting as the organisation's *interpreting agent.* This helped me to define my role to ensure that the design of the organisation enlisted the directed motivational intent of the human resources, systems and *management technologies.*

To become successful in resolving presented problems it was essential to have the ability to drill down to find the root cause of the problem. The developed process for successfully achieving this competency was to *think organisationally* as it allowed me to address the behavioural requirements of the organisation. It allowed me to separate out and identify the dysfunctional distracting organisational behaviour induced by that organisation's dysfunctional problem solving and decision-making practices.

Developing a theory in practice I began to identify basic tenets that assisted in focusing my development. For example, the notion that the organisation is the common denominator clearly identifies that the organisation is not there for the employees or the *management technologies,* it is there to satisfy a primary delivery service. That service is the notion that the individual, the systems and the *management technologies* have at all times to work in harmony and to collectively complement the organisation's delivery performance culture. These tenets are important in that they allowed me to understand that when designing high performance organisations you design the organisation from the service delivery end, allowing all the other activities to support and reinforce that identified delivery performance culture.

These basic concepts are applicable and are generally accepted, yet the real issues that had to be addressed were the induced anxiety and the harmonisation of the technical along with the social needs of the individual and the workgroup (teams) to collectively satisfy the organisation's need to respond to its environment. Therefore, the created environment within the organisation provides the context for all these developmental activities. This requires that the development of the organisation, the development of human resources, all *management technologies,* systems, procedures, practices and decision-making are understood to be within the context of that organisation's developmental responsive needs. It was the gained understanding of these contextual relationships that allowed me to improve my own *intuitive cognitive organisational awareness* for successfully solving induced organisational problems.

Positioning myself to apply these basic assumptions creates a requirement that when the organisation is in transition; all other activities are also required to work through a parallel transition process. The developed understanding of these basic concepts identified the need to create an applied process for managing the induced anxiety that inevitably surfaces when individuals and sets of political power cabals are required to change their current protective practices.

To address these issues I developed an organisational transition for a change process that acknowledged the existence of these behavioural practices. It is these developed processes that I want to share with you to enable you to understand these practices. This developed understanding will enable you to develop your *intuitive cognitive organisational awareness*, decision-making implementation and to significantly improve your own and your organisation's performance.

The benefits of using this approach are enormous in that it enables multiple problems to be resolved simultaneously through the reduction of dysfunctional practices. It improves cost by not having to service these dysfunctional practices. It effectively harmonises the social and the technical and focuses everyone's motivational intent. It has the capacity to reduce induced organisational stress, fatigue, sickness and absence, high labour turnover, poor productivity, quality and service delivery. It significantly improves the strategic, operational decision-making and, importantly, the successful implementation of those decisions, which have been achieved through the clarity of a shared organisational understanding and developed common organisational dialogue. These developed processes are motivationally addictive and will leave you asking why you were not made aware of them earlier.

The "Power of One" is invested when executives change their mind-set and adopt an organisational approach to solve presented problems: their influence and power increases significantly.

Note of Terms Used

- Throughout this book we shall use the terms *leadership* and *management* as being two parts of the leader's role. Leadership is influencing the direction to the applied design of the organisation, the systems, the procedures and practices. As part of their role, leaders have to remain responsible for the management of the implementation processes: all leaders are finally measured on their ability to effectively deliver the decisions they make.

- The use of the term *groups* refers to the notions having been developed within a therapeutic environment.

- The term *workgroups* is being used as a collective term for this management technology, for discussing the general behaviour of groups, teams, meetings and committees, which all further differentiate by task activity. Their title and structures change according to their position in the ranking order within the organisations and the task they have to achieve. Often these attributed titles can distract us from the common behavioural dynamics that all of these listed practices display, hence the unified term.

- Throughout this book the convention applies of using *fantasy* to mean conscious fantasy and *phantasy* to mean unconscious phantasy.

- *Culture* is seen as "the customary and traditional way of thinking and of doing things, which is shared to a greater or lesser degree by all its members." (Jaques 1951)

- *Climate* is not itself an organisational process or area, but the outcome of the interaction of processes and areas. (Hutton 1972)

- A *BELIEF* is something we accept as true. A *VALUE* is a standard or outcome by which you determine if something is important to you. BOTH serve as guides for making decisions and are at work all the time.

List of Figures

Fig 1	Sustainable Comparative Performance Chart	Page 25
Fig 2	Evolutionary Growth of an Organisation	Page 46
Fig 3	Politics, Career and Overt Organisation	Page 52
Fig 4	"AS IF" Displaced Organisational Goals	Page 59
Fig 5	Overt Organisation, Career and Politics	Page 62
Fig 6	Defence Against Anxiety and Resistance to Change	Page 84
Fig 7	Boundary Management	Page 106
Fig 8	Internalised Thinking Processes (COA)	Page 108
Fig 9	Primary Task	Page 112
Fig 10	Representation Hourglass Strategic Thinking	Page 112
Fig 11	Managing Organisational Boundaries	Page 116
Fig 12	Boundary Control for Task Systems	Page 125
Fig 13	Assumptions from Experience	Page 135
Fig 14	The Role of Systems and the Individual	Page 137
Fig 15	Managing a Group at Work	Page 141
Fig 16	An "As IF" group	Page 142
Fig 17	Product Life Cycle	Page 145
Fig 18	Common Regions for the Individual and the Enterprise	Page 147
Fig 19	Organisational Behavioural Iceberg	Page 150
Fig 20	Leading Transition for Change Processes	Page 158
Fig 21	Managing Loss During Transition	Page 165 / 166
Fig 22	Internalising Personal Change	Page 167
Fig 23	Role Ambiguity and Confusion	Page 171
Fig 24	Mapping Career Decisions	Page 180
Fig 25	Continuum of Leadership Behaviour	Page 184
Fig 26	Characterised Leadership Styles	Page 184
Fig 27	Leadership Roles (Interpersonal Content)	Page 185

Fig 28	Turbulence, Competencies and Role Relationships	Page 192
Fig 29	Communicated Message	Page 199
Fig 30	Adaptive Organisational Leadership	Page 206
Fig 31	Group's Cognitive Organisational Awareness	Page 215
Fig 32	Interdependency and Dependency of Workgroups	Page 233
Fig 33	Task Groups Orientation	Page 236
Fig 34	Invasiveness of Technologies	Page 245
Fig 35	Contract Management – Role Positioning	Page 266
Fig 36	Maslow's Hierarchy of Needs	Page 302
Fig 37	Kolb's Experiential Learning Cycle	Page 334
Fig 38	Kolb's Developed Experiential Cycle	Page 337
Fig 39	Evaluation Model	Page 356
Fig 40	Decision Processes Model	Page 390
Fig 41	Clinical Service Support Model	Page 439
Fig 42	Clinical Service Support Model (modified)	Page 470
Fig 43	Millennium Dome	Page 503

List of Tables

Table 1	Individual Role Difference	Page 229
Table 2	Task v Maintenance Roles	Page 229
Table 3	Herzberg's Hygiene Factors	Page 299

Acknowledgments

Geoffrey Hutton; there are not enough words to describe my gratitude for the insightful wisdom that Geoffrey used to encourage me to recognise my innate ability to lead transition for change. He had the ability to identify and bring to the fore those innate drivers that influenced my own organisational leadership behaviour. I value those inordinate skills that Geoffrey used to influence my thinking and personal development through widening my understanding of the complexity of organisational behaviour.

My fellow MSc students, who have, through their own research and questioning, influenced my understanding and applied organisational thinking for which I am eternally grateful.

My extensive list of colleagues that I have worked with over many transitions for change programmes; I value their positive contributions. I am gratified to understand that they also benefitted and wanted to take their personal development further.

Pauline Dewberry, for her patience, immense skills, commitment and accurate work turning my original manuscript and life's work into a much more attractive and readable publication. I wish her every success with her own future publications.

Last but not least my partner Margaret, who has encouraged, endured and supportively enabled me to produce this publication.

INTRODUCTION

For an organisation to perform effectively, to avoid decay and to survive, it has to constantly renew itself through a continuous process of responding to its environment. Working through these processes should enable you to make the connection that the organisation is leading the change. You, as its "agent" (Argyris, 1999), are required to interpret those needs and have the capacity to develop the supportive organisational processes that effectively match the identified responsive behaviour. This creates an expectation that the adopted style of leadership matches the organisation's developing responsive performance needs. The adoption of an organisational leadership approach challenges existing leadership theories and practices by identifying that *people are motivated by the purpose and not the person.*

We need, in today's mercurial business environments, to be able to evaluate and agree our strategic intent, to make quicker decisions that can be achieved through having in place effective business environmental scanning. MBA studies teach us to assess, decide and execute; we need to reduce the time spent on this process. It is reported that leaders spend 50% of their time using management technologies interrogating the data, checking the facts and assessing it. They spend 30% of their time in discussion to achieve consensus. This leaves only 20% of an executive's time for implementation, which is often delegated. Yet a leader's performance is measured not on their decision-making but how they implement those decisions. Executives often don't get directly involved in the *transition for change processes*, as they are often too busy managing the politics, *management technologies* and the demands of the imposed systems protocols.

Adopting an organisational approach demands that the organisation becomes the common denominator for all decision-making. The organisation is the vehicle that enables us to collectively cooperate to satisfy the organisation's needs. It also provides the opportunity to harmonise the two technologies – the social and the technical. This approach is designed to satisfy that fundamental need for individuals, within social environments and their organisations, to understand what something means. This is critically important, as all organisations and the management technologies they employ cannot make decisions. This is the prerogative of those who design and operate them.

The organisation provides the platform and reference point for all decision-making. These are applied assumptions that require that those individuals and management technologies employed by an organisation be deployed to satisfy that organisation's needs. It also implies that when designing the organisation you do so to enlist the *motivational intent* of all your employees.

Our failure to keep pace with the organisation's responsive needs creates a tendency to employ out of date management practices. These redundant practices cause us to become stuck in the past. "We are all redundant if we have yesterday's skills." Developing your capacity as an organisational leader and problem solver is immediate, as your organisation needs to remain responsive and will not wait for you to develop these skills. Doing what you have always done is no longer an option.

The transition from a systems led approach to an organisational led approach requires a mind-shift from one perceptive state to another. The structure of this book has been designed to enable you to make that necessary transition. Working through this transition process creates an opportunity for you to begin to *think organisationally* and develop your *intuitive cognitive organisational awareness*; allowing you to develop your capacity to *adapt your organisational leadership style* to satisfy the presented situation. These developed practices and applied skills will improve your strategic and operational decision-making. Critically your ability to implement strategies significantly improves by delivering predictable performance outcomes. All leaders are finally judged by their ability to implement decisions, not how they make them.

Part One: Dysfunctional Organisational Behaviour

It is essential to begin by deconstructing the current systems thinking and to provide support to make the necessary transition from one state to another. We begin by identifying, in Chapter One, how the current systems led decision-making practices create dysfunctional organisations and unpredictable outcomes. In Chapter Two, we examine the evolutionary development of an organisation to identify those critical transition stages. This creates *states of flux*, which when not understood and, therefore, not managed and regulated, lead to further dysfunctional practices. This causes leaders and managers to service the requirement of the control systems and the created displaced *organisational goals*. Chapter Three, from a behavioural perspective, identifies the enemy within and why change fails. This provides an opportunity for us to examine the behavioural responses when individuals and groups are affected by change. It is an introduction to the social behavioural dynamics that can create resistance to change initiatives. Working through the above processes, you become aware that using a systems approach to formulate decisions is innately flawed, as the two systems, the social and the technical, have a dependent relationship demanding they must work as close to harmony as possible.

Part Two: Developing a Theory in Practice

Chapter Four, Part One, provides an opportunity using an organisational approach to re-structure how we think about organisations. Developing a theory in practice reinforces our understanding of what is being led and managed in organisational terms. Chapter Five, Part Two, examines the inter-related behaviour of the individual, the group, the organisation and their environments. These chapters are designed to further develop your *organisational thinking*, by providing a contextual understanding, in organisational terms, of what needs to be led and managed. These developed practices are designed to improve your intuitive feel of the organisation and the behavioural dynamics when leading transition for change.

Part Three: Leading Transition for Change

Chapter Six is structured to enable you to ground some of these notions to make them tangible and therefore you are asked to work through the proffered *transition for change processes*. The theories and notions explored in Chapters Four and Five have been used to support the development of this organisational led approach. These processes are designed to reduce the degree of induced anxiety and therefore resistance to change. The realignment of the organisation identifies and eliminates those multiple problems created by the dysfunctional organisational behaviour. The time frame for identifying and developing a sustainable solution is considerably shorter and, importantly, does not have to be reworked in other guises. The improved performance curve, Fig. 1 (using an organisational approach), is sustainable where the systems approach, on the other hand, will have a much shorter and depleting life cycle.

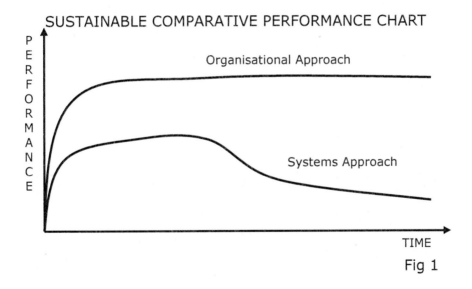

SUSTAINABLE COMPARATIVE PERFORMANCE CHART

Fig 1

The application of the developed *organisational leadership* and *organisational thinking* practices will be used to enable you to successfully lead and manage *transition for change*. It also identifies why we as organisational leaders have to adapt our behaviour to match the changing presented situation. Having worked through these chapters you will develop a clear understanding as to why using an organisational led approach provides consistent predictable outcomes.

Chapter Seven specifically explores why we must adapt our leadership practices. When an organisation is in transition, the style of leadership has to adapt to the changing presented situations. A military command style would be inappropriate for leading and managing a creative laissez-faire organisation.

Chapter Eight supports and reinforces this necessary adaptive leadership practice by exploring leadership positioning within workgroups and teams. Leaders and managers spend the majority of their time in some form of workgroup (teams), making it essential that we have a clear understanding of group dynamics. To enable you to translate your understanding of group dynamics in the context of an organisation, we consider these workgroups as micro organisations. They are task systems and they have inputs, translations and outputs back into that micro organisation's environment. These processes are designed to enable you to connect the collective decision-making processes to support and reinforce the organisation's overall performance.

Having worked through and developed your ability to think organisationally and improve your own cognitive organisational awareness, it enables you to create, within your workgroups, their collective *cognitive organisational awareness*. This significantly improves organisational, interdepartmental, inter-workgroup and inter-personal communication through a developed shared organisational language and dialogue that focuses on effectively resolving organisational problems.

These processes are designed to create learning organisations. For organisations to learn from their implementation practices they require effective feedback loops, designed into the decision-making processes, to enable you to *monitor to manage*. This practice of *monitoring to manage* enables you to retain control of your organisation's direction and performance. It enables you to continually appraise not only those activities that are not particularly successful, but to also learn from your successes to develop those practices further. We often experience success but don't always understand how we achieved it; in not understanding the processes we lose the opportunity to learn, develop and apply that successful practice further.

Developing organisations require structures and systems; management technologies that can either support your strategic intent or, as in some cases, create displaced systems and organisational goals. To avoid these unwanted outcomes and to ensure you remain in control, specific *management technologies* have been selected to demonstrate how they can be effectively employed. They have been selected to demonstrate that when leading transition for change they have to be designed to respond and support the changing organisation's performance culture. The primary message, when you are leading and managing transition for change, is to ensure that all *management technologies* are designed and employed only to reinforce your overall organisation's performance.

Part Four: Technology Change and Managing the Consequences

Chapter Nine examines the employment of new *management technologies*. We explore how the employment of *management technologies*, particularly computerised information technologies, affects change and how you manage their invasive consequences. We identify the unwanted consequential effects of using the flawed approach of using *management technologies* to drive change.

Chapter Ten explores the decision-making when outsourcing and their related contractual practices. The process examines the preliminary decision-making before outsourcing. We examine whether outsourcing creates distinct business advantages, is a fad or is a means for displacing intrusive legislation or dumping intractable problems. These two chapters overlap to a degree, particularly when examining the initial decision-making and the developed contractual management practices.

Chapter Eleven explores the relationship of remuneration and motivation, leadership behaviour and how they inform decision-making and the consequential performance of an organisation. This chapter is not designed to provide a definitive process for designing a remuneration system. It is being used to demonstrate how using an organisational approach enables the development of a notional cognitive model of the behaviour of executives created by the remuneration packages. It allows the identification of a behavioural practice that can act as an indicator as to when an organisation is being poorly led and managed. There is attached expectation that all the assumptions have to be tested before adopting an alternative approach. One of those assumptions that need to be tested is the payment of bonuses as an incentive for improving executives' performance; we discover that there is a mismatch within the bonus culture and improved performance.

Chapter Twelve explores the need to constantly re-examine how development, training and recruitment must continually reinforce the changing performance culture of your organisation. It offers an insight into alternative developmental organisational leadership practices where the outcomes directly translate into the organisation's performance.

Part Five: Case Studies

A number of case studies have been selected to demonstrate how the employment of an organisational approach enables you, in different organisational environmental settings, to identify sustainable solutions. These case studies range across the consequential executive decision-making when accelerated new technologies introduced dramatic transitional change within the brewing industries. These case studies demonstrate how using an organisational approach significantly improved the management of a major capital project, and provided a working solution to a displaced technical manifestation of introducing a new technology.

There are case studies employing an organisational approach, providing opportunities to explore the behavioural dynamics of leading and managing transition for change within the National Health Service. We also examine why an elderly Transitional Nursing Care service failed to protect a patient. The analysis within this case study demonstrates that, when using an organisational approach, these unwanted practices could be prevented. Enabling us to also explore how an organisational approach works can significantly improve the letting and management of contracts. Within the financial sector we are able to explore how the introduction of new *management technologies* using a systems led decision-making approach can *displace organisational goals*.

We look at the development and operation of an organisation through a case study of the Millennium Dome visitor attraction. It provides us with a unique opportunity to examine the life cycle of this project's development from a brown-field site through to the operational performance, closure and final disposal. It allows us to demonstrate the forensic capacity of using an organisational approach for the early identification of inappropriate practices and their unwanted consequential outcomes. This case study, using an organisational approach, demonstrates the early identification of potential fraudulent behaviour.

We finally explore how an organisation, Canary Wharf development, learned from a disastrous experience and effectively employed management technologies to ensure that they protected themselves from further failures.

These various case studies are designed to draw out and reinforce the lessons we have learned from the process of working through this book. They are works in progress and you are able to observe the various theories and notions being effectively applied throughout the *organisational thinking* and organisational development processes. For example, the reduction in dysfunctional behavioural practices enforces changes in an individual's leadership style, enabling them to use the *created intellectual and psychological space* to improve their own *organisational leadership* practices.

The success you will experience when you competently use these processes will motivate you to want to learn and develop your *organisational leadership* skills further. It is a tough process but extremely rewarding, and once experienced you will begin to ask yourself why you had not been made aware of these processes earlier. You will not want to regress to your old practices, as the success achieved through adopting an organisational leadership approach becomes addictive.

To maximise your *organisational thinking* and ability to employ these beneficial practices, it is recommended you work through each of the chapters in sequence.

SECTION ONE

Background, Understanding and Developed Organisational Thinking

PART ONE

Dysfunctional Organisational Behaviour

CHAPTER ONE
Identifying the Problem

CHAPTER TWO
Why Organisations Become Dysfunctional
(A System's Perspective)

CHAPTER THREE
The Enemy Within and Why Change Fails
(A Behavioural Perspective)

GOALS

- To provide an insight into the evolutionary processes that lead to dysfunctional organisational practices.
- To demonstrate how increased dependency on systems detaches leaders from the organisational processes.
- To explore how single systems decision-making creates displaced organisational goals.
- To identify the evolution of cyclical problem solving and how it becomes part of your organisation's culture.
- To introduce the notion of how our own behaviour can influence our decision-making and how this creates unwanted consequential outcomes.
- To create a degree of dissatisfaction that encourages you to want to explore how using an organisational approach will improve your decision-making and leadership skills.

CHAPTER ONE

IDENTIFYING THE PROBLEM

Many executives think of themselves as individuals whose greater grasp of the available information and greater insight removes the uncertainty from the situation. The increased use of computer-based Information Technology (IT) has further fuelled this belief. Even a casual observation of most business decisions usually reveals the fallacy of this view. Substantial uncertainty is more often the rule than the exception.

"The only sure thing in this world is the past, but we all work with the future."
Augusta Detoeuf

The rate and frequency of change and, at times, the mercurial nature of the external influences further increase the degree of uncertainty. The introduction of different forms of *management technologies*, which includes information technology, has increased the level of dependency and further removed executives from the reality and needs of the organisations they lead. This increased complexity is further compounded by the fact that many executives and managers lack a developed understanding, in organisational terms, of what they are leading and managing. All of which directly affects the *intent, processes* and quality of decision-making, which includes existing implementation practices.

Many organisations do not have effective decision-making processes that have the capacity to test validity, the consequential effects and the potential success rates. The intent of this book is to take some of the uncertainty out of the process and significantly improve the predictability of decision-making. The application of an *organisational approach* provides a process framework for testing decisions and their consequential effects.

To enable this process to be developed in the minds of executives and managers, it is essential that they work through the *transition for change* processes to ensure they have a fundamental grasp of what they are, in organisational terms, leading and managing. The existing problem this book is attempting to address is the fact that many leaders and managers have become so engrained and comfortable with the existing flawed *single initiative systems approach.*

"Organisation theory can be defined as the study of the structure, functioning and performance of organisations and the behaviour of groups and individuals within them." (Pugh, 1971.) This definition, in the light of current practices and experience, needs to include the influence and behaviour of systems and boundary management, along with a developed intuitive socio-technical design of organisations. This becomes even more prevalent when we consider the proliferation and invasiveness of management technologies, particularly Information Technology (IT), which in turn creates administrative production systems. The behavioural characteristics of these administrative production systems have a number of similarities to manufacturing and production processes that need to be understood.

Thinking about Organisations

Writers have been attempting to draw together information, practices and distil theories of how organisations function and how they should be led and managed. "They have tried to discover generalisations applicable to all organisations" (Pugh, 1971). Experience shows that this pursuit for a generalised systems application causes managers to seek panaceas to presented problems rather than develop their intuitive organisational leadership and management skills that match the specific needs of the organisation they are leading and managing. This practice of searching for quick packaged fixes will be examined to identify why in social systems they consistently fail. These and other practices detach leaders and managers from their organisations, which impairs their decision-making. Consequentially, many strategic strategies for change and performance improvements fail to achieve their desired outcomes.

"There is nothing more useless than doing efficiently that which should not be done at all."
Peter F Drucker

The concept of organisational behaviour is basic to the study and understanding of how much an organisation needs to control behaviour necessary for effective functioning. Fuelling a continuing debate are two factions. There are those who use a structured bureaucratic systems approach to maintain control and ensure efficiency. They claim, on the one hand, that the efficiency can be achieved through clear lines of authority, specialisation, clear job definitions, and standardised routines and practices; this is sometimes described as the machine model where people are seen and treated as part of the mechanistic processes.

There are those, the behaviourists, which include social science thinkers, who maintain that the continuing attempt to increase control over behaviour is self-defeating and counter-productive. They suggest these structured systems approaches, with their inherent rigidity, when coupled with the technologies employed, neglect the informal relationships and the need for individuals and groups to manage induced anxiety.

They suggest that the mechanistic methods achieve short-term gains but at the cost of increased resistance to change. This increase in resistance and alienation significantly compromises an organisation's ability to effectively respond to change. In response to an increase in resistance to change, you can observe an identifiable cyclical practice, of further *management technologies* being employed, which has the effect of losing sight of the real issues that need to be addressed. (Refer to Chapter Three, "The Enemy Within and Why Change Fails".)

The advocates of a structures systems approach indicate that social science thinking often fails to translate into effective practice, even though Pugh (1971) claims it to be a "major force." Managers often consider these academic pieces of research to be inaccessible as they are not able to translate the ideas into practice. Attached to these views is the notion that these researchers don't understand the reality of day-to-day leadership and management. For example, the excellent clinical analytical work of Menzies (1970) – "The Functioning of Social Systems as a Defence against Anxiety" – is often referred to in many academic papers but there is little evidence that the lessons have been translated into practice. Even so these ideas and unconscious practices can be seen to exist and be acted out, by both the individual and within the group process, as these phenomena exist within any social organisation.

Harmonisation, Best Fit

Both approaches have their merits; the important lesson is for the benefits of both approaches to be examined, modified and developed to satisfy the identified needs for leading and managing an organisation. The intent is to examine how it is possible to develop the intuitive processes for creating the appropriate arrangements for managing the product of "two technologies, material and social" (Burns, 1963). These "two technologies" have a dependent relationship and therefore, have to work as near to harmony as practicable.

The Need for Organisations to be Responsive

The claim and need for intuitive organisational leadership and management skills being developed, is consistent with the fact that organisations have to continuously respond to their specific and possibly mercurial environments. The desire to find a generalised systems application is dissipating and inappropriate, as indicated earlier. It is counter-productive, as organisations need to continually scan and evaluate their environments to service the strategic decision-making and adaptability of an organisation (Porter, 1980 & 1985 and Tapscott & Williams, 2006). The outcome of this scanned evaluation has to be translated and used to support the design of the organisation to enable it to respond appropriately to these external forces and to prevent decay.

The failure to lead and manage organisations effectively has led to dysfunctional practices, creating a market for the quick fix. This has been populated by books that offer panaceas for all the ills of existing business organisations. These observations are discussed in more detail in Chapters Two and Three, which should enable you to develop an understanding as to why organisations systematically become dysfunctional. The dysfunctional behaviour of organisations is what most people experience during their working lives. This, over time, has become accepted behaviour with many authors as they offer solutions in the form of a single initiative that further compounds the existing presented situation. These solutions are often the wrong solution for the wrong problem, which serves to compound the existing problem and buries the real problem even further. This, in turn, feeds a spiral of having to identify a solution to solve the problem created by the previous solution. The real organisational problem has been buried under increased layers of failed single initiative solutions.

Single Initiatives

For the purpose of discussion and to develop the argument against the use of single initiatives, two iconic authors have been identified that either take the mechanistic systems approach or leadership and motivational approach. The choice of these authors is based solely on the fact that they are well recognised and have both responded to their experiences of attempts to improve organisations' and managers' performance. Each of their experiences has directly influenced their adopted approaches to solving the same problem.

Systems Approach

Michael Hammer and James Champy (1993), in "Reengineering the Corporation", express their frustration with the constraints and inflexibility of corporate management. Attempts to introduce computerised technologies, with little success, directly influenced their practices and attitudes. They state that "America's business problem is that it is entering the twenty-first century with companies designed during the nineteenth century to work well in the twentieth." They identified a redundancy factor that is still prevalent in many of today's organisations.

The emergence of the Japanese ability to compete effectively on quality and service was one of the international market influences that fed into identifying the current failings of American corporations. To catch up with the Japanese they suggested, "We need something entirely different." At the heart of business reengineering lies the notion of "discontinuous thinking" – identifying and abandoning the outdated rules and fundamental assumptions that underlie current business operations. "Discontinuous thinking" translates into developing the ability to recognise and get rid of outdated methods and practices within an organisation.

What they have not addressed is why these outdated practices are maintained. To provide an insight as to why these practices are often maintained, refer to Chapters Two, Three and Four. Without this understanding of how social technical organisations work they, in their ignorance, advocated revolution when evolution would be more appropriate. They say, "Every company is replete with implicit rules left over from earlier decades: Customers don't repair their own equipment. Local warehouses are necessary for good service." Merchandising decisions are made at headquarters. These rules are based on assumptions about technology, people and organisational goals that no longer hold.

Fundamentally, reengineering is about reversing the industrial revolution. Reengineering rejects the assumptions inherent in Adam Smith's industrial paradigm – the division of labour, economies of scale, hierarchical control and all the other appurtenances of an early-stage developing economy. "Reengineering is the search for new models of organising work. Tradition counts for nothing. Reengineering is a new beginning." This statement prompts the question, beginning of what?

Although Hammer and Champy are eager to declare that classical organisation theory is obsolete, ideas such as the division of labour have had an enduring power and applicability that reengineering has so far failed to demonstrate. Reengineering is a *management technology*, yet Hammer and Champy are surprisingly vague about the details. They say, "Reengineering must focus on redesigning a fundamental business process, not on departments of other organisational units." They specified that the concept of reengineering is a revolutionary approach to business change and supports the idea that broken processes are good candidates for the employment of reengineering.

There is a high degree of resonance with the five focused steps used in the *Theory of Constraints* proffered by Eliyahu Moshe Goldratt, physicist and management consultant. *Theory of Constraints* is based on the premise that the rate of goal achievement is limited by at least one constraining process. Only by increasing flow through the constraint can overall throughput be increased, i.e. identify the constraint, the resource or policy that prevents the organisation from obtaining more of its goals.

Interestingly his frustrations stem from his experience and the realisation that the habits and assumptions of employees and managers prior to using the software were still prominent and negatively influenced results after implementation. The circumstance for developing the *Theory of Constraints* stems from similar experiences of Hammer and Champy when introducing computer based technologies. In either case they are simply saying: find the block to improving performance and do something appropriate about the situation. The developed solutions were to introduce a mechanistic, cost driven, systems approach for providing solutions. Experience provides evidence that these and other single strategic initiative constantly fail.

Deming (1986), who was the forefather of the practice of Total Quality, would rail against these purported practices. His philosophy was summarised by his Japanese proponents with the following (a) or (b) comparison:

(a) When people and organisations focus primarily on quality, defined by the ratio that quality tends to increase and costs fall over time.

Quality = Results of work effort / Total Cost

(b) However, when people and organisations focus primarily on costs, cost tends to rise and quality declines over time. Cost benefits are derived from the quality of the work and the delivery of services. Cost driven single initiatives that become the primary function will produce short-term gains (Fig. 1) but over time will become less beneficial. For example, poor quality products will be returned and create additional costs and loss of sales. Quality products coupled with quality services will automatically service the management cost and profitability. (These systems behavioural issues are further explored and reinforced in Chapter Nine, "Technology Change and Managing the Consequences".)

Social Reactive Consequences

There are many moderating factors that influence the outcome of leading and managing major organisational transition for change programmes. The way in which the initiative is implemented, especially one that disrupts core routines even though they create new relationships and responsibilities, significantly alter existing power relationships. This is one of the main, although not always overtly expressed, sources of resistance and can even lead to the sabotage of change initiatives. (Refer to the Avonmouth and Greenwich District Hospital case studies.) Reengineering creates significant disruptions of routines and may increase differentiation by incorporating new professional or quasi-professional positions, for example, techno-managers responsible for IT within a department. Increasing the level of unit differentiation has been associated with higher degrees of conflict and may lead to dysfunctional behaviours (Lawrence & Lorsch, 1967).

A similar idea was advocated by Davenport and Short in 1990. Unbiased reviews of a company's business processes and reengineering were rapidly adopted by a huge number of firms that were striving for renewed competitiveness, which they had lost due to the market entrance of foreign competitors, their inability to satisfy customer needs, and their insufficient cost structure. Even well-established management thinkers, such as Drucker and Peters, were accepting and advocating reengineering as a new tool for achieving success in a dynamic world. During the following years, a fast growing number of publications, books as well as journal articles, were dedicated to reengineering, and many consulting firms embarked on this trend and developed reengineering methods.

However, the critics were fast to claim that reengineering was a way to dehumanise the work place, increase managerial control, and to justify downsizing that equates to major reductions of the work force, and therefore was a rebirth of Taylorism under a different label. (Refer to Chapter Ten, "Outsourcing and Contractual Practices", for examples.) Interestingly Frederick Taylor suggested in the 1880s that managers use process-reengineering methods to discover the best processes for performing work. Each of the reengineering processes was being driven by the development of technology, the former, industrial, and the latter, information technology. Hammer's process allows for design process across function and departments, which was not available, with the prevailing technologies of the time, to Taylor. It is unsurprising that this process and its application have been branded as a product of a neo-Taylorist movement.

As a consequence one of the risks of reengineering is that a company becomes wrapped up in internal politicking and internalises its behaviour; it fails to keep up with competitors and/or predatory threats. The internalising is a function of people defending themselves against the induced anxiety caused by the rapidity and nature of the changes being experienced and the felt sense of chaos.

American Express, when tackling a comprehensive reengineering of its credit card business, lost out to MasterCard and Visa who stole the march and introduced a new product – the corporate procurement card. American Express lagged a full year behind before being able to offer customers the same service. This approach is often presented to corporations as a quick fix and, while it may provide you with major short-term financial gains (Fig. 1), it will, over time, leave you in a worse position (Leth, 1994). Wheatley describes the appeal of reengineering as a sign of "collective desperation" (Drown, 1994).

Davenport (1995), an early reengineering proponent, stated that: "When I wrote about 'business process redesign' in 1990, I explicitly said that using it for cost reduction alone was not a sensible goal. And consultants Michael Hammer and James Champy, the two names most closely associated with reengineering, have insisted all along that layoffs shouldn't be the point. But the fact is, once out of the bottle, the reengineering genie quickly turned ugly." Michael Hammer similarly admitted that: "I wasn't smart enough about that. I was reflecting my engineering background and was insufficiently appreciative of the human dimension. I've learned that's critical." They write: "Winning companies know how to do their work better," echoing Fredrick Taylor. This is a belief that Thomas Peters and Robert Waterman would also share.

Leadership and Motivational Approach

There is agreement between Michael Hammer and James Champy and Peters and Waterman (1982) with a shared desire to eradicate the latent practice of industrial organisations. Peters and Waterman explained, "Start with Taylorism, add a layer of Druckerism and a dose of McNamaraism, and by the late 1970's you had the great American corporation that was being run by bean counters." *In Search of Excellence* by Thomas Peters and Robert Waterman (1982) satisfied a market need, created by these deemed dysfunctional organisations. The differences are that Peters wanted to put "people first" and Hammer used a mechanistic systems approach.

Peters and Waterman need to be complimented for identifying that there was a profitable niche market created by the dysfunctional practices within many organisations. They also identified that through these motivational aphorisms, managers wanted to be excited by the possibilities that these books offered: the can-do attitude and the promise of liberation of the existing corporate strait-jacketed practices. The injection of their ideas has spawned a whole raft of quick fix can-do literature that is designed to satisfy felt and identified failings of dysfunctional organisations. The created market stimulated the production of many other books, which together all beat the leadership and motivational drum. They stimulated a market for many "Son of Excellence" books.

The main message within *In Search of Excellence* is simply People, Customers and Action. There are eight themes that also form the eight chapters of the book:

1. A bias for action, active decision making – "getting on with it".

2. Close to the customer – learning from the people served by the business.

3. Autonomy and entrepreneurship – fostering innovation and nurturing "champions".

4. Productivity through people – treating rank and file employees as a source of quality.

5. Hands-on, value-driven – management philosophy that guides everyday practice – management showing its commitment.

6. Stick with the knitting – stay with the business you know.

7. Simple form, lean staff – some of the best companies have minimal HQ staff.

8. Simultaneous loose-tight properties – autonomy in shop-floor activities plus centralised values.

In reality most people would generally agree with these expressed intentions. A major concern exists with the effective delivery of these expectations, in other words the "how". This concern is further exacerbated when they propose the use of the McKinsey flawed "7-S" model:

1. Structure

2. Strategy

3. Systems

4. Style of management

5. Skills – corporate strength

6. Staff

7. Shared values

These management techniques, when evaluated using an organisational approach, are unworkable. This is indicated by the order of the list. Structure is listed first, when it is a given that form follows function. Corporate strength is an analytical practice that would be undertaken before defining the strategy. It also provides an insight into the internal activities that need to be addressed before implementing a strategy. Shared values have to be developed at the beginning of any change strategy otherwise the motivational drive of the individual is unsupportive. Developing the individual and collective motivational drive is basic to any change initiative if success is to be achieved. We have to remember the main focus of *In Search of Excellence* is leadership and motivation through putting people first. What is evident is that *In Search of Excellence* did not produce the proposed revolution, as Hammer still wanted to revolutionise the same "blocked" corporate activities.

What has emerged from these brief explorations is that Hammer became frustrated with the deployment of computer technologies that were being introduced to improve the efficiency of what he considered to be outmoded management techniques. In other words, computer technology was being used to drive change. On the other hand Peters' approach of using leadership and motivational techniques to "put people first" is, in effect, his *management technology* for also driving change. Peters also makes the implied assumption that individuals have the authority to enact his proposed aphorisms. When you examine Chapters Three, Five and Six, which discuss individual and group behaviour, you will find that most people find it extremely difficult to step outside the existing *normative behaviour*.

Paler Louis (1999) discusses the development of normative behaviours in the experiment "Monkey See and Monkey Do":

Monkey See and Monkey Do

Albert Einstein once observed: "It's the same kind of thinking that created the problem in the first place." This observation can be made clear by the following example.

A group of behavioural psychologists recently conducted an experiment with a group of monkeys in a setting with one-way mirrors. A dozen monkeys were placed in a room, in the centre of which was a pole with a bunch of bananas on top. Above the bananas, mounted in the ceiling, was a showerhead. When one of the older monkeys climbed the pole the scientists sprayed her with ice-cold water. The monkey retreated.

An hour or so later another monkey made a quick dash for the top and was also hosed down. At this point unbeknownst to the monkeys, the scientists changed three things: they removed one monkey from the room; they brought in a new one; and they disconnected the showerhead.

Soon, the new monkey in the room tried to climb to the top but was stopped by others. Eventually all the monkeys were replaced and each time the new monkey was stopped when they started climbing. Finally, though no monkey remained who had been present for the spraying, no one ventured up the pole. Thus they never realized that conditions had changed and the bananas were there for the picking.

The moral of the story is that experience is the best and at times the worst teacher. So, if we are to solve new problems we must develop and adopt new attitudes, new patterns of thinking that are suited to the situation set within Its own context. Viable solutions will require new ways of seeing new modes of action, a new vocabulary, and a new set of images, new perspectives, and new sensibilities. With the emergent attitude there comes commensurate perspective and leadership. (Paler Louis 1999).

What has become evident is the frailty of a *single strategic initiative approach* when introducing and leading *transition for change* programmes. This further reinforces the conclusions in Chapters Two and Three that neither the systems nor the behavioural approach produce appropriate and sustainable solutions. As both authors have suggested, we need an alternative approach to replace our current practices.

Each approach offered panaceas and neither have lived up to that expectation. What they have achieved has unwittingly added to the existing confused and dysfunctional behaviour within many organisations. They, as with many other writers of the same ilk, fail to appreciate the unconscious behaviour of individuals and groups. They have not understood the consequential effects of their proposed decision-making and implementation processes. These social processes, within organisations, have to be understood.

Psychoanalysts who study organisations and group processes can usefully provide different perspectives and insights that do help to improve our understanding of these processes. Developing an understanding of these social group processes and how they affect decision-making is important as it can help to work as a predictor of future performance outcomes.

CHAPTER TWO

Why Organisations Become Dysfunctional
(A Systems Perspective)

Before attempting to address the issue of why organisations become dysfunctional it would be useful to answer the following question: "Why do we organise?" There is no other compelling reason than to successfully cooperate, to effectively complete increasingly complex tasks. In other words, the organisation is the means, the vehicle, which enables you to collectively succeed. The organisation is the vehicle that provides a performance platform that enables your business to perform effectively. Focusing on the organisational processes provides the purpose that everyone can identify with, collectively and individually. It becomes evident from an examination of these processes that *people follow the purpose and not the person.*

Working with these organisational processes also identifies that the organisation needs to respond to its environment and therefore, leads the *transition for change.* We therefore, as Organisational Leaders, have to develop an almost *intuitive understanding of the organisation's needs,* which is referred to as having a well-developed *cognitive organisational awareness.* This enables us to design our organisations, to satisfactorily respond and behave, to meet our organisation's specific transitional needs. It is for these reasons that we must develop the use of an organisational approach for decision-making and problem solving, as this will simultaneously resolve many of the presented problems.

This demands that we develop the ability to *think organisationally* and adapt our *organisational leadership* approach to significantly improve *our decision-making* and *organisational problem solving.* Failure to do so can have direct or insidious unwanted consequences for your organisation. Understanding why organisations become dysfunctional is important as it provides an insight into why some organisations perform better than others. It also supports the development of your *cognitive organisational awareness*.

Tracing the evolutionary growth and development of an organisation will assist in identifying why and where the management of an organisation becomes progressively dysfunctional. This process will also identify what can be done to manage your organisation's development and avoid these unwanted, crippling, dysfunctional behavioural practices. It also addresses why we need to change our management thinking and address the question, "Why we need to adopt an organisational approach?"

Evolution of Dysfunctional Organisational Behaviour

A notional modified model, Fig. 2 (R. Stewart) will assist us to trace and identify some of the processes and critical transition points. These transition points introduce the organisational processes, what can be referred to as a *state of flux*. There is a state of fluidity that needs to be regulated and managed effectively and in terms of the organisation's needs.

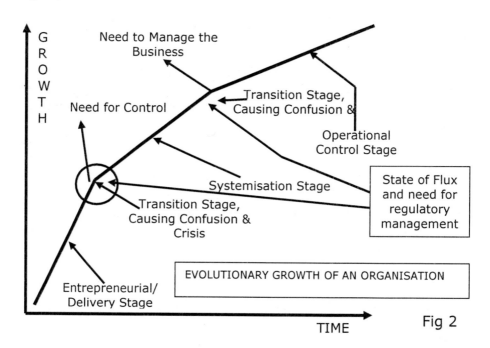

Fig 2

At the *entrepreneurial delivery stage* the task and desired outcome is clear and can be even felt by that entrepreneur, as they are still in touch with their market and customer base. At the entrepreneurial delivery stage there are few people, little formality, quick growth along with loyalty and rewards, which are identifiable with ownership.

To satisfy a larger market demand, organisations are required to respond appropriately. With an increase in throughput there is a need to introduce staff with specific skills and to differentiate tasks to enable those new employees to *contribute to the organisation's overall performance*. During this initial transition stage there is a need for improved control to overcome the felt confusion created by crisis management. The need for control comes from, "It's getting too big", "We need guidelines to reduce firefighting", along with the need to clarify priorities.

Systems Management

Usually when we feel we need to control activities we begin to introduce systems, practices and procedures, which may be referred to as the *systems stage*. These will also include such activities as the introduction of organisational charts, and other *management technologies* and the development of specialist departmental functions that we begin to consider as techno-managers. Often these necessary transitional stages are the genesis of where many organisations' problems stem from.

With further business development there is an increased need to manage the business organisation. This introduces another transitional stage that is further influenced through increased crisis management and felt confusion. This is often identified with losing touch with customers, too many meetings, too much paperwork, "low risk attitudes" (Nyquist, 2009), political power game playing and the old and familiar empire building, leading to silo structured organisations. This is the stage where executives start to become detached from the business of their organisation through the increased dependency on *management technologies and systems*. This introduces a further transition stage, that of operational control where the executive and management become increasingly anxious, which develops from a concerned need to retain control. This felt need to retain control and to relieve executives' and managers' anxieties, causes parallel systems to be introduced centralising the control.

Systems Dependency

A phenomenon that develops in organisations is the dangerous practice of becoming *systems dependent*. The reliance on systems management has the effect of developing a mind-set where the management directs and remotely controls the organisation through the developed control systems.

This could be compared with a pilot depending on the automatic piloting systems, with the difference being that the employed automatic systems are more predictable and reliable. An important critical difference is that the pilot has a vested personal need for the systems to work, where executives and managers have a vested interest but not the same level of personal dependency other than to enable them to defend themselves against their own anxieties. Another concern is that systems introduced into organisations are often designed to fit already dysfunctional organisations. This further contributes to an already dysfunctional organisational culture that leaders and managers become familiar with and accept. (Refer to the observations entitled "Monkey See and Monkey Do" by Paler Louis (1999) above and reflect on how quickly we become part of the existing fabric of that organisation's dysfunctional performance culture.)

This style of *systems management* has the effect of disengaging executive leaders and managers from the management of their organisations. Nyquist writes when discussing "Military Decrepitude", "Modern communications and computer processing have transformed command and control so much so that generals can monitor real-time movement of troops and materials around the world. All too often these 'virtual' commanders second-guess combat leaders in the field, destroying morale. Few are concerned that the over-reliance or misuse of new technologies may produce a false sense of security. In fact, security may be totally compromised when advanced systems fail."

For example, the earlier reference to pilots and their relationship with their technology has changed through the over-dependency on the computerised control technology. The US Federal Aviation

Administration (FAA) has become concerned about the loss of control in flight. In the industry this is expressed as "lost situational awareness". A report published in 2013 concluded that the pilots were losing touch with their aeroplanes: the computers that control them were so accurate and reliable that the pilots built up a huge level of trust in them whilst losing confidence in their own ability to manage the aircraft. Under certain circumstances the computer cannot cope and transfers the controls to the pilot by disconnecting the autopilot. The FAA reports there is a fundamental misunderstanding between the pilot and machine.

Pilots are still trained to fly traditional electromechanical aircraft but are given computerised ones. Pilots are trained to navigate using traditional means but then rely on global navigation satellite systems (GNSS) and computers, where they lose the mental ability to cope when they have to revert back to basics. The FAA's report identifies a number of skills pilots lose, which includes all the basic skills a pilot is expected to have. When the autopilot relinquishes control to the pilot they quickly lose control of the aircraft. This is evidenced by the fact that when an aircraft's "black box" is eventually recovered it often reveals that the pilots had become confused by a momentary loss of flight information.

The Royal Academy of Engineers identified that the over-dependency on these data network technologies – which also includes financial trading systems, shipping, agriculture, railways, and emergency services – has become a problem, because the GNSS signal is not only at risk from geomagnetic storms but also from human interference on account of the weakness of the signal. This is equivalent to picking up light from a strong bulb at a distance of 20,000km. They suggest that powerful jammers that cost as little as £20 operated from a tall building or from a balloon could knock out the GNSS across the whole of Southern England.

The above examples emphasise the consequential outcome of over-dependency on technology but critically it clearly indicates that both the pilot and the executive lose that all-important "feel" of how their craft or organisation is actually performing.

Executives often only receive filtered selective information that, subordinates perceive, will satisfy that executive. Often, when discussing systems, we automatically think of high technology computer systems, yet in the case study entitled "Transitional Nursing Care" we find that the repression of a damaging report combined with the failure to use specific action triggering language, such as "abuse", completely negated the reporting and monitoring processes, leading to endemic neglect and abuse of a patient. These practices are prevalent when you have a politically functioning system dependent on a decision-making culture that places an emphasis on the "appearance of success rather than the reality."

Skills Redundancy

A trap that many executives and managers fall into is "trying to use out-of-date organisational systems for coping with entirely new situations" (Burns, 1963), in what may be referred to as the skills redundancy factor. Today's business environment is demanding that appropriate alternative organisational arrangements are developed to cope with increased change and complexity. Yet experience shows that many organisations still revert to out-of-date management technologies and practices. It is at the *systems and operational control* transition stages (Fig. 2) that many dysfunctional practices are introduced and compounded, which begin to adversely influence the performance of an organisation's control and decision-making.

There are two elements that stem from the above discussion that need to be further explored:

Firstly there is the issue of using out-of-date systems for new situations. There is a degree of sympathy with these managers in that the existing training and education also follows the same practices. They have not had the opportunity to develop an understanding of their organisation's behaviour or to develop their *cognitive organisational awareness*. To overcome this dilemma the following discussion is designed to develop your organisational thinking processes.

The second element is that when employing new management technologies, leaders lose sight of their organisation's needs through being immersed in the management of the protocols of the systems. These systems do not make decisions, those decisions are always the preserve of those systems' "agents" who employ, design and manage these systems.

Performance Culture Continuum

The consequential effect of not having a clear perspective over their organisation's *performance culture continuum* causes executives and managers to become detached from the delivery end of their organisations. They tend to lead and manage the presented created dysfunctional organisation, as that has now become their operating leadership and management environment. This can be described as the developed corporate *executive vicinage*. The development of this detached state of executives and managers can be better understood through Miller's (1959) concept of *technology, territory and time*, which he used for identifying and differentiating complex production systems. Developing the use of this concept further enables the introduction of the idea of how performance cultures change over a continuum of technology, territory and time, which can be referred to as the *performance culture continuum*:

When advanced, technologically supported, sophisticated communication and process systems are employed it becomes essential to gain a clear understanding of the performance culture changes that will occur over the *performance culture continuum*. Nyquist, when discussing the performance culture of the U.S. military, observes, "The weakness of the U.S. military stems from shared societal pathologies and the phenomenon of widespread narcissism. This places an inordinate emphasis on the appearance of success rather than the reality." Within organisations this represents servicing the politics and one's own career and then whatever is left for the overt organisation (Fig. 3). In other words, this dysfunctional decision-making process compounds the existing dysfunctional organisational practices.

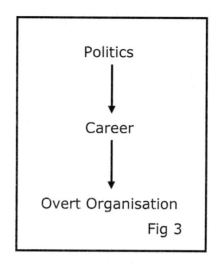

Politics

↓

Career

↓

Overt Organisation

Fig 3

At the other end of the *performance culture continuum* the reality for those on the ground in a combat zone or, say, delivering an emergency clinical procedure, the performance culture is real, personal and immediate. Within many organisations, where the executive is detached from the delivery end of their business – which could include the U.S. military (Nyquist) – it becomes very easy to observe the following decision-making practices expressed in Fig. 3.

At the executive end of an organisation's *performance culture continuum* a developed decision-making practice exists, which takes the form of: *politics – career – and then the overt organisation.* (Fig. 3.) This political decision-making process develops unconsciously and becomes pervasive in many organisations.

Within, for example, the combat zone (the delivery end of the process) this political model for decision-making would only serve to compromise performance and put lives at risk, as immediacy and direct involvement will influence decision-making practices. As Nyquist writes, "Too often the generals are micromanaging their troops from the rear – far from the realities faced by those 'charged with leadership', causing role confusion and conflict." Perspective of the performance culture, along the command time-line, will change over the *performance culture continuum.* In organisational terms a clear understanding of what is being managed, to improve leaders' *intuitive feel* of what is being led and managed becomes essential. This *intuitive feel* can only be achieved through the effective development of your *cognitive organisational awareness.*

The generals need to define the system's purpose and its underlying *intent*. Is it an information system to support the decision-making of the leaders on the ground or is it a direct command and control system? By implication each system will employ very different performance boundaries that need to be understood and managed.

The performance cultures at either end of the *performance culture continuum* will be directly influenced by the choice of how systems are designed and employed to achieve the defined *intent*. That choice will directly affect the complementary or shared *primary task* at each end of the *performance culture continuum* along with the organisational design, style of leadership and management. The notion of territory, technology and time has to be taken into consideration when evaluating the design of any organisation and its systems. (This discussion is developed further in Chapter Nine, "Technology Change and Managing the Consequences" and in the case studies for the development of hospitals and financial services.)

The value of this notional model is that it assists in identifying the transitional stages that an organisation makes when developing and responding to its environment. Organisations are in constant transition, and as a consequence, they have to continuously work through the different transitional phases of their development. Transition analysis allows you to identify and examine these critical transition processes your organisation is experiencing. This process has an enormous value as an analytical practice for identifying the nucleus of a problem. These nuclei are identifiable places within the processes and are referred to as *"states of flux"* (Fig. 2).

The value of this process is that, when designing your organisation, it identifies those critical transitional *states of flux* in advance. Having identified these critical transitional *states of flux* enables you to design your organisation, its structures, processes, systems, procedures and practices to specifically manage and regulate these transitional stages effectively.

It is desirable to view these transition points as being in a *state of flux* as becoming unpredictable if not led, regulated and managed appropriately. It is useful to have a mental picture of the process for smelting iron. Initially you are managing a number of stable solid ingredients. These various ingredients are mixed and their temperature is raised to create liquid iron. The critical stage for the smelting process is the management of the created *state of flux*, the molten metal. The consequential effects of misjudging this *state of flux*, when pouring, will create significant problems further along the production process. This may lead to poor product quality, waste, recycling, low productivity, de-motivation and additional costs. These analytical processes and their consequential outcomes can be applied to any systems process within any type of organisation, not just manufacturing.

Developing a regime for managing this process around these *states of flux* prevents these potential failings. This practice of analysing organisation and process decision-making can quickly identify the potential consequential effects. An example of displaced consequential effects has been expressed by Senge (1993), where he suggests, "The cure can be worse than the effects." "Sometimes the easy or familiar solution is not only ineffective; sometimes it is addictive and dangerous." Senge, for example, identifies that the development of alcoholism may start as social drinking that is being used to overcome a problem of low self-esteem or work related stress. Gradually, the cure becomes worse than the disease; among other problems it makes self-esteem and stress even worse than they were to begin with.

The long-term, most insidious consequences of applying non-systemic solutions, and the understanding of how society, individuals and political investment (power brokers) can be missed, create further problems developing from the solution that will require further solutions to be generated. Using the notion of a *performance culture continuum* you will automatically explore the whole system through to delivery and its consequences before enacting the proposed solution. This approach not only has the capacity to provide operational solutions, it can and will migrate across your organisation's boundaries into your organisation's environment. Acting as a predictor, this whole organisational approach can prevent unwanted and unexpected outcomes.

BP's Safety Record

In December 1965, BP's oilrig Sea Gem was being moved when two of its legs collapsed causing the rig to capsize. Thirteen members of the crew were killed.

In March 2005, BP's Texas City's refinery, one of the largest refineries, exploded causing fifteen deaths, injuring one hundred and eighty people and forcing thousands of nearby residents to remain in their homes. The explosion caused all the casualties and substantial damage in the rest of the plant. Importantly this incident was the culmination of a series of less serious accidents at this refinery. The engineering problems that contributed to these incidents were not addressed. In fact the maintenance and safety budgets were reduced as cost saving measures at the plant. The responsibility was ultimately that of the London based executive. (Baker Panel Report 2010). The consequences of these accidents have severely damaged BP's image through the mismanagement of the plant. The most recent scathing report by the US Chemical Safety and Hazard Investigation Board (US Chemical Safety and Hazard Investigation Board 2010), found, "... organizational and safety deficiencies at all levels in the BP Corporation." They also said that these management failures could be traced from Texas to London. (McClatchy Washington Bureau 2010)

April 2010 an explosion on the BP offshore deep-water drilling rig in the Gulf of Mexico resulted in eleven deaths and sixteen injured. Another 99 survived without serious physical injury. The explosion caused the Deepwater Horizon to burn and sink leading to a massive offshore oil spillage in the Gulf of Mexico, estimated to be the biggest oil spillage in the history of the US.

Two immediate examples are BP and Barclays bank; BP for its safety record, whereas the FBI in the USA was investigating the traders of Barclays bank, eventually leading to the Libor scandal in the UK. In each case the CEOs were forced to resign and in each case the warning signs were there and went unheeded.

This, in turn, enables the identification of the critical task and roles that have to be completed to successfully manage the process. *Transition analysis* and the use *of performance culture continuum* are two parts of the practice used in the development of what is referred to as *socio-technical systems* and design. Do not be put off by the language, as you will find that it is a process that will assist in developing that elusive harmonisation between the technical and the social behaviour within organisations and other social systems.

Cognitive Intuitive Organisational Awareness

Executives and managers often lose that important *intuitive feel* that is necessary when leading and managing organisations; basically they become detached from the real needs and activities of their organisations. (Refer to Chapter Eleven, "Remuneration and Motivation".) *Intuitive feel* refers to an organisational leader being in tune with their organisation's responsive behaviour, which is developed when practising *organisational leadership* and management of an organisation. This intuitive organisational feel is achieved when you think organisationally and develop your *cognitive organisational awareness*. Achieving this state clarifies your intent, informs your attitudes and your own personally directed motivation.

Wageman et al. (2008) provide a useful example, when discussing executive team members' roles: "Just let me focus on my real job rather than waste time in endless meetings that accomplish nothing." The "meetings that accomplish nothing" are the ones where the executives consider the direction and future of the organisation. This suggests that these executives are not collectively aware, in organisational terms, of what they are required to lead and manage. There has been a complete failure to develop the whole of the executive's *cognitive organisational awareness* and, as a consequence, their ability to lead and manage their organisation effectively.

This detached managerial phenomenon contributed to the catastrophic collapse in 1995 of Barings merchant bank that was trusted with the finance of royalty and aristocrats for over two hundred years. It was apparently brought down by the covert activities of one rogue trader, leaving the bank with losses of around £850 million. It is well known that systems, if not directed and controlled, will begin to develop a life of their own. In other words, these systems begin to service their own need and not that of the organisation. When there is a developed dependency on systems there is always a risk of inappropriate activities developing (an example is the Libor rate fixing scandal). This becomes particularly true when either the systems prevent a person from doing "their job" or it becomes evident that the systems are functional or designed as a defence against anxiety, and are not *monitoring to manage* the practices.

Barings' bank trading practices were not designed *to monitor and manage* the *performance culture continuum*, allowing practices to become inappropriate and corrupt. This is confirmed in the Bank of England's report of the enquiry into the collapse of Barings Bank (1995): "The losses were incurred by reason of unauthorised and concealed trading activities within BFS (Barings Futures Singapore). The true position was not noticed earlier by reason of serious failure of control and managerial confusion within Barings."

The case of the Millennium Dome fraud, which we will discuss in more detail later, can be attached to functional monitoring and poor boundary definition and management creating an opportunity for corruption should a person have those intentions. They may not start with an intention to use fraudulent practices but the temptation can be such; if the risk of identification is perceived to be low, people will begin to take advantage of the given situation. Whatever level of systems operation the system will be, if poorly designed, misused and lead to corruption of the system. (These consequential outcomes are further discussed in the case studies, "Transitional Nursing Care", "Outsourcing Contractual Practices", "The Millennium Dome" fraud, and Chapter Nine, "Technology Change and Managing the Consequences".)

The failure to design appropriate monitoring and management systems for control can create an environment that almost "gives permission" for misuse and inappropriate decision-making. There are occasions where the discovery of inappropriate fraudulent practices is not prosecuted, in the interest of protecting the company's market credibility. At an individual level the information may be repressed to protect reputations and careers. Each of which further creates a political environment that further compromises decision-making and in fact notionally gives permission for the misuse of systems. "This places an inordinate emphasis on the appearance of success rather than the reality" (Nyquist, 2009).

An example: the anti-terrorist law, framed in statutes, intended for combating international terrorism in the United Kingdom, which has been inappropriately employed for surveillance purposes. The surveillance powers have been used to monitor people that may be infringing minor local government regulations, which were not related to any terrorist activities.

Earlier reference was made to the fact that the corruption of systems occurs for two reasons: one, if the systems are inappropriately designed and two, if there is intent to defraud. In the case of an Assurance company, the central computing systems were inappropriately designed, disrupting the formal operational system by failing to deliver the necessary regulatory information. Employees developed alternative unofficial systems to overcome the inadequacies. The second instance is that when poor management practices exist and the system does not respond to enforcing the appropriate timely monitoring for control.

This is a systems management failure and invites employees to use their creative skills to benefit themselves. This can be expressed in misuse such as inflated expense claims (restraint is being practised regarding the United Kingdom's Parliamentary expenses scandal, 2009), claiming additional hours when completing time sheets, claiming pay when not on site, repressing critical reports, manipulating statistics to influence decision-making and many others. The gap between this behaviour and the wholesale fraudulent deception and very low-level infringements, are very small. Over time these "low-level" infringements can, when not detected, lead to catastrophic events; a good example of this insidious behaviour is the collapse of Barings Bank.

Induced Anxiety

Even though extreme examples have been used, it takes little to consider that at a personal level the operators of these systems can and will develop and use them to defend themselves against anxiety and at the expense of the organisation. We can assume that the systems have been unconsciously corrupted for a purpose not fully for the benefit of the overall organisation. This introduces the notion in practice of systems developing a life of their own and beginning to operate independently of the organisation they are supposed to service. We can track this system's "goal *displacement*" (Fig. 4) development in that the system becomes the organisation rather than servicing the organisation. The consequential outcomes of this misuse of *management technologies* can be shown in the following example. The United Kingdom's government spent £26 billion introducing Information Technology (IT) into the public sector. Government reports indicate that only 13% to 17% of the expenditure converted into viable programmes.

DISPLACED ORGANISATIONAL GOALS

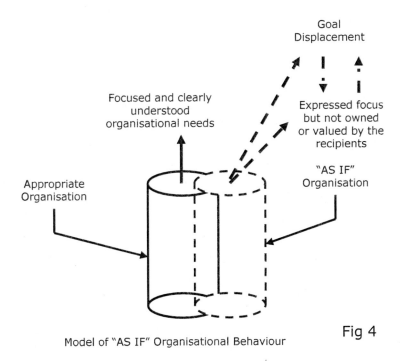

Model of "AS IF" Organisational Behaviour

Fig 4

This evolutionary process of the system is part of the need to regain control, to manage anxiety, which in turn gives too much credence to the system and leads to increasing systems dependency and *"goal displacement"* (Fig. 4). System dependency begins to develop when the management feel that the organisation is becoming too large, too complex and too difficult to monitor and control (Fig. 2). The failure to understand the concept of "territory, technology and time" (Miller, 1959), and how this can affect the performance culture over the developed *performance culture continuum*, adds to the already confused thinking and indicates why leaders and managers seek panaceas to relieve their anxiety. Goffman (1974) observed, "We tolerate the unexplained but not the inexplicable." It is essential that these concepts be understood to provide a means for evaluating and managing the various external and internal influences along with our own behaviour.

Without an understanding of what has to be led and managed, in organisational terms, leaders will make inappropriate decisions, further contributing, although unwittingly, to any existing dysfunctional practices. The induced ambiguity adds to the negative spiral of poor and inappropriate decision-making, which in turn induces higher levels of stress within the decision-making processes.

Defence against Anxiety

There are a number of behavioural forces at work, directly affecting the organisations' and systems' behaviour, and when not understood, compound the felt need for further personal controls, which introduces a great deal of anxiety and confusion, leading to "pathological behaviour" (Burns, 1963). The consequential *goal displacement* (Fig. 4), from managing the organisation to managing the systems and socially structured political practices, eventually renders the social processes "mentally sick" (Rice, 1958). It is important to recognise that it is the need to manage induced anxieties that directly influence the way decisions are made and are implemented, which affects the way people, systems and the overall organisation behave.

Menzies (1970) writes, "A social defence system develops over time as a result of collusive interaction and agreement, often unconscious, between members of an organisation or to what form it should take. The socially structured defence mechanisms then tend to become an aspect of external reality with which new and old members of an institution must come to terms." These practices are the unconscious felt need to defend against anxiety that is created when an organisation is forced to respond to environmental forces and social needs or simply to find a solution to a presented problem. (Refer to case studies and "Overview" of the "The Brewing Industry".) Menzies (1970) observes that "…Between members of an organisation or to what form it should take" is important, as these unconscious social defence systems will, in an existing dysfunctional organisation, compound the existing dysfunctional practices.

Any proposed change to existing practices will be vehemently resisted. Menzies (1970) and Jaques (1955) stressed that resistance to social change can be better understood if it is seen as resistance of groups of people unconsciously clinging to existing institutions because changes threaten existing social defences against deep and intense anxiety. When leading and managing transition for change it is important that these social dynamics be understood, even felt.

Sir Winston Churchill said on this issue,
"The further back you can look, the further forward you can see."

For example, it is important before leading and managing a process of transition for change to examine the recent history of the institution to gain an understanding of *"the here and now"*. It is important to develop this process of thinking organisationally when discussing the introduction of new management technologies and/or negotiating with one or multiple trade unions (refer to the Avonmouth case study.)

Developed Organisation's Performance Culture

These induced dysfunctional management practices developed over the evolutionary stages of an organisation become indelible and part of your organisation's *"corporate organisational performance"* culture. Often within business organisations there is an acceptance that this is all part of corporate life and creates the psychological box we are all extolled to think outside of.

Wageman et al. (2008) identifies these corporate cultural differences when describing an executive's experiences of attempting to integrate two different organisations. "For some, especially those who had 'grown up' with Applebee's, the ideal culture was one, as one executive put it, 'of Midwesterners trying to do the right thing.' Others, especially those who had worked for large more traditional long-established companies, were at home in a culture that fostered a structured, formal, and silo approach." The acceptance of an organisation's corporate performance culture encourages other dysfunctional practises to be introduced, further depleting the performance of your organisation. The management of the organisation is seen as that of managing systems, procedures and practices, all of which have attached ownership and power inappropriately attributed to those who sponsor and manage these systems.

Decision-Making Process

These developed management practices, identified earlier, influence a decision-making process of *Politics – Career – and then the overt Organisation* (Fig. 3). This model of decision-making is imprecise, confusing, depleting and distracting, all of which significantly detracts from your organisation's overall performance as it introduces *displaced goals* (Fig. 4). A *displaced goal* could be the need to service "the appearance of success rather than the reality." In organisational terms this is a dysfunctional organisational decision-making process. The aim must be to reverse the above practices and begin with the *Overt Organisation – Career and finally the politics* (Fig. 5). "It would be unwise for anyone to ignore the politics. Critically the politics of an organisation has to be alternatively managed in terms of the organisation's needs" (Johnson, 1983).

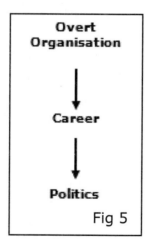

Fig 5

It is essential that these processes be recognised by those responsible for leading and managing the organisation. To change the current decision-making practices, it is necessary to develop the skills and competencies by using an *organisational approach*. We can now begin to provide an answer to the question posited at the beginning of this chapter, "Why do we organise?" – "To successfully cooperate, to complete increasingly complex tasks effectively." This question has been partly answered through this brief exploration of organisational development and its pathology. The identified compounded and failed decision-making practices are not providing the results anticipated, strongly indicating that we need to change the way we think about, lead and manage our organisations.

You may have observed that when discussing single systems from a systems point of view it becomes very difficult not to discuss the behavioural elements, as they are intertwined and totally dependent on each other. In Chapter Three we shall explore why organisations become dysfunctional from a behavioural perspective.

CHAPTER THREE

The Enemy Within and Why Change Fails
(A Behavioural Perspective)

In Chapter Two we explored how systems dependency caused organisations to become dysfunctional. Identification of how systems are designed and behave directly influences the behaviour of individuals and their decision-making within their organisations. The explorations of these inappropriate practices identified executives and managers consciously and/or unconsciously defending themselves against any induced felt sense of anxiety. This provides an opportunity to examine how these various practices affected the behaviour and motives that influence those making and implementing strategic and operational decisions.

During the process of examining systems behaviour we naturally made a brief excursion into social and group dynamics. As we work through this chapter we shall find that the reverse process will take place; we shall naturally stray into systems behaviour. These natural transgressions confirm that these two practices have a dependent relationship and have to be considered simultaneously.

By developing these concepts, their relationships and making the connections between these various activities, we will begin to provide a framework of "organisational thinking" to improve decision-making. To begin with, the two main issues that need to be addressed are *organisational leadership* and *managing transition for change*. When developing these ideas, the concepts already discussed will be further teased out and put into context.

The exploration throughout this chapter is designed with the direct intent to persuade you, as organisational leaders, to examine your own behaviour and how that affects your decision-making and others' behaviour. If your experiences involve working in dysfunctional organisations and politically centred organisations you will need to make a personal transition from that redundant frame of reference to that of *thinking organisationally*. Any change in behaviour and decision-making requires that the individual or workgroup make a personal transition from one state to another.

Organising Chairs

The function of organisational leadership requires you to have the capacity to design effective organisations. To develop the idea of organisational design, it is useful to consider the simple process of rearranging a set of chairs in readiness for an event. When doing so it is important to consider the arrangements, the design, and pattern to satisfy the desired *intent* and the necessary performance outcomes.

They can be arranged in lines, in classroom or school assembly format. This is usually used when a structured one-way instructive outcome is desired, a hierarchical structure to acknowledge authority and to control the situation. Another arrangement could be a crescent shaped auditorium, which is designed to provide a focal point for the attention of each individual attending. This can be a lecture or a surgical procedure and is used with the intention of imparting very specific detailed information.

Another outcome is the engagement of the individual in a developmental exploratory process. The chairs can be arranged in a circle with the intent of creating an equal, collaborative discursive format for problem solving. This egalitarian arrangement has a designed intent of reducing hierarchical barriers to encourage free and open discussion.

A further example, within a Gestalt therapeutic setting: two chairs could be used where the client would, when acting out roles, transfer from one chair to the other, to experience the different feelings of two conflicting characterisations, within the same person. The designed intent of this arrangement of chairs is to encourage and support the resolution of conflict within an individual.

Three chairs may be arranged and used in a triangle with the designed intent of facilitating third-party negotiations and/or the resolution of interpersonal conflict.

These are obvious examples; they do have the practical value of demonstrating the process of the designed strategic *intent* to successfully achieve an identified desired behavioural and performance outcome. The various performance outcomes identified in these examples enlist a particular behavioural performance expectation from all those in attendance.

It also indicates that leaders in different situations will also play different roles that have to match the designed *intent*. These arrangements of chairs may be reconfigured through the introduction of *management technologies*: for example, teleconferencing or, say, a medical procedure being pre-recorded and distributed by various mediums for each person to study individually. Whatever approach is employed, the leader has to adapt their role to fit the created remote and less interactive situation, created by the employed management technology. (Refer to Chapter Seven, "Adaptive Organisational Leadership" to further explore role adaptability.)

Each of the chairs creates different forms of social organisations and enlists a different leadership style that automatically and appropriately flows from the *intent*. In organisational terms the *intent* is to satisfy the "primary task". The designed arrangement of the chairs automatically evokes expectations in the participants, and has implied values along with personal and required social group behaviour. It may have become evident that when we fail to design the social organisation to satisfy the *intent*, we create anxieties that are induced through the created confusion and dysfunctional behaviour.

We all need to *make sense of our environment* and these dysfunctional practices serve only to deny us that opportunity, which introduces confusion, personal conflict and a felt sense of anxiety. By making the connection we identify why individuals and/or their workgroup find cause to reorganise their activities to defend them from induced anxieties. If these defensive social practices are further denied sickness and absence begin to increase. For example this is prevalent in nurses who no longer have the ability to delegate upwards as means of "defence against anxiety" (Menzies, 1970), to relieve the projected feelings when working with patients.

This process of organising chairs, although simple, identifies the qualities that are used when thinking about, designing and implementing strategies, leading and managing transition for change within any organisation. When implementing strategies it is important to create the appropriate organisational vehicle to achieve the intended changes and ensure that the appropriate performance delivery outcomes are achieved. Experience, time and time again, demonstrates that the lack of understanding and the ability to design your organisation appropriately directly contributes to the compromise and even failure of many strategic intentions.

What complicates the processes are, of course, the size and complexity of an organisation. Scale, geography, relative complexity, rate of change, the nature of the technologies employed and market behaviour, along with acquired social personal experience within an organisation, all adds to the mix and the sense of being overwhelmed.

Thinking in terms of the organisation enables these complex mixes of influences to be simplified, which reduces the complexity of decision-making, the relative ambiguity and critically induced anxieties. It helps organisational leaders to make sense of the potentially chaotic mix of influences, by helping those to decide what blend of influences are needed to support and improve decision-making. The added value is that the reduction of complexity and induced anxiety that creates the tendency for leaders to develop organisations as a "defence against anxiety" (Menzies, 1970) is dramatically reduced.

Environments of Social Organisations

Goffman (1974) observed, "We tolerate the unexplained but not the inexplicable." When considering how leaders may react when faced with complex and unfamiliar situations, such as a need to lead and manage *transition for change*, it elevates the desire to create defences from induced situational anxieties. Having introduced the idea that many leaders and managers, in organisational terms, are unfamiliar with what they should be leading and managing suggests the following situation will prevail.

When presented with the need to manage transition for change, lacking an understanding along with experience, there is a shift along the continuum from the "unexplained" towards the "inexplicable." This is particularly prevalent when the same task is undertaken in a political and personality structured game-playing organisation. (Refer to the "Millennium Dome" case study.)

Understanding what is being led and managed

"To understand what something means is the major goal of sociology, but it is also the fundamental role of existence for the human species" (Phillips, 1973). Experience proves that being able to make sense of what is being dealt with and having a means for developing an appropriate *structure for testing decision-making is critically important*. Lagadec (1993) writes, "Our ability to deal with chaos depends on structures that have been developed before the chaos arrives. When the chaos arrives, it serves as an abrupt and brutal audit: at a moment's notice, everything that was left unprepared becomes a complex problem and every weakness comes rushing to the forefront."

These breaches in the defences opened by a crisis create a vacuum. The negative nature of a vacuum will automatically draw in any available resource to fill it. Often this vacuum, in line with current management thinking, creates a desire to search for panaceas. These remedies – often inappropriate systems solutions – are imported and employed, serving only, over time, to further compound and lose sight of the original problem. (Refer to Chapter Nine, "Technology Change and Managing the Consequences", where we identify that the government has spent circa £26 billion on failed IT computer systems. Also Chapter Ten, "Outsourcing and Contractual Practices", where problems are often inappropriately transferred or even dumped.)

The Hatton Cross Rail Disaster, when examined in organisational terms, is an example where historic decisions affected the current operational activities of the trains and the track. When we use the notion of *dependent relationships* it is impossible, in organisational and technological terms, to separate the trains and the track. It is a simple *dependent relationship* and to have two different organisations operating the trains and the track separately is ill-conceived. The decision was made when the government of the day chose to privatise the national railway network. The basic rule in any organisation is that you design your organisation to regulate any *states of flux* created by making a transition from one state to another. The dependency of the trains on the track is self-evident.

Separating these two dependent elements creates an unnecessary *transition and a state of flux* from one organisational culture to another. This, in effect, requires another organisation that specifically manages the regulatory management of that *transitional state of flux* between the services that run on the track and the need to install and maintain the rail track services. These include all the track safety procedures and practices. The failure to regulate this transition can lead to confusion and even the need to translate the language from one organisational culture to another.

The executives introduced and compounded the earlier inappropriate decision-making error, which confirmed that the executives had little understanding, in organisational terms, of what they were leading and managing, which led to the decision to outsource the track maintenance. This in turn introduced a further transitional *state of flux* created through the need to translate from one organisational culture and its language to another.

It is unsurprising to learn that the Inquiry into the crash found that the maintenance staff had reported a defect at Hatton Cross Station. Yet the outsourced contracted maintenance staff attended a problem at the other end of the station. The defective track remained, which caused the fatal accident. The potential for these incidents reoccurring still remain through the inherent initial organisational design, even though they have subsequently taken that particular outsourced maintenance contract in-house.

Two situations can be identified: that of a catastrophic nature and also the insidious situation. In either case, these can introduce devastating unpredictable outcomes. To bring these processes into "sharp focus" the practice of Situational Awareness will be used to assist in developing our understanding. Even so, what must remain at the forefront of every leader's mind is the fact that most catastrophic events are the result of the insidious lack of awareness and consequential outcome of the executive leadership's decision-making processes. (We should be able to make a connection with the earlier example of the developed, but insidious, mismatch with pilots and the employed computer technology causing them to report "lost situational awareness".)

Nimrod Enquiry: Flawed, Sloppy and Complacent

The inquiry into the fatal fire on RAF Nimrod XV230 where 14 servicemen, serving in Afganistan, died on 2nd September 2006, chaired by the lawyer Charles Haddon-Cave QC, found a lamentable trail of avoidable error. It is, simply, a devastating tale of a department that has lost its way. The Nimrod Intergrating Project Team and the Ministry of Defence itself, was stricken by an "organisational trauma" induced by the overwhelming objective of finding savings. He added: 'A sacred and unbreakable duty of care is owed to the men and women of the Armed Forces. Concluding, Mr Haddon-Cave QC said that, 'financial pressure and cuts' forced the MoD to put 'business and financial targets' ahead of 'vital safety' and airworthiness issues'. 'The catastophe was caused as much by organisational culture as the faulty fuel seal. Financial pressures and cuts drove a cascade of organisational changes, which led to distraction from vital safety and airworthiness issues as the top priority.' BAE interest in winning contracts with the MoD was their business priority. 'Internal promotion resulted not from being on top of safety but being on top of budgets.'

For example, the Nimrod Enquiry (2010) was ten years in the making, yet was simply avoidable. (See inset.)

Toyota's difficulty with the safety of their vehicles and their fall from grace, creating a self-inflicted corporate market crisis, can be traced to the executives' decision-making. For example, Toyota chairman, Akio Toyoda, said when responding at a Congressional Hearing in the USA, "the Company has expanded too quickly and the three priorities, safety, quality and volume may have become confused." The confusion can be traced to the *consequential effects* of Toyota doubling their volume in five years to become the world's largest vehicle manufacturer and supplier. In doing so, the executives and management were not able to effectively manage the "supply chain quality" to the adopted standards they had assiduously developed to achieve their formidable record of product reliability.

Situational Awareness

The study of *situational awareness* can assist us to make sense of catastrophic failings, as it provides an insight into the possible mind-set and "organisational thinking" (Hutton, 1972) that organisational leaders need to develop. Endsley's definition (1995b), that "the perception of elements in the environment within a volume of time and space, the comprehension of their meaning, and the projection of their status in the near future", is firmly established and widely accepted.

It can be proffered that this perceptive state should be the outcome when considering and using Porter's (1980 & 1985) five simplified strategic elements. *Situational awareness*, in the context of organisational leadership, involves being aware of what is happening to your organisation and around you, understanding how information, events, and *even more so, your own behaviour* will impact on your decision-making and therefore the intent and the performance outcomes of your organisation, now and in the near future. It also requires that we are aware of the *consequential effects* when implementing any strategic decision.

Situational Awareness is a field of study usually concerned with perception of the environment critical to decision-makers in complex dynamic areas, from air traffic control and power plant operations, to military command and control. Lacking situational awareness or having inadequate situational awareness has been identified as one of the primary factors in accidents attributed to human error: Hartel, Smith, & Prince (1991), Merket, Bergondy, & Cuevas-Mesa (1997), Nullmeyer, Stella, Montijo, & Harden (2005); emergency response and military command and control operations: Blandford & Wong (2004), Gorman, Cooke, & Winner (2006); and offshore oil and nuclear power plant management: Flin & O'Connor (2001).

These studies and the notion of *situational awareness* fit well with the developed ideas and practice of *cognitive organisational awareness*, as the latter directly shifts the onus onto the organisational leader to become aware of their own behaviour, particularly with regards to their own decision-making and how their behaviour affects other's behaviour and subsequent decision-making. (These issues are further discussed in Chapter Seven, "Adaptive Organisational Leadership" and Chapter Eight, "Workgroups – Leadership Positioning in Groups".)

It is unfortunate that such devastating disasters have to be used to make "stark" the failings of leaders and managers of organisations. These examples are of value as they focus attention and encapsulate the way organisations had been led and managed. These reports often identify the insidious depletion of inappropriate leadership and management prior to an accident. It provides stark reminders that all organisations are open to the precipitation of any underlying weaknesses. In the above example, the Hatton Cross Rail Disaster, underlying weakness was within the basic organisational and systems design, a situation that stems from not understanding *interdependent and dependent relationships*. These weaknesses are often within the decision-making processes, caused by the lack of understanding as to what is being led and managed and the human processes that subsequently affect our behaviour when working with social systems such as organisations and groups.

"Human beings, who are almost unique in having the ability to learn from the experiences of others, are also remarkable for their apparent disinclination not to do so."
Douglas Adams

When these same levels of failures occur in, for example, retail or knowledge-based organisations, the catastrophe is confined to loss of market position or profit, or skilled people leaving the organisation, all of which are extremely important. Although the failures in the introduction of information technology supporting the knowledge base have not only been extremely costly, it is mainly the institutions acquiring the technology that have felt the consequential effects. The suppliers have, other than their reputation, generally escaped the full financial consequences and go on to purvey the same technologies, creating the same predictable failings. This suggests that there is a complete lack of any effective process of learning from these substantial failings. It is reminiscent of the adage used in the newspaper industry: "If it bleeds it leads", which implies that if it

72

doesn't bleed it goes unreported and lessons are unheeded. (These issues are further examined in Chapter Seven, "Technology Change and Managing the Consequences".)

The process of dysfunctional decision-making, in either situation, is just as important as what the differences are and the identified consequential outcomes that may or may not become public. When catastrophes occur, they are reported and become public knowledge: "If it bleeds it leads." These research and inquiry findings, by their nature, are retrospective, and can only act as "stark reminders". Identifying corporate weaknesses that lead to catastrophic events, although well researched, does not provide the solutions for rectifying these failings. This becomes evident when the affected organisations fail to implement the changes recommended in even judicial reports, for example the Hatton Cross Rail Disaster and the ill-fated flight of the space shuttle "Challenger".

If we accept that these claims are reasonable it may evoke a feeling of being helpless, which stems from leading and managing within an environment that is unfamiliar and not understood. The intent through this book is to demonstrate how the use of an organisational approach to organisational leadership and problem solving clearly provides an opportunity to learn from these situations and to provide a working method for testing decision-making practices. It also provides an opportunity to *audit your current practices* enabling you to avoid predictable failures.

Reality

Situational awareness is particularly important in work domains where the information flow can be quite high and poor decisions may lead to serious consequences – for example, piloting an airplane, functioning as a soldier, or treating critically ill or injured patients, or the need to lead and manage the *transition for change* when improving the performance culture of an organisation. There is a sudden demand for information when presented with the realisation of the critical condition of an organisation faced with its potential demise, e.g. Barings merchant bank (1995). Northern Rock UK, during the 2007-2009 financial crisis, was suspended from the London Stock Exchange, and in September 2007 was nationalised. (Refer to

Chapter Six, "Leading Transition for Change", and the "Overview of Case Studies".)

The United States sub-prime financial crisis saw the eventual demise of Lehman Brother Holdings Inc., a global financial service company. It was, in 2008, the largest bankruptcy in the history of the United States. When an organisation is, by necessity, having to manage scheduled or unscheduled change, degrees of chaos are introduced: "…It serves as an abrupt and brutal audit." The devastating event that beset Toyota, which has compromised its reputation for quality and reliability, is an abrupt and brutal audit for that company.

A distinction that needs to be made is that these *management technology* driven activities are all managed within an organisational envelope and its environment. For example, the political influence of the UK government's identified *intent* created an "overwhelming objective of finding savings" causing "organisational trauma" (Nimrod Enquiry 2010). The evidence shows that, as with this and many other disasters, decision-making and failed corporate practices are identified as the prime reason for these failings. The use of the idea of situational awareness remains important, as it provides a working definition of the mind-set of *organisational thinking* that executives and managers need to develop to become effective *organisational leaders and managers.*

"Doing nothing is making a decision which retains an attached ownership and accountability."
A. Johnson

There are two possible dynamics that may separate these technology driven activities from that of managing at the corporate level within an organisation. One is that the immediacy of the activities of the employed technologies and the dangers they import should, by their very nature, demand attention. The second, the slow insidious depleting dysfunctional activities – ten years in the Nimrod case – and the protracted inappropriate practices of Lehman Brothers, which infect an organisation, are far more difficult to identify and therefore manage. These infectious dysfunctional cultures become part of the "corporate performance culture" that old and new members learn to live with and not challenge. They become risk adverse and career orientated (Nyquist, 2009). (Refer to Chapter Eleven: "Remuneration and Motivation", along with the case studies "Transitional Nursing Care" and "Greenwich District Hospital".)

The developed, although dysfunctional, corporate culture can detach leaders from the *primary task*. In the Nimrod case this was the cost recovery rather than airworthiness. What is amazing is that this problem of cost developed, precipitously, over a period of ten years, which begs the question – why? It is difficult to believe that a cost monitoring practice did not exist, which raises a series of new questions: why was it ignored, and who was giving permission and not being held accountable for these massive cost overruns?

The value of using an organisational approach is that it clearly defines the *primary task* and provides an understanding of the nature of the boundaries to be managed, which along with those influences that can mutate and become infectious, can be anticipated, clearly defined and managed.

Leadership and Organisational Behaviour

In an attempt to provide answers to the above questions it is necessary to identify the underlying human involvement in the decision-making processes. This is an area in which psychoanalysts can make a major contribution because they approach the subject with different assumptions, namely that the everyday behaviour of individuals in social institutions is heavily influenced by unconscious processes. It is important to explore the emotional behaviour of the individual when they are faced with these chaotic events. Before doing so it would be useful to identify the leader's roles in social organisations.

Leaders are generally regarded as people who, by direction and encouragement, help others to achieve group goals. Without them social cooperation and therefore civilisation would be difficult, if not impossible. A popular belief is that society behaves *as if* individuals and their social institutions run on rational, understandable, conscious lines, which is amazing because, wherever you look, the evidence is to the contrary. Decisions are made on arbitrary and illogical criteria; the obvious is often denied.

These kinds of behaviours can be identified in this example. A senior executive, who was a qualified brewer, displayed the following behaviour. The technical problem was the over-carbonation of keg beer as a consequence of stratification caused by fermenting high gravity beer in vertical vessels, which were over sixty feet tall. At a senior executives' meeting to discuss the presented problem of poor dispensing in the trade outlets, the senior executive denied that when fermenting beer it generated carbon dioxide (CO_2). Other qualified brewers failed to challenge his pontificating and the basic assumption that was clearly not true, as CO_2 is a natural by-product of the fermenting process. "The important thing about pontification is that although an intellectual exercise, its origins are emotional. Closely allied to pontification is the no less hazardous 'cognitive dissonance'. This uncomfortable mental state arises when a person possesses knowledge or beliefs which are in conflict with a decision he has made" (Dixon, 1976).

There were two main reasons that affected the dynamics of this meeting and the subsequent projected behaviour. One was that the main board of executives had realised that during the rationalisation and development of a central brewing process and distribution Greenfield Site, their power base had geographically shifted to the executive body running the new centralised production distribution site. They were in the process of what can be, at best, called a "power raid" to reclaim some of the power and influence. The members of the new centralised production and distribution site occupied the senior roles with the consent of the main board members. The newly established order of things was being directly and forcefully disturbed creating career and life changing "chaos" for the incumbents of these posts. The executive referred to above, who made the statement, was extremely ambitious and would at all costs do almost anything to defend the career he had mapped out.

The extrinsic challenge to the newly established groups of executives is having their sovereignty and power challenged by an existing power group. Bion (1967), when introducing the notion of sovereignty and power, writes: "In small groups similar to those used here [for therapeutic purposes – author's note], power and sovereignty do not develop to maturity. The mature form is extrinsic and impinges on the group only in the form of invasion by another group." Often people feel their sovereignty, power and even identity has been violated when these invasive activities are imposed during the merging and or taking over of a corporation.

The other dynamic was that the technology being employed was advanced and relatively new within the brewing industry. The brewers were now the owners of the new technology and they had become the technicians employed to manage these new ground-breaking processes. They were unable to consider the possibility that the cause of the problem was within the brewing and fermenting process, caused by stratification. They projected all the blame onto the disparate group of trade outlets, who individually were unable to make their case and defend themselves. The trade outlets were being made the "scapegoats" (Jaques 1951 and Trist and Bamford, 1951). They, the brewers, could not be the cause of the problem and subsequently went into a state of denial.

The brewers, historically as the owners of the new technology, formed a closed group. Thus their sense of self, derived from belonging to a group and an institution, wore a layer of "psychological skin" to foster a sense of identity and security of belonging. Obholzer (1989) writes, "The so called 'logic' of everyday conscious behaviour is nothing but a badly applied veneer on the carcass of unconscious individual and group assumptions." These mental cooperatives take the form of ideologies and schools of thought, enlist compliance within the group, which directly affects the direction of decision-making, and when challenged they can be aggressively resisted. Obholzer (1989) confirms these phenomena exist, which makes it an important process that needs to be understood, particularly when attempting to influence and introduce transition for change. He writes, "A particular problem for intensely paranoid leaders is that any information or events which threaten to contradict their most cherished beliefs, may actually intensify rather than reduce their persecutory delusions. Deeply suspicious of the apparent contradictory evidence and incapable of admitting they are wrong." They are capable of becoming even more entrenched and allow their decision-making to become delusional, self-protective and distinctly inappropriate to the real task in hand.

This inability to rationally examine the presented problem was further induced by the "power raid" by the main board members. They had, as many of them were either qualified brewers or old brewing family members, become caught up in the process of denial, as historically they were never challenged. Collectively they all colluded with the brewer, who said, "CO_2 is not generated during the fermenting process." This example has identified that these unconscious processes do operate within social organisations. (Further details of the background to this induced situation and the eventual resolution are discussed in the case study entitled "Ullage, CO_2 and 'AS IF' Organisations".)

Why Leaders Mislead

Within the earlier exploration of organisations, three major factors emerge. The first is that many executives and managers in organisational terms are unaware of what they need to lead and manage. The second is the conscious or unconscious development of dependency on systems. The third is the induced anxiety that is felt by individuals and groups when operating within a social system, particularly when working close to the "inexplicable" end of the continuum. If we accept that, at the very least, the three factors are inter-dependent and will influence the decision-making processes that occur in any social organisation, it raises important questions: in what way are leaders likely to mislead and how that is likely to affect their decision-making? It becomes important, as we are all affected in different ways when we enter any social situation. How we respond will be dependent on our own life experience and developed coping strategies. (Refer to Chapter Twelve, "Development, Training and Recruitment", where this concept is further discussed.)

When considering these factors the leader is being required to deal with a high degree of ambiguity. Observations clearly identify how this situation can affect an individual. Dixon (1989) writes, "An additional problem for a decision-maker, political, military and business leaders is that of incomplete or ambiguous information. Faced with the fact that rarely, if ever, is sufficient information available on which to make important decisions." We can make the connection with Goffman's (1974) observations, "We tolerate the unexplained but not the inexplicable." That suggests, as we move along this continuum, our level of anxiety progressively increases when we are forced to deal with these unpalatable situations.

"Through denial of the unpalatable, misinterpretation, distortion or repression of the unacceptable, and a predilection for wish fulfilling fantasies, decisions tend to be based not on what is the case but on what we would like to be the case." Within this decision-making environment they are working at what is referred to as the *"assumption level"* devoid of what is necessary to evaluate and manage the presented situation. The implication is that leaders are likely to mislead particularly if they lack the understanding, in organisational terms, as to what they are leading and managing. This in turn, prohibits their ability to effectively evaluate the implications of their decisions. They are unable to determine the *consequential effects* of their *decision-making,* which contributes to the compromising factors that directly affects the consistent shortcomings of many strategic initiatives.

In Chapter Six, "Leading Transition for Change", we discuss the introduction of the process of *monitoring to manage* to alleviate these failures to evaluate and learn. Although a logical practice for leaders to adopt, it introduces a potential for leaders misleading through their inordinate desire to be seen to be *consistent and committed*. To some degree this behaviour may help to provide an insight as to "how they may deal with unpalatable situations".

Consequential Effects

Experience demonstrates that many of these compromised strategic practices are reworked under another guise. These cycles of events can be observed in many organisations; they are not only costly in financial terms but do have negative effects on employees who are likely to become increasingly resistant to change initiatives. The felt sense of failure can induce a desire to introduce further systems to achieve control of the organisational practices; reengineering and outsourcing are obvious examples.

Earlier we discussed the use of systems and the consequential effects when inappropriately or poorly designed. *Intent and motive* will influence the way systems are developed, which can lead to systems being designed to justify and support any decision owned by a paranoid leader. In other words they are designing these systems as a defence against their own anxiety.

"When considering the reasons why leaders lead people astray, pride of place must surely be given to those personality factors, which through self-selection characterise the potential misleaders. The argument is simple; people are attracted to and prosper in vocations that suit their mental make-up. As a consequence it is not surprising to find amongst the ranks of leaders some who are power-hungry, manipulative, extrovert, sensation-seeking, theatrical, exhibitionistic, devious, pragmatic, risk takers, and certainly not weighed down with moral scruples. For good or bad the natural characteristics of such people, encouraged by the job they are trying to do, will determine the decisions they make" (Dixon, 1989). Within dysfunctional corporate performance cultures, the old and new members learn to live with and do not challenge their decision-making behaviour, which allows people to act out their own fantasies. (Refer to Chapter Eleven, "Remuneration and Motivation".) When the need for transition for change is forced on the individual or groups, this disturbs any felt sense of equilibrium as it presents an anxious threat that needs to be managed and defended against.

The Individual and the Organisation

People do not exist as individuals. They are joined together in groups, small and large, and they interact in these groups both as individuals and as groups. An individual cannot exist in isolation, but only in relation to other individuals and groups. Even when alone, what that individual undertakes is, in a large part, a product of past relationships and anticipated relationships in the future. A baby is dependent on one person: its mother. Gradually assimilated patterns of relationships develop with the father and other siblings. As a child develops in childhood they begin to develop further relationships with other members of the extended family and family networks.

The first break with the family pattern is usually when a child goes to school and encounters, for the first time, an institution where they have to contribute as a member of a wider society. The hopes and fears that govern an individual's expectations of how they will be treated by others, along with the fears and attitudes on which they base their own code of conduct, will be developed. The developed codes of conduct, expectations, attitudes and beliefs and motives are directly influenced by their experiences, derived from those relationships that build the patterns that become that individual's personality. These developmental processes will directly influence how we react and make decisions when presented with the inexplicable. (Refer to Chapter Twelve, "Development, Training and Recruitment", where these issues are further explored.)

Managing the Inexplicable

When there is an element of confusion, for example, the availability and quality of information, change scheduled or unscheduled introduces degrees of chaos (Lagadec, 1993) the first impulse is to grasp for some explanation, any old explanation. And what we get hold of are the automatic explanations we have lived with longest and invoked most often. We often find the initial meaning of events by drawing inferences from how we feel (Weick). When a need for peace of mind takes precedence over that for survival the anticipated outcomes of a decision may well seem rosier than they deserve. Add to this the fact that the more emotionally important and the less warranted a decision the greater would-be attempts to justify it. Possible examples are the wars in Iraq and Afghanistan. The demise of major institutions, identified earlier, was avoidable or at the very least the damage could have been significantly reduced. The introduction of all-pervasive IT systems to drive change within both private and public sectors has created significant unwanted consequential outcomes.

Choosing the best possible options depends on *attitudes* and *motives* that are relevant to the desired goal, which in this discussion is improving the on-going performance culture of an organisation. "So when leaders are swayed by such egocentric desires as their need to be liked, the urge to strike a macho image, to boost self-esteem, to appear young and energetic, to distract attention from their shortcomings or to emulate some great leader of the past, the chances are that their decisions will be biased away from what is best for their followers. Since these motives are often synonymous with those which get such people to positions of power in the first place, they tend to be the stock-in-trade of leaders who mislead." (Dixon, 1989.)

There are others of a more malignant and intractable kind that are excessively paranoid or psychopathic, because they are grandiose and corrupted by enjoying too much power for too long, because they are driven by and acting out infantile complexes, or because they are trying to compensate for feelings of inferiority sown early in childhood.

A particular problem for intensely paranoid leaders is that any information or event that threatens to contradict their most cherished beliefs may actually intensify rather than reduce their persecutory delusions. Deeply suspicious of the apparently contradictory evidence and incapable of ever admitting they might have been wrong, leaders of this ilk become even more prone to initiating some dangerous action which seems, to them, justified as self-protective or retaliatory, which can be interpreted as bullying.

Not only do they interact with each other, magnifying the likelihood of wrong decisions, but also the stressful consequences of an *initial misjudgement can set off a whole chain of further errors* (Dixon, 1989). In Chapter Three we identified the same pattern of increasing dysfunctional behaviour generated from a systems behavioural approach, although in this case human behaviour. An example we can consider is the United Kingdom's government-created dependency on two major outsourcing contractors where the decisions have become irrevocable, through the misplaced vested personal and political power of individuals. (Refer to Chapter Ten, "Outsourcing and Contractual Practices".)

Physical Personal Experiences

Faced with an awesome choice it is highly likely that the decision-maker will be handicapped both physically and mentally by that biological anachronism: the adrenalin rush of a "fight or flight" emergency response. Such concomitants of stress as narrowed attention, perceptual distortion, impaired memory, slowed thinking, not to mention physical disorders ranging in severity from indigestion and headache to cardiac arrest, are just some of the symptoms, which could afflict even the most dedicated leaders. (Refer to Chapter Eleven "Remuneration and Motivation" where the rates of attrition for leaders are discussed.)

This reaction, ideally suited to those physical threats, which can be countered by the rapid expenditure of muscular energy – such as striking or running away from an attacker – is singularly inappropriate to the complex cognitive problems facing high-level decision-makers today. Having evolved over millions of years to cope with and survive in a habitat radically different from the present one, our brains simply don't work in the sort of ways that allow us to interact successfully or safely with modern technology (Dixon, 1989 & Goleman, 1996).

Defensive Mechanisms

The purpose of mental defensive mechanisms, either in the individual or the social systems setting, is to protect oneself from inner conflict and pain. Psychoanalysts describe this behaviour as splitting and projective identification. These terms are used to describe the process of disowning the negative aspects of oneself and identifying them with conviction in others. We all practise this defensive device of projecting and disowning aspects of the self and then identifying them in others. It happens not only in the individual but also in groups, including large and small organisations.

The following notional model (Fig. 6) should assist to develop your understanding of how instinctive relationships and the practice of defending against anxiety and resistance to change.

Karl E. Weick, Professor of Psychology, University of Michigan, who describes the nature and type of decisions leaders make when faced with the inexplicable, provide a possible insight into leaders' behaviour. You don't have to have a disaster to find the inexplicable; you can experience the dynamics of this phenomenon when you are engaged in the management of organisational *transition for change*. This feeling of confusion and anxiety when leading and managing *transition for change* processes are felt, particularly when things aren't going to plan, which can evoke primeval feelings that we all possess.

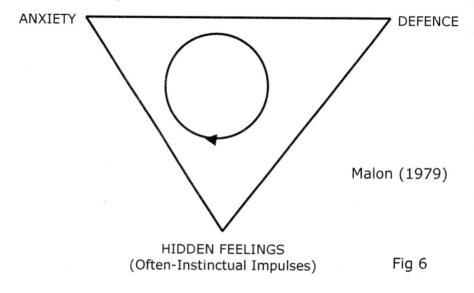

DEFENCE AGAINST ANXIETY AND/OR RESISTANCE TO CHANGE

ANXIETY   DEFENCE

Malon (1979)

HIDDEN FEELINGS
(Often-Instinctual Impulses)   Fig 6

Experience of managing major change programmes that had suddenly attracted external powerful political influences created chaos and confusion that was inexplicable as it did not fit the demands of the existing transition for change programmes. Trying to translate the presented organisational, political and individual motives became extremely difficult. When immersed and responsible for the outcome, it feels "as if" you are working in an asylum; the activities are insanely irrational, contradictory and confusing. Nearly every day, after working in this kind of organisation's environment, Erving Goffman's book, *Asylums: Essays on the Social Situation of Mental Patients and Other Inmates* was pulled forward and flagged on the bookshelf.

The feeling of isolation and threat is prevalent and if not managed can be extremely damaging to one's own health and well being. In essence, when managing major change it can feel like you are working in an asylum, particularly when the organisation has a personality/political structure. Where people are making irrational pontifications that directly affect decisions, which they compound them when they become aware of their errors, by further irrational decisions. (These themes are further developed in Chapter Six, "Leading Transition for Change" to provide a means for managing any possible induced but unwarranted decision-making practices.) (Refer to "The Millennium Dome" case study for an example of unwanted political influence.)

Dependency on Groups

These situations are stressful and do affect the quality of a leader's decision-making. It is clear that leaders do not work in isolation, as it is part of their role to give direction and leadership to cooperative individuals within groups, which introduces the need to explore the dynamics of the conscious and unconscious assumptions of individuals and groups (Bion, 1968).

There is a good deal that needs to be teased out through the research and writings of various psychoanalysts who have examined political leadership decision-making, organisations and the behavioural dynamics in groups. The importance of understanding the basics of individual and group behaviour becomes evident from the experience of managing major change programmes. From these organisational developmental experiences, it becomes evident that we all depend on group relationships for collective success. They also demonstrate how these dependant group relationships can be productive as well as restrictive. These experiences will be used to clearly demonstrate how these psychoanalytical processes are acted out during the process of leading and managing transition for change and the development of the individual.

"Top-level leadership today may be characterised in terms of a basically incompatible relationship – that between something warm, soft, slow, wet, sentient and unreliable and something cold, hard, fast, devoid of feelings but infinitely destructive. In other words, fallible human beings..." (Dixon, 1989). Agreement may not be achieved as to Dixon's description but what is important is that human beings are fallible. That fallibility is expressed in the need to belong to groups and also be subjected to the implied or expressed norms. It is, therefore, important that leaders are aware of how they *affect others and others affect their own behaviour.*

Developing a Sense of Self

Earliest relationships have as their task the containing of the child's anxiety and the fostering of a sense of self: the development of a *psychological skin*. In the formative stages this serves both as a physical boundary for a sense of self and also as a psychological one. Thus a sense of self, of belonging to a family, a group, an institution, a nation, are all various layers of skin to foster a sense of identity, security and belonging. "Schools of thought and social structures are thus man-made devices to protect us from these anxieties. Put another way, they are social structures, which we join at birth, renewing or not (as the case may be) our membership as we go through life in order to have protection and rescue from isolation and breakdown." (Obholzer, 1989.) It follows that the unconscious fears are of a different and opposite state of mind: of not knowing, of being lost, boundary-less, out of control, at the mercy of hostile forces. They are ways of avoiding being lost in space, boundary-less, unconnected, psychotic; psychoanalysts describe them as ways of keeping psychotic anxieties at bay.

These processes and their consequential, at times unpredictable, outcomes underwrite the need for this book as it enables you to create appropriate organisational environments that attempt to limit these unwanted behavioural outcomes. This is achieved by providing a framework for testing decision-making, understanding how they influence practices and behaviour, which, in turn, determine the likely performance outcomes, but critically provide an opportunity for an individual to learn from their decision-making behaviour and take appropriate developmental action.

These "mental defensive cooperatives" take the form of ideologies or schools of thought. What they all have in common is that they will act defensively on our behalf, to keep the unspeakable and unthinkable at bay: for example, the brewer who denied CO_2 existed in the brewing process. The greater the anxiety, it becomes more prevalent, the greater the pseudo-clarity of insight and the resulting self-righteousness (Obholzer, 1989).

Membership of these social defensive systems, whilst comforting in the short-term, can in the long-term become a damaging activity, because it leads to inevitable escalation of internal personal conflict and pushes the individual, group and organisational problems further away. This reduces, over time, the ability to identify the original cause of the problem, which now becomes the problem. "It's the same kind of thinking that created the problem in the first place" (Albert Einstein). Unfortunately these processes considerably reduce the chance that the problem can be acknowledged and worked upon.

A problem cannot be addressed until it is acknowledged, and preferably defined in clear terms and personally owned. Therefore it is essential that all of us in both our personal and organisational roles constantly work at further developing a frame of reference where all decisions can be tested in terms of our organisations. It is in the nature of our personal and social defence mechanisms that denial will constantly encroach on awareness of the dangers. It is a consequence of our denying these qualities in ourselves and perceiving them only in the other side by a process of projective identification.

The price to pay for membership of these mental and social structures is not to question their functioning but to go along with the system in an unthinking sort of way. (Refer to case studies, "Transition Nursing Care", "Avonmouth" and "Greenwich District Hospital".) "These structures then do the denial on our behalf – it is as if the contract is along the lines of 'don't worry your head about uncertainties, anxieties, fear of death, annihilation, extinction, etc. – join and in return for your allegiance we will provide you with a ready-made system of denial and defence – leave it all to us. All we want from you is unquestioned allegiance to our way of doing things." Corruption occurs when a person appears to be complying, but behaves differently and/or represses information that may disturb that balance. "Personal thoughts and questioning therefore invalidates membership and returns the anxiety to us for us to deal with individually" (Obholzer, 1989). (Refer to case study, "Transitional Nursing Care".)

For example, a fish in a goldfish bowl, set on an island, observes to another fish in the water around the island, "It is kind of restrictive but I like the security." The real message is that the fish in the bowl is dependent on others for support and feeding and even its survival. The fish in the sea is free to make its own decisions in terms of how it scavenges for food and survives within its own wider environment.

Psychological Contract

This is sometimes referred to as the *psychological contract* between the individual and the organisation, the group and the fish with its keeper. Benefits of compliance are sometimes expressed through pay structures and in particular bonus structuring. An example as to where this approach becomes contradictory was within the developed practice of the New Millennium Experience Company (N.M.E.C.). Not insignificant bonuses were offered to deliver on time. At the same time it was repeatedly reinforced that any untoward practice of a possible fraudulent nature had to be reported, depending on who was committing the offence as to whether it would be reported, particularly if your bonus could be compromised. It needs to also be said that everyone was on short-term contracts, which influenced and determined attitudes.

The essence of these systems of social organisations is that they will practise denial on our behalf. In other words, that they will act as a mental cooperative for our own defensive structures; a mass-produced skin of denial is somehow more credible than a home-produced individual one, and others doing it lends a supposed credibility to the process.

When, for example an organisation introduces a Safety Officer or Human Resources (HR) Manager there is a tendency for perceived responsibilities to be deferred to those roles. Where individuals had, for example, all accepted and took responsibility for safety for themselves and one another, the development of the role of Safety Officer saw those same people cede that responsibility for safety to that individual. Where they would normally have taken action, they deferred to the Safety Officer. In one situation, the Safety Officer could not cope with the resistance and volume of work. In an attempt to encourage the individual to accept responsibility further rules and regulations were introduced to enforce the practice. This led to conflict and even threats of strike action. This may be an indicator of why we have an over-regulating Health and Safety Industry.

Another example of HR management is that it can, if not defined appropriately and/or the HR manager wants to enhance their influence, cause precipitous role confusion and power transfer. The confusion can and does exist. The confusion is, for example, between

88

the line managers and the role of the HR department's responsibilities. The line manager is charged with the responsibility to lead and manage that element of the organisation. They are responsible for the performance, motivation, and discipline of those individuals that work within that line manager's responsibility.

When for example a line manager needs to discipline an individual, they have to refer to the HR department, who automatically bring to the discussion a completely different set of values. (Refer to the "Greenwich District Hospital" case study.) Many HR departments manage systems that are designed to create conformity across the organisation, to prevent wage/salary-drift, and to enforce equality of practices, usually influenced by interactions with Trade Unions and interpretation of regulatory legislation. These systems solutions often create a situation where the line managers become less effective. Their authority is compromised by the need for conformity to the non-line HR manager's pervasive influence and their one-fix-all control systems. Both the Safety Officer's and the HR manager's roles are, in reality, there to manage the boundary of the organisations and protect the organisation against litigation.

The two roles of the safety officer and the HR manager have been used to demonstrate possible role confusion and conflict. When you identify all the different parties that many line managers have to defer to, you start to develop a sense of the depletion of the line manager's ability to act independently.

Leadership and Management Development

Accepting that these processes and practices are played out within social organisations we can begin to examine the reasons why the majority of management and leadership development and training does not translate into improving the performance of the sponsoring organisation.

Understanding why these development programmes do not transfer enables a better understanding of resistance to many change initiatives. It becomes evident when you accept the defensive behavioural dynamics discussed above, that membership of these mental and social structures defines the operating culture that you are attempting to change. Even though these leadership and management development programmes are professionally delivered and in many cases valued by the participants, they are rejected by that organisation's social culture. The developed concept and understanding do not transfer from the classroom to a participant's place of work, as the implied performance cultures are at odds.

These new ideas disturb the time-developed social systems for defending against induced anxieties. This demonstrates why, in many cases, the content of the leadership and management development programmes fails to translate into the recipient's organisation. It is useful to consider this process acting "as if" transplanting an organ; if the match is not absolute, the opportunity for rejection is considerably higher. When the transplant's profile is not a complete match, the degree of maintenance, through the use of medication, or, in organisations, the development of alternative systems is considerable.

When, for example, *management technologies* are used to drive change they will, as identified in Chapter One, disturb the existing balance within the developed social systems. It is due to these disturbances that the practice of reengineering is being unconsciously employed. The practice of the initial dysfunctional decision-making and subsequent, induced organisational behaviour increases resistance whilst individuals attempt to make sense of these events (Philips 1973). The failure to match socio-technical needs creates a demand that the systems be modified to achieve the systems performance. This mismatch of the socio and the technical systems can be compared with the need to employ medication to offset and prevent the organ or the technical system being rejected. Overlaying the technical drivers for change on top of an existing dysfunctional organisational performance culture causes the mismatch between the socio and the technical systems to be further compounded.

The statement that any change will disturb the existing balance indicates where there is a need to have a well-developed ability to *think organisationally* to enable the consequences of these disturbances to be understood, regulated and managed. The technology must have the *intent* to improve the existing situation. But if you want to successfully achieve performance improvements you have to begin by designing the organisation to match the desired intent. Automatically, as discussed and reinforced earlier, you design all the systems, procedures and practices to create an environment where individuals and workgroups can collectively direct their contribution to the overall organisation's performance.

To assist in clarifying the point that the design of the organisation must lead the design of the systems, procedures and practices can be explored through examining the process of designing and fitting an electrical loom into a car. It would be inconceivable to design the electrical loom for a car before you agree the function, design and shape of a car. To take a loom from another car and attempt to fit it to a newly designed car would not cross anyone's mind as it would be impracticable, and at best a compromised expensive alternative. Simply, until you determine the behavioural performance outcome and function of your organisation you cannot complete the design until you have a clear understanding of the performance outcome your organisation needs to deliver. Therefore, the systems and management technologies, which include training and development, need to be designed to complement and reinforce, as with the car, the function and design of your organisation.

The above example of overlaying technologies onto an existing dysfunctional organisation fails to complement and reinforce the identified organisation's delivery performance. The consequential outcome is that each party renegotiates some form of alternative solution to make the system work, which invariably introduces cumulative compromises that can virtually make the system redundant. "Make the system work" has been underlined to draw your attention to the focus of the problem being resolved, that of the system and not in terms of the organisation. We have discussed at length situational problem solving and this is a good example that is not being resolved in terms of the host organisation's needs.

We are servicing an "as if" (Fig. 4 "Displaced Organisational Goal") organisation that has evolved to maintain the system and not the organisation. Understanding this concept and the associated behavioural dynamics is critical when you need to improve an organisation's performance and employ technologies to support and reinforce the identified organisational performance improvements. (Chapter Nine, "Technology Change & Managing the Consequences", examines the consequential outcomes of failing to understand this basic concept.)

When books such as, 'In Search of Excellence,' Peters and Waterman (1982) extol managers to manage change, innovation, leadership, creativity, entrepreneurship and many other practices, they are, in fact, asking leaders and managers to step outside their social groups. As we discovered earlier this is risky; we feel isolated, threatened and our primeval instincts can be invoked, which can be a very uncomfortable experience. Being an individual in such a group situation is so lonely as to be very frightening. There is fear that one's very existence is at stake. To take the risk you either have strong motives, the skill to manage the *transition for change*, invested authority and understanding the consequential outcomes before wanting to take the risk.

Remember that we all try to avoid pain, which we achieve by belonging to social groups, on which we become dependent, which also provides the protection and defence against anxiety. We should not, therefore, be surprised to find that when attempting to introduce strategic initiatives to achieve changes in performance there is resistance and many barriers to successfully managing *transition for change*. The provision of an organisational-led process directly reduces the degrees of this felt sense of organisationally induced anxiety.

Review

Having reviewed and explored some of the important issues and behavioural dynamics it quickly becomes evident that the current single initiative approach to leading and managing organisations is unsustainable. Rapidly changing organisational environments that are constantly influenced by changes, in particular, knowledge and information technologies, global marketing, political, raised expectations and naturally economic fluctuations are all contributing to the need to understand what is being led and managed in terms of the organisation.

This developed understanding, along with the need to continually manage an organisation that is in constant transition demands that we adopt appropriate styles of organisational leadership that can be successfully identified through the use of an organisational approach. The current leadership and management practices are not capable of delivering a consistent shared approach for the exacting demands placed on today's organisations.

Experience of successfully managing major organisational transition and change, clearly identifies that the use of an *organisational leadership* approach consistently works in any organisational environment. It must be evident that we all need to "think organisationally" if we want to lead and develop successful organisations. In each organisation where an *organisational leadership* approach has been applied for managing *transition for change*, successful and sustainable outcomes have been achieved. (These concepts and processes have been further developed in Chapter Six, "Leading Transition for Change".)

The use of a single initiative approach is doomed to fail as evidenced through Hammer, Peters and many other writers, which has, over time, proved to be ineffective and can introduce serious consequential and unwanted outcomes. Peters' encouragement to claim and exercise various motivational practices cannot consistently work, because of the personal psychological risks, unless the individual has a very good understanding of the behavioural dynamics of their organisation. The inability to define the real problem that is presented inadvertently encourages further inappropriate management technologies and systems solutions to be harvested and applied. The effect of this practice is to add layers of solutions to the presented problem, in an attempt to provide a solution, which is often the wrong solution for the wrong problem.

It should be evident that if you choose either the behavioural or systems approach, using them as single initiatives, they will both produce the same degree of failure. It should also have become evident that the two practices are interdependent and that the appropriate combination has to be applied, which creates the demand that we harmonise the social and technical (socio-technical). This basic assumption and understanding applies to all social organisations and must by necessity become part of the design process of any organisation when leading and managing transition for change.

Phillips (1973) writes, "To understand what something means is the major goal of sociology..." hence the reason for developing the ability; for leaders, *cognitive organisational awareness* to enable them to understand, in organisational terms, what they are leading and managing. In these uncertain situations it provides a secure performance platform and critically a reference point for all decision-making.

PART TWO

Developing a Theory in Practice

Goals and Introduction

CHAPTER FOUR
Developing a Theory in Practice – Part One
(Understanding what is being led and managed)

CHAPTER FIVE
Developing a Theory in Practice – Part Two
(The inter-related behaviour of the individual,
The group, the organisation and environment)

GOALS

- To develop your capacity to *think organisationally*.
- To develop your *intuitive cognitive organisational awareness* that includes the development of your *social emotional intelligence*.
- To develop a contextual understanding of your role within a social organisation.
- To develop your understanding of boundary management, task systems and how they have to be collectively harmonised.
- To develop an understanding of how our personal development influences our decision-making behaviour within the context of an organisation.
- To enable you to identify and resolve complex problems and provide sustainable solutions through improved decision-making practices.
- To reinforce the need to be able to adapt your own behaviour to the presented situation and be aware of your own feelings.

Introduction

Chapter Four is structured to enable you to develop your understanding of the theories and notions that support the application of an organisational decision-making approach.

Chapter Five is structured to develop your understanding of how the different behavioural activities fit within an organisation and its environment. It provides you with an opportunity to explore your inter-related behaviour, develop your *social emotional intelligence* and how it translates within workgroups and within a social organisation's environment.

The developed understanding of how organisations behaves and operate is an essential capability. *The organisation is the vehicle* and common denominator that enables your organisation and you to succeed. The derived success of using an organisational approach is that you create an identifiable performance platform to support appropriate and consistent decision-making. It enables multiple, complex, and sometimes-compounded problems to be resolved simultaneously.

This approach has an evaluative, diagnostic and even forensic capacity that enables you to successfully examine presented organisational problems. The following chapters are structured to enable you to develop your own understanding and capacity to audit your own and your organisation's current practices.

CHAPTER FOUR
DEVELOPING A THEORY IN PRACTICE

(Part One)
(Understanding what is being led and managed)

This chapter is designed to provide you with an insight into the contextual nature of an organisation to support the development of your *organisational thinking*. The intention is to develop your *cognitive organisational awareness* to significantly improve your decision-making and organisational *leadership* competencies.

By comparing the negative flawed practices discussed earlier we are able to identify and avoid these unwanted outcomes. Enabling you to begin to develop your ability to design and create effective appropriate organisations.

For Kurt Lewin, there was "nothing as practical as a good theory" (1963), which is an important concept that needs to be developed, with the precept that there will be an identifiable performance improvement outcome. It is tested by its ability to effectively deliver the necessary service delivery performance outcomes. To feed the evolution of a theory it is essential that we have a clear understanding of the subject under consideration; that of the organisation and how it behaves.

Albert Einstein declared that he was "passionately curious." Essentially if you are passionate about a subject, in this case, improving your own and your organisation's performance, we begin to follow his example by developing and testing our theories. Hutton (1972), writes, "everybody has theories" and suggests "they pass under other names, like myths or fantasies or proverbs or prescriptions or personal constructs, schemata, concepts or frames of references."

He suggests that when some people make their notions or ideas systematic and discuss them publicly there is an assumed requirement that they have to begin to develop empirical data. To empirically test the ideas, he says, "We are entering into the field of scientific theory and research."

Hutton (1972) discusses the "function of a theory" in which he distinguishes at least five functions, "which brings the function of a theory closer to the function of other sets of ideas." He writes, "Theories are often used in order to allow people to continue operating at some enquiry or technological or professional endeavour." Importantly, "Theories which suffer fro m lack of elegance or lack of comprehensiveness or lack of refutability may still be quite useful to people at the applied end of the discipline." Experience shows that this is an important distinction.

"The second function, which can be quite explicitly recognised as being scientifically valid, is the function of suggesting or guiding research and enquiry. This is the *heuristic* function."

"A thing may look specious in theory, yet ruinous in practice; a thing may look evil in theory, and yet be in practice excellent."
Edmund Burke (1788)

The third is more generally understandable, "the function of a theory is that of bringing into order what otherwise appears to be disconnected items of information." This is often caused by the design of the organisation, which for example, "...keeps people from seeing important interactions" (Senge, 1993). Having the ability to think organisationally assists you to make the connections between what appears to be disassociated activities that present themselves in organisations. "Let us call this the *orienting* comprehensive function" (Hutton, 1972). This is the theoretical function used when working through and developing the practice of *Organisational Problem Solving*. The developed practice has the necessary ability of clarifying complex dynamics in organisational situations, to make the necessary connections and orientate your leaders' and managers' minds on "what matters" and will provide working decision-making solutions. The process of *"thinking organisationally"* automatically imbues the requirement to constantly learn about the organisation's responsive changing needs. This is ingrained into the developed performance culture of the organisations. Argyris (1999), when writing on the subject of organisational learning, writes that it "is a competency that all organisations should develop."

(Examples of the failure of organisations to learn from their created presented problems that have become immersed in the complexity of the existing dysfunctional organisation's dynamics and reactive management practices are discussed in the case studies, "Avonmouth", "Operating Theatres Conflict Resolution", "Transitional Nursing Care" and "Greenwich District Hospital".)

"The forth function is to reduce a mass of data to a simpler statement. This *reductive* function is an extension of the *orienting* function as we are now asking that the statements of the theory should be as elegant and simple as possible." This function will become an integral part of the process when applying the practice of organisational problem solving. This is important, as it becomes the initial and final justification for the investment in personal effort and raw costs. (In Chapter Six, "Leading and Managing Transition for Change" these quantifiable measures are discussed as part of the overall processes of monitoring to manage.)

"The fifth function is related to precise or direct 'explanation' of the sort that can be tested by prediction. This is the *explanatory-predictive* function of the theory to which the criterion of *refutability* applies. The highest test of the theory is to show that it, and no other, can logically specify the outcome of empirical observations." The aim of this book is to encourage the reader to apply, test and work toward the ability to achieve the explanatory-predictive function.

There is a developed progression of these five functions that can be effectively applied. When developing your own *organisational leadership* competencies you are required to have a well-developed *cognitive organisational awareness* that enables you to *think organisationally* to identify the seat of the presented organisational problems and have the capacity to provide sustainable solutions.

Evolution of a Theory

Executives and managers have indicated that they have worked through the theories and practices of various writers and found it difficult to correlate and make sense of their ideas, in terms of what they are required to lead and manage. These concerns are important and need to be addressed by putting these ideas and theories into *the context* of the organisation we are being asked to lead and manage.

Chapters two and three should offer, in part, an explanation as to why these theories of leading and/or managing organisations failed to translate. This chapter, combined with Chapter Five, should assist in putting these theories into the context of leading and managing organisational transition. There is a concern that many authors are writing from the reported experience of others and not *their experience* of personally being responsible for leading and managing *transition for change.* This lack of first-hand experience prevents them from *contextualising* the situation within the social organisation under discussion.

Within the context of this book authors shall be identified as they have influenced the development of this process of *organisational leadership* and *organisational problem solving*. The intent is to enable executives and managers to anchor some of these worthy ideas and theories when working through and developing these processes for leading and managing organisations in transition.

Experience of working in a variety of organisational settings, for example, research, designing and developing large mechanical handling production systems, in process production, project management, strategic planning, financial services, the brewing industry, health care, administration and event project management repeatedly confirmed that these structural prescriptions were not directly transferable from one organisational performance culture to another. What had become evident from research and experience led, through practice, to the development of an applied theory of *Organisational Leadership and Management for Organisational Problem Solving* that has developed into an effective organisation decision-making and implementation process.

Theory Defined and Application

The organisation is leading the change, therefore, those leading and managing that organisation are its "agent." They have to interpret and service that organisation's transitional needs to an effective operational delivery performance; this capacity is defined as *organisational leadership*. Organisational leaders have to have the capacity to specifically design their organisation to effectively achieve the identified *"primary task."* All activities must be designed and developed to reinforce the identified organisation's *operating delivery performance culture*.

A competitive rowing eight would expect oarsmen to synchronise their collective intent and effort to enable their water borne vehicle to effectively compete. This is a simple obvious example; organisations must have the same complementary *intent* to enable the organisation to compete effectively.

To assist with the understanding of the development of this theory and how it can be applied, a number of interactive elements are identified. These elements will be discussed to demonstrate how they interact and have influenced the development of this applied process and practice.

Purpose of Organisations

Simply, we organise and co-operate to complete complex tasks effectively. For effective cooperation, individuals have to participate, develop, own and share a common understanding, to "understand their world" the appropriate performance outcomes of their organisation and their own input. This provides each employee with the necessary purpose and motivational focus. "The principle of supportive relationships" defined by Likert (1961) is a good working arrangement that is enabled only by the use of an appropriate organisational design. This means that the *business and management technologies* are harmonised with the social needs of that particular organisation. We have discussed both micro activities of cooperation and motivation within the macro organisation where we create the appropriate setting for individuals, to motivate themselves, which in turn enables them to contribute effectively.

Environmental Activities

An organisation has to respond to its specific and changing environment. It has to respond as an 'open system', Miller & Rice (1967) by receiving information, which it uses to interact dynamically with its environment. Openness increases its likelihood *to survive and prosper* (Bertalanffy, 1968). This concept applies equally at personal and organisational levels. There is a need for it to appropriately respond to its specific environment to ensure that, the *product service* continuously satisfies the needs of the market and customer expectations. These environmental influences are constantly in flux and need to be interpreted in terms of the responsive needs of your organisation (Porter 1980 & 1985). Essentially the organisation, in its need to respond to prevent decay and survive, will want to react to these external influences. For an organisation to perform effectively it has to have the ability to continuously manage *transition for change*.

These assertions regarding the need for the organisation to be in a constant state of transition (constantly renewing itself) by implication, demands that the leaders and managers of that organisation create by design, "learning organisations" (Argyris, 1999). This can only be achieved when the leaders and managers of those organisations have a well-developed understanding of the business environment and those external forces that directly or indirectly influence their organisation's operational performance. They have to understand the consequential effects these environmental forces may have on their organisation's performance. This developed understanding enables them to regulate and manage the *states of flux* that these environmental forces create at the boundary of the organisation.

Doing nothing is not an option, as these external forces will continue to permeate your organisation's boundaries. Over time you will begin to experience the conflicting behavioural dynamics of your organisation's drive and its need to respond appropriately. The case studies will provide you with an opportunity to sense what it feels like to experience an organisation that needs to respond, which has limited executive *organisational leadership*.

Primary Task

To begin the process of design it is essential that the *primary task* of your organisation is collectively identified and understood. The concept of the *primary task* as originally defined by Rice (1958, 1963), Hutton (1962) and Miller and Rice (1967) "is essentially heuristic, which allows us to explore the ordering of multiple activities (constituent systems of activities where these exist)." They suggest, "It makes it possible to construct and compare different organisational models of an enterprise based on different definitions of the *primary task* and to compare the organisations of different enterprises with the same or different *primary task.*"

Experience confirms that the *primary task* of an organisation is fixed and does not change. If the *primary task* changes then the nature and responsive behaviour will also change. In essence if the *primary task* changes you have a different organisation to lead and manage. Any sub-organisations, departments and functions will have different *primary tasks*. Critically the sum of all the *primary tasks* must complement and reinforce the *primary task* of the overall business organisation. Whatever the size or complexity of an organisation it will have an identifiable *primary task*.

This definition of the use and nature of the *primary task* departs from those described by Miller and Rice (1967), where they suggest, "...in a factory, the production system that converts raw materials into finished products has long-term priority, and the *primary task* is the conversion of the raw material into products." They postulate that, "If the machinery breaks down the *primary task* of the conversion system shifts from producing goods to repairing machinery." Experience shows that the *primary task* of the conversion system should the machinery break down, does not transfer to the maintenance activities' *primary task*. The *primary task* of the maintenance activities must be designed and focused to reinforce and complement the *primary task* of the primary conversion system.

This is an extremely important concept that directly affects the way we think and approach the development of individuals, teams, workgroups and the overall organisation. How they fit and complement one another and have the same focused intent is the responsibility of those "agents" leading and managing the various parts of the organisation.

The *primary task* plays a critical role in clarifying and improving the organisational leader's decision-making in that it acts as a reference point for all decision-making. It enables the ability to identify the nature and value of the external environmental forces at the boundary of the organisation. Therefore enabling these potential *states of flux* to be identified, regulated and managed to avoid unwanted influences.

Developing an Organisational Perspective

We need to tease this concept a little further in relation to the constant notion of "building shared vision" that people can follow (Senge, 1993). There is an implied assumption that having a vision is an important motivational factor that people will sign up to. There are difficulties with this neat idea, in that where the individuals are positioned within an organisation will influence their perspective and personal vision. It is similar to walking up a mountain, as you progress towards the top the perspective changes. You gain a wider view of the landscape at the top. When at the bottom your view is limited to a localised perspective. We can make the connection with the notion that throughout this hierarchical structure there is a developed *performance culture continuum* from top to bottom, which has to be understood and managed.

When at the top of an organisation not only is the perspective enhanced but also the role demands that you interpret the wider perspective in terms of your organisation's operational needs. The organisational leaders and managers in different parts of your organisation will develop a perspective gained from the position that they inherit. That is, they will interpret their perspective of the organisation from where they are positioned. The executive needs to intellectually create a link to their organisation's internal environment through the developed use of a *culture performance continuum*. This provides them with an appropriate perspective at all levels within their organisation.

Wherever you are positioned within the organisation's hierarchy, those leaders and managers of the whole organisation and any sub-organisations are required to scan their organisation's environment enabling them to effectively manage their organisation's boundaries. This practice applies at all levels within the organisation. The perspective within the sub-organisation is developed from scanning both the internal and external environments. The host organisation, where the sub-organisation exists, influences one part of the sub-organisation's boundaries along with external influences impacting on its externally connected boundaries (Fig. 7). Fig. 8 is a notional model that has been produced to help develop a mental model for us to understand and develop an internal perspective of what we are leading and managing.

BOUNDARY MANAGEMENT

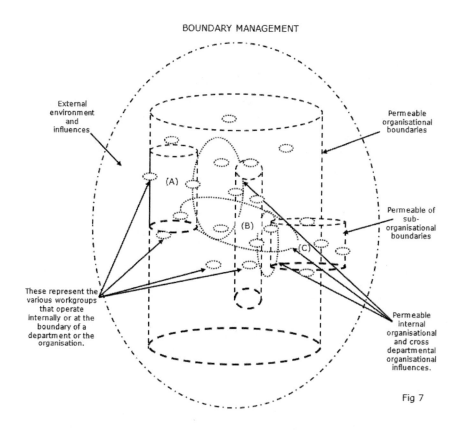

Fig 7

Grounding this exploration brings the discussion back to a *shared motivational intent*. Experience and successful application clearly indicates that people are motivated when they have a shared understanding developed, in organisational terms, as to what is being led and managed with an attached intent. It is a basic human motivational requirement to make sense of our world, that of our organisations and work environment. These organisational and personal developmental processes are designed to provide the contextual understanding that we all need to enable us to make sense of our working environment.

Creating a shared understanding of what the *intent* of the organisation is and having well-developed *organisational leadership* and management competencies enables an understanding of what has to be achieved and what is required of them. In other words, how they fit and contribute. The developed understanding of the demands of each of the complementary roles that have to be enacted, coupled with the developed ability to understand and lead their organisation, frees them to act with assurance, competence and *directed intent*.

The *intent* is always to find ways of designing that part of their organisation to continuously reinforce the overall organisational performance outcomes. Everyone has a well-developed expectation and *motivational intent* generated from their own appropriate perspective of how they can contribute effectively to the overall organisation's performance. This leads them, through awareness and *intent*, to being able to manage their own motivational behaviour that can be directed towards reinforcing the organisation's overall performance.

The development of the various notions and ideas emanating from research and backed up in practice suggest the following model for *personal motivation in social organisations* acts as a model for *personal change*. This notional model (Fig. 8) enables the individuals to attain awareness and understanding, and to make sense of their environment by organising and interpreting sensory information. This developed competency identifies individual and group expectations and the intent of their individual or group motivational actions. This is referred to as a developed collective *cognitive organisational awareness*.

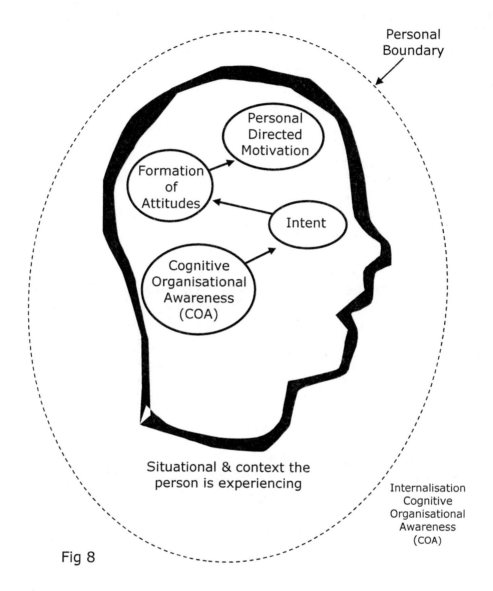

Personal Boundary

Personal Directed Motivation

Formation of Attitudes

Intent

Cognitive Organisational Awareness (COA)

Situational & context the person is experiencing

Internalisation Cognitive Organisational Awareness (COA)

Fig 8

Personal Motivation Model in Social Organisations
(A Model for Personal Change)

The term cognition (Latin: *cognoscere,* "to know" "conceptualise" or "to recognise") refers to a faculty for processing information, the ability to feel, or be conscious of events, objects or sensory patterns and applying the knowledge for changing preferences. Cognition, or cognitive process, can be natural or artificial, conscious or unconscious. With the development of the "feel" of the organisation and how it should or is behaving – this becomes a natural and almost unconscious intuitive process.

From the above explanation the model (Fig. 8) describes the process of developmental thinking. It begins with the development of your *cognitive organisational awareness* that feeds the *intent*, which informs and formulates our *attitudes* that *direct our motivational* intent and actions. To service this personal motivational model we are charged with the task of designing and developing our organisations that individuals can identify with and want to subscribe. The organisation is the motivational performance platform that we can all use to improve our own personal directed motivational performance.

Genesis of Thinking Organisationally

When developing an organisation's performance culture, it is essential to start by asking, "Why does this organisation exist, what is its purpose, what is its reason for being?" In other words, what is its *primary task?*

Confusion exists in the literature; for example, Beckhard (1985) uses the term 'Core Mission' and suggests this is "your reason for being." The distinction between the Core Mission and the Primary Task is that one has a transformational value and the other is static and does not change.

For example, missionaries are specifically dispatched to preach, teach and importantly, convert. To convert implies a change in an individual's religious perspective and a change in the society and how it is organised. The *primary task* does not change and has no requirement for any change, hence its value as a benchmark, for testing all organisational decision-making.

The *primary task* never changes and should there be a requirement to do so, it immediately implies that you are about to lead and manage a very different organisation. An example, the failure to differentiate the *primary task* of the host nursing care practice and that of a new service being introduced in the form of a transitional nursing care service caused abusive and unnecessary discomfort to the patient. (Refer to case study "Transitional Nursing Care".)

To understand and apply this notion of the *primary task* can be further expressed through the following imaginary flawed situation. If you arrive to play a particular sport, for example, football, and someone throws on a rugby ball, or to play lacrosse, and hockey sticks are issued, confusion will ensue. The equipment is part of the employed technologies and will not fit the operating practices of these various competitive sports. The common shared expectation for each of these sporting activities is to win by defeating their opponents. In each case the way you organise and employ any developed sports' technologies and applied collective competency will be specific to that sporting activity. The performance culture for supporting these sporting activities will be very different, even though they share the same desire to defeat their opponents. There on the pitch, strategies and organisation specifically developed to win will be very different. The employed sports' technologies, training and development along with that sporting activities' environment, will define the *primary task* and *the strategic intent* for each of these sporting activities.

The value of defining the *primary task* is that it provides a constant fixed reference point, for all organisational decision-making. Mission statements change over time, with the development of events. Importantly, because of an individual's positional perspective within their organisation, this prevents them from relating and making these mission statements meaningful.

Identifying the Primary Task

The process of determining the primary task, which is essentially heuristic, is to examine the primary services that are to be provided. The factors that service this enquiry are the marketplace, the customers and the technologies employed to create the product/service. These are the primary critical factors that give purpose to an organisation.

Of course, an organisation can be created once you have identified a market that will be dedicated to developing a product/service to satisfy that market need. An innovative technology may also need to be marketed. An organisation could be developed that will identify an existing market and or develop a new consumer need to satisfy that product and service delivery.

Having worked through either the product development or market-creating route there will be a need to create an operational organisation that can satisfy the market place using the employed technologies. These heuristic processes are interdependent and directly influence the nature and performance culture of the developed delivery organisation. They directly influence the definition of the primary task (Fig. 9) that in turn influences the created performance culture and all the activities that are needed to reinforce the desired organisational performance culture.

The Value of Defining the Primary Task

The process of identifying the *primary task* assists in defining the values, intent, performance culture, roles, division of tasks, performance expectations, authority, responsibility, and accountability, along with the style of organisational leadership and management. It is important to understand that both authority and responsibility are delegated functions. Accountability is the reverse in that the individual, in accepting authority and responsibility, is accountable to the delegating authority for the agreed performance delivery.

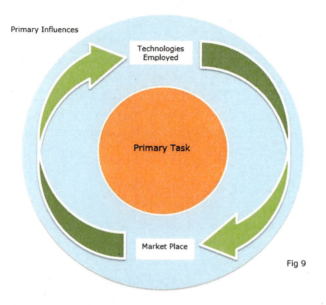

Technologies
Employed

Primary Task

Market Place

Fig 9

The *primary task* provides the scope of the design of the organisation, the *intent* and responsiveness for enabling the organisation to accommodate the effects of an organisation's environmental forces. Critically it is the reference point and filtering link between the environmental influences and the design and development of the delivery operational practices (Fig. 10).

REPRESENTATIONAL HOURGLASS STRATEGIC THINKING PROCESS

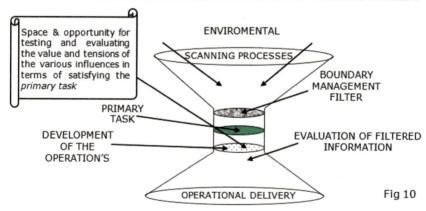

Space & opportunity for testing and evaluating the value and tensions of the various influences in terms of satisfying the *primary task*

ENVIROMENTAL

SCANNING PROCESSES

BOUNDARY
MANAGEMENT
FILTER

PRIMARY
TASK

DEVELOPMENT
OF THE
OPERATION'S

EVALUATION OF FILTERED
INFORMATION

OPERATIONAL DELIVERY

Fig 10

It not only provides a *frame of refer*ence for all decision-making, it creates an opportunity to test any assumptions in terms of the decisions being made. An additional important and valued derivative from identifying the *primary task* is that it works across national and cultural boundaries.

It, critically, provides what is often referred to, illusive "compelling purpose" (Wageman et al, 2008), i.e. that focused element that people can identify with, own and *motivate themselves* to contribute. Cary Cooper, professor of organisational psychology at Lancaster University, reinforces this critical element; "People need to feel some sort of ownership of their own destiny for a leader to influence their attitudes and behaviour." Fritz Pearl says, "It makes the leader's direction compelling, it gives people something to figure out, feel part of and gives people a sense of stability as they interact with the leader."

The *primary task* provides that focus along with the ability of each individual identifying how they can contribute to their organisation's overall performance. The focus is achieved through *clarity of purpose* and a *common organisational dialogue* that is derived from the created *organisational performance culture*. The organisation's behaviour provides this definition and it is for the *organisational leader* to interpret these responsive needs for others to share and own. This needs to include "The principles of supportive relationships ... that yield favourable attitudes" (Likert, 1961), which requires that the organisation be designed to enlist and reinforce these motivating factors.

Specificity of Design

The *primary task* provides the function and scope of the organisational design. These are essential elements when considering the needs for creating and developing the specific design for an organisation. To develop this concept there is a need to consider the organisation as the vehicle, which enables complex tasks to be completed effectively. All vehicles have to be designed specifically for a task.

The design for a formula one car would not be adopted for heavy-duty off-track weight carrying duties. Ships, aircraft and railways, for example, are required to operate within different environments. They each employ different technologies to satisfy the demands of the operating environment and the task to be completed. These designs are, in turn, further differentiated for more refined tasks.

The design of a single seated fighter aircraft is distinctly different to that of a passenger or cargo carrying aircraft. Although a sailing craft and a large cruise liner or even an aircraft carrier experience a similar watery environment, they are all designed to complete specific and even unrelated tasks. Each of these combinations of task and the technologies employed will develop their own internal delivery performance culture.

There is little need to labour this point any further, except to say that *form will always follow function*. A simple example of the use of this principle is when considering the structure of a building. If the heavy plant were to be sited, for process reasons, at the top of a structure rather than on the ground floor, the design of the structure, to support the additional weight, would have to be strengthened and configured to accommodate the process plant and the additional weight. If the plant were situated on the ground floor the designed structure could be configured using lighter materials.

Designing Downwards or Upwards

The maxim, *"form follows function"* brings to mind a question that executives have often asked, "Do I design downwards or upwards?" The whole of the design has to have *intent* and that intent has to be the product service delivery, whatever that may be. The need to translate the product services has to satisfy the market and therefore the customer, which by definition defines the *intent* and function of the organisation. If form follows function the design has to satisfy identified functions, which exist at the *transactional boundary* of the organisation. This automatically indicates that you *design upwards*.

What may introduce a level of confusion is the felt need to develop control systems of information to enable the ability to direct and manage the overall on-going processes. These systems are often developed with *intent* to control rather than *monitor to manage*. The first intent to control invariably acquires systems that are designed centrally and from the top down. When the *intent* is to monitor to manage, the systems are invariably designed bottom up, from the service delivery end of the business. These examples have been used to deliberately demonstrate how the *expressed intent* will directly influence how we think, *make decisions and critically implement those decisions*. (Refer to Anscombe's definition of "intentionality" Chapter Six, "Leading Transition for Change".)

Boundary Management

The development of the *primary task* is derived from the interactive transactions of the market place and the *employed technologies* to provide the *product service delivery* (Fig. 11). Many authors writing on management issues will provide a list of external influences that are affecting, directly or indirectly, your organisation's behaviour. For example, changes in technology, the market place, economic, political, resources (materials and people), pressure groups, people's expectations, and social change. There are others that may be industry specific, for example seasonal changes (Fig. 11).

It is important to make the connection between projected events that are being played out within your organisation's environment. For example, in the United Kingdom, June 2012, it was reported that the Unite Union's General Secretary was plotting a leverage strategy against those companies that opposed his demands. He was reported to hail this strategy as "the future of the movement." Connect this strategy to the political cluster, as the Unite Union is the opposition Labour Party's largest donor. It is important to make these connections and to develop strategies for managing any projected outcomes.

All of these broadly identified elements have local, national and global influences. You can directly observe the accelerating effects that these local, national and global influences are having through the availability of the almost immediate responsive communication technologies. Information can be almost instantly reproduced Trans-continentally, as these technologies have no respect for cultures or national boundaries.

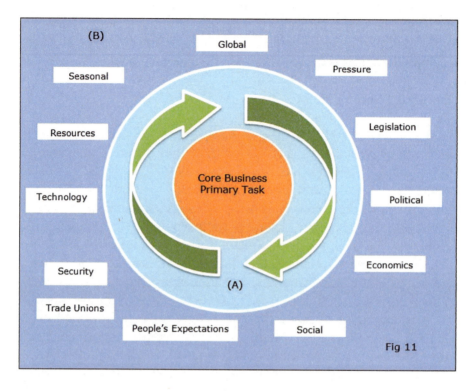

Fig 11

Managing Organisational Boundaries

The above listing, within (Fig. 11), is simplistic and only addresses the obvious environmental influences. Porter (1980 & 1985) adds to the discussion by further including the need to develop and sustain a competitive advantage. He addresses corporate rivalry and neatly introduces his five forces. They are:

1. Competitive rivalry within the industry
2. Bargaining power of suppliers
3. Bargaining power of customers
4. The threat of new entrants
5. The threat of substitute products

An additional element (6) has to be considered – how your organisation has been behaving within its different cultural and operational environments. An example of a projected influence into your organisation's environment is the poor safety record of BP.

It is the role of executives and managers to understand how these various influences are likely to impact on the organisation's business performance and to factor their interpretation into the responsive operational design of the organisation. The failure of BP's chief executive to scan his organisation's environment and become aware of this threat caused him to be replaced.

These environmental issues combine, adding to the complexity of their development, which is not within the remit of this book. Porter's book is a very good starting point for understanding and scanning the environment. These various external influences support the process of defining the focus, role and scope of responsibility of the senior executive team. These external influences will, in open systems organisations, permeate the organisation's boundaries, subtly or directly influencing the internal activities of that organisation. When uncontrolled or unrecognised, these external influences, borrowing from computer technology and Nyquist (2009), can infect your organisation.

An example of this need to scan the environment is provided in Tapscott and Williams' book *Wikinomics* (2006) where they discuss the notion of mass collaboration they claim, "Changes everything." Collaboration is cooperation, which is the bedrock of any successful society and social group. It is why we create organisations to use our collaborative skills to collectively succeed. In essence this is nothing new; it is the way we survive and succeed.

"Changes everything" is an overstated claim, but do remember Wikinomics has a proprietary *intent*. The use of a wider range of resources to access information provided by the available technology of the Internet can be beneficial. The benefit of this technology is unaffected by cultural or national boundaries. We share and accept the excitement and the potential that these writers express to encourage executives to change the way they lead and manage their business organisations. The examples they use to highlight this change in attitude is interesting as it introduces a number of ideas that apply to the development and thinking about organisations.

Rob McEwen, the CEO of Goldcorp Incorporated, was essentially under threat as the gold market was contracting and the current geological evaluations were not at all promising. This small Canadian gold mining company was struggling, "besieged by strikes, lingering debts, and an exceedingly high cost of production, which had caused them to cease mining operations. Conditions in the market place were hardly favourable" (Trapscott and Williams, 2006). For McEwen, the "shoe was pinching" (Hutton); he was presented with a forced choice to consider closure or find some radical solution. He was introduced to the idea of sharing the company's historic data on its geological explorations on the Internet to encourage other geologists to share their knowledge and skills to provide further analysis. Breaking with the existing secretive conventions proved to be extremely successful.

We all enjoy these success stories yet when you examine the decision-making, the executive, in organisational terms, was simply scanning his organisation's environment to maximise the benefit to his organisation. Of course the available technology of the Internet provided that opportunity. The ideas and encouragement provided by reading this book cannot be ignored, as that is the reality. An important issue it raises is – how do you interpret and employ this management technology? It is important to get this right as it can easily distract you from your *primary task* and lead you to create inappropriate dysfunctional organisations. (Refer to Chapter Nine, "Technology Change and Managing the Consequences".)

Failure to Manage the Boundaries

When these various boundaries are not managed effectively, inappropriate influences can be "infectious" (Nyquist, 2009). These infectious influences can deflect the focus and attention away from the *primary task* of that organisation and create *displaced goals* (Fig. 4).

"There's a strange thing goes on inside a bubble. People inside it can't see outside, don't believe there is an outside."
Lucy Prebble

An example can be identified through the UK government's practice coupled with an 'overwhelming' 'objective of finding savings' causing 'organisational trauma'. (Nimrod Enquiry 2010). The overriding demands were caused by a drive to recover costs estimated at £1bn budget overrun, accumulated over a period of ten years. The consequential effect expressed through the examination of the Trident disaster in 2006 identified that there was a breach in the assured airworthiness of the aircraft and the safety of service personnel on board. "Internal promotion resulted not from being on top of safety but being on top of budgets" (Nimrod Enquiry 2010).

The combined governmental pressure and the "overwhelming objective of finding savings" (you can substitute a group board and/or main board of business organisation for government) and the desire to attract further lucrative contracts, created a toxic combination, redefining this service organisation's activities where safety was no longer the priority. This practice of servicing displaced goals (Fig. 4) can be observed in many organisations.

Nyquist (2009) discusses how political influences have produced "too many of today's generals that are political" which is infectious and has a contaminating effect on decision-making "forestalling timely action" that would ensure the US war-fighting capability.

Nyquist (2009) writes, "They know what side their bread is buttered, and they avoid risks that may hurt their chances of promotion. This in turn, promulgates a culture of risk aversion in a profession that depends for success on taking calculated risks. At the same time, America's generals tend to kill reform, kill money-saving measures, and oppose truth telling. For many years the U.S. Army has needed reorganisation and new ideas. For example, the systems used in today's chain of command were devised in the nineteenth century and needs to be shortened. There are too many generals. Each unnecessary link in the chain of command adds friction to the flow of vital information, which contaminates the decision making process and forestalls timely action."

These politicised examples clearly demonstrate the disastrous effects of failing to effectively manage your organisation's boundaries, allowing decision-making to become contaminated, creating adverse consequential effects on that organisation's operating performance. Experience of working in a variety of organisations shows equally dysfunctional behaviour except that the consequential failures only tend to cause decay and in some cases the demise of an organisation.

These tragic cases introduce two other factors – that of speed and the tension of the various influences. In this case political, with a capital P, and economic financial constraints had caused the reported, "organisational trauma." We can learn from this particular case that when environmental changes are not anticipated the consequential effects can be terminal. We can refer, for example, to the demise of Lehman Bros. business organisation in the USA. When these dramatic situations are anticipated we often collectively find the capacity to cope with the enforced choice. The slow *insidious depleting dysfunctional activities*, ten years in the Nimrod case, infecting your organisation are far more difficult to identify and therefore manage.

Quick fixes and Panaceas

This difficulty with current management thinking and practices is the search for quick fixes and panaceas, coupled with political decision making, acts to overlay a solution onto the existing problem. The failure of a systems solution approach is that it does not, in organisational terms, identify the cause of the problem. As a consequence, executives and managers choose to overlay a solution to a presented problem. This practice of layering of adopted solutions has a strong potential for creating further dysfunctional practices and the development of further problems that will need to be resolved. This invites further layering and has the effect of burying the original problem that, in turn, becomes difficult to identify when attempting to resolve a presented problem.

Experience of observing this cyclical practice, which can develop over a number of years, clearly demonstrates that managers are managing the problems created by the solution to the unspecified initial problem. These compounded multiple failed solutions insidiously develop and become part of the dysfunctional management culture and daily activities being played out in the Nimrod example. The use of an organisational approach is designed to break this cycle of events and quickly identify the root cause of the presented problem. (Further examples of areas of mismanagement of organisational boundaries can be found in Chapters Nine and Eleven, "Technology Change and Managing the Consequences" "Remuneration and Motivation" and the "Avonmouth" case study.)

Organisational leadership

To lead and manage an organisation it becomes essential to, in effect, create a firewall that enables you to manage the resulting behaviour of these external influences. In other words, managing the permeability of the organisation's boundaries. Essentially the person responsible for leading and managing the organisation, the "agent" must have the responsibility to scan the organisation's environment, interpret the information in terms of the organisation's business and primary task and then translate how those influences will complement your organisation's directed delivery performance (Fig. 10, "Hourglass Strategic Thinking").

The management of these influences are defined in terms that infer it is only the responsibility of the executive management to provide direction and a "compelling purpose." It is their responsibility, but it is essential that we consider that these influences affect, in different ways, many parts of your organisation. We need equally to understand and manage the consequential effects of these various influences, as single activities and/or when they are combined. The application of boundary management applies at all levels within an organisation, including all workgroups and individuals (Fig. 7, "Boundary Management"). For the purpose of simplifying this discussion teams are being incorporated into the term workgroups.

For example the maintenance function discussed earlier has its own environment and boundaries, part of which is influenced by the overall organisation; it is part of the service provision, behaviour and values. Other parts of the maintenance organisation's boundaries will be influenced across its own external boundaries, scanning for available technologies and other influences, for example, legislation, or Health and Safety Regulations that impact on the specific activities of this sub-organisation's practices.

For these practices to be understood it becomes essential that we have some concept of our boundaries in relationship to others, when working in workgroups, inter-departmentally and across the whole organisation. It is important that we understand how the organisation relates to its environment and also the inter-related behaviour of the individual and the workgroups within the environment of the organisation to support the development of our organisational leadership skills. An exploration of the contextual relationship and inter-relationship are explored in more detail in Chapter Five.

CHAPTER FIVE

DEVELOPING A THEORY IN PRACTICE

(Part Two)
The inter-related behaviour of the individual
The group, the organisation and its environment

"To understand what something means is the major goal of sociology, but it is also the fundamental role of existence for the human species" (Phillips, 1973). Lagadec (1993) writes, "Our ability to deal with chaos depends on structures that have been developed before the chaos arrives."

We constantly strive to make sense of our environment, which in the context of this book, is the socio-technical environment of our business's service delivery organisation. This exploration is an attempt to show the inter-relations and congruence between the most primitive levels of the individual's unconscious behaviour and how they feature in organisations. To ground this exploration, in particular the notion and application of boundary management, it is essential that we examine the inter-related behaviour of the individual, the workgroup and the organisation.

Fig. 7, "Boundary Management" attempts to provide a notional overview of the permeability of the boundaries and how the individual, the workgroup and the sub-organisations interrelate and are influenced by one another, the overall organisation and its environment. It should help us to understand the inter-dependence of the individual, the group, the organisation and their environments.

The purpose for working through these particular relationships is to ensure that you, as organisational leaders and managers, develop a full grasp of these complex relationships. The other motive for asking you to work through this process is that there is a requirement that you, as the "agent" are able to interpret and respond appropriately to the organisation's needs. To be successful, you need to understand how you respond in different organisational situations, the impact you have on the behaviour on others and how their behaviour affects you.

The notion of the individual and the group as a task system are borrowed from organisational theories developed from the understanding of the behaviour of organisations. Using the notions from general systems theory should demonstrate that the processes of the individual, the group and the organisation are task systems along with their inter-dependent relationships.

Systems Theory

In Systems Theory (Bertalanffy, 1950), the organisation must interact with the environment to exist. To achieve this it uses a system of import from the environment, a conversion process and export of finished products back into the environment. These exports further influence the business environment of your organisation. For example, the introduction of containerisation for bulk transportation dramatically affected work practices all over the world.

The systems of importation – conversion – export (Katz and Kahn, 1966 and Hutton, 1972), implies that some form of trading across boundaries is taking place. Therefore, by definition the system must have a boundary where transactions take place between it and its environment (Fig. 12).

For the system to survive it is essential that the boundaries are adequately managed, because improper trading across boundaries can cause the system to become unstable and fail to achieve a "steady state" (Bertalanffy, ibid). Closed systems by definition do not trade with the environment and eventually will arrive at a state where they have no additional capacity to do any work other than to maintain themselves. This implies that the organisation should be appropriately designed to manage these various task systems that are applicable to your organisation.

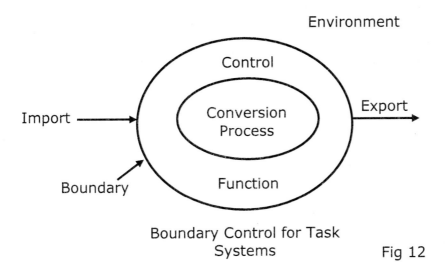

Environment

Control

Conversion
Process

Import

Export

Boundary

Function

Boundary Control for Task
Systems

Fig 12

Organisational Behaviour

We discovered in previous chapters that an organisation could become a mechanism for defending us against induced anxiety. This can be detrimental to the accomplishment of the *primary task* through the creation of *displaced goals* (Fig. 4). The formation of traditions, the structure of work and the method by which people deal with each other will be influenced by the way in which anxiety is, and has been, dealt with. Menzies (1970) found that: "The need of members of an organisation to use it in the struggle against anxiety leads to the development of socially structured defence mechanisms which appear as elements in the structure, culture and mode of the functioning of the organisation. A social defence system develops over time as the result of collusive interaction and agreement, often unconscious, between members of the organisation as to what form it will take."

These forms of defence mechanisms make change in organisations difficult "because change threatens existing social defences against anxiety" (Jaques, 1955). Menzies (1970) also found that this occurred "when social defence systems are dominated by primitive psychic defence mechanisms." Hence the reason for developing and employing an organisational approach, which enables the understanding and management of these socially interrelated activities that develop within social organisations.

Burns and Stalker (1961) in their study of the management of innovation in the burgeoning electronics industry, found a great deal of resistance to change. Even carefully considered tactics designed to break down the authoritarian structure and to serve as a medium for "organic" procedures would be thwarted by the "single-minded deviation of a whole group of executives to clear cut mechanistic procedures" (Burns and Stalker, ibid)." (Refer to the "Avonmouth" and "National Health Services" case studies, where similar practices were experienced.)

This kind of behaviour is a case of the executive management failing to manage the boundaries of their organisation and not changing the conversion processes to accommodate the new technology and its attending performance culture. Managers who act in this manner can be working towards stability, but the price they have to pay is the loss of ability to adapt to environmental changes. Kets de Vries discusses in "Struggling with the Demon" the role of the leader is the willingness to "know self." He writes that many of the executives he has known are stuck, "governed by the past" and locked in a "psychic prison". The consequences of this executive behaviour can translate into reducing their own and the permeability of their organisation's boundaries. This reduction in the permeability of the organisational boundary stems from the induced anxiety of the managers being asked to change their own behaviour.

The outcome of this behaviour can be identified by the following example expressed by Lagadec (1993). When there is an element of confusion in, for example, the available and quality of information, uncertainty as to what the future holds; change, scheduled or unscheduled, introduces "degrees of chaos", and the first impulse is to grasp for some explanation, any old explanation. And what we get hold of are the automatic explanations we have lived with longest and invoked most often. These notions resonate with Kets de Vries' observations above.

The use of models providing images helps to develop notional mental frameworks that should help you make sense of your own organisation, particularly when *leading transition for change*. This discussion is intended to provide you with an insight into how the theories in this book have been researched, developed and successfully employed over time. Importantly, it should provide you with an opportunity to take these ideas and develop them further to improve others and your own leadership and organisational problem solving skills.

"Everyone thinks of changing the world, but no one thinks of changing themselves."
Leo Tolstoy

It is important for this discussion to reiterate that you need to understand how *your own behaviour* can or might impact on your decision-making, on others' behaviour and your organisation's performance. In Chapter Three we discussed how leaders mislead and should act as an indicator to the potential hazards we might unconsciously introduce. This is one of the reasons for drilling down into the literature to provide you with an insight and opportunity to consider how you may respond in particular roles. (Refer to Chapter Seven "Adaptive Organisational Leadership" and Chapter Eight, "Workgroups, Leadership and Positioning in Groups" to further explore the process and application of organisational leadership.)

We can learn a great deal from, for example, studying nurses and their working environment as every organisation has something to teach us. For example, for nurses to manage their anxieties they delegate upwards (Menzies, 1970). When nurses are denied this ability, through inappropriate organisational design and practices, nurses become stressed, and consequently sickness and absenteeism dramatically increase. Attached to these levels of anxiety and related sickness and absence are significant reductions in patient service quality with increased cost implications.

Often we find an inverse ratio where poor quality of service produces an increase in costs. When you reverse this inverse ratio and focus on service quality the costs will, over time, reduce (Deming, 1986). The value of this example is that it directly relates to how the organisation behaves and how it impacts on those working within it and how it can create a negative or positive outcome.

Digital Computers Ltd UK was formed with the expressed intent that innovation should be the driver of the organisation's service provision. That the technical computer engineers were, at the customer interface, making the innovative decisions was productive and appropriate. Yet, when acted out, the executives were unable to adapt their leadership and management styles to accommodate these innovative practices. The decision-making that was driving and affecting the organisation's growth and development was being made at the technical engineering level within the organisation and not within the executive level.

The executives, within this organisation's innovative culture, were experiencing difficulty even though it was appropriate. Many of the executives were innovative computer engineers and had difficulty understanding the need for the control of the organisation to be managed through the decision-making being made at a middle and senior management level. They failed to understand that they were required by the organisation to scan the environment and to monitor to manage the practice of direct customer intervention of providing solutions at source. This practice required that the decision-making be managed at the customer interface. Therefore, the executive role was to support and enable the innovation to thrive at the customer interface. The result of attempting to rescue the decision-making back to the executives caused a great deal of confusion and conflict between those trying to deliver an innovative service to the customers and the executive. This infighting within the organisation depleted its performance and reputation, eventually forcing it to merge with another organisation to survive.

The example of the executive group's collective behaviour (Burns and Stalker, ibid) indicates that they were working as an "as if" group, that is, in reality, leading and managing the displaced organisational goals. When a group is operating in this manner it takes on the characteristics of a closed system and, therefore, has little energy to give to understanding the real problem. All the time the internal problem is unresolved, the process of projection will act to relieve the group's anxiety and this can be achieved by finding a "scapegoat" (Jaques 1951 and Trist and Bamford 1951).

Burns and Stalker (ibid) found that this form of anxiety resulted in inter-group conflict and different departments becoming "scapegoats." When people in a group are being persecuted, they develop precise and equally strong dislikes of their persecutors (Jaques, 1955). He also found that the "scapegoats" could be found from outside the organisation, for example, union officials, suppliers and/or competitors. It is evident that a visiting consultant could be cast in the role of "scapegoat." (Refer to case studies, "Avonmouth" and "Greenwich District Hospital".)

The leader or the consultant must understand these processes and be able to assist the individual and/or the group to discharge their anger, which is often projected onto the person they perceived to have created the disruption. The leader and/or the consultant, in turn, should understand the processes of these social dynamics, not to own the projected anger, but to be able to act as an emotional conduit to discharge the projected anger.

Internal Persecution

An organisation that insists on persecuting itself is unable to distinguish between reality and fantasy. Retaining this kind of organisational mentality neglects to adequately manage its boundaries, which has a tendency to compound the internal difficulties of its members. (Refer to case studies, "The Brewing industry" "Ullage, CO_2 and "as if" Organisations" and "NHS District Works, Leading Transition for Change".)

This lack of social and psychological satisfaction will lead to sub-optimal performance (Miller, 1953), and the confusion about organisational boundaries will eventually render the social processes "mentally sick" (Rice), which could, if not rectified, lead to eventual failure. (Refer to Chapter Ten, "Outsourcing and Contractual Practices".)

Fig. 7 is a notional model of how boundary management applies throughout an organisation. Without complicating this model any further it is essential for all managers to understand that the managing of boundaries also applies to each employee. Within the model sub-department (A) (Fig. 7) abuts the boundary of the organisation, which infers that it is directly affected by external influences. It is also influenced by the internal activities of the organisation, other departments and functions along with corporate systems and procedures.

Likewise, the workgroups' boundaries are also influenced by the activities of the sub-department and the overall organisation's behaviour. With sub-departments, the workgroups also work at and across the boundaries of the organisation they work within. Some workgroups have a more complex relationship as they work across the boundaries of not only the sub-departments but also the whole organisation. This may all appear to be complicated but when evaluated and understood in terms of the organisation it becomes intuitive and matter of fact. The purpose of this exploration and the use of this notional model is to assist with the development of a mind-set that thinks in terms of the organisation.

The position of the various sub-parts of the organisation and the workgroups, by inference, will have to develop their own organisational culture, styles of leadership and management. Some of these sub-organisations will, as they are affected by the various internal and external influences, have to manage transition and change more often than other parts of the organisation. If the management systems are a one size fits all by nature these departments will have difficulty responding appropriately to these external boundary influences.

We can make a connection with BP's drive to reduce costs, initiated in London and taking effect in Texas. The local management were in a situation similar to the Nimrod example; they were cost oriented, displacing their organisation's goals.

An example of this type of myopic behaviour can be seen when examining the history of IBM and General Motors. At the top of these mammoth organisations the executives were insulated from the changing technology and market influences. They were making large profits and were not on the cusp of survival, and this cushioned comfort introduced a degree of inertia and complacency whilst everything was changing around them.

When you lose the sensitivity of your organisation's environment, for example, your market place, you are no longer in touch with your business and client needs. This could be described as a closed system creating a detached internal environment with a closed or reduced permeable boundary. It is essential for an open system that it works towards achieving a *steady state* for it to survive and develop.

Steady State or Homeostasis

Often there is confusion with the notion of the organisation being in a constant state of responding to its environment and the notion of maintaining a *steady state*. The following explanation is an attempt to help differentiate and clarify these complementary conditions.

Steady state or homeostasis, from the Greek 'standing still', is the property of a system that regulates its internal environment and tends to maintain a stable *steady state*. All homeostasis systems have control mechanisms, used to maintain a *steady state*, which takes the form of three interdependent components for the variables to be regulated. The *receptor* is the sensing mechanism for monitoring the environment. When a receptor identifies a stimulus, it sends information to a 'control centre', which sets the range at which a variable is maintained.

This, in organisational terms, is the environmental scanning process undertaken by the organisational leaders (the 'receptors') who then determine, in terms of the organisation's needs (the 'control centre'), the range and level of permeability of that organisation's boundary. The control of the response to the stimulus takes place within the 'control centre' where the executive leaders, "the interpretive agents", determine the appropriate response. (Refer to Fig.10, "Representation Hourglass Strategic Thinking".)

The 'control centre' determines the appropriate response to the stimulus, which then sends a signal to an effecter that may be a muscle, an organ or other structures; in this instance an organisation's operating system, which has the capacity to receive and respond to the control system's signal. The receipt of the signal, that a change has occurred, stimulates a process of responsive activity to either enhance the response with a *positive feedback* or a *negative feedback* to further control the effects. This responsive process has the deliberate intention to engage with the environmental stimulant to enable the organism, or in this case the organisation, to attempt to achieve a developed *steady state*. This is achieved through the effective regulatory behaviour of managing the permeability of your organisation's boundaries.

This condition of closed boundaries has been observed when working with executives who have suddenly found that they have to lead and manage an organisation that is being forced to dramatically change. Some have responded by developing their understanding of their organisation's transitional dynamics during the change process. They were open, their personal boundaries were open, and they survived and flourished.

Others were locked in their own personal anxiety "psychic prison" and unable to learn and change their style of leadership. Anxiety had closed their personal boundaries and as a consequence failed to survive the imposed changes. It could be observed that their withdrawal was causing confused decision-making. This led to people taking responsibility for their own functions and only communicating what the confused leader wanted to hear. The following will be familiar to many in that these self-regulating sub-organisations were based on politicking, power-centred and competitive career creating opportunities, with little attention to the overt organisation (Fig. 3, "Politics, Career and Overt Organisation"). These political personality-driven organisations dissipate the potential of any organisation. Eventually they are either taken over, dramatically overhauled, or fail.

An open system, if it is going to survive, cannot randomly trade with the environment and needs to regulate at its boundaries. A system is distinguished from an aggregate of activities by the existence of regulations (Rice, 1996). Regulation relates to activities to throughput, ordering them in such a way as to ensure that the process is accomplished; that the different import − conversions − export processes of the system are related to each other and that the system, as a whole, is related to the environment. (Fig. 12, "Boundary Control for Task Systems" attempts to identify some of these relationships.)

Connect this notion to the discussion on design, where we identified that we design the organisation to scan the market place, translate and create an organisation that can continuously and effectively respond. This is, in reality, a simple import − conversion − export process (Fig. 12), described by Rice. You may have begun to make the connection with the notion of creating a *performance culture continuum* that spans the whole of this transactional process. (Refer to Fig.10, "Representation Hourglass Strategic Thinking".)

Organisational systems are developed to achieve a *primary task* – the task it must perform to survive (Rice, ibid). For a system to achieve a task it must have all the necessary facilities for obtaining it. This can be called a task system. This is an important notion in that the identification of the *primary task* provides *direction and intent* for the task system. Further developments and how they *fit*, having identified the *context, direction and intent*, enables, for example, the individual and their role to be clearly examined and understood. Working through these processes progressively contributes to the development of our *cognitive organisational awareness,* our ability to *think organisationally* and the development of our *organisational leadership competencies.* (Refer to the developed processes outlined in Chapter Six, "Leading Transition for Change".)

The Individual as a Task System

Lawrence and Lorsch (1976) considered that the behaviour of members of an organisation is interdependent in terms of the task to be accomplished, the personalities of the other members and the unwritten rules about appropriate behaviour for the members.

This view of life in an organisation and the entire overt inter-related and complex relationships poses the question: where does one begin any form of analysis? To begin with, one must have a fundamental understanding of the behaviour of an organisation, the social behaviour of an organisation and the social behaviour of the people in it. "A group, whether small or large, consists of individuals in relationship to one another, and therefore, the understanding of personality is the foundation for understanding social life. To do this it is necessary to investigate how individuals develop from infancy into maturity" (Klein, 1959).

For the purpose of understanding your own transitional development, we should take a cue from Klein and begin by looking firstly at the individual, then at the development of workgroups and finally, the organisation. There is a specific reason for exploring these developmental ideas, which stems from the need for you as a developing organisational leader, to understand your own developmental behaviour. Goleman (1996) in his highly acclaimed book 'Emotional Intelligence' encourages you to understand your own relationship with others and in different social groups. In social organisations, the appropriate behaviour needs to fit your organisation's social developmental needs, which requires that you have a well-developed *social emotional intelligence* that complements your *developed cognitive organisational awareness*.

Therefore, the focus of your *intuitive development* is deliberately set within the specific context of effectively leading and managing your organisation and its environment. This developed intuitive competency can be described as having a felt sense of what is being enacted by your organisation. This intuitive sense is achieved through your developed *cognitive organisational awareness*. Our capacity to achieve a well-developed *cognitive organisational awareness* is a direct function of our own experiences, developed personality and *social emotional intelligence*. (To ground the understanding of the development of our *social emotional intelligence,* refer to Chapter Twelve, "Development, Training and Recruitment".)

It is important for us to have some understanding of our own developed behaviour and how it transfers across an organisation's boundaries. We discussed and identified in Chapter Three, "The Enemy Within..." that we consciously and unconsciously influence the way decisions are made and are implemented. "When considering the reasons why leaders lead people astray, pride of place must surely be given to those personality factors, which through self-selection characterise the potential misleaders. The argument is simple; people are attracted to and prosper in vocations, which suit their mental make-up" (Dixon, 1989). This is important as Dixon identifies our "mental-make up" is influencing our decision-making and can, in some cases, prevent an individual making the transition from their bounded professional role to one that may ask them to open their own personal boundaries that is necessary for becoming and effective organisational leader. (Refer to Fig. 24, "Mapping Career Decisions".)

If an individual is unable to make the transition from their bounded professional role they will have a tendency to mould the organisation to fit their bounded psychological need and induced anxieties, rather than adapting their behaviour to fit the presented organisational needs. It is useful to keep in mind that the organisation is not there for you; you are there for the organisation to act as its "interpretive agent."

Fig. 13 ("Assumptions from Experience") is a useful notional model that can assist us to understand and review the assumption and subsequent attitudes that we have developed from our experience. Being aware of the processes that influence our attitudes provides us with an opportunity to also change them in the light of further experience.

Our attitudes inform our motivational behaviour and intent. When being asked to contribute to the overall organisation's performance, our attitudes and motivational intent have to be directed to ensure they contribute to the organisation's overall performance.

ASSUMPTION FROM EXPERIENCE

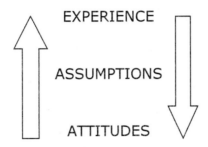

EXPERIENCE

ASSUMPTIONS

ATTITUDES

Fig 13

From an organisational leader's perspective we keep in mind this notional model. When designing our organisations we are making choices as to how we want individuals, workgroups, sub-organisations and the whole organisation to behave. If we design our organisations that only enlist automated responses (machine model), people may act in a way that will negate their contribution, which may cause them to only work within the prescriptive requirements (tick box mentality). They may even engage in developing alternative practices to relieve the boredom and/or to beat the system.

For example, in some company call centres individual call-rates are automatically monitored. Some individuals simply initiate the automated call system and as soon as the connection is made they disconnect. The recipients of these bogus calls know these as nuisance calls. This registers a call completed hence that individual's work rate appears to be acceptable, yet there has been no business transacted.

Change the design to enlist the collective intelligence and the behaviour will change, with individuals being motivated to contribute to the overall organisation's performance.

Influence of Working Environments

These differences in organisational climates have the notional effect of switching individual's attitudes and therefore their directed motivational *intent*. It should start to become evident that the way we perceive and understand how organisations work is crucial to how successfully we translate our leadership practices into the organisation. In simple language we can either turn people on or turn them off; we have the choice, we have to have the developed competencies to know when and how we do this.

An example of how our working environments can influence our behaviour is provided by Menzies (1970), from her studies of nursing services in general hospitals. Menzies found that: "Intimate physical contact with the patient arouses strong libidinal and erotic wishes and impulses that may be difficult to control. The work situation arouses very strong mixed feelings in the nurses: pity, compassion, love, guilt and anxiety; hatred and resentment of the patient who arouses these strong feelings; envy of the care given to the patient." This study of nurses brought out the fact that nurses were displaying very primitive feelings, which were greatly influenced by their environmental conditions. This could be claimed to be a specific situation but these primitive feelings are displayed in all kinds of social organisations. To explore these experienced induced feelings further it is useful to examine an individual's behaviour using general systems theory.

General Systems Theory and the Individual

For the individual to successfully develop, it is essential that they manage the processes of projection and introjection. Projection occurs when a person unconsciously attributes to another a person's characteristics, which are, in fact, their own. What was originally an internal threat is now experienced as an external threat and can be dealt with in the same way as any other external threat. The real source of anxiety remains within the individual. The action of projection does not resolve the cause of the anxiety and it remains within the individuals to resolve their own internal conflict. An example of introjection is where a manager identifies with the failing of his subordinates as a reflection of his own skills. When an individual is employed these personally developed behaviours are also imported across your organisation's boundaries.

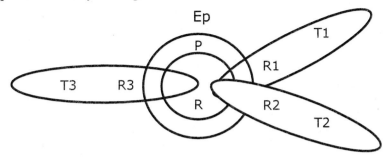

Ep	= External environment of individual
P	= Ego function
R	= Internal world of individual
T1, T2, T3	= Tasks
R1, R2, R3	= Roles

The Role System of the Individual

Fig 14

The capacity of the individual to manage these conflicting feelings lies in them being able to define the boundaries between self and the outside world and perceiving what is inside and what is outside and acting appropriately with this knowledge. Ill-conceived introjections and projection can distort the boundaries and action then becomes based on distorted facts and on unreal perceptions of the situation. This is an area where "leaders can mislead."

The mature ego is the means that can be used to define the boundaries between what is inside and what is outside and can also regulate the transaction between one and the other. This can be diagrammatically represented as a system of roles, Rice (1969) (Fig. 14).

The ego function is located in the boundary control region, checking and measuring intake, controlling conversion activities and inspecting output. It uses the senses as instruments of import systems: thinking, feeling and other processes, to convert the intake, then action, speech, or other means of expression to export the output.

The individual is not just a single activity system with easily defined primary tasks. The person is a multi-task system capable of multiple activities. The activities become bounded and controlled task systems when they are directed to perform a specific task to fulfil some specific purpose. The difficulty is the controlling of internal boundaries and the dealing with activities not related to the task performance. The built-in attitudes and beliefs formed through previous experience (Fig. 13, "Assumptions from Experience") act as a means of regulating against elements, which may or may not be relevant to the specific task.

A role requires the carrying out of specific activities and the export of particular outputs. This concept developed by Rice (1969) is useful in that an individual sets up a task system, which requires a project team composed of relevant skills, experience, feelings and attitudes. It is the task of the ego function to ensure they are adequate and available. When the role changes the project team disbands and reforms to support the new role. Each of the roles the individual has to take requires different capabilities and can be related to different parts of the environment and will need different kinds of management control. It is possible to recognise people who act or appear to be quite different in separate and distinct situations (Lawrence and Lorsch, 1967). "The ego function could be said to be exercising different kinds of management" (Rice, ibid). (Refer to Chapter Seven, "Adaptive Organisational Leadership" where these "different kinds of management" are, by necessity, being exercised.) (Chapter Twelve, "Development Training and Recruitment" examines and develops these behavioural attributes further to assist in clarifying the nature of successful developmental social and leadership practices.)

To practice and become an *effective Organisational Leader* it is essential this concept is understood, as each organisational situation will require a different style of leadership and management to enable appropriate decision-making that is required for the organisation to function effectively. The progressive process experienced when leading and managing of transition for change will require the adoption of different leadership roles to facilitate the transition process.

Dislike of the role and/or the activities or behaviour required in it, and the demonstration of the dislike by attempts to change the role or modify behaviour, or the intrusion of feelings or judgements that contradict role requirements inevitably distorts intakes and modifies conversion processes which can only result in inappropriate output.

Menzies (1970) illustrates these kinds of role modifications when discussing the attempts by nurses to eliminate decisions by ritual task performance and delegating upwards when making decisions. These are methods of regulation that are used for defending against anxiety. When a group of individuals all experience anxiety they unconsciously collude to effect changes that defend them against anxiety. To understand this phenomenon it is necessary to examine the individual's role in a group and the group's behaviour.

Agyris (1986) in his article "Skilled Incompetence" identifies how managers who are skilled communicators, but who want to manage the potential risk, employ the use of ambiguous communication. The receiver of the communication clearly understands the ambiguity and responds accordingly. This ritualistic behaviour is also part of the developed corporate working environment that we all over time fit into and do not challenge. It is also a direct function of managers defending themselves from the induced anxiety of the organisation attempting to respond to its environment and not knowing what to do. This suggests these people do not have a well-developed *cognitive organisational awareness* leaving them exposed and needing to revert to safe internalised organisational cultural practices. This all contributes to the collusive behaviour discussed by Menzies (1970). This example has been used to simply demonstrate that these behavioural practices present themselves in different forms.

The Individual in a Group

Hutton (1971) said that people differ in the way in which they perceive and react to other people because of and to do with the way in which they have worked over their own internal organisation.

As a member of a group, a number of different dimensions affect the individual. They are part of the environment as well as the group. They have, as identified above, their own standards derived from their developed experience as well as belonging to other groups, such as family and friendship allegiances.

The individual has not only to use their ego function to control transactions across their own boundary, but also between their role and that of others. "When the ego function fails to locate boundaries precisely and fails to control transactions across these boundaries confusion is inevitable, confusion of roles and the authority exercised in the roles. To be continuously confused about role/personal boundaries or completely unable to define and maintain boundaries is to be mentally sick" (Rice, 1969). For the individual member, the problem is that of reconciling his hopes, fears, aspirations and personal objectives, with the demands of the group and these may be many, Bion (1968). (Refer to case study, "NHS, District Works, Leading Transition for Change" for an example of people being subjected to these conditions through inappropriate systems-led practices.)

These transactional relationships can best be demonstrated by the use of a diagrammatic model developed by Bridger (1978) (Fig. 15). The large circle straddling the group boundaries represents the "Me" in the group. This person's identity and private needs are derived from family, education, background, career, standards and values, religion and all other things that go to make up the person who is partly inside and partly outside any one group, which emphasises the elements and areas to be defended. These are used when a person engages in the balancing and optimising process when committing to a group task.

Before discussing group behaviour it is useful to look at why groups are formed. Most groups, as with any organisation, are formed to service or achieve a specific task; by definition this must be a task system. A task system in this context is a system of activities, plus the collaborative human and physical resources to perform these activities. In effect they are micro sub-organisations that have to be developed to _fit_ into the overall complementary practice of contributing to the overall organisation's performance.

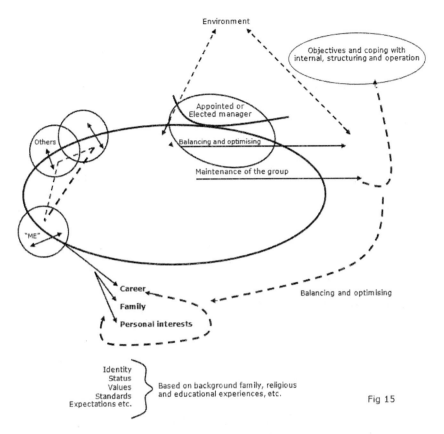

Fig 15

Group Behaviour

Bion (1968) describes the group as operating at two levels: one level contains the task group and the second level contains the basic assumption or "as if" group. The group and the "as if" group each assume a different state exists when it does not. The following diagram best demonstrates this concept (Bridger 1978) (Fig. 16). You may want to make the notional connection, as you progress through this book, with the fact that groups can be seen as micro organisations and when organisations are dysfunctional are working in a state that can be referred to being "as if", which creates *displaced goals* (Fig. 4).

Bion (1968) has described three distinct emotional states of groups from which three basic assumptions can be deduced. The three basic assumptions that are part of the group's developmental behaviour are:

Fight / Flight – To attack or run away from somebody or something.

Dependency – To obtain security from one individual.

Pairing – To reproduce itself, or to produce another leader.

Only one of these basic assumptions can be operating at any one time, although it can change frequently or persist for some time.

When a group feels threatened, anxiety causes it to take action to preserve itself and its integrity. The basic assumption gives meaning to the behaviour of the group as a whole, yet the assumption is not overtly expressed even when it is being acted on.

AN "AS IF" GROUP

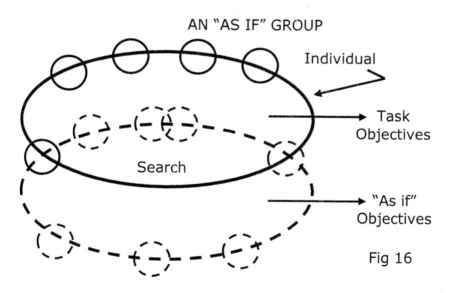

Fig 16

One condition of an effective group is that it is in contact with reality and knows the boundaries between what is inside the group and what is outside. The group can become ineffective when, through projection, it blurs the boundaries and projects its own internal problems. By realising that the sources of its anxiety are within the group, the group removes a major obstacle to achieving an effective performance. This can be likened to an individual not being able to change until they recognise and own their own internal conflict.

Bion (1968) has shown that in a group the basic explanation of a group action lies in the consolidated individual behaviour resulting from the inter-connection of individual projection processes. It is also expected that the group mentality would be opposed to the avowed aims of the individual members of the group. Margaret Rioch (1970), comments that the idea that rational forces dominant in a group is "rare and perhaps even non-existent in pure culture."

Any rational attempts to investigate the dynamics of the group are perturbed by fear and mechanisms for dealing with them that are characteristic of the paranoid-schizoid position. In other words, when the group faces persecutory anxiety, then the individual members unconsciously collude with one another in the process of splitting and projecting identification. This suggests that the group is behaving as a whole in the same manner to that of individuals subjected to the same anxieties. With this kind of group collective collusion it can be expected that this process would be apparent in society and organisations.

The group, any group, organisation, or society, needs and evolves a structure of tasks, roles, procedures, rules, and ascribed status (what Bion referred to as the "group culture"), in order to contain the anxiety of the unknown and the responses that, unconsciously are mobilised to defend against that unknown. Within the group, Bion believed one can see operating a number of powerful unconscious and unlearned, quasi-instinctive, strategies and denial as constituting what he termed a "group mentality", opposed to the conscious aims, intentions and effort of individuals. No group, no organisation and no individual, however sophisticated, are ever wholly outside the sphere of group mentality in this sense. Paradoxically, Bion believed, this is at least partly because the ability of the group to mobilise group mentality is a powerful unlearned source of co-operation (Armstrong, 1995).

The Organisation as an Open System

Some notions of general systems theory have been used to illustrate the processes at work within the individual and the group. An organisation and its processes can also be further analysed by using this approach.

For an organisation to exist it must continually import material and people from the environment. The imports are used to facilitate the conversion process and the end products are exported into the environment. These combine to form the technical and the social elements that need to be harmonised. With any open system the organisation maintains a "steady state" only as long as it continually changes and adapts to the forces from the environment.

This process can be compared with a product cycle (Fig. 17). The product is designed, developed and marketed to satisfy an identified market and social need. Over time the market will change and so will the interest in the specific product. The curve in (Fig. 17) shows the product decline and the need to renew, either by: – redesigning the product to satisfy the new social needs, or to design and develop an entirely new product. In this case the product is the transitional development of the organisation, workgroups and individuals. Tracking these cycles is important to keep the product/service fresh to meet the changing environmental needs.

The same applies to the organisation in that it has to constantly learn from its environment and remain responsive, as with the products, to the changing identified needs. In business terms the operation of the organisation develops and maintains its effectiveness as long as it is sensitive and reacts to the changing needs of the market and society. By regulating and managing the exchanges across the organisation's boundary, this enables the appropriate behavioural response to be achieved.

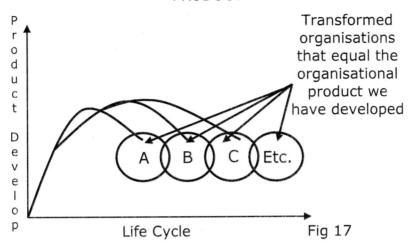

PRODUCT

Transformed organisations that equal the organisational product we have developed

Product Development (vertical axis)

Life Cycle

A B C Etc.

Fig 17

(Refer to Fig. 10, "Representational Hourglass Strategic Thinking".) Examining the nature, number of processes, and their imports and exports, reveals the variety of relationships that an organisation, or part of an organisation, makes with different parts of the environment and also within itself and its different parts. The different parts can themselves be referred to as sub-systems, having the same properties as total systems (Hutton 1972 and Katz and Kahn 1966).

The whole enterprise and sub-systems are all task systems. It is equally important that the boundaries and transactions are also managed and controlled effectively for each of the sub-systems. The simple diagram (Fig. 12, "Boundary Control for Task Systems") has demonstrated the process, where Rice (1969) describes task management as essentially 1) The definition of boundaries between the task and system and 2) The control of transactions across boundaries.

The connections we need to make with these various task systems is that they are all dependent and/or interdependent, depending on their relationship to one another. This creates a demand that these social and task systems relationships are understood when designing and connecting these various task systems to complement the overall organisation's decision-making processes, for supporting the developmental performance of an organisation.

Organisational Development

Just as individuals become more complex as they grow and develop, so does the complexity of organisations increase with their size and differentiation (Lawrence and Lorsch, 1967a).

The operating system (Hutton, 1969; Rice, 1969), is the system of activities that is in the mainstream of the dominant import – conversion – export process by which the primary task is performed. When an enterprise has more than one operating system, a differentiated management system is required to control and coordinate the activities of the differentiated systems. (Refer, for an example, to the case study, "Transitional Nursing Care" where they failed to understand, regulate and manage the differentiated service delivery systems.)

The Individual and the Organisation (Adaptive Roles)

To manage the various task systems of an activity, people in the organisation occupy positions and belong to "role sets" (Handy, Katz and Kahn). When assigning positions, the organisation cannot pre-determine the sentience of the various groups to which each individual belongs. These observations reaffirm the need for leaders and managers to be able to interpret and adapt their behaviour to satisfy the demands of the various roles these individuals, workgroups and role sets occupy. When working through the *transition for change* process, there is a need to move from one state to another. Through this journey the behaviour of those affected will change in response to the felt levels of anxiety, understanding and the eventual ownership of the new demands and working relationships.

Ownership can only be achieved once the individual has a well-developed *cognitive organisational awareness* (Fig. 8) that must include the acceptance that the organisational leader is the "agent" of the organisation. The model begins with the development of your *cognitive organisational awareness* that influences the *intent*, which informs and formulates your *attitudes* that *direct your motivated* activity. You may want to make the connection with the notion of

(Fig. 13, "Assumptions from Experience") which infers that you can change your motivational attitudes by re-examining your basic assumptions. (These personal developments and changing relationships are further teased out and applied in Chapter Six, "Leading Transition for Change" Chapter Seven, "Adaptive Organisational Leadership" and Chapter Eight, "Workgroups – Leadership and Positioning in Groups".)

The Individual in the Organisation

Hutton (1969) has developed a conceptual view of the individual in an organisation, which has the capacity to identify some of the boundary activities and role relationships that feed into the development of your *cognitive organisational awareness*. It is useful in that it represents the individual and the organisation as a system of behaviour and activity. The convention used in Fig. 18 by Hutton represents the individual and the enterprise as areas and boundaries.

To make full use of this model it is essential to understand the notion of roles as applying not to the individual but to the social system they participate in. It is "outside", not as a tangible object but as something belonging to a system of higher order. The individual enters into or plays a role. This is important, as already identified; individual personalities do affect 'how' leaders and managers and others play roles, some of which are pre-determined, although individuals may interpret them in different ways.

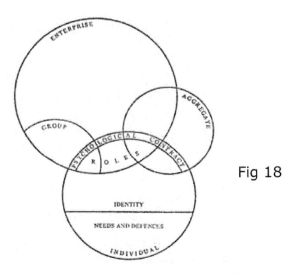

Fig 18

Common Regions for the Individual and Enterprise

The model uses the same concept employed to demonstrate the individual in the group, of the individual and the aggregate straddling the organisation's boundaries. This implies that the individual is not wholly in the organisation – physically yes, but not psychologically. The individual balances and optimises their relationship with the enterprise, in much the same way as they are a member of a group, to maintain their identity and integrity. In the study of the behaviour by Menzies the socially structured defence mechanism tended to become a part of the external reality with which all old and new members of the organisation must come to terms.

Why an Organisational Approach?

Simply stated, it enables us to effectively influence the expressed experiences and unexpressed behaviour that can be experienced when leading and managing social organisations. Therefore, Chapters Four, Five and Six need to be connected to the practice of leading and managing organisations. It should have become evident that a great deal of behaviour is induced by the situation experienced created through their social and working environment. A poor experience of an organisation in transition for change will influence that individual's future expectation and defensive response. A good experience will generally encourage that individual to embrace transition for change with a more open attitude.

The employment of an organisational approach is a deliberate tactic to enable leaders and managers to positively influence what may be considered the covert behaviour discussed in the previous chapters. The development of the ability to *think organisationally*, the development of your *cognitive organisational awareness*, the developed ability to *design your organisation* and *adapt your leadership* style (using your *social emotional intelligence*) is collectively employed to improve your organisational leadership skills. These collective developments are designed to enable you to positively influence the covert behaviour in social organisations.

We have identified that we have to understand and manage the overt as well as the covert organisation. To assist in putting this into context it is useful to consider the notion of an iceberg and then to connect this to another concept, that of the Pareto Principle or the

80/20 rule. Essentially by using and connecting these two notions we emphasise the need to improve our ability to lead and manage the overt twenty per cent to maximise our ability to positively influence the covert eighty per cent.

Consider an iceberg (Fig. 19), where we can place those observable, overt, activities above the water line and those not directly observable, the covert, activities below the water line. An iceberg is approximate eighty per cent under water with only twenty per cent exposed (80/20), which may suggest that when we are not aware of what we are leading and managing we only have intellectually access to only twenty per cent of what is available in organisational terms.

Pareto Principle

Using the notion of the Pareto Principle, also known as the 80/20 rule, and the law of the vital few states, for many events, roughly eighty per cent of the effects came from twenty per cent of the cause. We can use our imagination and consider that to affect and gain a form of access to the eighty per cent we need to use all our skills and competencies when working with the twenty per cent directly available to us.

The value of this image is that anyone who attempts to introduce new technologies, new strategies, or lead transition for change programmes would be well advised to develop an understanding as to how individuals, groups and teams may function in different social organisational environments.

It is important that we not only manage the overt tangible elements and their interactive relationships but also that we also do so with a clear understanding of how we want to effectively influence the covert behavioural activities and how they contribute.

In other words we need to design our organisations to create a working environment where individuals motivate themselves to contribute effectively to the organisation's overall performance. This requires that the technologies employed be designed with that *intent*. This brings us to the expectation that the technology and the social systems are working in harmony for the collective good of the individual and the overall organisation's performance.

ORGANISATIONAL BEHAVIOURAL ICEBERG

Formal (overt) aspects: -

Policies
Goals, targets, objectives
Technologies
Systems and procedures
Structures
Perceived skills and ability
20%   **Financial Resources**
Human resources

Informal (covert) aspects: -

Attitudes, value and perceptions
Feelings of anxiety, anger, fear, and despair
Dis-empowerment, confusion, incompetence and
impotence
80%   **Interactive feelings**
Group behaviour
Politics and career aspirations

Fig 19

NOTE: - The overt and the covert could be described as the conscious and the
unconscious behaviour of an organisation

SECTION TWO

Application of an Organisational Approach

PART THREE
Leading Transition for Change

Goals and Introduction

CHAPTER SIX
Leading Transition for Change

CHAPTER SEVEN
Adaptive Organisational Leadership

CHAPTER EIGHT
Workgroups
(Leadership and Positioning in Groups)

GOALS

- To provide a frame of reference for successfully leading transition for change.
- To enable you to begin to make the mind-shift and personal transition from a system to an organisational-led decision-making approach.
- To examine your own behaviour when responding to presented situations and how that affects others.
- To understand why you need to adapt your leadership style to satisfy the changing needs of presented situations.
- To explore your adaptive role when leading and developing workgroups and teams.
- To develop your understanding of leading and developing effective workgroups.

Introduction

Chapter Six is a distillation of the previous chapters that have been used to develop your understanding of how organisations, workgroups, individuals, systems and management technologies behave. Using this developed *cognitive organisational awareness* has enabled the identification of an effective process for successfully leading transition for organisational change. That has the capacity to consistently deliver the necessary strategic delivery performance outcomes. This applied organisational led approach provides you with an opportunity to work through the processes for *leading and managing transition for change*, and provides you with a framework to focus the *directed collective motivational behaviour* and for you to attach the various *management technologies*.

Chapter Seven provides an opportunity to understand and develop the need to adapt your leadership practices to satisfy the presented situation within the context of your organisation and its inherent workgroups. Understanding group behaviour is an essential attribute, as related workgroups need to complement one another's activities and their contribution to the overall organisations performance.

Chapter Eight examines workgroups and leadership positioning as leaders spend much of their time in some form of workgroup where they formulate decisions and strategies for implementation. Workgroups are the means for you, as the "interpreting agent" to enlist the collective intelligence, to inform decision-making and effectively develop implementation tactics. We have to keep in mind that when implementing these decisions they will affect other parts of your organisation, also the behaviour and decision-making of other workgroups. These connected *contextual decision-making processes* are important, as they are the way we effectively enlist the collective intelligence for us to formulate decisions and develop successful implementation practices.

These three chapters provide a frame of reference that when employed, automatically stimulate and influence positive behavioural practices within workgroups, your organisations and your own success.

Your performance will be significantly impaired without an understanding of these necessary competencies as they have a dependent relationship that requires that you understand their relationship and any consequential behaviour. This developed cognitive understanding is designed to reinforce your *organisational thinking and your cognitive organisational awareness.* The primary *intent* for asking you to work through these processes is to significantly improve your organisational leadership practice, decision-making and your organisation's service delivery performance.

CHAPTER SIX

LEADING TRANSITION FOR CHANGE

A Change in Performance Culture Requires A Transition from One State to Another

We are constantly extolled to learn to manage change. Often the approach to this clarion call is that leaders and managers begin where they are with the current dysfunctional practices. We have consistently identified that many of the solutions are to resolve problems created by the previous solution. We also discovered that these systems led approaches significantly increase resistance to change, leading to many single strategic initiatives being seriously compromised.

To overcome this negative cycle of events it should be evident that we have to go back to basics and address the organisation's needs, as that is our performance platform. The following approach is being proffered as it provides an initial working frame of reference where we can direct and attach the influences created by the motivational behavioural practices and management technologies.

Developed Mind-Set

To begin with we have to use a process where we start where we want to finish. This provides us with a developing organisational model that services those transactions that convert all the previous activities into viable outcomes. To start this process it would be useful to share a general model for leading and managing transition for change that has been consistently used within a variety of organisational situations. We shall be working through these processes using various workgroups and management technologies that all make demands on your ability to lead and manage the presented situations.

The process that predates the use of this model (Fig.20) is the analytical process of examining 'the recent history to understand the here and now,' the scanning of that organisation's environment, the employment and differentiation of technologies, and the translation and management across your organisation's boundaries. These have to be understood without any judgemental intent (refer to *detached engaged positioning*, Chapters Seven and Eight, "Adaptive Organisational Leadership" and "Workgroups".) otherwise you will begin to spiral into the history of activities that serves only to play the blame game.

These preliminary activities service the development and the ability to test the competencies of your existing organisation, workgroups, systems, practices, decision-making processes and the competency of those employed to deliver the developed strategy for effectively *leading transition for change*. Working through these preliminaries also provides you with an insight into the potential areas of conflict. This developed process provides you with an opportunity to use the information to ensure that the strategic *intent* is not derailed or compromised, preventing the identified performance outcomes being achieved.

Using the Organisation as the 'Third Party'

"In any disagreement deal only with the current situation."
A Johnson

When leading transition for change, there will always be challenges and areas of conflict. The value of using an organisational approach is that you can use the organisation as the 'third party' for conflict resolution. The primary development is that of the organisation, which requires all the employees, management technologies and their systems, procedures and practices, all work in harmony to reinforce the organisation's needs. The organisation needs to employ people to work and complement its focused collaborative activities, but the organisation is not there for the employees.

This dependent relationship between the employee and the organisation has to be managed to ensure both parties benefit one another. That makes the human side of work the most important aspect in any consideration of jobs and organisations. For example, organisations are made up of people; the work, of course is done by people, and the result of the work is for people, whether they be direct recipients, patients in hospitals, customers; or the indirect recipients, namely, other employees or members of the wider community.

Even so the base line is that organisations need to respond to their environment and for those employed to be enabled to respond to the identified organisational needs. Therefore when resolving conflict it is essential that it is completed in terms of the organisation's needs.

In conflict resolution the organisation becomes the 'third party' and is used to redirect the conflicting issues to be addressed in terms of the organisation's needs. Often the conflict is generated by differences either in the personalities, professional background, or ownership of a power cabal that is being disturbed, and different developed perceptions from these individuals' experiences. Irrespective of these differences the common denominator is the servicing of the development of the organisation. By redefining the conflicting issues in terms of the organisation's needs, the personality content is redirected away from personal confrontation. If not addressed, this become infectious and depleting, not only for the organisation but also for those individuals involved.

Leading Transition for change

A precautionary note regarding the use of the following diagram (Fig. 20). – This diagram has only been produced to provide a structure to attach and discuss these connected intellectual processes. These attached processes are being used to evaluate their dependent or interdependent relationships, that feed into the *development of the performance culture continuum* and to identify the various *states of flux*. It is a collective intellectual process where all of those taking part have or are working towards the development of their collective *cognitive organisational awareness*.

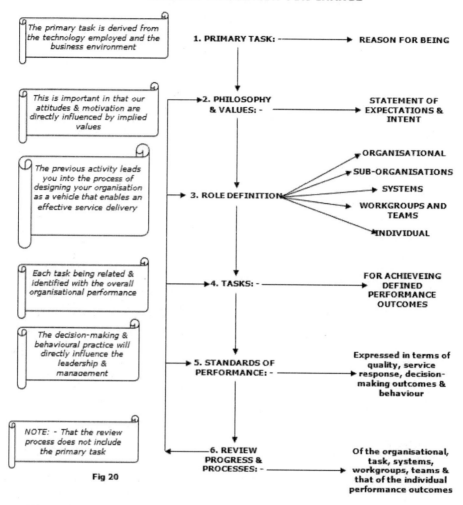

Fig 20

The concern is that this becomes a prescriptive practice rather than an evaluative decision-making process that enables you to make the connections with various dependent and interdependent activities as they emerge. It is not a linear process; it is a continuous process of analysis and review to ensure that you test all the assumptions against previous decisions. It provides an opportunity to further review and modify your decision-making and implementation strategies.

Consistency and Commitment

The above processed when written appear to be logical and simplistic but as with the chart above it carries a further precautionary tale. The potential behaviour attributed to the overwhelming desire to appear to be *consistent and committed* requires a cautionary note when dealing with nonlinear decision-making processes such as leading transition for change. The employment of processes to *monitor to manage* the consequences of our decision-making is also part of the need to develop a knowledge based learning organisation. This process of *monitoring to manage,* for some leaders, maybe counter-intuitive and the following behaviour may be experienced.

There are at least two parts to this potential dilemma; one is avoiding pain and the other is the felt sense of being seen to be *consistent and committed.* These factors can induce a defensive response of justifying your earlier decision. Once committed to an action and a stand had been taken, the need for consistency pressures the individual to bring what they thought and believed into line with what they had already done. "They simply convince themselves that they had made the right choice," Cialdini (2007)

"Inconsistency is commonly thought to be an undesirable trait. That person who believes, words, and deeds don't match they seem to be indecisive, confused, two-faced or even mentally ill. On the other side, a high degree of consistency is normally associated with personal and intellectual strength. It is at the heart of logic, rationality, stability, and honesty," Cialdini (2007).

This expectation when internalised generate a sense that it is in our interest to be consistent, we easily fall into automatic responsive behaviour to such an extent that we apply it to situations unthinkingly even when it is not sensible, *consistency* can be disastrous. Nevertheless, *consistency* along with its attached component *commitment* has its attractions.

Cialdini write, "Like most other forms of automatic responding, it offers a shortcut through the density of modern life. Once we have made up our minds about an issue, stubborn consistency allows us a very appealing luxury: we don't have to think about the issues anymore. We don't have to sift through volumes of information we encounter every day to identify relevant facts; we don't have to expend our mental energy to weigh the pros and cons; we don't have to make any further tough decisions. Instead all we have to do when confronted with the issues is to turn on our consistency tape, and we know just what to believe, say, or do. We need only believe, say, or do whatever is consistent with the early decisions."

The attraction is that it allows us a convenient, relatively effortless, and efficient method of dealing with complex daily environments that make severe demands on our mental energies and capacities. Is not hard to understand, then, what automatic consistency is a difficult reaction to curb. But, it is essential that we rigorously re-examine the performance outcomes of our decisions to ensure that they are achieving the desired intent. Failure to do so introduces undesirable practices that create dysfunctional organisational practices caused by those factors that cause leaders to mislead. (Refer to Chapter Three, "The Enemy Within and Why Change Fails".)

This process of leading transition for change requires that you are working to understand where to want to finish, referred to as the *future state*. This process enables us to begin to work "as if" we are working in that created organisational environment. The fundamental reason for adopting this approach is that it has the capacity to enlist all the future fears of those affected. The participants are beginning to play out their concerns as they experience them, therefore providing an opportunity for these anxieties to surface, be expressed, understood and managed. It brings those covert concerns and resistance to change activities to the surface, enabling them to be addressed at source, rather than covertly and inappropriately influence the proceedings. (Refer to Fig. 19, "Organisational Behavioural Iceberg".) It is easier to deal with these issues at this stage of the proceedings than to attempt to rework the unwanted outcomes at a later date.

Working through these Processes

Stage 1 (Fig. 20), identifying and collectively agreeing the *"primary task."* (Refer to Chapter Four). Working through this process, participants may find they are outside their own comfort zones. Also, individuals and the workgroups they belong to will be working through their own transition processes that can prove to be frustratingly difficult. Even so, it cannot be circumvented, as it is particularly important for improving and managing the decision-making and implementation processes.

It is part of the process where the participants develop and take ownership of the transition for change processes. In reality it is a process for *working for clarity* and identifying the *intent* of the organisation, which enables the participants to make sense and understand what something means (Phillips 1973). When working with systems, they tend to use linear logical processes. Human beings do not work along logical processes, as they need to test assumptions and continually test their understanding of the contextual requirement of their working environment before they can "let go" and "internalise change" (Fig. 21). It is all part of the process of understanding and making sense of what something means. Working through this process and identifying the *primary task* provides the scope and benchmark for testing all decision-making and implementation processes. The quality of decision-making and having the ability to effectively implement any decisions will underwrite not only your organisation's performance but also your own.

Working through the processes of identifying the *primary task* develops the capacity of the executive decision-makers to improve their collective understanding of their organisation's role, their individual roles and, importantly, the development of the necessary collective *organisational and leadership* language that supports the dialogue for the on-going development of their organisation.

Stage 2 (Fig. 20) is where you identify and agree the *intent*, philosophy and values of your business organisation, which is all part of the process of *developing a shared cognitive organisational model* that each person can own and effectively contribute toward. When thinking through these processes, the values of the organisation are identified and become imbued in the governance and practices of your organisation. It becomes explicit within the design of your organisation's leadership and management processes.

The process of role clarification, that of the "Agent" Argyris (1999) leads naturally into the intellectual use of the notion of the *open-ended hourglass* (Fig. 10) where at one end, the external influences are scanned and processed in terms of the organisation's identified responsive needs. The scanning process includes testing their values and importantly what attention needs to be attributed to each of them. The other end of the hourglass is the service delivery end, where the organisation is designed to ensure that the operating processes are satisfying the customer's service delivery expectations. This includes the process of identifying sub-organisations, their boundaries, their dependent and inter-dependent boundary relationships and the nature of their complementary and task working relationships.

Stage 3 (Fig. 20). This practice of clarifying roles is important as it assists in identifying and reducing role ambiguity, confusion and conflict, which all lead to the incumbent becoming demotivated, destroying morale and creating low risk attitudes (Nyquit 2009).

When working through role clarification we need to keep in mind the notional process of working through either intellectually or physical processes of *variation analysis*, which assist in developing an understanding of the organisation's *performance culture continuum*. These processes identify those critical *states of flux* that need to be regulated and managed. The identification of these *states of flux* informs the way you develop and structure your organisation and the roles leaders, managers, workgroups and departments have to adopt. Many of these *states of flux* are created by the need to transact across various *task systems*, discussed in Chapter Five, creating a requirement that these transactions and created *states of flux* are regulated and managed. All of these processes inform the nature of the structure of your organisation and the ability to effectively transact and communicate across these *task systems boundaries*.

When working through these processes discussed above, including those preliminary activities, we have to keep in mind the induced and potential behavioural outcomes. The human side of work is the most important aspect in any consideration of jobs and organisations. When leading transition for change, there is an absolute need to understand human behaviour within social organisations. We must keep in mind that the employed technologies and all the management technologies, including information technology (IT) do not think for themselves; they have to have an "agent." How you interpret, adapt and respond, as the "agent" will directly affect your decision-making and ability to effectively implement strategies. The "agent's" *intent* is important, as this will directly influence the design and use of these management technologies and their eventual behavioural outcomes. (These concepts are further developed in Chapters Seven and Nine, "Adaptive Organisational Leadership" and "Technology Change and Managing the Consequences".)

The above should have evoked the notion discussed earlier that we need to harmonise the social and technical to ensure that we achieve the best fit that complements the organisation's needs. These socio-technical considerations are essential to ensure they not only complement the overall organisation's performance but also the behaviour of the individual and the specific technologies. (The reasons why these two activities have to be harmonised have been fully explored in Chapters One, Two and Three.)

Intent and Choice

An important concept that we need to grasp is what Anscombe (1957) suggested, that we "act under the intentionality of a person's actions." Anscombe wrote, "Human action is intentional" and if you ask the question "Why?" the individual should be able to express what they intended, which should also reveal what consequential effects they wanted to evoke.

This concept holds good when examining the processes adopted for decision-making within organisations. For example, is your intention to control or monitor to manage? Or to make the choice of using technology to drive change, or adopt an organisational approach where the technology is employed to reinforce the *intent* of the future organisation's performance? Whatever approach you choose to adopt will directly affect the behavioural *intent* of your organisation and those employed within. It will directly influence the design and the behaviour of the participant's role within any decision-making processes and protocols of the operating systems.

Of course, when working through these transition processes, the financial and cost management systems are being evaluated alongside these considerations. It is important that these and other *management technologies* are developed and used to reinforce the "intentionality" of decision-making processes, not to usurp them. To prevent these systems from these unwanted practices it is essential when designing them to clearly express their *intent*. It is important when defining the *intent,* as it will affect the attitudes and directed behaviour of not only those designing and managing the system but also the behaviour of the systems and those operating it. (Refer to Part One, "Dysfunctional Organisational Behaviour," Chapters One, Two and Three and Chapter Nine, "Technology Change and Managing the Consequences" to further develop your understanding as to how leaders begin managing displaced organisational goals.)

Personal Transition

Reflecting on defining and managing the *intent* requires that we consider the other consequential outcomes experienced when individuals, workgroups and departments are outside their comfort zone caused through the need to make a transition from one state to another. The experienced discomfort can often be attached to an individual, workgroup and/or departments having to adapt to new roles that have been identified within this process, causing them to want to regress (Fig. 21, "Transition Curve" nodes 1, 2 and 3) to what they understand and are most familiar with. The process of making not only at the organisational level but also at the personal level, a transition from one state to another stimulates these behavioural dynamics. These stimulated behavioural practices have to be understood to enable them to be processed and managed in terms of the individual and organisation's needs. They can become the genesis of resistance to change if not understood and managed. (These contextual relationships have been discussed in Chapter Five: "The Inter-related Behaviour of the Individual, Group, the Organisation and Environment" refer to this chapter to understand the context of these behavioural dynamics.)

The Need to "Let Go"

Leading transition for change is not a linear process; you may have to rework parts of the process, as people will regress whenever they perceive an opportunity to relieve their anxiety. These non-linear processes can be better understood by considering that people have to make personal changes; not only to their inter-relationships, their work practices and their roles but also manage behavioural changes that are affected by the need to change attitudes and their directed motivational *intent.*

The need for individuals to make a transition requires that they *"let go"* of what they have become comfortable with and possibly used to defend themselves against anxiety. These anxieties are often a hangover from induced anxieties created through working in a dysfunctional organisation. These personal transitional needs can best be related by examining a transition curve that displays similar characteristics to a bereavement curve. In each case the individual is dealing with loss (Fig. 21). The loss takes the form of "letting go" of past practices and the historic mechanisms used for defending themselves against induced anxiety.

Being allowed to legitimately express their frustration and even anger is important, as it is one of the indicators that the transition for change is moving towards the rationalisation and integration stages. It is all part of "letting go" of the past and fully engaging in the future needs of the organisation and themselves.

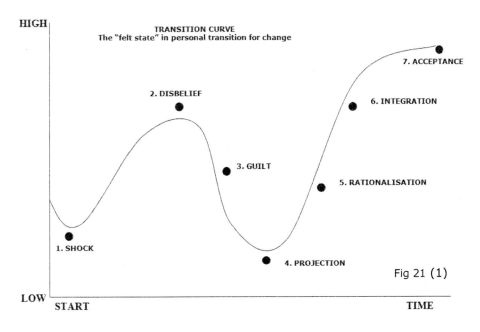

Fig 21 (1)

165

Individuals regress to relieve their generated discomfort by being outside of their personal comfort zone. These influences cause this non-linear process that results from our natural desire to avoid pain. This becomes evident when the individual begins moving along the notional bereavement curve toward rationalisation and the integration stage. They begin to feel guilty about the waste of their working lives and this is often expressed with anger, which is sometimes projected onto the person who is instituting these changes.

Internalising Change

It is useful at this stage to briefly develop in your minds the concept of how individuals, workgroups and team members manage personal transition. Having a developed notion that you can also relate to is important when you are asking others to make any changes to their work practices to satisfy the organisation's needs.

To achieve a successful *transition for change* it is important that individuals have the opportunity to develop a sense of ownership to *internalise the necessity for change*. This intellectual shift is important to achieve as the individual develops a personal understanding, by making sense of their world, to change their attitudes and motivate themselves to engage in the transition processes.

Experience indicates that internalisation seems to consist of three elements for achieving personal change (Fig. 22).

INTERNALISING PERSONAL CHANGE

1. PROVISION OF A NEW COGNITIVE MODEL

2. APPLICATION AND IMPROVISATION

3. VERIFICATION THROUGH EXPERIENCE.   Fig 22

The use of the notion of cognition for these purposes is the mental act or process by which knowledge is acquired, including perception intuition, reasoning and judgement. In the context of leading and managing organisational *transition for change*, it becomes the knowledge that results from the use of *organisational thinking* processes that are employed for the parallel development of your organisation and those employed.

In practice it is important to keep in mind how we internalise change. Fig. 22 demonstrates the internal processes we adopt when internalising change. Working through the transition for change processes of any organisation, we begin with the identification of the *primary task*, which starts the process of creating a new *cognitive organisational* mode, in terms of the *future state* that those affected can relate to and own. Fully engaging those affected in the *organisational transition processes* enables them to experience the *application and improvisation* used to design and develop future practices. That can be *verified by their experience* of working through this transition process. With experience they will verify that the design of the organisation is appropriate (Fig. 22). (For examples of how this applies in practice and where this has been successfully employed, refer to case studies "Avonmouth", "Greenfield Development Project" and "NHS, District Works, "Leading Transition for Change".)

Working through these processes of internalising change complements the "Assumptions from Experience" model (Fig. 13) enabling the individual to simultaneously test and change their assumption through their experience. These are processes individuals and workgroups appear to work through when using an organisational approach.

These transitional and behavioural experiences are felt at all levels within an organisation. For example, if the executive workgroup fails to make the necessary intellectual and behavioural changes they will become locked in a historic model of performance expectations and continue to use redundant *management technologies*. Transition for change is not a one off push and then you sit back; this is when complacency sets in and you and your organisation lose that edge of the organisation responding effectively. Continuously leading transition for change enables you, as suggested by Kotter (2008), to remain alert and retain a sense of "urgency." It prevents what Kets de Vries' emphasises in *Struggling with the Demon* where executives are stuck, "governed by the past" and locked in a "psychic prison."

It is for these reasons that these preliminary evaluations and working through these processes become absolutely essential as it enables you to appropriately identify and learn to manage potential resistance to change. Importantly these abilities need to be imbued within the future development of the executive and all the managers.

Resistance to Change

The failure to understand and manage the parallel transition process induces further anxiety and resistance to change (Fig. 6. "Defence against Anxiety and Resistance to Change"). We identified in earlier chapters that there are a number of behavioural forces at work directly affecting the organisation's and system's behaviour. When not understood, they compound the felt need for further personal controls, which introduces a great deal of anxiety and confusion, leading to "pathological behaviour" Burns (1963). This is compounded when "change threatens existing social defences against anxiety" Jaques (1955). With increased insecurity, sectional loyalty and people considering their careers as important as the needs of the organisation, clear conflict of interests can arise (Burns, 1963). He also found that this form of anxiety resulted in inter-group conflict and different departments becoming "scapegoats." When people in a group are being persecuted they develop precise and equally strong dislikes of their persecutors (Jaques, 1955).

Change can destroy the accepted career structure that has undesirable consequences. A factor, which adds to the climate of uncertainty, was identified by Merton's (1940) studies that

"Competition within organisations occurs within closely defined limits. Evaluation and promotion are relatively independent of an individual's achievement." This increased political manoeuvring causes the more ambitious people to become overtly ruthless, very often at the expense of others. "The breakdown of the career structure and the attendant behaviour introduced a great deal of neurosis. The climate over the period of this experience had changed from caring, paternalistic, almost indulgent pattern of management to a punishment centred bureaucracy" (Gouldner, 1955A). These potential behavioural outcomes resonate with the reported behaviour experienced within NHS hospitals and the provision of nursing care. (To further your understanding of the dynamics of these consequential outcomes, refer to case study, "Transitional Nursing Care".)

Emery & Trist (1973), observed that confusion created by unresolved problems leads to acts of "superficiality", called "trivialisation" where anything is tried, which may effectively achieve a reduction in complexity. All of these activities service the dysfunctional political decision-making models (Fig. 2, "Politics, Career & Overt Organisation" and the creation of "displaced goals", Fig. 4).

Should these levels of confusion exist within the leader, the organisation's "agent", those factors that influence why leaders mislead come to the fore. Should there be a failure to develop their *cognitive organisational awareness* to fit their new role, symptoms of "Why Leaders Mislead" (Chapter Five) will begin to emerge as their levels of anxiety increase.

The consequential effects are that many well-meaning strategic and operational initiatives fail to deliver the desired performance expectations. These initiatives become, to accommodate the above political defensive activities, heavily compromised to pacify the various political cabals. These initiatives become derailed, serving only to compound the problems they were initially developed to resolve. The use of an organisational approach has the capacity to identify, limit and enable you to manage these spirals of defensive behaviours. The identification and management of these behavioural responses to ensure the decision-making processes are not subverted and create dysfunctional practices.

Processing Within a Workgroup Setting

With these sets of behavioural dynamics it is important that we do not isolate the individual, as this may be unacceptable and intolerable to that individual. Yet, in organisations and workgroups, leaders and managers are asked to do just that without the knowledge and experience of any therapeutic process or understanding of the consequences. Why are we surprised that resistance, resentment and even entrenchment are the outcomes? The reason these transition processes are conducted in workgroups is derived from Bion's (1968) assumption that when working with workgroups, which can help individuals make a difference to their behaviour, it is always and only with the understanding of the individual-in-the-group, never the individual alone.

Managing Boundaries

As you are working in workgroups it is essential that you understand and manage the transactions across the various task boundaries. During the organisation's development process we identify and create specific interpersonal, workgroup, interdepartmental and technological boundaries that all need to be regulated and managed to ensure they complement and reinforce one another.

It is important to understand these notions of boundary management as they will and do directly influence the task that a task system is attempting to achieve. For example, workgroups do not work in isolation, they have to interact and will influence other workgroup activities. This requires that we have a clear understanding of the dependent and interdependent relationships so that they can be developed and managed to ensure that they do reinforce and complement one another.

Fig. 23 is a set of notional boundary models that become useful when attempting to understand interpersonal role relationships and how they develop. Working through these at an interpersonal level we can translate these ideas into the context of an organisation, sub-departments, and workgroups and systems relationships. It is useful to examine the boundaries, for the purpose of this discussion, as systems boundaries are attached to management technologies.

Fig 23

Fig. 23 (A) represents the boundaries of a couple's relationship. Each has their own identity and needs that have to be satisfied in terms of the couple's developing relationship.

The harmonious commonly shared space Fig. 23 (A) (H) is where the two individuals share and experience life together. It is a complementary experience and like any group has to be maintained along with a shared directed *trusted intent*.

When the boundaries increasingly overlap as indicated in Fig. 23 (B) the relationship has changed. One party or the other has moved into the other person's space either by invitation or circumstance. If one of the individuals is, for instance, unwell the other person may, during the reparative period by necessity, have to develop a more supportive role. The position shown in Fig. 23 (A) is established once recovery has been achieved.

Within an organisation we can observe these practices where other departments may overlap. This tends to occur when there appears to be a failure by one or other of the departments to complement the needs of the other. (For examples in practice, refer to case studies, "Avonmouth" and "NHS District Works, Leading Transition for Change".) This form of relationship can develop when the executive generally promulgates a blanket strategic initiative. For example, when a blanket ten per cent cut in all budgets is imposed irrespective of a department's respective performance. BP is an example where their cost cutting practices led to poor safety management. Their authority, real and implied, compromised the operating decision-making in the USA, with disastrous consequences.

Fig. 23 (C) indicates that these two people do not have a direct relationship but may be influenced by each other, subject to their presence. This indirect relationship will always be governed by the

171

circumstances they are both experiencing. It may be flirtatious, menacing or someone that is entertaining and amuses you in passing; each leaves an impression. We can make the connection with the developed relationship of those that belong to the executive or "Corporate America" Sculley CEO of Apple, for example, whose vicinage is where they use other executives as their *reference points* can be those *significant others* who are in comparative work. (These relationships are further discussed in Chapter Eleven "Remuneration and Motivation".)

Fig. 23 (D) indicates that there is no direct relationship yet one person's behaviour may, indirectly affect the other, say, by the introduction of new legislation that can indirectly influence your working and/or your social life. A further consideration is the introduction of new technologies that can be extremely invasive and have little respect for a person, workgroups, sub-organisations, whole organisations and even national boundaries. For example, the widely used containerisation for transporting products has had enormous consequential influences on the docking industry, the design of container ships and the recipient industries using these practices.

These sets of induced behavioural activities have to be understood and managed to avoid unwanted consequences. "When there is an element of confusion in, for example, the availability and quality of information, change, scheduled or unscheduled introduces degrees of chaos." This proffered organisational approach has been designed to enable you to understand and be prepared to effectively manage these induced behavioural activities that are derived from the differentiated needs of your organisation.

Stage 4 (Fig. 20) provides the opportunity to discuss tasks that have to be completed. In Chapter Five we discussed task boundary management and task systems and how they fit into the overall organisation's development. The notion of roles and tasks naturally overlap and the reason for discussing roles first is primarily the roles that are derived from the organisation's developmental processes. The tasks are in turn derived from the complementary roles of the individuals, the workgroups, the sub-organisations and the employed technologies, along with all the *management technologies.*

It is necessary when *leading transition for change* to ensure that all these task systems reinforce and complement one another. Doing so reinforces the development and maintenance of the *performance culture continuum*. The use of *variation analysis* identifies the *states of flux* and the consequential effects of decision-making, also identifying the tasks, their boundaries, task sets and their dependent and interdependent relationships. To ensure success, review feedback loops are introduced to enable you to determine that all the activities complement and reinforce one another to achieve the identified outcomes.

This practice of ensuring task systems reinforce and complement one another is important as this evaluative process informs not only the boundaries of the tasks, but also the performance standards that need to be achieved. These performance standards need to be understood by all parties and be owned by all affected parties to ensure the appropriate collaborative behaviour. It is important that these standards are derived from the identified interdependent and dependent relationships of the various task systems. These complementary activities are all designed to develop and reinforce the overall organisation's *performance culture continuum*.

Stage 5 (Fig. 20) provides an opportunity to discuss standards of performance that should be expressed in terms of service response, quality, decision-making, outcome and behaviour. These general parameters also apply to the employment of management technologies.

A confusion experienced in many organisations is the understanding of ownership and the inappropriate use of performance targets. It is pointless defining a targeted standard of performance if those recipients who have to deliver them are not in control, or are not party to setting and agreeing those targets. Simply, there is no ownership which raises the issues of delegating responsibility with authority and accountability, discussed in previous chapters. If you make someone responsible for the delivery of a targeted performance standard you must delegate the responsibility along with the authority and means for achieving those targets. If you fail to do so, the ownership for achieving those standards and targets remains with the person assigning the responsibility.

If you are given the task of driving a car you have to be able to make the decision and react to events on the road. You are responsible for achieving the identified targeted destination, the standards of performance, the regulation of the car's speed, and responding to the conditions of the road, the weather and other traffic. Therefore, you are responsible for the performance for safely arriving at the targeted destination. By being in control of the vehicle, it assumes you have the authority to drive it. In all cases you are accountable for your performance, your passengers, other road users, pedestrians and the regulatory authorities.

If the targeted time of arrival is unreasonably short the driver is being asked to violate some of these criteria. Should they have the delegated means to make alternative arrangements, they may take their passengers by other means of transportation, allowing the person to still achieve the desired targeted delivery outcome. If they are denied the means for making alternative choices they are unlikely to be able to satisfactorily achieve the necessary performance standards when attempting to achieve the targeted outcome.

The target is the end product of an aim that you constantly work to achieve. Pilots of an aircraft leave one airport for another targeted airport that may be on another continent. Pilots do not fly direct to their targets, they are constantly accommodating and making adjustments to the prevailing environmental conditions. The trace of an aircraft, when plotted, is not a straight line, it will often curve and displays the relative position of the aircraft pointing away from the targeted airport. The value of understanding this notion enables us to differentiate between aims and targets. When you are examining and testing for performance you are always evaluating the aims and their *intent* in terms of the targeted achievement.

An important issue is that the pilot is in control and is responsible for making the decision to ensure the targeted performance is achieved. When a remote authority sets targets the ownership belongs to the remote authority. There is no ownership by those responsible for achieving the set target and this is the primary reason for failure and not achieving the set target. Remote control of the decision-making and second-guessing those delivering the services creates role ambiguity, confusion and conflict, which all leads to the incumbent becoming de-motivated, destroying morale and creating low risk attitudes. This is similar to the US generals who remotely micro manage the operational end of the conflict (Nyquist 2009).

These forms of remote target setting have had devastating consequences on the quality of care in NHS hospitals. The politically set targets are remotely defined and do not translate to the specific delivery of these care services. (For examples, refer to the case study, "Transition Nursing Care" and the Public enquiries summary report of the Mid Staffordshire NHS Foundation Trust.) This disastrous approach for improving and controlling performance is further compounded by the introduction of financial penalties, imposed when targets have not been achieved, to organisations and service departments that are already cash strapped. These forms of blanket solutions have the potential to demotivate and redirect the motivational intent of those affected. The redirected motivation will be used to defend themselves against the induced organisational anxiety along with the introduction of activities such as "trivialisation." (For further examples, refer to case studies, "District Works: Leading Transition for Change" "Operating Theatres: Resolution of Conflict" and "Greenwich District Hospital".)

Stage 6 (Fig. 20) reviewing these processes is not just in terms of the final result – it includes a process for learning. It provides an opportunity to examine and debrief what went well and those issues that did not go so well. The *intention* is to feed and reinforce the continued development of the organisation and the individual. It provides an opportunity to understand why an event was successful, so that we can successfully repeat and further develop our competencies. We do not always understand why a process or an applied technique works in one situation and not so well in another. Understanding this outcome of the applied processes enables us to be consistent in our preliminary thinking and evaluation before determining the leadership and management style we need to adopt.

When reviewing it is important that those affected are involved to ensure that you tap into the collective intelligence of your employees. This, for some, may immediately take the form of designing a questionnaire and/or introducing suggestion boxes that has the effect of further detaching you from your employees. We must never forget the value of creating informal social meeting points, around for example, a water dispenser, or vending machines where people can informally and openly discuss presenting issues.

It is quite useful to imagine Fig. 20 having a spiral around each stage sets. That each of these spirals also loop together as you will need, as events unfold, to renegotiate the boundaries of your authority, responsibility and accountability, to constantly ensure you can achieve the identified performance outcomes.

It is not a one-off process that you undertake when leading and managing change; it is a continuous process of performance evaluation. In terms of the individual's own performance it allows that person to understand where they are succeeding and where they may need to further develop their competencies. This allows the individual to begin to work on those areas they need to improve rather than wait for the annual review where these items may be discussed. There could be a delay of up to almost a year before any remedial action is taken, which makes it pointless, as these events have become unrelated. (The need to change the way we evaluate and reward performance is further discussed in Chapter Eleven, "Remuneration and Motivation" where we discuss "Bonus Culture – Mismatch" and Chapter Twelve, "Development Training and Recruitment".)

The above transition for change process has raised other issues that need to be further developed. These are leadership adaptability and the understanding of behavioural dynamics of group development. Your capacity to understand and effectively employ these competencies is essential for your own organisational leadership development.

CHAPTER SEVEN

ADAPTIVE ORGANISATIONAL LEADERSHIP

Throughout, we have identified that the organisation is leading the change; it is the *organisational leader* who becomes the "agent" and translates these environmental influences to enable the appropriate designed responsive development of their organisation. In that context, your organisation's environment has to be constantly scanned and its boundaries regulated and managed. The management of your organisation's boundaries ensure that the various influences are weighed and the appropriate attention attributed to them. You determine the permeability of your organisation's boundaries to prevent any unwanted influences affecting the performance of your organisation.

Endsley (1995b), when examining the consequences of disasters, offers the following definition: "The perception of elements in the environment within a volume of time and space, the comprehension of their meaning, and the projection of their status in the near future." This places the problem situation within a contextual setting that has to be understood. The contextual setting is within an organisation and the organisation within its environment. (Refer to Chapter Four, "Developing a Theory in Practice" part one and Chapter Five, "Developing a Theory in Practice" part two.) These processes enable you to define the role of your organisation, its position in the marketplace and to reposition your organisation to effectively respond to these influences. It, importantly, retains the appropriate *intent* for identifying sustainable workable solutions that fit your organisation's specific responsive needs to external influences to remain competitive. This is the strategic thinking phase of your organisation's future development, and stage one of the *transition for change.*

Having determined the direction and the relative position within the market place, this enables you to reposition yourself intellectually, and to understand your role positioning, for you to begin the phase. Phase two is where you begin to design the operational process and practices (Fig. 10, "Representation Hourglass Strategic Thinking"), where you design the organisation to match the identified *intent*. This includes the systems, procedures, practices, policies and use of management technologies to improve and reinforce your organisation's overall service delivery performance. These processes, as you work through them, will define the performance culture, the espoused values and the required styles of leadership and management.

The general model (Fig. 20, "Leading Transition for Change Processes") should indicate that as we work through these processes they present us with different intellectual situational positioning; for the simple reason that you are moving along the *culture performance continuum* that we experience when moving up and down and through any organisation. This places a demand that we develop our roles to fit the presented situation wherever we are physically or intellectually positioned along that continuum. With a well-developed *cognitive organisational awareness* you will be well positioned to sense, interpret and understand the requirement of the role that the organisational situation is requiring you to adopt. All of these activities are designed and employed to improve your decision-making and ability to effectively implement those decisions.

When discussing "Assumptions from Experience" (Fig. 13), we should have developed our understanding that our decision-making practices are influenced by our experiences and our assumptions. When positioning ourselves at the point where the decision has to be enacted, the context of the experience will influence our assumptions, attitudes and decision-making. This process enables you to understand what the demands are, in organisational terms, and "what matters" to satisfy your organisation and its workgroups needs, wherever you are positioned on the *culture performance continuum*.

Mant, when discussing leadership styles, writes, "Leadership is nothing to do with charismatic personality and everything to do with identifying what matters." In previous chapters we have identified and connected those practices that will improve the quality of your decision-making and implementation processes. Effective decision-making and the implementation of those decisions are the two factors that influence how all leaders are finally judged. These collective practices provide you with the appropriate processes to *think organisationally*, enabling you to constantly *work for clarity* and to "identify what matters" as people follow the purpose, not the person.

Working through these organisational transitional development processes enables you to identify the real issues that "matter." This process of *working for clarity* enables you to peel away those layers of presented problems that were once the solutions to the original problem, to allow you to identify the root cause of the presented problem.

Role Transition

In the previous chapter we discovered that when the organisation is in transition we also have to make a personal transition, which includes those who are leading and managing the processes. The personal transition we make enables us to adapt our behaviour to fit the presented roles that develop during these transition processes. The other situation is when we move vertically through the organisation. This may be referred to as the *vertical intellectual transition* that is from the technical functional role to becoming an *organisational leader*.

Role transition occurs when a person has to make the personal transition from one discipline to another, e.g. engineering, IT techno-managers, HR, marketing and finance, whose roles are either dominated by the employed technology or the main, specifically differentiated, management technologies. (Refer to Fig. 24 "Mapping Career Decisions".) There are cases when we find that if an individual from one of these disciplines has been promoted to the Chief Executive's role, for example, they have to make even more of a personal transition. The transition is from the technical representational role of their specific department and technical discipline to their new role as *organisational leader*.

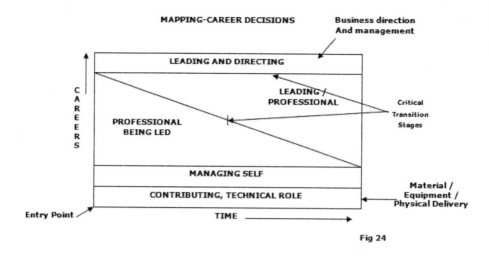

Fig 24

Should there be a failure to effectively make the transition from their previous discipline and not fully develop their *cognitive organisational awareness* to fit their new role, symptoms of "Why Leaders Mislead" (Chapter Five) will begin to emerge as their levels of anxiety increase.

The consequential effects of not making that transition are that we become anxious or find we are more and more exposed to the unfamiliar, "We tolerate the unexplained but not the inexplicable", Goffman (1974). Considering how leaders may react when faced with complex unfamiliar situations such as a need to lead and manage transition for change elevates the desire to create defences from induced situational anxieties. Having introduced the idea that many leaders and managers, in organisational terms, are unfamiliar with what they should be leading and managing, suggests the following situation will prevail. When presented with the need to manage transition for change, and lacking an understanding, of their new contextual environment along with experience, there is a shift along the continuum from the "unexplained" towards the "inexplicable."

This is further compounded by Dixon's (1989) observations, "An additional problem for a decision-maker, political, military and business leaders is that of incomplete or ambiguous information. Faced with the fact that rarely, if ever, is sufficient information available on which to make important decisions. Through denial of the unpalatable, misinterpretation, distortion or repression of the unacceptable, and a predilection for wish fulfilling fantasies, *decisions tend to be based not on what is the case but on what we would like to be the case*." When there is an element of confusion in, for example, the availability and quality of information, change, scheduled or unscheduled introduces degrees of "chaos" creating a desire to revert to what we are most familiar. How often do we observe an organisation becoming cost driven when the chief executive has been promoted from a financial background? This profession has only been chosen for this example yet the same behaviour can be observed when other professions are elevated to the role of chief executive.

We often find the initial meaning of events by drawing inferences from how we feel. When a need for peace of mind takes precedence over that for survival, the anticipated outcomes of a decision may well seem rosier than they deserve. Add to this the fact that the more emotionally important and the less warranted a decision, the greater would-be attempts to justify it. The demise of major institutions, identified earlier, was avoidable or at the very least the damage could have been significantly reduced. (To reinforce these notions refer to Chapter Five, "The Interrelated Behaviour of the Individual, the Group, the Organisation and the Environment".)

The above situation can cause these new executives to withdraw (refer to the Assurance Company case study), and/or myopic behaviour can begin to take root when an individual has not made the transition and does not have a well-developed *cognitive organisational awareness*. Having a well-developed *cognitive organisational awareness* will provide you with a reference point – an organisational platform – enabling you to understand the context of the decision-making situation, which indicates how you need to act to satisfactorily resolve any presented problems, be they organisational, workgroups and or individual.

Fig. 6 ("Defence against Anxiety and or Resistance to Change") reminds you of the processes experienced when anxieties tap into your hidden feelings, causing you to defend yourself from the induced anxiety. If you are unable to reduce the anxiety the cycle can start all over and raise your defensive behaviour to a higher level. When you connect these notions to the above discussion you should begin to develop a sense of how it can spiral out of control and directly affect your decision-making. This process of developing your *cognitive*

181

organisational awareness is designed to enable you to be positioned to reduce the constant inducement of anxiety. (We can, in Chapter Eleven, "Remuneration and Motivation" identify the executive referring to an external reference vicinage that satisfies their sense of isolation and being displaced.)

A Felt Sense of Redundancy

The above observations can be exacerbated by the experience of working through these personal transitional processes, which can, at first, create a sense of being redundant. This *sense of redundancy* stems from the fact that you are no longer servicing the dysfunctional organisational practices and fire fighting. You are able, through the developed individuals and workgroups competencies, to take up the appropriate *organisational leadership* role and the associated activities that will include *thinking organisationally*. This developed *intellectual space* should be used to *think organisationally* and develop the strategies for maintaining its urgency, vibrancy and direction. It is important that this created *intellectual space* is not squandered.

Leaders and managers, when faced with this dilemma and the unfamiliar situation to think organisationally, will feel both anxious and "redundant"; they will want to regress and start to take back some of the day-to-day activities to relieve their anxiety. You employ people to do the job so let them do it to the best of their ability.

Being aware of this phenomenon is an advantage. During the developed transition stage these role changes can be identified and the leaders and managers can be prepared by working "as if" they have made the transition. (Refer to Fig. 13, "Assumptions from experience".) There is also the process of "Letting Go" where individuals may want to regress by adopting their previous practices. (Refer to Chapter Six, "Leading Transition for Change, Fig. 20".) Having an experience of their new role assists in reducing induced anxiety and these unwanted regressive practices.

You may have made the connection that this feeling of "redundancy" can cause managers to resist the change in response to managing their own anxieties. Experience of managing major organisational transition for change has repeatedly demonstrated that the middle and senior managers are more likely to resist change for all the reasons we have previously discussed. These anxieties that are engendered when managing transition for change are further compounded when they begin to perceive this felt sense of redundancy. Developing their new organisational leadership and management roles, in parallel with all the other transitions during the transition process is critical to allay their fears.

The practice of working through the transition for change processes enables these managers to develop their understanding of their new role. Their repositioning requires that they use this intellectual space to *think organisationally* and consider its future developmental needs. It provides an opportunity to service the "hygiene factors" that need to be completed to ensure the motivational vibrancy of our organisations. This will include the need to continuously scan our internal and external organisational environments.

Role Variation

Without making the appropriate personal transition (Fig. 20, 21 and 22), the induced sense of isolation and being out of control will induce anxieties and the behaviours discussed above. The career-mapping model may help with the understanding of the different roles and attached expectations because they exact specific leadership behavioural requirements.

To assist in the process of interpreting and understanding the types of roles, they are generally identified in (Fig. 25). The following modified Tannenbaum & Schmidt (1973) model is an attempt to display some of the general role variations that we as organisational leaders will have to adopt and develop to satisfy the presented situation in the context of the organisation's needs.

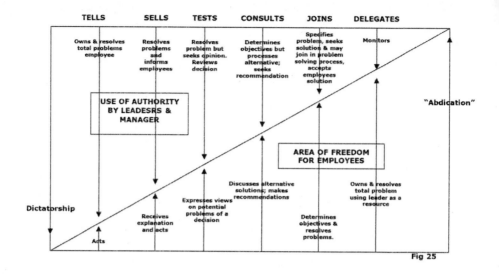

Fig 25

The fundamentals underpinning situational leadership (Hersey, and Blanchard, 1969) is that there is no prevalent style of leadership. They propose that effective leadership is task-relevant and the most successful leaders are those who adapt their style of leadership to fit the maturity of individuals, groups and the organisations they are attempting to lead and manage. These situational tasks have to be understood in terms of the context of the organisation to determine "what matters" and needs to be achieved.

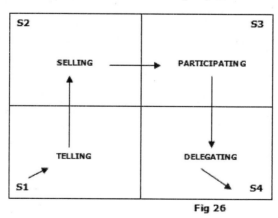

Fig 26

Hersey, & Blanchard (1969) define four main categories and this is evaluated by the amount of commitment and competence, which will identify the appropriate style that needs to be employed for each situation (Fig. 26).

They also characterised leadership styles in terms of the amount of task behaviour and relationship behaviour that the leader provides to their followers.

These leadership styles are categorised into four behavioural types, which are S1, Telling, S2, Selling, S3, Participating and S4, Delegating, which fits well into the more expansive model of Tannenbaum & Schmidt (Fig. 25).

Mintzberg identified ten leadership Roles, which he classified as the essential roles that managers undertake (Fig. 27).

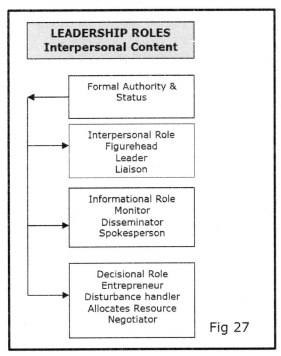

Fig 27

These ten leadership and management roles can be used as a frame of reference for developing and evaluating your own performance as an organisational leader. They provide you with some sense of the need to adapt your role to the presented situation and processes that you need to lead and manage.

Style, Behaviour and Displaced Goals

This is important, even if the decision-making process is appropriate; how you enact and implement the decision will predetermine how successful you are in achieving the expressed performance outcomes. This brings us to the issues of situational leadership (Hersey & Blanchard, 1969), and how it operates within an organisational setting. The difficulty with the simple notion of situational leadership, within the context of an organisation, is that it implies that you only deal with the presented situation. Often in organisations the presented situation is the dysfunctional organisational situation, which causes leaders and managers to solve presented problems, created by the systems solution used to solve a previous problem. This layering effect buries the problem and you end up solving the problems caused by the solution to the previous problem.

Albert Einstein once observed,
"It's the same kind of thinking that created the problem in the first place."

These problems can range through, for example, behavioural (individual, workgroups, teams, sub-organisations, whole organisations), inappropriate leadership (leading to lack of commitment, under achieving, poor productivity, high sickness rates and absence, along with political game playing), systems failure, inappropriate policies, failure of strategic initiatives and many others. Invariably, these stem from the historic dysfunctional practices within an organisation.

This notional "as if" model (Fig. 4, "AS IF Displaced Organisational Goals") should help to demonstrate why we often address the wrong problem. The displaced "as if" dysfunctional organisation will naturally have displaced goals and associated behavioural activities. The displacement of the organisation and its goals leads to the identification of the wrong problems and the provision of the wrong solutions (Einstein). Referring to (Fig. 4) you can mentally envisage these "as if" states, being realigned, which should infer the degree of complexity we are dealing with. The complexity of an organisation and the decision-making processes, are compounded by the dysfunctional practices and consequential induced behaviour of the leader and the organisation.

What becomes important from this discussion is the fact that when you develop your *cognitive organisational awareness* you are not developing it in terms of the dysfunctional behavioural practices you may have experienced.

It should have become evident that situational leadership has to be understood in terms of the situation being created within the *context of the organisation* and how that organisation's behaviour creates the situation. The distinction is that, when developing your *cognitive organisational awareness*, it can only be achieved after you have worked through the whole process of identifying the *primary task* and other elements of the *organisational transition process* discussed earlier (Fig. 20). This enables us to stay focused on the true organisational needs, "what matters" and not servicing displaced goals.

Positioning to Manage the Behavioural Dynamics

Strategic and operational decision-making is a dynamic process that takes shape over time, and influences across boundaries at multiple levels within an organisation. It affects the social, political, and emotional and increases anxiety and stress caused by the potential discontinuity and disruption of power bases. "While cognitive decision-making tasks may prove challenging for many leaders, the socio-emotional component is often their Achilles heel." (Roberto, 2005) Putting these issues into the context of your organisation enables these socio-emotional components to be simplified and understood, which in turn makes it easier to find appropriate solutions.

To deal with these "socio-emotional components" it is important that you are positioned, both physically and intellectually, to adopt the appropriate role to manage the processes for dealing with presented issues. Having a well-developed *cognitive organisational awareness* provides you with a sense of the appropriateness of expressed behaviour and how it is affecting the decision-making and implementation processes. Interpreting the presented situation enables you to *adopt the appropriate role and leadership style* to match the presented behavioural and task needs.

When these socio-emotional components are not contained they can be expressed through withdrawal, bullying and/or projecting their discomfort by finding a "scapegoat." A further component that we can observe, in the individual, is that they are organisationally, socially and/or technically displaced and as a consequence feel incompetent, which is masked by adopted defensive behaviour. This created sense of self is, as Obholzer (1989) writes, "The so called 'logic' of everyday conscious behaviour is nothing but a badly applied veneer on the carcass of unconscious individual and group assumptions."

Success is a function of both the quality of decision-making and effective implementation of those decisions. To be successful at both these activities you must develop an understanding of those people you are leading and managing. A leader's ability to navigate through the personality clashes and social pressures of the decision-making process often determines both of these activities.

The above discussion begins to frame and define the personal decision-making process that you have to make to ensure that you have developed your understanding of your role relationship and tasks that you need to undertake to be an *effective organisational leader*. The development of these *decision-making processes*, which is the responsibility of the *organisational leader,* can be examined through Roberto's (2005) observations on J. F. Kennedy and the fateful Bay of Pigs Invasion of Cuba:

"In 1961, President J. F. Kennedy authorised U.S. support for the Bay of Pigs invasion, an attempt by 1,400 Cuban exiles to overthrow Fidel Castro. It proved catastrophic. Kennedy asked his advisers: "How could I have been so stupid?"

The president's team didn't lack intelligence, but its decision-making process was deeply flawed. Veteran CIA officials advocated forcefully for the invasion. They filtered information that only Kennedy saw and excluded officials who might have exposed the plan's weaknesses. The president and cabinet often deferred to the CIA "experts" downplaying their own reservations. *{Deskilling is often observed when individuals are dealing with the unfamiliar.}*

Afterwards, Kennedy completely overhauled his foreign policy decision-making process. He urged advisers not to participate as departmental representatives, but as "sceptical generalists." He invited lower-level officials and outside experts to participate. He split advisers into sub-groups to assess alternatives. He assigned close confidantes as "devil's advocate." He chose not to attend preliminary meetings to encourage free discussion. When the Cuban missile crisis arose in 1962, these changes helped to ensure a more successful outcome.

The above re-evaluation of previous decision-making indicates Kennedy's desire to change his role by, for example, not attending preliminary meetings, with the *intent* to directly improve the quality of decision-making.

"Any decision is not complete until it has been implemented and the outcomes evaluated."
A Johnson

Roberto (2005) identified that by defining your decision-making process, you acquire four levers of power. They are:

1.   ***Composition***. Who participates? What value is a participant who can provide data, information or a fresh point of view others don't possess? Will they play a critical role in implementation? Have you included trusted confidantes as sounding boards? Have you considered demographic diversity appropriately? If your decision requires creative thinking, and your usual advisers are susceptible to groupthink, seek more diversity. But if implementation necessitates intense coordination and your advisers have trouble reconciling contrasting views, lean toward homogeneity. *{All of these considerations have to be placed in the context of the type of decision being made, and also relate to that part of the process you are managing.}*

2.   ***Context***. What norms and ground rules will control the deliberations? *{These can be determined by working through Leading Transition for Change processes.}* Structural context includes reporting relationships, control mechanisms, and reward/punishment systems. Psychological context (behavioural norms and situational pressures) can be more fluid. Work to

create a climate of psychological safety, in which people will take personal risks, share information, admit mistakes, request help, identify "taboo" topics, and express dissent. Lead by example. Acknowledge your own fallibility. *{Creating the appropriate organisational climate is achieved when you lead and manage the transition for change effectively.}*

3.   ***Communication.*** How will participants exchange information, generate alternatives, and evaluate them? A structured approach dictates detailed procedures for offering viewpoints, comparing alternatives, and reaching conclusions. With an unstructured approach, managers discuss ideas freely. This fosters strong commitment. Add structure to foster more divergent thinking and productive debate. *{Within an organisational context we have to ensure that there is a clear intent that is shared by all the participants.}*

4.   **Control.** How and when will you introduce your own views? Some crisis situations may require early intervention. Should you play a special role during the decision process? Will you be the "steadying force" who tempers overconfidence, or the "devil's advocate"? Research suggests it's useful to cultivate a "symphony of distinct roles." Encourage subordinates to play some of them (Roberto 2005). *{How you place yourself will be dependent on the nature of the decision being made. Experience has demonstrated that by developing a role that has been referred to as being detached/engaged is extremely useful. It allows you to observe the processes and measure when to make a contribution or intervention.} {Author's observations, in italics}*

It all makes good sense and provides a framework for thinking through the processes that are appropriate for different strategic and operational decision-making. It also suggests that J. F. Kennedy wanted to develop a "learning organisation", Argyris (1999). It also services your own personal decision-making on how to adapt your role to fit the decision-making processes being managed. It critically identifies the need for the other participants to modify their roles to "fit" and satisfy the presented needs of the decision-making and implementation processes.

Competency, Maturity and Role Positioning

The Competency Maturity, modified model, Hersey & Blanchard ("Continuum of Leadership Behaviour" Fig. 25), provides an opportunity to develop a sense of where your workgroups maturity and commitment exists and should any weakness exist that prevents you doing your job, you can take remedial action. It is your responsibility to ensure that your executive workgroups are competent not only in their specific disciplines but also have high shared complementary *cognitive organisational awareness*. Having a shared *cognitive organisational awareness* is essential for those who are preparing to take over the mantle of leading the organisation at whatever level they are positioned. As the Chief Executive these competencies beside business awareness are absolutely essential.

The examples of J.F. Kennedy earlier, and Roberto's (2005) observations are all designed to develop the competency of the various workgroups to ensure that they effectively service the quality and appropriateness of the decision-making processes. This will be determined by the presented situation and its context and on the developed *workgroup's organisational competency* that you are to lead and manage. This role adaptability applies at the executive, the operational and delivery end of any organisation, to satisfy the developing *performance culture continuum*. The understanding of workgroups, how they function and how you can determine the roles you play, the position either being *detached/engaged* that determines your role position is developed further in Chapter Eight ("Workgroups – Leadership and Positioning in Groups").

Turbulence, Competencies and Role Relationships

Fig 28

The above practice, of *organisational leadership*, makes sets of demands on your role that requires you to constantly interpret and adjust your leadership style. When scanning the environment, implicitly you are working in that environment. At the same time you are leading and managing the strategic and operational performance. Fig. 28 characterises two extreme roles that will change, by degrees, according to the level of *turbulence* in your organisation's environment and the level of developed *cognitive organisational awareness* of your executive management workgroup.

In role (A) we can assume that the environment is reasonably stable and manageable, hence the presence and time the *organisational leader* can be in the organisation. The more turbulent the organisation's environment role (B), the higher the demands for the organisational leader to deal with those environmental issues "that matter" to ensure the future of the organisation.

A well-developed *cognitive organisational awareness* within your executive and management workgroups enables you to confidently address these turbulent environmental issues. For example, whether you are responsible for a national or multinational organisation, you become part of any of the sub-organisation's environment. In these circumstances you influence those organisation's boundaries and how you perceive and enact your role will directly influence geographically displaced and local behaviour (e.g. BP's UK centralised cost control initiative, influencing unwanted behaviour in the USA and Nimrod's displaced goals, with disastrous consequential

192

outcomes). (These situations have been further explored in the following case studies: the "Greenfield Brewing Site Development" "Avonmouth" "Greenwich District Hospital" and "Transitional Nursing Care".)

The performance of a subdivision of your overall organisation, whatever its geographical locations, structure, size or type of business, will be directly affected by the central leadership style and behaviour.

If you are perceived to have a leadership style that follows the Political – Career – Overt organisation (Fig. 3), a cost led *intent*, using technology for change, or you run an overt organisation – Career – and then Political (Fig. 5), people will respond to each of these *perceived intentions*. These changes demonstrate your organisation's *intent*, created by the organisation's "agent", when appropriate, and will encourage others to improve your organisation's performance.

These translations will occur and need to be understood to prevent unwanted deviations and lapses into dysfunctional practices. It is important to check your assumptions as to what is being reported, to fit the deeds in real terms. (This concern is addressed by the use of the feedback loops and processes identified in Fig. 20, "Leading Transition for Change" Chapter Six.)

Managing the Decision-Making Processes

Roberto (2005) asks us to consider the dialogue within many organisations: "Candour, conflict and debate are often conspicuously absent during decision making." Managers feel uncomfortable dissenting. Groups converge quickly on one solution. Critical assumptions remain untested. Creative alternatives never surface. Leaders hear "yes" too often, or hear nothing when people mean "no." Their organisations don't just make poor choices: They may leave unethical choices unchallenged. This behaviour can lead to a situation that is referred to as the Abilene paradox.

The Abilene paradox is a paradox in which a workgroup of people collectively decide on a course of action that is counter to the preference of any of the individuals in the workgroup. It occurs through the breakdown of workgroup communication in which each member mistakenly believes that their own preferences are counter to the workgroup's and therefore, do not raise objections, in fear of "rocking the boat."

Within groups, Bion believed, one can see operating a number of powerful unconscious and unlearned, quasi-instinctive, strategies of evasion and denial. Bion saw these as constituting what he termed a "group mentality", opposed to the conscious aims, intentions and efforts of individuals (Armstrong, 1995). (Refer to Chapter Seven, "Remuneration and Motivation" where other financial, power and/or career interests influences this collusive paradox.)

There is a need to make a connection with the fact that we actively act to avoid pain and in doing so, we create defences that causes us to collectively collude to protect us from these induced anxieties. Obholzer (1989) writes, these 'mental cooperatives' take the form of ideologies and schools of thought, and enlist compliance within the group, which directly affects the direction of decision-making and when challenged, they can be aggressively resisted. Not wanting to be the focus of the potential aggressive behaviour, there is a tendency to avoid open conflict.

It is for these reasons that the use of an organisational approach is employed as this provides the common organisational dialogue that allows potential conflict to be managed using the organisation as the *third party for conflict resolution*. (Refer to Chapter Three, "The Enemy Within and Why Change Fails" to re-examine these collusive practices and the way they develop; see also Chapter Six, "Leading Transition for Change.) When making these connections you are constantly updating your *cognitive organisational awareness*.

Of course, conflict alone isn't enough: Leaders must also build consensus. Consensus doesn't mean unanimity on all facets of a decision. Nor does it mean surrendering leadership. It does mean people will cooperate in implementation even if they're not fully satisfied with the decision. Consensus requires strong commitment to the chosen action, and strong, shared understanding of its rationale. Commitment helps prevent opponents from derailing implementation. It promotes perseverance in the face of obstacles. Common understanding of the decision rationale helps individuals coordinate and act in the "spirit" of the decision. Conversely, commitment without deep understanding can amount to "blind devotion."

Individuals may dedicate themselves to implementation, but work at cross-purposes because they understand the decision differently.

Unfortunately, if executives engage in vigorous debate during the decision process, people may walk away dissatisfied with the outcome, disgruntled with colleagues and less dedicated to implementation. How do you foster conflict to enhance the quality of decision-making while simultaneously building the consensus needed for effective implementation? The consequential outcomes of not having vigorous debate and challenging assumptions are discussed in the case study, "Transitional Nursing Care."

Managing Conflict

Addressing Roberto's question and having to lead and manage these developing and fluid situations is one of the reasons for sharing this process of using an organisational approach. Using an organisational approach provides you with an opportunity to test these expressed differences in terms of the organisation, without repressing debate. It allows and safely encourages focused dialogue in terms of the organisation's overall delivery and performance needs. It assists in developing the appropriate primary organisational language to support the dialogue of continuously improving the overall organisation's performance.

Using an organisational approach has the ability, for example, when dealing with personality conflict, to refer the adversaries to define their concerns in terms of the organisation's needs. They, when addressing the organisation's needs, find that they have to redirect their energies to the presented issues that have no personality content. Using an organisational approach is extremely useful when you need to keep everyone's minds on "what matters." These behavioural outcomes are not the preserve of the executive; they are acted out throughout your organisation. (Refer to "Using the Organisation as the 'Third Party'" for process for managing conflict within an organisation, Chapter Six.)

Implementation of Decisions

The above raises the question of implementation of these decisions. Within the processes of decision-making there are two elements, the decision being made and the need to effectively implement that decision. When you consider that the appropriate decision may become *lost or changed in translation*, there is a need to ensure all the translators are using the same language, within the same context, and have a well-developed *cognitive organisational awareness* and are *thinking organisationally*.

The decision-making may be satisfactory but the implementation needs a good deal of consideration, as the failure to manage the implementation process will lead to unexpected and even unwanted outcomes. In fact, when developing the decision-making processes, it is essential to incorporate the evaluation process of examining how effectively the decision can be implemented and managed. The failure to do so and just hand over the decision for someone else to implement enlists Deming's (1986) claims, "The worker is not the problem. The problem is at the top, management." (Refer to "Leading Transition for Change" Chapter Six, which discusses the way strategic and operational change are successfully implemented.) *Leaders are judged not on their decision-making skills but on their ability to implement those decisions effectively.* J.F. Kennedy's example above is a case in point where he did not want to fail through poor implementation.

Translation of Leader's Intent

For example, when conducting active research and experiential workshops you can clearly observe the executive and/or senior managers and those having to negotiate, on their behalf, across organisational and workgroup boundaries, translating the central expressed message markedly differently. Observation of a leader who had a clearly expressed style of leadership, which was toward the consultative end of the spectrum, is translated as autocratic and almost dictatorial, all of course under the title of the leader, in this case, the Chief Executive. This raises the issue of the developed competencies of those within your workgroups and particularly the executive workgroup. (The consequence is discussed, in more detail, when examining "Technology Change and Managing the Consequence" Chapter Nine.)

These same reinterpretations can occur when you are developing your organisation and the systems and procedures are being redesigned. The example of the Chief Executive above should indicate to you that if these same people were responsible for overseeing the design of the systems, they would design the systems to fit the style they have interpreted, not the *intent* expressed by the Chief Executive.

These communication mismatches often translate into dysfunctional systems and organisational behaviour. Even though you have led and managed the process for making the decision you still have to oversee the management of the implementation processes. This separates those leaders who perform and deliver from those who don't.

Managing Displaced Systems Goals

We can be working for the system rather than the organisation, which means that we are servicing the displaced systems goals discussed above. For many managers, managing systems is far more comfortable and predictable than managing individuals and workgroups. One of the drivers that influences executives' decisions for introducing new technologies, stems from Roberto's observation, "...the socio-emotional component is often their Achilles heel." The unwanted and even disastrous consequences of this decision-making approach are examined in Chapter Nine ("Technology Change and Managing the Consequences").

We can observe many executives and managers consciously introducing new technologies to overcome some of these "socio-emotional components" which, in turn, increases the dependency factor on the correct functioning of the *management technology* being employed as discussed in Chapter Two. The inability to manage the "socio-emotional", which creates a level of anxiety, causes leaders and managers to employ systems as a defence against induced anxiety, which detaches them from their organisation's operational activities (Fig. 2). Often we can trace the induced anxiety to the "Political, Career and Overt organisations" decision-making process (Fig. 3) where there is a necessity to translate the intent of the political and career implication, creating a high degree of uncertainty.

Creating an Organisational Dialogue

Often you can observe within the decision-making process people working with different frames of reference, which are influenced by their experiences, background, and their roles within the organisation. For example, if you ask each person within a workgroup to write down his or her definition of quality, experience indicates that each person will define the topic differently. Generic language, if not specifically defined, assumes everyone is singing from the same hymn sheet, which is often not the case. We are often working at the assumption level, which should encourage us to make the connection with Agyris (1986) in his article "Skilled Incompetence." He identifies how managers who are skilled communicators but want to manage the potential risks, employ the use of ambiguous communication.

Using an organisational approach provides the necessary common language and the ability to maintain an effective dialogue about the continuing performance of an organisation. It allows you to determine when someone is inappropriately influencing the decision-making processes. Using an organisational approach safely allows you to ask that individual to refocus their contribution to satisfy the organisation's needs.

Interpersonal Relationships

Within the context of the situation being examined it is important that we have well developed interpersonal skills. How well we influence others is dependent on how well we communicate with others. Therefore an important, parallel development, for significantly improving your *organisational leadership* skills is the ability to "read people" McCormack (1984). He writes, "Whether, I'm selling or buying; whether I'm hiring or (in the capacity as a consultant) being hired; whether I'm negotiating a contract or responding to someone else's demands, I want to know where the other person is coming from. I want to know the other person's real self." He also suggests that, "Shrewd insight into people can be gained simply through the power of observation. In most business situations there is usually more to see than meets the eye, a whole level of personal dynamics operating just beneath the surface." (Refer to Fig. 19, "Behavioural Iceberg".)

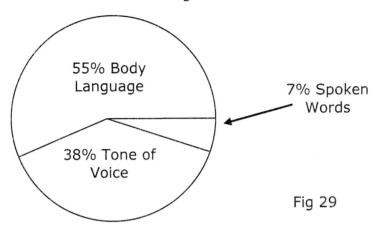

Communicated Message

55% Body
Language

7% Spoken
Words

38% Tone of
Voice

Fig 29

For example, 55% of indirect messages are translated through your body language and 38% through tone of voice, and what you actually say translates into only 7% of the communicated message (Argyle et al. 1970), Fig. 29. It is what you do that makes sense to others, the receivers, which has the greatest impact. Should your true *intent* be one thing but expressed in a way that identifies another, say to soften the impact of the information, the recipient will pick up the true *intent* and respond accordingly. You only have to make this mistake once or twice and trust begins to dwindle along with your authority.

INTENT
"The truth can be expressed through our internal self as well as through others."
A. Johnson

The above behavioural interpretation should underwrite the requirement that *we understand how we affect others and how they affect us.* To that end it would be useful to connect this discussion of inter-related behaviour by recalling the content of Chapter Five ("The Inter-Related Behaviour of the Individual, the Group, the Organisation and Environment"), where we discussed how the created organisation's environment would influence the felt experience, the assumptions being made, individuals' and workgroups attitudes along with their directed motivational *intent* and maturity.

McCormack (1984) surveyed a number of executives, some of whom were chairmen of a variety of business organisations. He reports: "Almost without exception, and often at the top of their list, they said, 'Learn to be a good listener.' This has to be coupled with the following understanding: the responsibility for effective communication is with the messenger. In the case of organisational leadership, if there is no common language the receiver of the message (who becomes the translator) can be working at cross-purposes. Well-developed listening skills will enable you to determine whether your message has been translated effectively.

The processes of reviewing, debriefing and testing assumptions demands that you become a good listener and that your own personal boundaries are open to alternative points of view. Developing a common organisational language enables everyone to engage and communicate more effectively the difficulties they are experiencing with the organisation. In many organisations the discussions about improving organisational performance emanates from the position, experience, perceptions and the attached language of that part of the organisation. The language is therefore differentiated and specific to those parts of the organisation. The message may not be as eloquent as you would like but it is important; they have taken the risk of expressing their views, as they are often appealing for you to improve the situation.

For example, the perception of the organisation's activities and the attached language when viewed from the top of the organisation is different to perception and language at the middle and bottom or delivery end of the organisation. This situation has elements of L. P. Hartley's book "The Go Between" where he opens with the "The past is a foreign country: they do things differently there." "In times of drastic change it is the learners who inherit the future" (Eric Hoffer). The non-learner usually finds him or herself equipped to live in a world that no longer exists.

These quotations raise the issue of the time lapse between the top and bottom of an organisation; those at the bottom are dealing with different issues than those emanating from the top. "They do things differently there" which infers that the technologies and the market place are influencing that part of your organisation differently. Be aware that these differences can be placed along the *culture performance continuum* to test whether they are appropriate and fit your *cognitive organisational awareness model*.

There is also a redundancy factor in that these changes create within, "...A world that no longer exists." If you are not responding to the needs of your organisation and its environment, your leadership skills and ability to effectively act as its "agent" will become redundant as they no longer fit your organisation's responsive needs. For example, the executives of General Motors, through myopic vision and closed organisational and personal boundaries, caused their organisation to lose their market share. Aviva suffered humiliating shareholder revolt at its annual meeting 2012 by not supporting the controversial proposals for executives' pay. The revolt forced Andrew Moss, the chief executive, to stand down. One of the shareholders complained that the board was more concerned about remuneration than about growing the business. (These situations are further explored in Chapter Eleven, "Remuneration and Motivation".)

Corporate executive life can cause executives to relate to what may be referred to as the executive worth club, or as John Sculley, Apple's ex-chief executive, referred to as "Corporate America." John Sculley, when having to make the fateful decision to sack the founder of Apple, Steve Jobs, said, "That's what Corporate America would do." He was referring to the practice of other American company executives that had sacked the founder of the company they were running. These decisions are often influenced in terms of these executives' exclusive vicinage that causes them to become detached from the real life of their organisation, where matching or even competing pay packages becomes their centre of egotistical attention. Unfortunately these external influences can cause executives to lose sight of the true purpose of their organisational role. In doing so they are no longer capable of effectively engaging in a dialogue for communicating the need to continuously improve their organisation's performance. They speak a different language.

When individuals have a well-developed *cognitive organisational awareness* they are likely to want to influence their organisation's performance and Hoffer would offer the following advice to them: "The only way to predict the future is to have the power to shape the future." This is the genesis of the process of inverted organisational leadership. It is important that you are open to any alternative proposals; it may even redirect the direction and performance of your entire organisation. To enable these influences within your organisation it is important to develop the primary skills of a good communicator and that of being a *good listener*.

To become a good listener it often requires you to be aware of your own feelings and at the same time have the ability to suspend them when receiving information. This is particularly true when you receive unwanted information. The practice of suspending your own feelings and listening to the message enables you to evaluate the information in terms of the organisation's development needs.

The value of working with a well-*developed cognitive organisational awareness* (Fig. 8, "Internalised Thinking Process") enables you to suspend any concerns regarding organisational issues. You can observe executives who do not have a well-developed *cognitive organisational awareness* becoming preoccupied with the *management systems* issues rather than listening to the individual and engaging in a created common dialogue.

"The mind is like a parachute, it works better when it's open."
Anon

This preoccupation, whatever it is, prevents you from listening effectively; this is known as conducting your own internal dialogue. It is similar to someone talking over you when you are attempting to discuss a particular point. Or someone completely changing the subject before you finish what you are saying, creating the effect of ignoring you and indicating that what he or she is saying is more important. These people are externalising the internal dialogue. These individuals are simply not listening to you and negate what you are attempting to communicate. When you are conducting your own internalised dialogue you are unable to *effectively listen*. Argyle (1978) explores these various forms of exchanges in detail, to develop a more in depth understanding, which should be read to further complement this discussion.

The other important issue that needs to be expressed is the need to test assumptions before jumping to any conclusions, "over responding to conventional interpretations, or reading meaning into things where none exists" (McCormack, 1984). Keeping an open mind and testing the assumptions against your developed *cognitive organisational awareness*, enables you to ask the right question to constantly *work for clarity* to determine the speaker's actual *intent*.

Having a well-developed *cognitive organisational awareness* provides you with a reference model that you can use to test the information's value in terms of the organisation's needs. It reduces the ambiguity that leaders experience when being asked to make decisions through lack of information. It also creates a common language that enables you to have an *effective dialogue*, when testing assumptions, regarding the improvement in performance of your organisation, workgroups, individuals and your own.

LISTEN TO THE MESSAGE
"The truth may be outrageous but try not to be outraged, listen to what is being said."
Anon

This may require that you receive unconventional wisdom instead of telling you what you want to hear. What would it be like to hear what people thought rather than have them say what they thought you wanted to hear? It may provide you with unconventional wisdom that may secure significant performance improvements in your business organisation. All achieved through the development of organisational leadership skills and the ability to test these unconventional views against your well-developed *cognitive organisational awareness*. And in turn, motivate your work force to collectively contribute to your organisation's overall business performance, simply because they know that they are *being listened to and valued*. Enlisting the fundamental human motivational need identified and experienced, during the Hawthorne Experiment (1923), William James captured this fundamental need in the following: "The deepest principle in human nature is the craving to be appreciated."

Tapping into the Intellectual Capacity

The above allows you to *tap into your organisation's intellectual capacity* which is part of the development of your organisation's working climate that you have created to enable individuals to become self-motivated, and to use their *motivated effort and intent* to service and reinforce your organisation's overall performance. For these individuals to be able to successfully direct this focused effort they have to understand the nature of the organisation they are trying to create. They have to have, for their specific role, a level of *cognitive organisational awareness*. (For example, this process is achieved through the linked orientated activities of the various workgroups discussed in Chapter Eight.)

When these individuals have a shared *organisational awareness* they also acquire the attached language and therefore have the ability to engage in the dialogue about the organisation's performance. This engagement allows the intellectual intelligence of your whole organisation to be used as a significant developmental resource. You need to make the connection with leading the transition for change processes and the attached practices (Fig. 20), which clearly demonstrates a review feedback and action loop. These feedback cycles have been deliberately designed to improve your capacity to monitor, debrief and evaluate the performance of your implementation strategy and of course the quality of your strategic decision-making. These feedback loops are also designed to improve your organisation's capacity to *continuously learn* and tap into the whole of your organisation's intellectual resources.

The added value of this approach when employing new recruits is that they don't sit back because they find that they cannot influence the existing organisation's performance culture. Their ability to influence, or create opportunities to contribute and improve your organisation's overall performance by, for example, using *inverted leadership skills* is repressed. (In Chapter Twelve, "Development, Training and Recruitment" we further discuss the development of organisational leadership's skills through supervised experience to resolve existing live-presented organisational issues.)

Leadership Competency

Attempting to define leadership is an inappropriate task as it changes with the individual, the situation and the context of that situation, which has so many variables it is pointless pursuing a single definition. We are, therefore, not going to trawl through the numerous theories as they can be simply accessed in other articles to fit your developmental needs. We shall just touch on the prevalent theories to provide an insight into their intent and history. When doing so we may need to be aware if they are proprietary, the *intent* is to sell a product and not necessarily provide you with a genuine *process* for developing your own leadership capabilities.

Competency is a function of the degree to which an individual is aware of their impact upon others and how those people affect them. This is particularly true when you need to be able to interpret, match and influence a situation as well as the ability to solve problems in such a way that they remain solved. Therefore, your ability to move in and out of the organisation or workgroups will depend on the competency of the other members of your workgroup and their ability, in organisational terms, to translate your expectations. (Fig. 28, "Turbulence, Competency and role Relationships".)

This is one of the main reasons for developing an organisational approach, as the organisation's development is the only common element that everyone has to be able to relate to which should be the only preoccupation of any well-developed *organisational leader*. If others are not able to effectively engage in an organisational dialogue you should begin to express concerns about their ability to translate, in organisational terms, what needs to be accomplished, as it enables that all-important clear and consistent communication of the message, and how it is understood and effectively acted upon.

When we distil these theories of leadership the contextual element is missing, and it is this factor that is influencing behaviour of not only the organisation but your own. The process of leading and managing the organisation places a demand for leaders to adapt their style and behaviour to fit the presented demands of the organisational situation. For example, it would be inappropriate for a military command structure to be employed when running a creative research laissez-faire organisation.

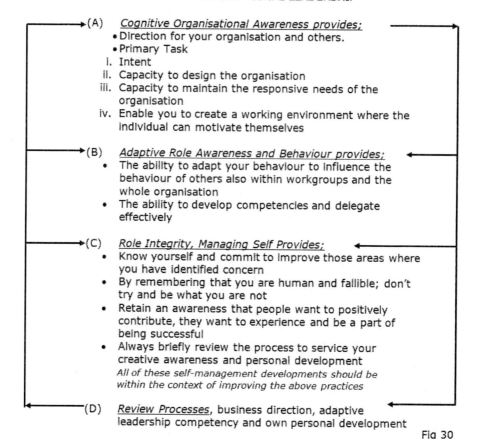

(A) *Cognitive Organisational Awareness provides;*
- Direction for your organisation and others.
- Primary Task
i. Intent
ii. Capacity to design the organisation
iii. Capacity to maintain the responsive needs of the organisation
iv. Enable you to create a working environment where the individual can motivate themselves

(B) *Adaptive Role Awareness and Behaviour provides;*
- The ability to adapt your behaviour to influence the behaviour of others also within workgroups and the whole organisation
- The ability to develop competencies and delegate effectively

(C) *Role Integrity, Managing Self Provides;*
- Know yourself and commit to improve those areas where you have identified concern
- By remembering that you are human and fallible; don't try and be what you are not
- Retain an awareness that people want to positively contribute, they want to experience and be a part of being successful
- Always briefly review the process to service your creative awareness and personal development
  All of these self-management developments should be within the context of improving the above practices

(D) *Review Processes*, business direction, adaptive leadership competency and own personal development

Fig 30

Fig. 30 is a model of the general processes that we mentally develop to ensure that we fit and complement the demands of the organisation. This general model (Fig. 30) has two feedback loops that enable us to provide information that indicate changes that we need to be prepared to lead and manage. This adaptive model is also designed to indicate when there is a mismatch between the presented situation and your cognitive understanding of how the organisation should be behaving. It provides an opportunity to test assumptions and move from the assumption level to the task level that needs to be addressed.

When making strategic decisions and preparing for them to be implemented it is important that you have the ability to identify the appropriate processes that support the context and nature of the decision being examined.

The intent of this book is to improve your *organisational thinking* and *organisational problem solving* and to persuade you to develop your *cognitive organisational awareness*. This will not happen until you commit to your own organisational leadership development. Remember:

"Until one is committed there is hesitancy,
The chance to draw back, always ineffectiveness."

"Whatever you can do or dream you can do, begin it, boldness has
genius power and magic in it, begin it now."
Goethe

It is what you do today that sets the direction of what can be achieved tomorrow; you have to start today. There is a good reason for immediacy, your organisation is not going to wait, even more so in today's business environment, for you to develop your organisational leadership skills. It is important you start now to ensure the future effectiveness of your organisation. Remember your organisation relies on you as its "agent" as its organisational leader; it cannot think for itself.

CHAPTER EIGHT

WORKGROUPS
Leadership Positioning in Workgroups

Executives and managers report that they spend fifty to ninety per cent of their time in some form of meeting/workgroup activity. It is common knowledge that workgroups are the engines of any organisation and how well they perform and collaborate can directly affect your leadership performance, the quality of your decision-making practices, your interdepartmental performances, your organisation's performance, productivity and quality of working life for those involved. They determine your leadership competency and how successful you are, as they are used to manage the implementation of your decisions.

Workgroups are used to facilitate the organisational leader's decision-making processes. They provide an opportunity to enlist those individuals that have the ability to effectively contribute to the decision-making process, depending where the workgroup is situated within the organisation, its tasks, responsibilities and the nature of the decisions that are under consideration.

In the previous chapter we determined that the ability for you to effectively lead is directly dependent on the *competency of the respective workgroups* you are required to lead and manage (Fig. 28). Understanding the functioning of workgroups is fundamental for the development of your own *cognitive organisational awareness*. A grounded understanding of workgroup behaviour enables you to adapt your role and position yourself to facilitate the workgroup's development and maturity.

Drucker (1977) wrote, "Business enterprises must have a government. This usually takes the form of a board of directors who are responsible for the governance of that enterprise." The nature of the decision they have to address should relate to issues relating to evidence derived from the scanning of the organisation's environment, the *intent*, direction, and strategic capacity of the organisation to operationally deliver its services.

As you migrate down the organisation the workgroups will be responsible for different decision-making activities. These activities should be collectively and collaboratively directed towards reinforcing the overall organisation's performance. These workgroups are required to translate the executive's decision-making into viable operational practices.

Fundamentally, workgroups are required to support the leaders' decision-making processes. The leader remains responsible for making the final decision. "Leadership is not consensus and consensus is not leadership but that does not mean you do not consult. It does not mean to say you do not seek advice. But at a point there is a time when someone has to say – right, I have listened to you all and I respect what you have to say but for the following reasons we are going to go down this path." (Sir Charles Court).

The workgroup still retains the collective responsibility for the effective development of the implementation strategy. This requires that each member have an agreed understanding of their roles, and a well-developed *cognitive organisational awareness*, enabling them to translate and collectively contribute to the overall organisation's delivery performance.

Developing an Understanding

It is for these reasons that this chapter is attempting to develop common ground, which enables workgroup behaviour to be understood, and to transfer into improved leadership and management of all forms of workgroups. To begin this process, it is extremely useful for leaders and managers to have a basic understanding of the processes of group development and behavioural dynamics identified by social scientists, psychoanalysts and in particular Bion. It is also useful to have an understanding of the contextual environment these various workgroups operate within. This developed understanding is required to enable you to focus and facilitate the transitional development of your various workgroups.

Often these constituent parts are missing from the understanding, experience and practices of most leaders and managers. The purpose of this exploratory chapter is to bring these practices together and to create an opportunity for you to develop an improved understanding of these processes. The focused intent of introducing this process is to significantly improve your ability to successfully lead and manage various types of dynamic workgroups. The collective improved performance of leadership and management of the various workgroups will directly translate into the overall improvement of your organisation's performance.

To assist your developmental understanding we shall explore how these various workgroups operate and contribute within an organisation. We shall look at the intra-group and inter-group behaviour to determine why workgroups within organisations become dysfunctional. Armed with this information and understanding of how workgroups function you will be able to design and develop your own organisation and develop your own workgroup leadership skills, to manage these processes effectively.

Leaders and managers are often apprehensive and have little knowledge about working with groups. Most leaders and managers concentrate their effort on managing individuals rather than building effective workgroups. This stems, in part, from the misunderstanding that appears to exist between the managers and social scientists, identified earlier. Another contributing factor is that managers like events and activities to be regulated where workgroups should and need to be dynamic and change with the changing needs of the organisation.

In the context of this book we need to examine workgroups, teams and meetings in organisational terms. To that end workgroups and teams are all sub-organisations and systems that are set up to effectively complete a specific task. (Fig. 12, "Boundary Control for Task Systems".) If they do not have a clear specific and related task, you have to ask why they exist.

In many ways groups resemble a car engine. The output of a workgroup, like the output of an engine, depends on the operation of the total moving parts (physically in the case of the engine, physically and psychologically in the case of the workgroups). Should one part of the engine malfunction, the total performance of the engine is impaired. Any one of these faults may even prevent all the other components from operating at all.

The analogy with an engine has distinct differences, in that it does not have a social conscience, or any personal psychological baggage, which all social groups do. It does not have to work and complement other workgroups or work across transition boundaries that all workgroups have to do to collectively reinforce their organisation's overall performance. A workgroup can be considered to be a micro-organisation, where they cooperate to effectively complete an identified task, which, in turn, enables other workgroup's tasks to be successfully completed. (To put these notions into context and develop your mental model of workgroups in organisations, refer to Fig. 12, "Boundary Control of Task Systems" and Fig. 15, "Managing a Group at Work".)

When working through the transition for change process of any organisation we are attempting to realign the organisation and remove the dysfunctional practices. In doing so we are asking the existing dysfunctional workgroups to make a transition from one state to another. It is the same form of *organisational thinking* we apply to the whole organisation and any of its constituent parts. To be affective we have to have a developed understanding of inter-groups and intra-group behaviour provided by those researchers who specialise in the study of group behaviour.

We discussed the development of an individual and found that as they develop their personality they also bring to the workgroup all their personal history. Any anxieties that may exist for an individual could be amplified by joining a workgroup. Particularly if it is dysfunctional, which is more likely as we identified earlier that leaders and managers, more often than not, have limited knowledge of how workgroups function.

Often these workgroups are operating within an already dysfunctional organisational environment. The developmental

211

behaviour of many workgroups is directly affected by their social experiences and from their environment within their organisation. The development of these workgroups can be notionally compared with the development of an individual's personality. We need to keep these sets of situational behavioural dynamics in mind when we attempt to improve the performance culture of any workgroup. The *recent history* is a good starting point.

It takes little to imagine that these workgroups are working with displaced goals and working "as if" to satisfy their existence rather than contributing to the overall performance of the organisation. These kinds of behavioural practices resonate with Argyris' (1986) observations regarding management practices, which he entitled "Skilled Incompetence." The development of your understanding of your social organisation's behaviour will enable you to clarify the activities of your workgroups to focus, perform and contribute effectively.

When attempting to change any workgroup's performance behaviour you need to keep in mind the issues discussed in Chapters Four, Five and Six ("Developing a Theory in Practice" and "Leading Transition for Change"). We identified that we must pay attention to resistance to change being augmented by the discontinuity of the power structure that can be real or perceived when working through these processes. "Thus, when culture change is accompanied by a shift of power resistance can be compounded" (Ansoff).

Also you need to keep in mind that all the time the internal problem is unresolved the process of projection will act to relieve the group's anxiety and this can be achieved by finding a "scapegoat" (Jaques 1951 and Trist and Bamford 1951). Burns and Stalker (ibid) found that this form of anxiety resulted in inter-group conflict and different departments becoming "scapegoats." When people in a group are being persecuted they develop precise and equally strong dislikes of their persecutors (Jaques, 1955).

In the same way *management technologies* are used, as defences against anxiety, workgroups are not in any way exempt. When you consider that belonging to a family, a group, an institution, or a nation, these are all various layers of skin to foster a sense of identity, security and belonging. "Schools of thought and social structures are thus man-

212

made devices to protect us from these anxieties. Put another way, they are social structures, which we join at birth, renewing or not (as the case may be) our membership as we go through life in order to have protection and rescue from isolation and breakdown" (Obholzer, 1989).

Membership of these social defensive systems, whilst comforting in the short-term, can in the long-term become a damaging activity, because it leads to inevitable escalation of internal personal conflict and pushes the individual, group and organisational problems further away. This reduces, over time, the ability to identify the original cause of the problem, which now becomes the problem.

The developed processes for improving workgroup's performance are designed to enable you to successfully steer your way through these generated issues that exist in different forms within different types of workgroups. Developing your ability to *think organisationally* and your *cognitive organisational* awareness provides you with a sense of the organisational environment that you are attempting to service and complement. The intention of working through these processes is an attempt to translate the excellent work undertaken by social scientists and psychoanalysts. In particular Bion (1968), who identified processes that leaders and managers can transfer into their skill-set to improve their ability to effectively develop, lead and manage workgroups.

This is not a one-way process. You have to also make a personal transition to enable your own mind-set to transfer from your existing understanding of leading and managing an organisation to the development of your *organisational thinking skills* and your developed cognitive *organisational awareness*. There is a good deal of work for you to undertake. There are no panaceas; these *processes* have to be worked through, to ensure you continue your own and your workgroup's developmental journey.

Conflicting Perceptions

Vast quantities of energy are spent on trying to make managers aware of what research and literature has been produced by behavioural sciences. Yet, evidence suggests that relatively few decisions concerning people in organisations are, in fact, influenced

213

by these sciences. Various explanations have been put forward. Academics claim the managers are tradition bound and inflexible in their outlook. Managers argue that academics are unable to communicate in simple language and their 'ivory tower' research has little bearing on helping to run a business.

Both arguments have an element of truth but they are too simplistic to explain away why applied behavioural sciences are not applied. But even with focused effort to educate managers through a variety of agencies it has not been possible to bring managers and behavioural scientists together.

Perhaps the explanation as to why behavioural scientists do not influence business decisions is because *managers and behavioural scientists view people differently*. Managers would assume everybody is different, which is not unreasonable, but those individuals when entering a group, the study and understanding from a behavioural scientists standpoint, is of group dynamics, not the individual. There is an understanding, which derives from working with groups that could at best make a difference to the behaviour of their members, which is the understanding of the individual in the group, never of the individual alone (Bion 1968 and Alexander 1995).

We need to consider the recent history of those who are required to lead and manage workgroups. For example, the journey of a behavioural scientist is very different to that of the organisational leader and manager. Our professional development and our personal life experiences contribute to the way we make decisions.

For example, engineers can generally be described as quantitative decision-makers, where architects may be biased towards the qualitative end of the spectrum. When these two professions meet there can be confusion and conflict because of the way each party makes decisions. Differing decision-making practices will exist between the social scientists and leaders of organisations, which may partly provide an understanding as to why these important contributions are not so readily understood and employed within organisations. Employing an organisational approach provides a common language that enables these differences to be harnessed in terms of the organisation's developing performance needs. (These

214

decision-making processes are further developed in Chapter Nine, "Technology Change and Managing the Consequences".)

Workgroup Dynamics

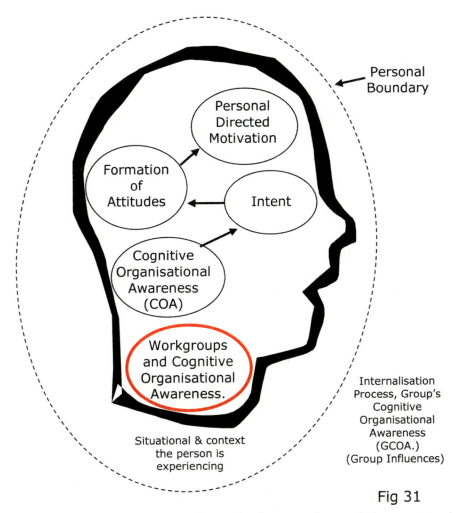

Fig 31

When workgroups are formed they tend to follow general development processes that need to be understood and worked through. In Chapter Nine we discuss how these group dynamics are exerted on the individual (Bion, 1968). These behavioural dynamics can be experienced when being part of and observing a leaderless group as the individuals work through these group development processes.

Bion's contribution is extremely important as it provides you with an insight into how groups work. These behavioural practices can be observed from experiencing these types of unstructured and leaderless groups, which bring the unconscious into our *cognitive awareness of workgroup's behaviour* and notionally an insight into what is happening under the waterline. (Refer to Fig. 19, "Organisational Behavioural Iceberg".) It provides you with a frame of reference for understanding group behaviour, in the context of *organisational leadership* and acts as another point of internalised reference (Fig. 31, which is a modified Fig. 8). Fig. 31 should help to place the developed understanding of workgroup behaviour in relationship to, and contributing to, your developed *cognitive organisational awareness* and the collective mind-set.

Workgroups as Micro-Organisations and Group Processes

It is useful to view workgroups as micro-organisations, as they are task systems that have to have a focused intent and productive outcome (Fig. 12, "Boundary Control for Task Systems"). We have to develop our sensitivity as to how they work in exactly the same way we develop our understanding and develop our *cognitive organisational (workgroup) awareness* (Fig. 31) to effectively lead and manage workgroups within social organisations.

The distinction, one has to make, is that these are specific social organisations that are required to successfully operate within specific service delivery organisation environments. We need to understand how each member of the workgroup responds to their experience of being a member and how they respond to different behavioural dynamics, which will exist in differing and other workgroups.

Changes in the task, the intensity of the task to be achieved, the social environment and/or changes in the membership will in some way influence the behavioural dynamics of that workgroup and/or the individual's behaviour. The dynamics of workgroups are not static, as with any social organisation, the nature of the task, the workgroup's environment, changes in personnel and the management systems they employ will automatically change the workgroup's behavioural dynamics.

These influences on the dynamic behaviour of workgroups should further reinforce the need to understand that these processes exist, in the sense that the individual and social behaviour are seen to be profoundly, if not exclusively, driven by emotional experience and defences, which individuals and social groups mobilise to contain or ward off the burden of anxiety such experiences arouse (Armstrong, 1995).

According to Bion groups operate on two levels; these are the task groups, which are reality-oriented and carry out the task, and the other is the basic assumption group or group mentality (Fig. 16, "An "AS IF" Group"). Both levels have survival as their objective, but that survival means different things. "The internal world of a group is made up then, first of the contributions of its members to its purpose and second, of the feeling and attitudes the members develop about each other and about the group, both internally and in relation to its environment" (Miller & Rice, 1975).

Members may pair up with each other as they resonate with unconscious needs, values, and more conscious convictions, the leader included. These collusions may play out through the mechanisms of dependence, pairing, and fight-flight (Bion, 1960), in splitting, scapegoat and marginalising some members of the group. This directly infers that you have little choice but to develop an understanding of these social defence mechanisms if you want to develop your *cognitive organisational awareness* and *intuitive feel* of what is happening or likely to happen when leading and managing the development of workgroups.

Bale (1950) identified, when examining communication patterns, that there were similar patterns of behaviour to those identified by Bion. Bale suggests that the following linear processes exist and are acted out:

First, the group discussion tended to shift relatively quickly between the discussion of the group's task and discussion relevant to the relationship between the members. He believed that oscillating between these two needs was the product of an implicit attempt to balance the demands of the task and its completion and the group cohesion, under the presumption that the conflict generated during the task discussion caused stress and anxiety among members, which must be released through positive rational talk.

Secondly, the task group discussions shifted from an emphasis on opinion exchange, through alternativeness to values underlying the decision, to making the decision. The implication is that the group goes through the same series of stages in the same order for any decision-making group that he refers to as the linear phase model. We can make the connection with the notion of the workgroup making a *transition from one state to another*.

Third, the most talkative person of a group tends to make forty to fifty per cent of the comments and the second most talkative between twenty five to thirty per cent, irrespective of the size of the workgroup. As a consequence, large workgroups tend to be dominated by one or two people to the detriment of others. Quieter members of these workgroups may not necessary lack ideas, but either lack confidence to express them or feel intimidated by those who do most of the talking. It is important for workgroup leaders to understand how these dynamics work and learn to manage them to improve not only the processes of the workgroup but also the quality of decision-making by tapping into the total workgroup's intellectual capacity. We can make the connection with group development processes where we can observe individuals competing for leadership and/or they may be managing their own anxieties.

This linear phasing was replicated by Fisher (1970) who demonstrated that groups sequentially work through an orientation stage, a conflict stage in which a decision emerges and finally a stage where the decision is reinforced.

Workgroup Contextual Relationships

A further difficulty, which adds to the confusion, is that the training for workgroup development neglects to place the workgroup's behaviour in the context of your organisation, which by its very essence is the workgroup's external and contextual environment. With any organisation it is influenced by the immediate and extended organisational behaviour.

One experience of leading a major project was where every member of the workgroup was required to take responsibility to produce the minutes. A set of minutes was produced that did not record the discussion verbatim but only recorded the decision and why and who was going to take action, which received an institutionalised request for the minutes to be in the formatted standard practice. The standard practice had over time become a defensive mechanism, as there was little trust, hence the desire to maintain a verbatim set of lengthy records of events.

The purpose, within the project team, of sharing the duty of producing minutes had an egalitarian element and was part of that workgroup's collegiate development.

The interesting issue that stems from this example was that the minutes were brief, clear, and unambiguous and importantly were read and acted upon. The structure of the minutes had in-built operant regulatory practices that ensured all the participants worked and delivered on time the agreed activities. The traditional style was extensive and often not readable as they were tedious, which meant that individuals arrived ill-prepared, working with what they remembered of the previous meeting. To overcome this obdurate behaviour two sets of minutes were produced, one as a mask to manage the politics, and the other a working document.

There is another side to this obdurate behaviour, which can be related to Argyris' (1986) observation regarding management practices, which he entitled "Skilled Incompetence" where he says, "Managers who are skilled communicators may also be good at covering up real problems." He asks, "How can skilful action be counterproductive?" We can begin to answer this question by briefly examining Ashkenas & Shaffer's (1982) article published in the Harvard Business Review entitled "Managers Can Avoid Wasting Time" where they report managers often spend time on unproductive work, which they do to avoid job related anxiety. Some of this time wasting is achieved by attending non-productive meetings; they read and pick up every detail of the previous minutes, write to the secretary or chair of the group with corrections; all of these activities may be being used to defend that individual's own anxiety. They become professional meeting attendees and game players, who have the capacity to dissipate the energy of any workgroup activity (refer above to Bale, 1950). They do not want the action and responsibility to be clearly expressed as this may expose their own failings. These examples of ritualistic practices are employed defensively against anxieties. These and other avoidance behaviours have the capacity to deplete not only the performance of that workgroup but also the overall organisation's decision-making performance.

There is another practice that has been particularly observed in NHS hospitals where members of a committee attend because they do not trust the decision-making process. These situations encourage senior, well-paid clinical consultants to attend these meetings to protect their clinical practices. This practice exists, in other organisations, but has a particular resonance because of the political dynamics played out in NHS hospitals.

Positioning Workgroups within Your Organisations

This exploration has been used to show that when leading and/or being a member of a workgroup it is essential to become aware of the groups external environment and its *contextual role* within the whole organisation. When viewing workgroups as micro-organisations within a host organisation, you soon become aware that it is a system of inputs, conversion and outputs. The input is scanning to understand the organisation's needs for managing the decision-making and implementation processes; the output is the delivered action, which should be designed to reinforce the overall host organisation's performance (Fig. 12, "Boundary Control for Task Systems").

Contextualising the group's existence enables you to begin, as with any organisation, to develop its direction, task, role, ethos, *intent* and contribution to other workgroups within the host organisation. You are able define how it can and must service the overall organisation's decision-making practices. Leading and managing these processes is the responsibility of the workgroup leader who has to remain *detached* to work at the boundary to scan and interpret those influences that may affect the workgroup's performance. The developing leadership role not only has to remain *detached* but also *engaged* to service the developing competence of that workgroup. (The practice of being *detached/engaged* has been defined in previous chapters. Refer to Fig. 28, "Turbulence, Competencies and Role Relationships".)

Linked Action and Decision-Making

For example, the decision-making processes of each workgroup and how they interconnect and influence one another and the overall behaviour of the organisation has to be understood. Sometimes the relative "seniority" of the workgroup may unduly influence the behaviour of the subordinate workgroups even when the situation has dramatically changed. An example that will help to explore this notion of connected decision-making is to briefly examine the decision-making processes that led to the ill-fated flight of the space rocket "Challenger."

On 28th January 1986, the space shuttle Challenger exploded over Florida, killing all seven crew. Their fate was set before they left the launch pad, many years before, and can be traced to the decision-making processes used for letting development contracts. During the flight preparation engineers discovered that a vital component of the twin shuttle rocket boosters seals may default.

The climatic condition at the launch pad was abnormal in that it was extremely cold the night before causing icicles to form under the launch pad. By morning the temperatures were 32 degrees Fahrenheit and if the shuttle launched that day it would have been the coldest day of any shuttle launch. The engineers realised that the ring seal fitted to the twin shuttle rocket boosters would malfunction at these low temperatures.

The contractors who produced the twin shuttle rocket boosters had realised the consequences but were unable to influence those making the flight launch decisions. These positional authorities, real or perceived, when placed in the context of the media, political funding support and the world's attention probably influenced individual decision-making behaviour and practices. In the heat and intensity of the moment these difficulties have to be understood and to enable the impending chaos to be effectively managed (Lagadec, 1993).

Remaining with the connected issues of the decision-making processes we discover that the fate of this flight was seeded at an earlier stage in the decision-making process. The twin shuttle rocket boosters were contracted to a company that was land bound and had no immediate access to suitable water borne transportation. The physical size of the twin rocket boosters precluded them being transported overland. The solution to overcome the problem caused by the contractual placement decision was to split the rocket booster cylinders into sections. This solution required that these sections, when refitted on site, had to be sealed to contain the rocket fuel. The design of these seals would have had parameters defined for the satisfactory performance of these seals, which would have included climatic changes. The climatic condition on the launch date was either outside or very close to these design parameters. The decision to launch stressed these seals causing them to fail with catastrophic consequences.

The initial decision to place the contract with a land bound contractor set this process in motion. If the contractor had access to water transport the design would have retained its integrity and this specific cause of this disaster averted. Water transportation would have enabled the twin shuttle rocket boosters to be manufactured in one piece without the need for any seals.

The above complex decision-making processes that were further compounded by the political environment should bring to mind, Lagadec's (1993) observations, "When there is an element of confusion in, for example, the availability and quality of information, change, scheduled or unscheduled introduces degrees of chaos." When these conditions are presented the decision-making must be influenced by those with the information, in this case the engineers who manufactured the seals. The parameters set by the design of the seals being stressed should have been automatically factored in to ensure that when a situation arose they became the lead decision-makers.

The lessons we can take from this unfortunate disaster are that the ranking of perceived and/or real authority can influence the ability to influence advanced decisions. At the other end of the spectrum, those with the authority may not have the ability to receive the information from these "subordinate" workgroups, in this case the manufacturers contracted to complete the twin shuttle rocket boosters. The relationship of these various hierarchical workgroups is that these structures authorising relationships can and do block effective communications.

Understanding inter-group behaviour will help to significantly reduce the potential for miscommunication. To support this proposed developed understanding of inter-workgroup's behaviour and the analysis of their decision-making processes, it is important to have evaluated the consequential effects that can be identified through the use of variation analysis, which in turn allows you to identify those *states of flux* that need to be regulated, managed and prioritised. It also allows you to immediately understand the changing priorities these variable activities have on the potential for directly influencing the appropriate decision-making. Critically the consequential decision-making, identified when examining the process of variation analysis, should enable you to identify the change in authority that relates to critical changes in a component's ability to perform safely.

For example, when there is a disaster such as the spillage into an environmentally sensitive waterway or there is a fire, say, at a factory, the CEO is subordinate to the responsible officer for containing and leading the reparative action. In other words, the responsible officer employed to deal with these issues is in command and, as a consequence, the CEO must take on a subordinate role.

When letting this contract, we find that it has introduced the need to compromise the integrity of our *intent,* which, in this case, is not to compromise the safety of the craft; we have to have the courage to review the decisions for letting of that contract. Or alternatively ensure the contract engineers have the positional power to influence the decision-making when the design parameters are likely to be compromised. The retrospective cost comparison would have easily challenged and influenced this contract letting practice. ("The Millennium Dome" case study is another example, of where political and time pressures caused the evidence of malpractice to go unheeded. The failure to respond to the evidence led to major fraudulent criminal activity.)

Developing the Primary Task

To identify the primary task of the workgroup the *employed technology* is the group's behavioural dynamics, which includes each individual's psychological baggage, coupled with the management technologies they employ. You do not have to become a psychotherapist but having a developed understanding of a group's behavioural dynamics is essential.

The workgroup's environmental market place is determined by its position within the organisation. Does it sit completely within the host organisation or does it live at the boundaries of the organisation where it is influenced by external events affecting the whole organisation and those specific influences that affect that workgroup's activities? (Refer to Fig. 7, "Boundary Management".) This process of contextualising the group's role within its host organisation determines its position, its dependent and interdependent relationships and its ability to influence, which directly affects its behaviour and activity. It determines the *intent* of that group when contributing to the overall organisation's performance. (These consequential outcomes are further developed in Chapter Ten, "Outsourcing and Contractual Practices".)

These processes for working for clarity are important particularly when "chaos" may strike, in that these ranking relationships may rapidly change. The person or workgroup that has the knowledge and information may suddenly move up the decision-making authority ranking to lead and influence the new decision-making processes. Those that were in the original senior role may now find that they have to take a subordinate role during the resolution of the cause of the chaos and/or confusion.

Ownership of Management Technologies

Transferred environmental influences will, at the very least, be the technologies employed, the management technologies (MT), HR, systems technologies (ST), IT, production technologies (PT) and cost and financial technologies (CFT). Those who attend the meeting will transfer these specialities and their incumbent behaviours into the workgroups, in other words, across the workgroup's boundaries.

For example, if production and HR management are in attendance along with financial managers each will bring to that group's development their own issues, anxieties and agendas that, in turn, will influence the practices and behaviour of that group.

For example, when we examine the relationship of the Works Department in a hospital it has to be non-intrusive even though the clinical staff are dependent on their service performance. The Works Department's role changed through the design and structure of the building, causing the role relationship and power shift to acquire a different emphasis. (This concept is further developed in the case study, "Greenwich District Hospital".) The building design created an exaggerated dependency that changed the relative power and working relationships. We can also make the connection at this point with the introduction of new technologies. (Refer to Chapter Nine, "Technology Change and Managing the Consequences".)

When a representative of a department has a fixed brief, let's say, a non-negotiable brief, the positioning and behaviour of that workgroup member will, as in the case of the talkative members discussed earlier, influence the direction of the decision-making. This creates a dynamic where the person providing the brief is externally influencing the outcome of the decision-making. These practices can be clearly observed when working in highly politicised, protective game-playing organisations.

When attending these kinds of meetings it is often difficult to discern what and who is influencing these workgroup processes. It is for these reasons you have to develop your *cognitive organisational awareness* and your *group cognitive organisational awareness* that supports and is as much to do with knowing when and how to express emotion as it is does with controlling it.

For example, Sigdal Barsade conducted an experiment at Yale University, where he engaged a group of volunteers to play the role of managers to agree and allocate bonuses to their subordinates. A trained actor was planted among them who always spoke first. In some groups, the actor projected cheerful enthusiasm; in others, relaxed warmth; in others depressed sluggishness and hostility. The results indicated that the actor was able to influence the group with his projected emotions. Where good feelings were projected, this led to improved cooperation, fairness and the overall group performance. In fact, objective measures indicated that the cheerful group were better able to distribute the money fairly and in a way that helped the organisation (Sigdal Barsade, 1998, reference Chemiss, 2000).

The dynamics will also be directly influenced, if for example, you change the constituents and remove one of the personalities and/or introduce another person. The dynamics of that workgroup's behaviour will change. Should a subordinate person join the group that person may begin to accept the sets of norms experienced in that workgroup. This is the same sort of behaviour observed in the, "Monkeys See and Monkeys Do" experiment (Paler Louis, 1999).

Implied Power and influence

On the other hand when, for example, a senior executive manager joins a lower order workgroup, the dynamics will change, even if that person declares that they want the other members to ignore the seniority of that person's rank. This is difficult to achieve and the reasons can be, in part, explained by the outcomes of the Milgram experiment.

The Milgram experiment on obedience to authority figures was a series of social psychology experiments conducted by Yale University psychologist Stanley Milgram, which measured the willingness of participants to obey an authority figure who instructed them to perform acts that conflicted with their personal conscience. Milgram summarised the experiment in his 1974 article, "The Perils of Obedience", where he wrote about his concerns of the main finding of the study that of the extreme willingness of adults to go to almost any lengths on the command of an authority.

Consider how this behavioural dynamic may play out in an organisation that has a political decision-making practice (Fig. 3, "Politics, Career and the Overt Organisation"). When considering Milgram's findings, take the opportunity to reflect on the Nimrod disaster, the BP disasters and the practice that will be discussed in Chapter Ten, "Outsourcing and Contractual Practices" the case study, "Transition Nursing Care" and the consequential effects of your own compliant decision-making practice.

For any senior person's influence to be effectively assimilated the existing workgroup members and the senior person have to jointly work through the new sets of dynamic relationships before the workgroup can begin to work effectively through their decision-making processes. The ability of a senior person being able to integrate into the working process of a workgroup is made easier when all the participants have equally developed *cognitive organisational awareness.* This common competency and using a common language facilitates the dialogue, enabling each participant to work on the "overt organisational" issues rather than being distracted by the potential political influences (Refer to Fig. 5, "Overt organisation, Careers and Politics" Chapter Seven, "Adaptive Organisational Leadership" and Chapter Twelve, "Development, Training and Recruitment" where the realignment of these activities are designed to support these workgroup developmental competencies.)

Leadership Positioning

This positioning is important and can be, particularly at the early stages of a workgroup's formation, difficult for the workgroup members, which includes you. This practice of detachment is important in the early stages of a workgroup's development, as you are required to suspend judgement, not to seek an agenda, take the lead or impose or create structures.

To adopt a detached role where the members work through the issues for themselves allows the workgroup's total intellectual capacity to be used and developed, and provides an opportunity for the members to gain a high degree of ownership. Suspicions may be aroused, when they view you as the leader or expert and you appear not to engage. If you are not leading, how can the group function and/or get to work and complete the task? They may assume you are playing some kind of game; surely if you are the senior responsible person for the workgroup's performance you should show the way forward.

Bion acknowledged these expectations but refused to comply, not through stubbornness, but because he was not clear as to why these needs needed to be met. The task of the group would be clear and did not need a leader since there were no immediate decisions to be made. He stated if there was no immediate requirement for a leader at this stage of the creative development of the group, the wish for a leader was not being based on any evidenced reality. It left the question, 'what was this need based on'? "The sucking in is a way for the group's members or individuals wanting to relieve their own anxiety" (Armstrong, 1995).

This conundrum follows something like this. "The group, any group, organisation, society… needs and evolves a structure of tasks, roles, procedures, rules, and ascribed status, that Bion refers to as the "Group culture", in order to contain the anxiety of the unknown and to defend against that unknown, which, unconsciously, is mobilised to defend against the unknown. The unknown is, at the same time, what is unknown and feared in each of us and what is unknown in the realities we engage with as we live and work." These behavioural influences and the need to reduce anxiety in new ventures, groups and societies tend to towards the formation of a "group culture" that can lead, if these dynamics are not understood, toward institutionalised behaviour that we follow even though we are instinctively aware that it is inappropriate. (Refer to "Transitional Nursing Care" case study.)

"Within the group" Bion believed, "one can see operating a number of powerful unconscious and unlearned, quasi-instinctive strategies of evasion and denial." Bion saw these strategies of evasion and denial as constituting what he termed a "group mentality", opposed to the conscious aims, intentions and efforts of individuals (Armstrong, 1995).

This practice of detachment and being engaged may sound like a contradiction but it works extremely well, in that it allows you to notionally be outside of the workgroup, which enables you to observe the various interactions and the overall group developmental processes. The role, when engaged, refers to you working within and influencing the developmental processes, as you are part of the group. "The task of leadership and the intuitive skills of the leader are to balance the requirements of the co-operation and structure in the service of reality, with the constraints inevitably imposed by group mentality in the service of defence" (Armstrong, 1995). This means that the leader has to not only ensure that the task is completed effectively but they also maintain and manage the group processes to enable it to survive and develop. And the roles of being *detached/ engaged* enable you to maintain the social needs of the workgroup and ensure it remains on track to successfully complete the identified contextualised task.

Group Process by Definition

Group process is the sequence of interaction patterns between the members of the group. This will include the verbal and non-verbal contribution of each member (Fig. 29, "Communicated Message"), how members contribute to solving problems and maintaining the workgroup's cohesion.

Bale (1950) demonstrated that individuals adopted different roles within groups and they were categorised as set out in table 1.

Bale also suggested some roles are concerned with group maintenance issues, while others are more assertive and concerned with getting on with the task that the group has to perform, which are shown in table 2.

Categories	Explanation (Table 1)
Proposing	Any behaviour which puts forward a new suggestion, idea, proposal, or course of action
Supporting	Any behaviour which declares agreement or support with any individual or their idea
Building	Any behaviour which develops or extends an idea or suggestion made by someone else
Disagreeing (may be testing assumptions)	Any behaviour which states a criticism of another person's statement
Giving Information	Any behaviour which gives facts, ideas, opinions or clarifies these
Seeking Information	Any behaviour which asks for facts, ideas or opinions from others

Task Roles	Maintenance Roles (Table 2)
Initiator	*Encourager*
Information seeker	*Compromiser*
Diagnoses	*Peacekeeper*
Opinion Seeker	*Clarifier*
Evaluator	*Summariser*
Decision manager	*Standard Setting*

These tables have been produced to assist with the process of observing the workgroup's process during the developmental and decision-making stages. It enables you to use these as a basis for structuring your observations. It is important when observing any activity that any assumptions you may make are tested. In other words, always test your assumptions, as they may not be as they appear; getting it right will maintain your credibility.

The two positions, *detached/engaged*, enable you to observe the processes and also contribute to the effective development of the workgroup's practices. It enables you to observe the interaction, the forming of cabals, those who are hogging the meeting, soliciting those that are unable to make a contribution, or see whether the workgroup is in a position to make and/or implement any probable decision, which will include the elements we discussed when making the connections with Bion and Bridger (Chapter Five, Fig. 14, "The Role of Systems and the Individual").

Engaging a New Member

Even though the group's constituents may change, the identified primary task remains unchanged. What becomes necessary is the need for new members to be provided with an opportunity to work through the development and identification of the primary task, the purpose of the workgroup.

How often have you been asked to attend a meeting that is ill defined in its practices and when you join the existing members continue as if you had attended all the other meetings? Your ability to contribute effectively is significantly compromised. We fall into ritualistic conforming normative behaviour and unwittingly contribute to the dysfunctional decision-making processes.

Developing an Organisational Dialogue

Engaging an individual into the processes of a workgroup is necessary to ensure they can effectively contribute to the overall performance of the group and the organisation. When they understand the task, the *intent* and the overall delivery expectations, the new member's productive contribution becomes equal to the other group members.

This process is even more effective when all the organisation's leaders and managers have developed their own *cognitive organisational awareness and cognitive awareness of workgroup behaviour* and acquire an attached common *organisational developmental dialogue*. The value of this developing dialogue is that you can introduce an on-going discussion that has the organisation and individual's performance improvement at the centre of the discussion. Dialogue is the nexus of all good communication between individuals, workgroups and the whole organisation.

Avoiding Technical Deference

We have to be particularly aware of our own behaviour when working with these technical elements as we may feel that they are outside our competencies. The risk is that we defer to these individuals or groups to the detriment of the workgroups and the decision-making processes. The skill is not to defer. This is a form of abdication of responsibility, but to ensure that the application of these skills is directed towards the true development of the workgroup and the overall organisation's performance. Having a well-developed *cognitive organisational awareness*, coupled with your *group cognitive organisational awareness* (Fig. 8 and 31), will enable you to attach these technical contributions and ensure they are designed and directed to reinforce the workgroup's and organisations overall performance. The devastating consequential effects of deferring will be examined and developed further when introducing new technologies. (Refer to Chapter Nine, "Technology Change and Managing the Consequences").

Conflict Management and Decision-Making Practices

It is useful, when attempting to achieve these personality mergers and to create an effective amalgam using all the available skills and experience, to have some idea of their potential decision-making processes. Referring to the earlier example of working in project teams where engineers and architects need to work together we found that they easily, even though politely, begin to position themselves causing them to introduce a degree of intransigent conflict. These practices affect the process and progress of achieving a consensus or an effective working decision-making arrangement. The difficulties that have to be recognised are that these two disciplines have different decision-making practices that, to a higher degree, develop from the individuals' own education and professional development.

These misfits of decision-making processes have to be recognised and managed, which means that neither is wrong; they are just different. It is when we are presented with these conflicting differences that we can defer to our *group cognitive organisational awareness* competencies and *use the organisation as a third party for conflict resolution*. The process of resolving these conflicts should enable you to, if necessary, redefine and modify your decision-making processes. (Refer to the example of J.F. Kennedy, Chapter Seven, "Adaptive Organisational Leadership".)

Using the organisation to act "as if" a third party for conflict resolution has the capacity to allow each party to freely express their views. They are each required to not criticise the other party's behaviour but to direct and express their ideas and concerns in terms of the organisation's needs. This approach reduces direct personalised confrontation. You can allow these conflicting exchanges, as this permits the various views to be developed and expressed. These exchanges will help each party to develop their own position even though they may not achieve agreement. The use of your organisational competencies can be employed to ask each party to make the same case, but in terms of how these proposals contribute to the workgroup's performance and within the context of the workgroup's need to contribute to the overall organisation's performance. When referring to the 'parties' it includes the managing of conflict within the various workgroups. This process, for conflict management can be applied when working at the inter-workgroup boundaries, to ensure their working relationships are focused and complimentary.

This focuses the mind on the organisational task and often introduces new concepts and possibilities. The other party is asked to do the same, without referring to the other's contribution, unless complementing and making a further contribution to the other party's observations. Focusing on the organisation's need reduces the need for the professionals competing as they are now on common ground and own the same task; that of collectively contributing to the overall organisation's delivery performance.

Inter-Workgroup Practice

We have briefly discussed some of the potential behavioural dynamics of the intra-workgroup behaviour. It is essential that all workgroups (also read interdepartmental) are able to work by transacting effectively across their own boundaries. This developed cooperative behaviour can be described as inter-workgroup behaviour. Other workgroups operate within the same organisational environment, and that environment will determine your workgroup's dependent or interdependent relationship. In terms of your organisation's need and your positioning within the whole organisation, these clusters and collaborative working relationships have to be identified.

Simplified model Fig. 7 ("Boundary Management") has been produced to emphasise these relationships. Fig. 32 ("Interdependency and Dependency of Workgroups") shows the interrelationships between other workgroups and your own, to identify the interdependent and dependent relationships, along with any possible tensions that differentiate the degree of attributed attention that needs to be observed.

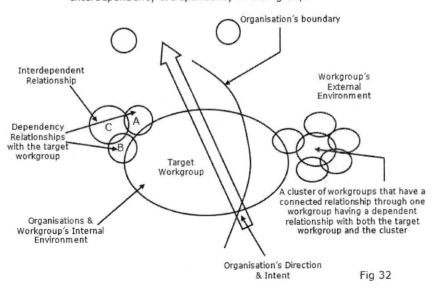

Interdependency & Dependency of Workgroups

Fig 32

233

The cluster of workgroups, for example, may be a project group, whose findings may influence the target workgroup's decision-making. The authority of this cluster has to be identified and declared to enable everyone to support and manage the cluster's deliberations. Workgroup's (A) and (B) (Fig. 32) relationships and degree of dependency has to be defined in relation to the task of the target workgroup. How you define these relationships and levels of dependency will create the appropriate tension between the target workgroup and the dependent workgroups. Working through these processes identifies their authority, responsibility, the related timeline for activities, and the established accountability of each of these workgroups and how they respond and relate to one another.

For example, the need to be clear with regards to the decision-making processes to support the progressive development of a major project identified that decision-making between the various workgroups had to be clarified and agreed. This process of clarifying the complementary decision-making practices examined the use of authority and where that was placed for particular decisions. In this case, the relationship with the main board, the management of the project teams, the technological innovation team and the operation's project management team all had to be clarified and understood to ensure each party were clear about the overall decision-making and delivery practices.

This meant that everyone was clear with regard to the nature of the decisions they were making and the timely link to the overall decision-making process. This was a necessary process that was developed to ensure that those that had to operate the plant and those who had to deliver the physical project were provided with a clear non-competitive and unambiguous decision-making process that enabled them to collectively commit.

The workgroups had to be designed to enable the individual to maximise their contribution, not only to the workgroup, but also be able to identify contextual relationships, in terms of each workgroup, and how they contributed to the decision-making process and overall organisation's performance. The failure to understand this critical practice is often identified when major disasters and catastrophes are retrospectively examined.

The above decision-making process has the capacity to prevent isolation, confusion and systems being developed for an unspecified reason, such as, protecting power cabals, leading to silo thinking, political game playing, "skilled incompetence", and "managers wasting time." This nesting of related activities works extremely well and avoids some of these depleting activities. (The case study, "Greenfield Development Project" identifies how these decision-making practices were successfully employed.)

It is part of the organisational leader's role to choreograph by planning and overseeing the movement, development and detailed orchestration of the various workgroups and individuals' contribution, by identifying, constructing and developing these clusters to ensure they remain contextualised and relative to the developing decision-making support processes.

For example, how often have you read reports after a disaster, where departments did not share information with each other? If they had, the disaster may have been prevented. The National Commission on Terrorist Attacks upon the United States (9/11 Commission) found that the attacks were carried out by members of Al-Qaeda and also found that intelligence agencies were inadequately coordinated to prevent the attacks.

The commission explains, "We believe the 9/11 attacks identified four kinds of failure: imagination, policy, capabilities and management." This infers, within the context of organisations, *organisational thinking, organisational leadership* and organisational problem solving were missing along with the failure to orchestrate their collective intentions and activities. Interestingly, several of the recommendations from this commission have yet to be introduced. These failures to meet the commission's recommendations are replicated in many other major disasters; they still maintain the identified and even dangerous dysfunctional practices. We can relate to the resistance to these recommendations as they transgress boundaries of existing political cabals. (These relationships are further discussed in Chapter Nine, "Technology Change and Managing the Consequences".)

Contextualising

The workgroup's leader has to have a developed shared understanding of the consequential related effects of their decision-making in the performance of the overall organisation. Understanding where these various workgroups fit into the overall organisational processes is important, for the purpose of orchestration and orientation.

Fig. 33 is an attempt to identify how these task workgroups may function and fit within an organisation but all share a common focused intent: the servicing and the reinforcement of the overall organisation's performance. The curved arrow is showing the direction of linked supported decision-making and the need to test assumptions regarding the information being provided, hence the two-way directional arrow.

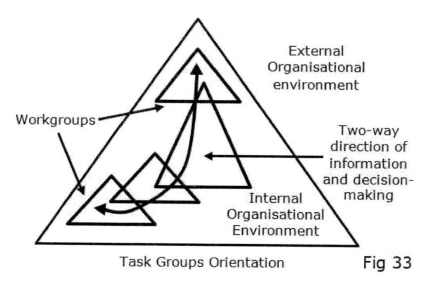

Task Groups Orientation   Fig 33

This notion of linking decision-making and activities also applies to departments and/or any sub-organisation, whether temporary or permanent. This is the developed practice of identifying the vertical performance culture continuum that must exist within any organisation. Having a clear mental image of this continuum enables you to link the various even disparate workgroup decision-making practices and task activities. It allows you to develop a sense of the variation analysis that enables you to determine the consequential effects of the decision-making of these various workgroup activities. The understanding of these connected, dependent and interdependent activities within your organisation enables you to identify and develop means for monitoring, to control your overall organisation's delivery performance.

Stifling Innovation

Many meetings are ritualistic and when you ask each individual what the purpose of the meeting is they often have different expectations to that of the other participants. These are the very settings where new recruits find that they cannot influence the situation and intellectually sit-back into the presented normative organisational culture, stifling innovation, creativity, learning and development, compressing everything into destructive ritualistic practices that we all eventually sign up to. We discovered earlier that it's extremely difficult to step outside of a group's normative behaviour.

Trainers tend to over simplify the behavioural dynamics of group formation and have distilled the processes down to a sound bite, forming, storming, norming, performing and adjourning, for team development, Tuckman (1965). Accepting that Tuckman acknowledges that understanding the group's process is of value, with the current quick fix mentality, there is an assumption that is all you have to understand, which is all part of the sound bite and panacea-seeking practices.

Even so, it has value, providing you accept the expressed reservation. The real value, that Tuckman explains, is that as the team develops maturity and ability, relationships are established and the leader changes their leadership style. We should also make connections with other models such as Tannenbaum & Schmidt's Continuum (Fig. 25), and Hersey and Blanchard's situational leadership models (Fig. 26) also identify the fact that leaders have to modify their style to the situation of the workgroup's relative maturity.

From the above we can make a connection with McGregor's 'X' 'Y' theory of leadership, which, in essence, defines a continuum from the 'X' dictatorial autocratic through to the various progressive forms where we arrive at what he refers to as a participative management leadership 'Y'. Leaders and managers work along this continuum and change their roles and styles as these workgroups mature.

Unfortunately these sound bite deliveries suggest that that is all you have to do, which in turn creates disillusionment when the practitioner fails to achieve the promised development and improvements in their group's performance. This feeds into the malaise discussed above that often exists. If not qualified that this is a simplification of the process it can, unfortunately, along with the current practices, create dysfunctional workgroup behaviour. We can relate this example to the failed employment of *management technologies* and their consequential unwanted dysfunctional practices. These examples reaffirm that these workgroups are micro-organisations that should be designed to enable each of them to be collectively developed to reinforce one another and your organisation's developing overall performance.

PART FOUR

Technology Change and Managing the Consequences

Goals and Introduction

CHAPTER NINE
Technology Change and Managing the Consequences

CHAPTER TEN
Outsourcing and Contractual Practices

CHAPTER ELEVEN
Remuneration and Motivation

CHAPTER TWELVE
Development, Training and Recruitment

GOALS

- Defining management technologies, identifying their invasive behaviour and when misapplied, their unwanted consequential outcomes.
- To examine outsourcing decision-making and implementation.
- To use an organisational approach to examine remuneration strategies, incentivised motivation practices and unwanted decision-making behaviour.
- To demonstrate the need to realign development, training and recruitment strategies to reinforce your organisation's responsive performance needs.
- To understand that when reducing the dysfunctional practices, this creates an initial felt sense of redundancy, requiring that the freed intellectual space be redirected and managed.

Introduction

Chapter Nine introduces the use and misuse of management technologies and their consequential outcomes. At the beginning of this book we identified that you have to design the management systems to service the identified organisational performance culture. Driving change using management technologies is a recipe for failure.

The following management technologies have been identified. They are "Outsourcing and Contractual Practices", "Remuneration and Motivation" along with "Development, Training and Recruitment." When not designed, developed and managed effectively they can and do create displaced organisational goals and in some cases have disastrous consequences.

Remuneration and motivation have been identified to provide an opportunity to demonstrate the evaluative use of an organisational approach. When working in large or complex organisations you need to develop a theory or concept that matches the presented situation. It removes the emotional assumptions usually attached to existing decision-making practices.

Development, training and recruitment are being addressed together as they all have dependent relationships. Each of these management technologies has the capacity to create unwanted conflict, role confusion and displaced organisational goals. They all need to be collectively employed to ensure the development of a candidate's *cognitive organisational awareness* along with the ability to effectively use their *social emotional intelligence* within the context of their organisation.

The experience of realigning your organisation changes the role of the leadership and management who may initially feel a sense of redundancy. This created *intellectual space* enables these individuals to re-employ their skills to address the needs of their developing organisation and the next generation of leaders and managers. This requires that managers supervise the individual's development, which in turn develops a need for those supervising training to improve their mentoring and coaching skills. It also requires that the promotional career opportunities be related to performance achievement.

CHAPTER NINE

TECHNOLOGY CHANGE AND MANAGING THE CONSEQUENCES

Management technologies are prolifically employed in all organisations for a variety of reasons and can be either beneficial or at the other end of the spectrum, disastrous. In this chapter we shall examine the processes for introducing management technologies to significantly improve the way they can contribute to your organisation's overall performance.

The purpose of this chapter is to reinforce the basic requirement that all *management technologies* must be designed to strengthen your overall organisation's service delivery performance. They must be designed to enable you to monitor to manage, and to control the direction and operational performance of your business organisation.

Technologies Defined

To ensure there is no confusion or ambiguity we need to restate and define technologies in terms of their use in organisations. *Employed technology* refers to the basic technology of the organisation for it to exist and function. This basic functional technology is part of and attached to the identification and achievement of the *primary task* (Fig. 9).

Management technologies are management systems that are employed to facilitate the strategic and operational performance of the overall organisation. The developed design and behaviour of the organisation creates the performance platform to ensure we deliver our services effectively. Most *management technologies* employ information technology (IT) in a supporting role, which demands that these developed systems be designed to reinforce the sub-organisations and your overall organisation's service delivery performance. Often imported support *management technologies* confuse the identification of the *employed technologies*. This is particularly prevalent in organisations that are dysfunctional and have *displaced goals* (Fig. 4), which are *systems dependent* and have impaired political decision-making practices (Fig. 3, "Politics, Career and Overt Organisation").

These imported technologies and the proliferation of *management technologies* (MT) is a collective term that includes, for example, Human Resources (HR), systems technologies (ST), computer based information technologies (IT), production and manufacturing technologies (PMT) and cost and financial technologies (CFT).

These management technologies can be further differentiated. For example with HR, remuneration systems, training and development programmes, managing employment and performance evaluation data, systems for managing and preventing wage and salary drift, disciplinary procedures, redundancy procedures, training and development, etc.

PMT can be differentiated by examining those systems that are introduced to control, for example, quality control, Just in Time, lean-manufacturing strategies, piecework systems, shift patterns, etc.

CFT can be differentiated by operational practices such as budgetary control systems, cost management, salary payment systems, etc. At another level the financial viability of the overall organisation has to be continually evaluated, to monitor the organisation's financial credit rating, evaluating the return on investments, etc.

The above listings are not intended to be absolute and have only been identified to provide a sense of the degree to which management technologies are differentiated and employed.

Organisations Demand Systems

In Chapter Two we explored the evolutionary organisational development and clearly identified the need for systems to support the growth of the business. These systems should be designed to enable the executive management to monitor and manage the organisation's performance. We also discovered that when systems are inappropriately deployed they contribute to your organisation becoming dysfunctional and develop the capacity to detach the leadership from the operating delivery performance of their organisation. Accepting that we need systems, it is essential that we ensure that they are designed to complement and reinforce your organisation's overall responsive performance.

The tenet that form follows function requires that we must design our organisations first, by working through the transition for change processes, to ensure the organisation performs effectively. All the systems can then be designed to reinforce the identified service delivery performance culture. It is the same applied logic of designing a vehicle or a building first before you design and develop the complementary wiring and other service systems. It would be unthinkable to do otherwise.

It is for these fundamental reasons that the executive leaders and all the other organisational leaders must not delegate the systems design. When you delegate you also delegate your ability to effectively monitor to manage and control along with the capacity to direct your business organisation's operational delivery performance. When you delegate this responsibility you create a situation where you only react to the *consequential outcomes* and not to those indicators that should influence strategic and operational decisions. This reactive practice compromises your ability to lead and manage the strategic, operational and service delivery performance of your organisation.

Abrogation of responsibility, to the professional or techno-managers, or to an outsourced service, is a fatal flaw. The consequential effects can be observed in those organisations where for example, the introduction of, IT technologies where whole organisations have experienced serious sub-optimal performance and even catastrophic failures. They were not prepared for the potential and created "chaos."

Invasiveness and Consequential Effects

Organisational leaders are the *interpretive "agent"* and have to remain involved and responsible for the direction, intent, design, implementation strategies and operational development of these major systems, to ensure they support and reinforce their organisation'overall performance. We must keep in mind, at all times, the fact that management technologies and their systems cannot think for themselves and the "agent" is responsible for their *designed intent*, behaviour and performance. The reason, why you, as the *organisational leader*, have to remain engaged, is that the introduction of any technology is highly invasive (Fig. 34, "Invasiveness of Technologies"), is disruptive, and has the capacity of creating *displaced organisational goals* and detaching the executive leadership.

This model is attempting to demonstrate that any technology that is imported into an organisation is invasive and affects the whole organisation, the sub-organisations the individual, and the groups' behavioural dynamics. How the technology is introduced and employed will directly affect the eventual service delivery performance outcome of your organisation.

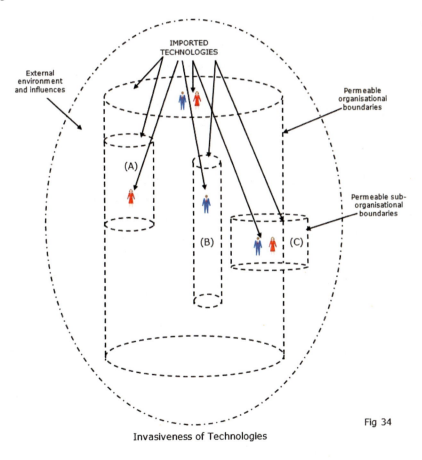

Fig 34

Invasiveness of Technologies

245

The created dependency on these systems creates a superficial sense of security and displaced attachment. The attachment is to the systems, not the process they are employed to support and service. As a consequence they become risk adverse and career orientated (Nyquist, 2009), having a tendency to service the dysfunctional political decision-making processes (Fig. 3). (For examples, refer to Chapter Ten, "Outsourcing and Contractual Management" and case study, "Transitional Nursing Care").

An example of technology detaching the user can be shown in the following experience. Within many public sectors there is a tendency to spend any underspend before the end of the year, irrespective of its value to the operation and delivery of the end product. A shortfall in qualified intensive care nursing staff, available funds and coupled with the purveyor's persuasive technological solution created the following situation. The new technology based patient-monitoring systems were introduced with little consultation to provide a solution. The consequential outcomes were that the existing nurses showed signs of frustration and stress induced through technological alienation. Obholzer's observation, regarding the dependency on these systems creates a superficial sense of security and displaced attachment, which became evident in this evaluative study.

Using an organisational approach, it became evident the new technology further detached the nurses from the responsive care they were trained to complete. The technology undertook all the monitoring and had attached alarm systems. The increased technology caused the nurses to manage the technology and become less responsive to the actual patients' needs. They were responding to the technologies' protocols that caused them to lose that all-important intuitive feel.

Simplifying the supporting technology, to little more than they were previously using, reversed the induced stress putting the nurses back in control of the patients' responsive care. In this case the leader, the nurses, had become detached from the appropriate care practices and service delivery. Because technology is available, it does not mean that you can simply employ it, as it can put patients at risk.

The abrogation of responsibility leads to the transfer of power to the techno-manager. The techno-manager is not trained to deal effectively with the organisational behavioural dynamics created by the introduction of these management technologies. These all-pervasive technology systems transgress boundaries of existing political cabals, systems and practices that have been introduced to reduce individual and group anxieties, divested authority and responsibilities. (Menzies 1970 and Jaques 1955). They naturally revert to what they know best and in turn defend themselves from any induced organisational anxiety.

We need to also keep in mind that membership of these mental and social structures want to retain control and define the operating culture that the techno-manager is attempting to change. It takes little to conclude that defensive conflict will ensue if the change processes are technology driven.

The term techno-manager not only refers to the person who manages IT, it refers to anyone who is responsible for designing and managing other management technologies such CFT, HR, PMT and other technology based management systems.

Invasiveness of Technologies

A senior researcher within an Oxford University research group, Bent Flyvbjerg, offered the following observations: "IT projects are so big and touch so many aspects of business, government and citizens' lives that they pose a singular new challenge for top management." These observations confirmed the need to understand and manage the invasive behaviour of IT and other management technologies, both on society's and your own organisation's behaviour. In other words, we have to have worked through and achieved the necessary degrees of clarity regarding the *consequential outcomes* of introducing these management technologies. (It would be useful to keep in mind the discussion in Chapter Five regarding the "Inter-related Behaviour of the Individual, the Group, the Organisation and Environment".)

In Chapter Three we identified that, "We tolerate the unexplained but not the inexplicable" (Goffman, 1974). That when faced with complex unfamiliar situations, such as the need to lead and manage transition for change, created through the introduction of new management technologies, this elevates the desire to create defences from induced situational anxiety. This is further compounded by

Dixon's (1989) observations, "Through denial of the unpalatable, misinterpretation, distortion or repression of the unacceptable, and a predilection for wish fulfilling fantasies, *decisions tend to be based not on what is the case but on what we would like to be the case*."

When there is an element of confusion in, for example, through the lack of what is being, in organisational terms, led and managed "change scheduled or unscheduled introduces degrees of chaos." The first impulse is to grasp for some explanation, any old explanation. And what we get hold of are the automatic explanations we have lived with longest and invoked most often. This can introduce a number of behavioural responses some of which are "trivialisation" "low risk attitudes" political power game playing and the old and familiar empire building, leading to silo structured organisations. Within this regressive process we revert to employing out-of-date organisational systems for coping with entirely new situations (Burns, 1963), that we identified, in earlier chapters, as the skills redundancy factor. This is the stage where executives start to become detached from the business of their organisation through the created dependency on *management technologies and systems* that relieves their anxieties. (Refer to Chapter Two, "Evolutionary Growth of an Organisation".)

Those that have a high degree of political influence may covertly or overtly misdirect the transition for change processes to defend themselves against any felt sense of created anxiety. The consequential outcomes compound the existing dysfunctional organisational behaviour by compromising the design and introduction of those management technologies being employed. (For further examples refer to case study one "The Brewing Industry".)

Work Life Balance

When we consider the invasive capacity of management technologies, in particular information technologies, they have no respect for existing organisational, workgroup or personal boundaries. Those boundaries are no longer sacrosanct and transgress your organisation's physical boundaries. These technologies, particularly mobile devices, have the capacity to become attached to the individual and therefore have the ability to enable that person to be accessed at any time.

When not employed appropriately, they can invade a person's life by constantly transgressing that individual's social and private life. For some this may be acceptable, which may also be a part of and nature of their employment. For others, it can be simply an unacceptable intrusion of their social lives. This raises issues of an individual's psychological contract and the ability to manage that all-important *work-life-balance*. Being unable to "switch off" can be stressful and lead to evasive unwanted outcomes, such as increased sickness, absence and low productivity.

Within Fig. 34 we have to consider that those people within the organisation are, notionally, never detached from your organisation and that your employed management technologies are attached to these individuals and operate beyond your organisation's boundaries. For example, by switching off your smart phone, your location can be established, messages, both voice and texts, can be stored and ready to immediately reengage you as soon as you open your mobile device.

Consequential Outcomes

Infusions of large management technologies are all-pervasive, and if not understood and controlled, introduce unwanted outcomes, and they can destroy individuals and companies. For example, well-known brands such as Kmart and the second largest car glass company spun out of control whilst attempting to implement large IT projects. Whole corporations such as Airbus, Levi-Strauss, Toll Collect and Hershey's have been on the brink of collapse because of out of control IT projects.

Government agencies face similar problems to those experienced within the private sector. The private sector failings, unlike the public sector, are not always available for examination. There have been a number of high cost, public sector IT initiatives, which have significantly overrun, under-performed or failed over the past twenty years including the Child Support agency's IT system, the IT system that would have underpinned the National ID Card Scheme, the Defence Infrastructure Programme, the implementation of the Single Payment Scheme run by the Rural Payment Agency and the National Offenders Management Scheme. These IT failings also affected, among others, the Criminal Records Bureau, Inland Revenue,

National Air Traffic Services and the Department of Works and Pensions along with many others.

The unhealthy reliance on *management technologies* to solve existing dysfunctional organisational problems is a part of the process of creating further problems from these systems driven solutions. Failure to understand these relationships and the application of new *management technologies* can have devastating consequences. (Refer to Chapter Ten, "Outsourcing and Contractual Practices" along with the 'Nimrod disaster' and BP's cost reduction policy on safety practices.) The consequential effects can be expressed not just in terms of reduced effectiveness and costs but also less tangible outcomes.

For example, these extracts from the Parliamentary Office of Science and Technology report (2003 summary report No 200), "Difficulties with IT delivery occur in both the public and private sector. A further survey across sectors found that only 13% of all projects, and less than 1% IT development projects were successful (on time, to specification and to cost). (Extract from the Public Accounts Committee, HC845, 2002).

Extract from the Public Administration Committee report, "Government and IT –"A Recipe for Rip-offs": Time for a new approach.

Arguably the government's IT needs are more complex than those of other organisations. Ian Watmore, Chief Operating Officer and head of the Efficiency and Reform Group in the Cabinet Office has been quoted as saying that "IT in government is as difficult as it gets." Jonathan Murray, a partner in an IT firm Innovia Ventures, highlighted the different challenges faced by the public sector:

It is recognized that public and private sector organizations serve different needs and are driven by different objectives. The majority of private sector organizations are motivated by a common set of financial performance objectives. Governance structures and business models can remain stable in private sector organizations for decades. These factors greatly simplify the process of identifying and implementing common best practice.

Public sector organizations operate in a reality that challenges many attempts to identify and transfer best practice. There is no homogeneity of objectives across government departments. The nature of the election cycle places severe constraints on the time window available for governance reform and acts to reinforce institutional resistance to change. The traditional - and understandable - constraints and conservatism of public procurement regulations and processes are antithetical to the speed with which organizations must adopt technology to support rapid change. Finally the political process has traditionally reinforced a stovepipe approach to governance where Ministers and senior civil servants are given autonomy and full authority over their departments to the detriment of more distributed and integrated approaches.

Size and complexity are often used as excuses. Deming identified that obstacles to progress are excuses, such as "our problems are different." These claims are supported by the committee report's extract above. Yes, they are large and complex but when you read Jonathan Murray's observation, in the above extract, you find these are mainly organisational issues that accumulatively undermine the ability to achieve success. There is confused organisational thinking, which is implied by the assertion that "...private sector organisations serve different needs and are driven by different objectives." "The majority of private sector organisations are motivated by a common set of financial performance objectives." This implies that the public sector does not have to have these sets of basic performance and management disciplines and objectives.

It becomes evident that the employment of IT does not resolve these problems, it tends to emphasise the current dysfunctional issues within your organisation. It may be useful to make the connection with the practices of reengineering and its consequential behavioural outcomes discussed in Chapter One. Reengineering and the employment of IT being used to drive change is a prescription for failure. (Discussed in detail in Chapters One, Two and Three.)

A further example of unwanted consequential outcomes is that in 2010 it was reported that £26 billion had been wasted. These failings affect the credibility of these services and also attract such observations that the UK has been described as "a world leader in ineffective IT schemes for government". The EU and the USA are also subject to similar catastrophic failings.

Intent

Often these programmes are driven by misplaced *intents*. When introducing large systems, you are managing a process of reframing your organisation's performance culture. That directly and dramatically influences the way individuals, workgroups, sub-organisations, other systems and your whole organisation behave and how it performs. (Refer to Chapter Five, "Developing a Theory in Practice" and Chapter Six, "Leading Transition for Change" where we discuss "intentionality of a person's actions".) When using a systems approach, as with the introduction of reengineering, to drive change, you will invariably experience unexpected, unwanted and uncontrolled consequential outcomes.

When you adopt an organisationally led approach and your *intent* is to design your systems to support and reinforce the desired performance outcomes, the identified organisational performance culture is predictably achieved. The maxim must be the system is employed to support and reinforce the desired organisational performance culture, not lead and drive the changes. If the systems technology is used to lead and drive the changes you will introduce displaced systems and organisational goals (Fig. 4).

Resistance to Change

These failures significantly increase the levels of resistance to any ideas of introducing new technologies and the inherent disturbing changes to work practices. This concern is expressed in the United Kingdom's National Audit office and Public Accounts Committee who scrutinise these projects, suggest that this can lead to a "risk adverse culture."

We should be able to make the connection with the fact that we all change our assumptions from our experience. When we experience the negative effects of failed change programmes, we shorten out sight lines and become "risk averse" introducing "low risk attitudes." (Refer to notional model Fig. 13, "Assumptions from Experience".)

Although IT projects have been identified as a stark reminder of the consequential effects, in the context of this book we need to keep in mind that the use of the term "technologies" includes other management technologies that also have the ability to compromise the performance of your whole organisation. For example, BP's cost reduction drive, which is the employment of a cost management technology, produced unwanted catastrophic safety disasters on other continents. This example demonstrates that national boundaries are not immune from the influence of these *management technologies*. In the example of the Nimrod disaster, rather than the airworthiness of the aircraft the preoccupation with the *displaced goal* of cost savings, created the fatal consequential outcomes.

Cycles of Dysfunctional Organisational Behaviour

Government and public sector organisations cannot fail in the way a business organisation can, so further measures are introduced to compensate for the ensuing failures. We should at this stage, begin to recognise the *cycle of dysfunctional organisational behaviour* being acted out.

The consequential effect of persisting with this dysfunctional approach for employing new technologies is highlighted through the following example. A £9.5 million High Court computer system in the UK, which was meant to 'speed up the flow of data across the Royal Courts of Justice,' is reported by the senior operational manager, to have said, "Initially good progress was made, however, over the past twelve to eighteen months significant problems with the systems have begun to emerge. The seriousness of those problems has become apparent, as has the likely cost of remediation." This culminated in the project being terminated with a further £9 million being committed to the introduction of a new system.

The above confusion relating to the introduction of new technologies brings to mind the story of someone who is lost in the remote countryside asking for directions from a farm labourer leaning on a gate. Question, by traveller: "How do I get to...?" The farm labour replies, "You can't get there from here." The not being able to "get there from here" is the disorientation process experienced when the decision-making begins by designing the systems to be employed to meet the presented organisational problems and drive the changes; creating a situation where the solution becomes the problem that serves only to further bury the existing organisational problems. We need to keep in mind that the reason for these systems being introduced was to resolve a presented organisational problem, not create a cycle of further compounded dysfunctional practices. These observable cyclical failures, of using a systems approach, prevent your organisation effectively responding to its environment.

Professor John McDermid, when contributing to a report compiled by the joint working group of Fellows of the Royal Academy of Engineering and the British Computer Society, observed that one of the problems with cutting-edge software is that it is often hard to visualise what the systems will do. "I wouldn't ask an engineer to build a 1000 meter long concrete beam suspended at one end because I know it can't be done as I have a physical perspective of it."

The lack of an organisational perspective introduces a high degree of confusion as the systems often do not "fit" the performance cultural demands of the developing organisation. The organisation's performance culture is in conflict with the developed system's culture eventually leading to a compromised unfulfilled manageable situation. The ensuing confusion and fear of failure leads to automatic explanations they have lived with longest and invoked most often.

Having a well-developed *cognitive organisational awareness* enables conflict and confusion, as it emerges, to be evaluated and sustainable solutions identified.

A lack of an organisational perspective within the decision-making process compounds the confusion, causing them to move towards the "inexplicable" (Goffman, 1974) end of the continuum, compounding the disorientation and the predictable reaction expressed by Lagadec. This usually leads to a regressive practice of employing a systems approach to defend themselves against increased anxieties and to apply solutions that further displaces the presented problem.

Techno-Managers and Increased Dependency

Often the techno-managers, particularly in the IT field, are recruited to fill a generated skills gap within your organisation. They are highly prized, as they are the 'one eyed person in the land of the blind, which makes them king.' The new owners of the technology have an IT system perspective that needs to be managed to ensure the developing systems do satisfy the organisation's responsive needs.

A huge amount of power and influence is divested, which is derived from the created dependency and the need to keep them on side. Not only has the power of influence and dependency shifted to the techno-manager it has also introduced the anxiety attached to these systems' susceptibility for technological failure. The design and use of these systems are such that a high degree of dependency is created and any failure can be "catastrophic" (Lagadec, 1993).

The created detachment is similar to the US generals who remotely micro manage the operational end of a conflict (Nyquist, 2009). This introduces an image of the general in his cocooned safe remote detached environment playing war games. It is unreal and detached, along with no generated ownership. (For further examples refer to Chapter Eleven, "Remuneration and Motivation".) The one who has the techno-skills is often the one who is promoted with the consequential effect of losing the experience and understanding of in-the-field, operational leadership practices. When "chaos arrives they are unprepared" (Lagadec, 1993).

Production Systems

The management of large quantities of generated data use management technologies that are supported by IT systems. These systems are by their very nature, *mechanistic production systems*; they simply process the data provided to a predetermined set of protocols. In large institutions the collection, storage and processing of data is required to service all the decision-making processes. The development of this knowledge base is to effectively service strategic, operational and service delivery decision-making. They must be designed to enable the executive to *monitor to manage* and therefore control the direction and operational performance of their organisation. Building into the design feedback loops within the data collection and conversion processes enables these systems to be monitored to confirm they are supporting the appropriate service delivery performance.

This is not a production process where tangible commodities are produced, in the conventional sense. It is nevertheless a data collection and conversion production system that is being employed to generate information to inform and record decision-making processes. It is an import, conversion and output systems process (Fig. 12, "Boundary Control for Task Systems"). These *management technologies* supported by IT systems are production processes that have replaced the manually recorded, data management and general information management processes.

The introduction of these technologies was to service the existing processes and improve efficiency. This leaves an unanswered question: to be more efficient at what? Usually this is coded language for reducing costs, labour and to institute regulated control. We can make a connection with reengineering being presented in a different guise (refer to Chapters One and Ten). These notional production systems have the potential, when not designed appropriately, of reducing the operative to becoming part of these mechanistic processes. With types of operative practices there is an ever-increasing desire to control the work practices, which introduces defensive "tick box" practices, further increasing unwanted operatives' technological alienation. It takes little to understand that these systems are being introduced as *control systems* not to *monitor to manage*. (For further examples refer to Chapter Ten, "Outsourcing and Contractual Management".)

The Desire to Control

In Chapter Two we identified through the use of Fig. 2, "Evolutionary Growth of an Organisation" executives crave control; and introduce systems to achieve that desire, further detaching them from their organisations.

At the other end of the organisation these practices have the capacity to alienate operatives who respond by adapting the systems to gain a degree of control over their own working environment. This operative behaviour evokes the agents of these systems to redesign them and introduce further protocols to control the operative's behaviour. It is little wonder we are experiencing what is generally referred to as the "tick box mentality." The operative as in any production system, has become part of the *machine model* that is experienced, for instance, when working on car production lines. The consequential outcome is the alienation of the operative and importantly the end user, the customer.

An amusing example of the machine model can be demonstrated in the following induction interview when completing an employment registration form. The new temporary employee had been brought out of retirement to complete a specific project. The outsourced company's young operative completed the interview and registration, the answers being recorded at a computer terminal whilst working through the computerised registration form. The name, sex and age was given, the age provided was seventy-four. The operative in front of the person could see that the woman was of mature age and had grey hair. When mindlessly trolling through the form she asked, "What are your career aspirations?" The interviewee responded, "To retire again." The computer operative unflinchingly accepted the answer.

These ritualistic practices create a myth that you are in control and well informed. The displacement provided by the system creates the comforting avoidance of the feelings attached to being disoriented. Yet, even a casual examination of these systems behaviours soon dispels the created myths. (These detached developed practices are further discussed in Chapter Ten, "Outsourcing Contractual Practices" and case studies, "Transitional Nursing Care" and "Greenwich District Hospital".) In the hospital case study, the emergency generators were institutionally tested and recorded for twenty-one years. On inspection of the practice it became evident that the generators had never been tested on full load. When tested it was discovered that there was a design fault which meant that the installed generators had never been fully commissioned.

From a behavioural perspective we need to make the connection with McGregor's X Y theory, where he identifies that leaders and managers that tend toward the autocratic (mechanistic) theory X approach, generally produce poor results. Enlightened leaders and managers use the theory Y approach, which is at the participative end of the continuum, and produce better performance outcomes and allow employees to grow and develop. (Refer to Chapter Ten, "Outsourcing Contractual Practices" where we discover that these profit centred organisations tend towards the control and autocratic end of McGregor's theory X, leading to poor service delivery outcomes.)

The monitoring to manage approach is more effective in that you retain a "hands on" feel of your organisation's performance through the ability to direct and control events. You are also able to constantly review the quality of your own and others' decision-making and when necessary, change the employed approach. (Refer to Fig. 20 "Transition For Change Processes".) Introducing these feedback loops has the advantage that you significantly reduce unwanted outcomes.

Creating an Informed Knowledge Based Organisation

To develop an *informed knowledge based organisation* we have to identify, convert and use the harvested data to create information that successfully informs our decision-making processes. The generated knowledge has to service the organisation's continuous developmental dialogue that has a focused *intent* to continuously improve your decision-making and your organisation's service delivery. To successfully achieve this, the design of the systems must have appropriate monitoring review processes that evaluate your organisation's true service delivery performance. The efficiency is derived from the data being processed in a timely, consistent, and an appropriate form, to enable, at the service interface, to effectively deliver the desired service performance and decision-making practices. We have to keep in mind that all organisations have a *service delivery outcome* and to ensure this we need to monitor to manage.

We have briefly addressed the development of production systems, which are invasive and demand our attention to service the developed technological protocols. The invasive nature of technologies has to be understood as it directly affects the behaviour of our organisations, work practices and the work-life balance of the employees. These practices, when overlaid onto an existing dysfunctional organisation, will directly influence the strategic decision-making processes and their outcomes. For example, the identification of services within that organisation that may be considered to be better provided by outsourcing these services. It takes little to begin to understand that these outsourcing decisions can be inappropriate.

The introduction of *machine model operative practices* often suggest that they can simply be outsourced, as it is a controllable ritualistic mechanistic process and sometimes they become defined as "commodities" (Lacity, Willcocks & Feeny, 1995). The example of the interview, discussed above, and the ritualistic practices, creates the displaced comforting myth of being in control and well informed. (A further example of inappropriate outsourcing decision is discussed in the "Transition Nursing Care" case study.) Outsourcing is often misused to transfer, displace and push away (dump) a problem rather than work through the *transition for change* processes to provide sustainable solutions.

External Influences

The above observations, particularly the strategic decision-making, for introducing new technologies, needs to be further explored. We have only explored the invasiveness of technologies when they are deployed within an organisation. We need to briefly explore the invasiveness of technologies from our organisation's environment. (Refer to Fig. 11, "Managing Organisational Boundaries".) Developed available technologies are one of the factors we have to examine when scanning our organisation's environment, along with the potential impact.

This environmental scanning process also services the search for solutions, panaceas and quick fixes, to resolve existing problems. These technological solutions are imported and others become invasive through their development and prolific use in other industries. The consequential outcomes are that these technological developments will act to influence your own organisation's behaviour.

An example that we can all relate to is the containerisation of goods for shipping. This was developed to satisfy the service of the supply-chain for manufacturing companies that employed Just-in-Time (JIT) management systems for the control and delivery of components. These management systems were originally introduced to reduce the capital stock holdings and to support the management and control of contracted suppliers.

The consequential impact of containerisation was the main reason for the London and other national docking facilities becoming redundant. The adoption of this new technology reduces the dependency on the dockworkers and their respective unions. This was a growing international technological influence that not only changed the docking industry, it changed the design of ships and the location of docking facilities to access deeper waters to accommodate these huge container carrying vessels. For these reasons, and this was repeated in other parts of the United Kingdom, the London Docks was closed and the containerisation docking facilities were moved further down the river Thames, out of London, to a new site developed in Tilbury, Essex. (Refer to case study, "Canary Wharf".)

Where Trade Union activity is either politically motivated or to do with preying on the vulnerability of an industry, they resort to making, what is considered to be, unreasonable demands with regards to pay and conditions. Those industries will vigorously scan their environment to search for available *management technologies* that will reduce their vulnerability and to reintroduce a degree of predictable control of their organisation. They may in conjunction with their environmental scanning also resort to funding the development of bespoke management technologies to resolve the presented problem of unpredictable collective bargaining. Essentially Trade Unions' behaviour often has the consequential effect of accelerating the deployment of new technologies.

An example of these processes has been recently experienced when the Transport Union RMT threatened strike action during the 2013 Olympic Games, to further their demands for additional payments during the games. Although this is not a judgement as to who was right or wrong, it did receive a reported response from the Mayor of London that he would accelerate the introduction of further automation.

Another response is to outsource services allowing the terms and conditions for those employees being radically changed to prevent unwanted collective action. One of the conditions is that many of these employees are on one-year renewable contracts. Potential troublemaker's contracts are simply not renewed.

In Search of a Solution

To find solutions to the unacceptable record of introducing IT systems, a joint workgroup was charged, under the chairmanship of Basil Butler, with the task of examining why many major IT projects fail. They identified there was a lack of professionalism in software engineering that could even be dangerous in safety-critical systems. They concluded that Britain is failing to produce software engineers and managers with IT and project management skills to commission and execute complex IT projects.

They identified that these designers needed to develop these skills but failed to understand that the recipient organisation's leaders have to have developed complementary skills to lead and direct these new competencies. The primary skill must be a well-developed *cognitive organisational awareness* that services their ability to lead an organisation and their decision-making processes, positioning these organisational leaders to understand that any *management technology* must be designed to support and reinforce the organisations service delivery performance, which in turn enables them to direct and control the activities of these well-trained systems designers.

The assumption, by the joint working group, that developing the systems designers' capabilities will provide the solution, however intended, is unworkable. Unfortunately it puts the cart before the horse. This can only lead to the conclusion that the current failures will continue to be all-pervasive unless the management of those skills is balanced and complemented by the development of effective *organisational leaders* with well-developed *cognitive organisational awareness* and good *organisational problem solving* skills.

The chairman is reported to have concluded, 'We looked at a range of studies showing that only around sixteen per cent of IT projects can be considered truly successful.' Even conservative estimates put the cost of such failures into tens of billions of pounds across the EU.

This created reliance on technology identifies a further issue, which is the inability to effectively apply the technology to service the overall organisation's needs. This can be demonstrated by the dilemma that Professor John McDermid, a member of the joint workgroup, had of 'not having a physical perspective'. This suggests that when introducing new technology these designers and the owners of these new technologies do not have a well-developed *cognitive organisational awareness* that fits that organisation.

Systems Design and Intent

The organisation is the vehicle that enables complex tasks to be completed effectively. The *intent* of these systems, by necessity, must be introduced to enable the executive leadership to monitor to manage and control the overall business direction and performance. By definition the systems design must follow the design and development of the future state of the organisation. The IT systems must have the capacity to remain responsive to that organisation's needs and enable that organisation to continuously respond to its environment.

The *intent* of the systems is to support and reinforce the decision-making and responsive performance of the organisation, which implies that the function of the organisation is developed and completed first. The systems are designed and developed to match the organisation's future performance culture. In each case the organisation and systems designers have to make a personal transition to enable the changes and future organisational responsive performance culture to be developed.

The maxim, is that when you need to improve your organisation's performance, you have to begin by leading and managing the *organisation's transition for change processes* before introducing any *management technologies*. The *intent* of the technology is there only to complement, support and reinforce the identified on-going performance delivery of that organisation. This practice translates into the maxim *form follows function*. This further translates into the practice (Chapter Four) where we addressed the enquiry, "Do we design downward or upwards?" We find that we define the service delivery requirements and then we design the organisation and its management technologies to service these requirements.

Systems are command led and those commands are a function of the *intent* of those who developed the brief, the designer's interpretation and those who operate and use them. It is these people who are making the decisions, not the systems. For example, the government needs to make changes to existing social care payment practices. These changes are at the customer interface and need to be understood in terms of how the system will need to respond to the service performance delivery. The service culture will change to satisfy the *intent* of the redefined care provision. To satisfy these changes the systems have to be redesigned to service the new service performance culture. The systems have to be redesigned to also service the strategic and operational decision-making practices. These changes are being used to alter the social dependency benefit culture.

Existing benefit recipients are being required to make the transition from dependency towards an independent self-supporting culture. These changes are not only organisational but are being used for social and cultural changes. The interface with the identified targeted client base must be sensitively managed. These changes at the interface with the targeted client base will generate anxieties in both the operative and the client. Usually these anxieties, experienced by the operatives, will be defended by the use of management technologies detaching the client, causing further frustration, alienation and resistance.

Often we find that because leaders and managers do not have a well-developed *cognitive organisational awareness*, they lack the ability to define the organisation's responsive future needs, to create a workable brief for the systems design and therefore, the ability to control and manage the invasive behaviour of the system. Deming (1986), places 85% of the responsibility and blame on the systems designed by management, with only 15% attributable to the workforce for unintended consequences.

These failures to understand the consequences of your decision-making and implementation strategies tend to reinforce the reliance on technologies to solve problems (Deming, 1986). It also creates situations where inappropriate deference is given to the techno-manager along with the transference of power. Interestingly Deming's 85% attributed percentage almost correlates, with the identified government and public sector IT systems failures discussed earlier.

Systems Behaviour and Decision-Making

We have extensively explored systems behaviour and how they can directly affect the performance of your organisation. Systems have to be employed, to enable you to effectively monitor to manage your organisation and to enable you to direct and control events. This can only be achieved by designing those systems to directly contribute to your strategic and operational decision-making, that must be designed to service your organisation's overall service delivery performance. There is a requirement, that these various systems complement one another, to prevent one system or the other conflicting and negating another system's performance. Simply, the control of the business performance is derived from the ability and *intent* to *monitor to manage* which in turn enables you to *control and direct* the performance of your organisation's service delivery.

We find that many systems are designed to control events rather than monitor to manage, which had the effect of detaching the leadership and management from their organisation. For example BP's UK based executive instituted a system of cost control. The consequential effects, played out in the USA, compromised safety practice. The accumulative effect of these disastrous events were not understood or heeded, leading to the Gulf of Mexico off shore drilling disaster and the eventual removal of the Chief Executive.

The above is an example of detached systems management, where a management technology is used to drive the changes, which, creates a displaced *intent*. In this case a cost management system introduced the consequential effect of compromising the safety systems and procedures. We cannot fail to recall Deming's inversion cost model, in

Chapter One, "Cost driven single initiatives that become the primary function will produce short-term gains but over time will become less beneficial." If we examine the enormous endless consequential litigation costs and compare this with the potential cost saving by reducing the safety budgets, we would not introduce these cost saving practices. We would, in turn, ensure through the directed *intent*, that the budgeted safety costs were being employed to effectively protect the company from litigation.

These conflicts of interest will automatically be felt and create anxieties because of the incompatibility of the conflicting cultures that are being generated by the systems and that of the organisation's requisite performance culture. This can create a situation, reported in Chapter Three that trying to translate the presented organisational, political and individual motives becomes extremely difficult. When immersed and responsible for the outcome, it feels "as if" you are working in an asylum, the activities are insanely irrational, contradictory and confusing. The symptoms of "Why Leaders Mislead" in Chapters Five and Seven, will begin to emerge as their levels of anxiety increase.

We should, also, make the connection with the Nimrod example, where the '...political influence of the UK government's identified *intent* created an 'overwhelming objective of finding savings' causing 'organisational trauma' (Nimrod Enquiry 2010). Substitute BP Head Offices in the UK for government, and you have created the same set of political dynamics.

These systems, when deployed, have attached to them the sponsors' perceived authority, and perceived power to influence career decisions, which can cause managers to abrogate their responsibility, and the organisations' performance, to the perceived centre of power. We, when introducing new management technologies, must be aware of the perceived political authority that becomes attached to these single initiatives and their misapplied consequential behavioural outcomes. These politically induced environments that the recipient of the instruction will respond to, introduce further dysfunctional decision-making practices. (Refer to Milgram experiment (1961) to develop an understanding of compliance, Fig. 3, "Politics, Career and Overt Organisation" Fig. 4 "Displaced Organisational Goals" refer to Chapter Seven, "Adaptive

Organisational Leadership" and Chapter Twelve, "Development, Training and Recruitment" where we discuss Merton's research on 'Performance Evaluation and Promotion.')

Contractual Role Positioning

The practice of letting, leading and managing the contract follows on from the processes of leading transition for change where the brief and scope of the contract is identified and defined. How you make and implement your decisions will directly determine how well your strategic intent is achieved.

Contractual role positioning is an important practice as it enables you to lead and manage the implementation of the contract for introducing new technologies, and to also ensure the technologies meet the contracted needs of your organisation's future service delivery performance outcomes. The contract manager and the future organisational leaders have to position themselves "as if" they are bridging between, even though they represent the client's needs, the contract supplier and the client. This is where the effective contract management must exist, as it's where the implementation processes are developed and managed effectively, Fig. 35.

ROLE POSITIONING

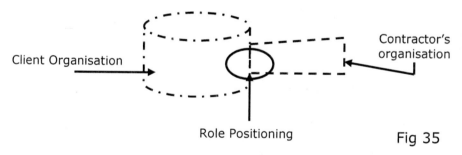

Role Positioning   Fig 35

This deliberate positioning is *on the boundary of the organisation,* where we are required to manage the permeability of our organisation's boundaries and those external influences, which can and do affect our overall organisation's performance. These practices are designed to ensure the contract is delivered on time and on budget and matches the scope of the brief for servicing the client's organisational service performance delivery needs. These expectations are pursued to ensure that the contractor is able and enabled to deliver the contract as specified and to also ensure that there is a *shared focused intent* that matches that of the client's organisation. (Refer to Chapter Ten, "Outsourcing Contractual Practices" where we discuss the necessary alignment of the contractor's activities to satisfy your organisation's performance needs.)

This intellectual positioning within the space between the client and the contractor can be better understood as managing and regulating, at the two boundaries, the transition from one organisational culture to another. That creates the *state of flux* that we are attempting to regulate and manage. The positioning of the project manager and the contract manager is an important practice to ensure the appropriate transference of the new technology. (Refer also to Chapter Ten, "Outsourcing and Contractual Practices" and the case studies; "The Millennium Dome" and "Transitional Nursing Care" to understand how precipitous dysfunctional practices develop.)

To prepare and successfully achieve the agreed outcomes there must be a clear and shared understanding of how you want the organisation to perform and behave once the technology has been introduced. It requires that you start where you want to finish in service delivery terms. We are addressing the question: do you design downward or upwards? This demands that you work through the transition for change processes, where we define the service delivery needs and the nature of the organisation that has to be designed to achieve those needs. This will enable you to determine the type and nature of the organisation you want to develop.

When working through the *transition for change processes* there is a stage where you begin to work "as if" you were working in that identified *future state*. It provides you with a conscious perception of your organisation developing an almost tangible sensory feel, and the development of that necessary intellectual and intuitive feel of the organisation you are about to lead and manage. (Refer to Chapter Six, "Leading Transition for Change".)

Within this process the systems, such as IT, can be evaluated in terms of its application and effectiveness. Effectiveness is determined by the system's ability to reinforce the identified future delivery performance culture and the on-going decision-making processes. For this to be effective, the systems need to be able to respond to the on-going responsive needs of your organisation. You avoid the current practice of introducing a one-size-fits-all system that is unresponsive to an organisation's need to continually respond to its environmental influences. You subsequently avoid the current practice of overlaying the technology onto an existing dysfunctional performance culture and the risk of it being rejected.

Having worked through these processes not only enables you to produce a contract that can be managed in terms of the organisation's needs, it defines the behaviour of not only the system but also the behaviour of the providing contractor. It is absolutely critical that the contractor's *organisational thinking* is aligned and managed to ensure that the design and developed systems reinforce your organisation's identified future state and the organisation's performance culture.

The problem with working with the existing dysfunctional organisation is that it has framed and created "mental models" (Senge, 1993). These "mental models" are, by association, in themselves dysfunctional. It is where leaders and managers retreat to when there is "chaos" that is introduced when leading transition for change caused through the need to introduce new technologies. With this in mind and having worked through the *transition for change processes*, you are now in a position to evaluate the nature and application of any technology. All of these activities are used to position your organisation and yourself to enable you to begin the processes of developing a clear achievable brief that has to be prepared before anyone is asked to tender.

From this position you are able to understand the real problems and needs of the organisation to provide a clear brief and terms of reference for engaging and contracting a provider. You are able to design and develop the contract to enable it to be let and managed effectively. A maxim that applies when letting a contract is that the way you develop and let the contract enables you to manage, monitor and control the contract. These processes support your ability to effectively implement the strategic *intent* through the introduction of new technologies. By working through these *transition processes* you would be contracting and applying the technology to the newly created situation and not overlaying the technology onto an existing dysfunctional organisational culture.

The techno-manager's role can be clearly defined in terms of them being able to develop and maintain these management systems to continuously reinforce the overall performance of your organisation. They don't become detached from these organisational processes and retreat into managing the systems for the system's sake. This practice of engagement has an important intent that is to prevent the systems creating displaced goals (Fig. 4), increasing dependency and you becoming detached from the operational performance of your organisation.

The benefits in time, cost and delivery service outcomes are enormous. At the very least it has to be far better than the existing practices where the current spend and cost of failed IT projects are inordinate. It is a practice that would significantly reduce the enormous financial losses and number of failed IT projects that are reported in the United Kingdom, the European Union and the USA. When looking at the presented problem from an organisational perspective, this becomes an obvious approach for providing cost effective, sustainable working solutions.

The case for using an organisational approach must be evident. It is an essential practice if you wish to significantly reduce the enormous level of IT project failures and the high revenue cost of introducing these systems. The process for introducing these systems is further developed in Chapter Six, "Leading Transition for Change." This is the way forward, but we do need a distinct mind-shift, to *thinking organisationally*, to create the necessary breakthrough in this endeavour by challenging the traditional, out of date redundant ways of systems thinking when introducing new technologies.

A Way Forward

The above observations require that those who are responsible for improving the organisation's performance must work through the *transition for change* processes before developing the scope and brief for designing the management technologies and computer systems. Working through the transition for change identifies the *primary task*, the business service *intent*, clarifies the scope of the brief of the systems to be designed, and importantly, the system's behavioural expectations. This approach will enable systems to be designed to service your organisation's future needs and not rework the existing problems in different guises.

Using an organisational approach has the added value of reducing the system's redundancy factor, by designing the systems to enable your organisation's needs to be continuously responsive to its environment. This adopted approach enables your organisation, which is your service delivery vehicle and performance platform, to be appropriately designed.

This requires a major paradigm shift from the current systems thinking for providing solutions to existing organisational problems, to a practice of *thinking organisationally* and using an *organisational led approach* to provide *sustainable solutions*.

It becomes obvious that the designers of these systems are being placed in an artificial situation, however well trained. They are applying their skills by interpreting the client's requirement on the hoof as the client invariably has a limited *cognitive organisational awareness* of that organisation's future needs and how these systems should behave at the delivery end of the organisation. The designers resort to what they know by tapping into other experiences of designing other systems. They know the expansive capability of their systems and the nature of this open situation encourages them to fully explore and deploy them. Their *intent* is to provide solutions to the presented problems but once again because of their training and systems orientation, they provide systems solutions and recreate the cyclic situation where the solution becomes the problem.

When designing cars, the shape and style of the car is designed first and the electrical control-wiring loom is then designed to fit that specific car's designed performance needs. Adapting another car's wiring loom to fit the new design would be unthinkable, as they know it would not work. The same principle applies to designing and developing your future organisation and its management systems.

This scenario is a recipe for failure no matter how well the IT professional has been trained in "system's architecture and project management." If the organisation has not been designed and structured to perform in the future-state, the system has no organisational framework for it to be attached. The designer is designing the system to match the dysfunctional practices that already exist and their efforts will only serve to further compound the existing dysfunctional organisational behaviour. (Refer to Chapter Two and Three, "Why Organisations become Dysfunctional" and "The Enemy Within and Why Change fails".) This is a waste of their enormous talent, which can be harnessed effectively through the use of an *organisational led approach.*

We can notionally consider that the problem was displaced onto the joint workgroup where they concluded that, "Britain is failing to produce software engineers and managers with IT and project management skills to commission and execute complex IT projects." While this may be true, the real problem must remain with those interpretive "agents "that are charged with the responsibility for leading and managing the organisation. They must have the skills to direct and enable the system's designers to design the systems to complement the future organisation's performance culture. The existing abrogated approach simply transfers the responsibility onto the system's engineers for the future performance of your organisation. This is an example of *goal displacement* (Fig. 4), where the problem and its solution are transferred onto the system's engineers.

The organisational leader is the interpretive "agent" and must remain responsible for the design, development and introduction of any management technology. They, through their well-developed *cognitive organisational awareness*, should bring to the management of projects that *intuitive physical perspective*. That is the intuitive feel, that missing perspective Professor McDermid expressed above. It cannot be overemphasised how critical a well-developed *cognitive organisational awareness* can be used for resolving the majority of the problems of IT systems failures, cost overruns and systems being developed that can be described as "not fit for purpose" for example the failed High Court computer system.

CHAPTER TEN

OUTSOURCING AND CONTRACTUAL PRACTICES

Decision Making and Implementation

This chapter is an exploration of the *management technology* of outsourcing, its use and misuse, examined from an organisational perspective. It provides you with an opportunity to explore the nature of strategic and operational decision-making. It should develop your understanding as to what you are outsourcing and why you need to specifically regulate and manage these services. The proffered organisational approach enables you to position yourself to design, develop, negotiate and effectively regulate all your contracts. (Refer to contractual practices and positioning in Chapter Nine.) This exploration should also enable you to decide whether this practice adds value, gives you that *business advantage,* is a means for displacing government regulations and transferring intractable problems and/or is it simply a costly management fad.

This chapter and the previous chapter overlap to a certain degree and should be considered together. The common denominators are the invasiveness of management technologies, their ability to detach the executive from the leadership, and management of the operational performance, along with the need to identify the decision-making processes, development, letting and the regulatory management of these *service provider's* contracts.

We identified in the previous chapter that the introduction of new management technologies that the executive authority must at all times remain fully engaged in the strategic and operational decision-making processes. The failure to do so can create unmanageable and even disastrous outcomes. The other issue we discussed was the fact that when you introduce these forms of management technologies, they often operate outside the boundaries of your own organisation's regulatory boundaries.

Understanding Outsourcing in Organisational Terms

Providers of outsourcing services are profit-centred organisations and will develop their systems and practices to minimise cost and to increase their profits, which requires that you develop the appropriate regulatory management practices in terms of your own organisation. Particularly if you accept that when a business is purely cost driven, quality is invariably compromised (Deming).

Regulatory practices are created when you transfer these services across the boundary of your organisation, which creates a transitional "state of flux" (Fig.2) from one operating organisational culture to another. (We can use Fig. 35, "Contract Management – Role Positioning" to notionally demonstrate these relationships.) Except that many of these forms of service contracts do cross the boundaries of your core business activities. Understanding these invasive practices is critical as they change the nature of the regulatory requirement that has to be instituted by the host organisation. As these practices translate into the process and practices of letting and managing these service contracts, knowing where your organisational boundaries of influence exist is important. It is at these boundaries that you, as the "agent" have to interpret and translate the created "states of flux" and their implications for your overall organisation's performance.

Within this critical decision-making process the "intentionality" has to be examined and clearly understood, as this will directly influence the decision-making behaviour of the outsourcing practices and your ability to achieve the desired improved performance (that desired business advantage). It is important to ensure and test that the service provider's organisation has the competence to complement and satisfy your organisation's service delivery performance culture. Throughout this chapter we shall explore the management of this *joint intent* to underwrite the importance of being clear about your organisation's *intent and your provider's intent* throughout the *decision-making processes* when deciding to outsource services.

Why Outsource?

Examples often used to explain outsourcing is that an organisation may outsource its landscaping function to a service provider that specialises in landscaping, as landscaping is irrelevant to the core operation of that company. The company may also be providing insurance or manufacturing services. The claim is that these companies can concentrate on their core functions. Companies and public services that outsource functions such as payroll management to those accountancy firms that specialise in payroll management, is another example.

These two comparative examples of possible outsourcing functions each have distinct contractual practices that emanate from their regulatory requirement. The failure of the landscape contractor to meet the contracted commitment will not directly affect your organisation's operating performance. Any failure by the payroll contractor will directly impact on the operating performance of your organisation. Simply, if employees are not paid appropriately they will redirect their attention to rectify the problem. You have to ensure that the personal and private information of each employee is secure and not sold on to others.

In organisational terms, you have, through this contractual arrangement, extended your organisation's management boundaries and created a *state of flux,* which needs to be regulated and managed to ensure you monitor to manage and control these processes. This practice of design in the regulatory practices ensures that, although you are delegating the responsibility and the authority, these contractors remain accountable for the quality of their service delivery.

To facilitate this practice it becomes essential to examine and understand the notion of *performance culture continuum,* along with the *dependent and interdependent relationship* of the service delivery arrangements. This developed information and understanding informs your decision-making, which enables you to develop your contracting practices to ensure the supplier meets and services your organisation's strategic decision-making and overall operational performance.

These examples have identified that the nature of the function being outsourced requires different corporate decision-making and contracted regulatory management. These practices ensure that the contracted service provision is provided within the context of your own organisation's service performance culture. In other words the outsourcing service provider has to design and develop their organisational management practices to reinforce and complement your own organisation's overall service delivery performance culture. If both parties do not understand these complementary arrangements, the level of regulatory management to ensure the provision of control significantly increases or you will lose control.

Why the Confusion?

It is argued that outsourcing is a cost saving strategy when used properly; that it can offer greater budgetary flexibility and control, and allows organisations to pay for the services they need, when they need them. That it also reduces the need to hire and train specialised staff, for example, provides access to fresh engineering expertise and reduces capital and operating costs. It becomes more affordable to purchase goods from companies with comparative advantages than it would be to produce those items internally. In essence, you are attempting to achieve a *business advantage* through improved product and service delivery. The critical difference we need to understand is that there is a reference to "goods" when most of today's outsourcing issues and contracts relate to the provision of services.

Manufacturing companies have been successfully employing these practices, obtaining goods and their attached service delivery, for many years, which form their supply chain and the ability to practice Just in Time (JIT). All of which have sound logical process decision-making, economic reasoning and distinct *business advantages*. These dynamic management technologies are strictly managed, regulated and controlled to assure their developed dependent supply chain. Critically, those companies that become part of the supply chain adopt and adapt their service delivery culture to fit that of the primary manufacturing company's service delivery performance culture. At the same time the primary manufacturing company will extend its regulatory boundary management into those supply companies to ensure that the specified contractual requirements are fulfilled at source.

Each of those manufactured products that have been contracted out to other manufacturers still service the core business needs of that organisation. For example, if a manufacturer providing components fails to meet the quality standards or the prescribed time frame, the whole of the manufacturing and assembly process could be affected. This may take the form of late product delivery, which may affect production and product delivery schedules. The poor quality of a specific product could create safety concerns and products being recalled. Without labouring the point any further, these two examples create customer dissatisfaction.

There may be contractual repercussions but these are retrospective and do not alter the current situation, that the core business service may have been disrupted and may have long term damaging consequences. (The Toyota example, discussed in Chapters Three and Six, is representative of the issues being discussed.)

The distinction we have to make when examining these comparative contractual situations, is that the supply chain deals with a physical commodity with an attached service provision. The current practice of outsourcing services that have less tangible outcomes has the created difficulty of measuring to monitor the necessary service performance delivery. As a consequence, they need a different form of contracted regulatory management practice to ensure they complement and service your organisation's overall delivery performance culture.

When you begin to examine these practices that have been effectively employed over a number of years we should ask the question – why has outsourcing become different to contracting other provisions? The existing process for supply-chain outsourcing within the manufacturing industry is simply based on creating and maintaining a *business advantage*. Outsourcing of services is attractive in that it fits the desire of many leaders and managers seeking panaceas to presented problems within an organisation, and not necessarily the achievement of a distinct *business advantage*.

When you examine the case studies it should become obvious that the current leadership and management practices do not have the capacity to effectively resolve presented organisational problems.

Often the current leadership and management practices are dysfunctional and serve only to compound existing problems. This resonates with Albert Einstein's observations; "It's the same kind of thinking that created the problem in the first place." The inability to resolve existing problems when using a systems approach and/or when seeking a panacea, outsourcing can become attractive, as a means of displacing and/or transferring a problem; "it's that same kind of thinking."

Fig. 28 ("Turbulence, Competency and Role Relationships") is useful in that when you inappropriately let an outsourcing contract you are creating a turbulent situation that will demand a good deal of your attention to regulate the ill-specified regulatory requirement. When you let the contract, to enable to monitor to manage and control there is less requirement for you to excessively regulate the process. This notion of competency is important in that when you introduce these forms of *management technologies* you control the degree of regulatory management and the time you have to invest. It is the same demand placed on a leader when developing their workgroups (Chapter Eight).

Before making the decision to outsource it is important to identify whether we are attempting to displace an unresolved dysfunctional practice or whether we are seeking genuine *business advantages*. This can only be determined by working through the *transition for change processes* as this has the capacity to identify those areas where your organisation has dysfunctional practices. The identification of the real and underlying problems allows sustainable solutions to be identified. The provision of a new frame of reference enables the systems and procedures to be realigned to reinforce the developing organisation's future performance culture.

Decision-Making and Implementation Processes

Working through the transition for change process enables the identification of the existing dysfunctional decision-making practices that are creating these unwanted outcomes. This initial evaluative process will inform your decision-making as to whether to outsource or not. The value of this approach is that it enables you to clearly define the service organisation, its leadership and management style, and the values that need to be imbued in the organisation's service provision. Subsequently the systems can be designed to ensure that the management processes can be managed and regulated. An important outcome of using this process is that it enables you to position yourself at the boundary of each organisation. This contractual positioning and working through the transition for change processes allows you to have an almost tangible, felt state (that all-important cognitive organisational awareness) of your organisation and its processes that enables you to effectively negotiate and regulate the letting and management of any contracts.

Current outsourcing decision-making practices create a detached dependency. A termination clause may be included within your contract, but may be extremely difficult to implement as you have limited alternatives to replace the existing services. This is an important issue as the clause is worthless if you are unable to implement it, leaving you feeling impotent, as you are unable to effectively hold the contractor to account. The following examples will identify the nature and degree of this problem:

Interestingly, when many of those outsourced contracts are let, we find that often the majority of those employed by the contractor are existing employees. This leaves the question – why is it that the contractor can improve the service being delivered when the majority of employees are from the original service organisation? The major effect of outsourcing is that the operatives' terms and conditions of employment are controlled by short term contracts, or have self-employed statuses, reduced hourly rates and that these employment practices are designed to displace increasing burdensome employment regulations. Often the service delivery is no better than the original in-house services but they may, in the short term, provide cost benefits. These cost driven decisions are often the nemesis of future presented organisational problems. (Refer to Deming's Cost/quality inversion model and outsourcing prison services.)

It is reported that two leading outsource service providers to the public sectors are suspected of "potential fraudulent practices." Serco has a £285 million contract to transport prisoners from their prison to appear in court. The Ministry of Justice conducted a detailed audit and as a result of an investigation into their tagging contract, subsequently identified that the Serco staff were recording prisoners as being ready for court when they in fact were not. As a consequence the Justice

Secretary has asked the City of London police to investigate alleged fraud. G4S, the other main outsourcing public service contractor, is also under investigation. The Justice Secretary has asked the Serious Fraud office to investigate potential overcharging by tens of millions of pounds.

The dilemma for the Justice Secretary is that these international contractors have created a huge dependency that makes it extremely difficult to terminate these contracts. The degree of government services that have been outsourced to these and other contractors is numerous and large, creating a situation where the contractor is almost immune to sanctions. In many cases the level of dependency makes it impossible to terminate these contracts. They have to resort to stopping other negotiations and potential contracts as a means for curtailing these huge international contractors. If you cannot regulate and control the contract you have to reconsider whether to let the contract.

A further examination of outsourcing practices has identified the use of contractual arrangements to satisfy political dogma that has compounded the inability to review and renew the practice within the provision of private prisons. The Labour Party had promised during a previous election campaign to return all the private prisons to the public sector (Harding, 1997). He records Jack Straw's (1995) reported comments on the subject, "The privatisation of prisons is morally repugnant... It must be the responsibility of the state to look after those the courts decide it is in society's interest to imprison. It is not appropriate for people to profit from incarceration." "The priority, in Labour's view is to implement the reforms recommended by the Woolf Inquiry (Woolf and Tumim 1991, "Prison Disturbances"), and their fear is that privatisation would cut across this primary objective. On the other hand the, the present government seems committed to further privatisation."

Harding asks – which of these competitive scenarios is the most likely? The answer is: neither of them. Whichever party wins the election, it will find its hands tied and its most radical positions unattainable. Labour will be inhibited by the terms of the Deregulation and Contracting out Act 1994, which is calculated to impose substantial cost constraints upon a U-turn in all areas of the UK's extensive privatisation programme. There would be complex legal repudiation in terms of the Act, and the expectation of prolonged litigation would be high. Whilst the principle of statute could be simply be repealed, in practice this might well incur too high a political cost (Harding, 1997).

Yet, Harding writes, "The Conservative government, on the other hand, will find the private sector somewhat reluctant to pick up contracts to run existing, operational prisons. The leverage which generally makes running private prisons financially viable is the opportunity, in staffing and structural terms, to 'start again': to eliminate old practices, rigid rosters, sick-leave expectation, open-ended overtime, and so on. Almost without exception, private operators have taken on prisons where nothing at all has been inherited – no staff, no prisoners, no programmes and no work practices. Yet employment rights and conditions at existing prisons are such that no government could deliver a 'clean' industrial situation for new contractors."

The current Conservative government's solution to these apparent intractable problems has been to institute a programme of disposing of existing penal institution for housing and commercial development. Creating a total dependency on outsourcing private contractors. The notion of dumping a problem rather than developing sustainable solution comes to mind.

Harding's observations reaffirm the fact that many organisations outsource intractable problems and create further dysfunctional intractable problems. The government is unable or unwilling to change the existing conditions of employment and work from a 'clean sheet'. Instead they have created a situation of providing guaranteed revenue stream for these private contractors to enjoy, even though they have still not been able to address the original problem within existing prisons. Had they had the understanding in organisational terms and had the ability to work through an appropriate transition for change process they would have been able to provide a sustainable working solution to the operation of existing prisons. This may have provided a working organisation model that would enable either government to find an organisational model that satisfies the primary task and their political agendas. Importantly the government of the day would have remained in control and not at the mercy of these international private operating companies.

The enactment of these historic political and defensive dogmas is not designed to achieve a business advantage but to block the imposition of the opposition's own historic dogmatic practices that of bringing many services back into the public sector. "The fears that privatisation would cut across this primary objective" (Woolf Inquiry) even if acted out, cannot be changed.

Even so these "fears" expressed, in the Woolf enquiry, are reasonable when you consider the Stanford prison experiment in which twenty-four normal college students were randomly assigned to be "prisoners" or "guards" in a mock prison located in the basement of the psychology building at Stanford University. The students quickly began acting out their roles, with "guards" becoming sadistic and "prisoners" showing extreme passivity and depression. Prisoners and guards rapidly adapted to their roles, stepping beyond the boundaries of what had been predicted and leading to dangerous and psychologically damaging situations. One-third of the guards were judged to have exhibited "genuine" sadistic tendencies, while many prisoners were emotionally traumatized and five had to be removed from the experiment early. Ethical concerns surrounding the famous experiment often draw comparisons to the Milgram experiment. One of the underlying reasons that this created prison environment rapidly deteriorated was the style of leadership and the created permissive custodial climate.

This brief exploration should provide an indicator as to why these private contractors can operate with a high degree of impunity, as they are the power brokers, even though the government is their paymaster.

These examples highlight the impossible position even the Secretary of State is attempting to regulate. The reality is that all the power is invested in those companies providing the services and from a United Kingdom Ltd perspective, is an inappropriate business model. It should be recorded that the UK government is not the only one who find themselves in the same inverse negotiating position.

A further reflection on the above dysfunctional decision-making is that these organisations, particularly as they contain vulnerable individuals, should not become political footballs for the two main parties to impose their political dogmas. A cross-party workgroup, jointly working on the presented issues using an organisational perspective, could have identified sustainable organisational practices that effectively managed the various needs of those incarcerated. Using this approach would have enabled those members of the workgroup to be able to express their political philosophies and have the opportunity, using the organisation as a *third party*, to translate their views into a common intent that serviced the delivery needs of these institutions. The potential outcome could have worked through the transition for change processes where the working practices were aligned to the true needs of the organisation. The quality of the service could be regulated, managed and controlled. Accountability could be easily exercised and appropriate sanctions applied. All of which amounts to a complete reversal of the existing and perpetrated dysfunctional decision-making practices and still satisfying either political interest.

The attached assumption to these observations is that, whatever party is in government they are responsible for leading and managing UK Limited. This assumes that they develop and employ an appropriate business model that works "as if" they were running a viable business. There is a failure to consistently provide education programmes within schools to develop our children to satisfy future UK intellectual and skill competencies that fit the future needs of UK Limited. That has led to skill shortages that have to be imported. Lord Baker, a former education secretary, writes: "It is a disgrace that after spending more than a decade in state schools, so many young British people do not have the skills to get a job. Meanwhile, companies are crying out for skilled workers and for young people from elsewhere in Europe to come here and get jobs."

The assumption that, whatever political party forms a government, they are responsible for the leadership and management of UK Limited. Applying an organisational approach would identify those service provisions such as prisons, health care and education that need to be designed to protect and support those vulnerable individuals that are required to use these services. Understanding this tenet will directly identify the necessary organisational performance culture along with the appropriate leadership and management style. None of these services can be developed on the whim of opposing political dogmas. Changing the way politicians view how these services are delivered will directly influence their decision-making and significantly reduce the depleting dysfunctional outcome we experience to date.

The above examples are not an attack on the contractors. Contractors have to have clearly defined boundaries of responsibility, authority and accountability. It is the responsibility of the person letting the contracts to ensure that the contract enables the service contractor to deliver the requirement of the contract within the defined boundaries. This means, for example, that the identified person responsible for delivering the contract must not be parachuted in once the contract has been signed. This allows you to ensure that the person representing the contractor is capable of delivering the service expectations. If you were requiring a person to head up a service within your organisation you would work hard to select the right person. (When you understand the influence of the employed leadership style used during the Stanford prison experiment you will soon begin to understand why this is critical.) If you allow the contractor to appoint whom they want in post you are allowing the contractor to dictate the leadership and management style. Remember they are reported to have better resources; this is one of the reasons for outsourcing. Therefore, it is only reasonable that you are party to the decision-making of who will lead and manage your service provision. The following exploration should reinforce these minimum expectations:

Consequences of not using an Organisational Approach

When working through the *transition for change process* you also identify the *performance culture continuum* that has to be developed across your entire organisation. This allows you to develop a perspective of how your organisation's services, departmental activities and technologies relate to one another. You are able to identify their dependent and interdependent relationships, and acquire an understanding of the consequential outcomes of how a decision and change made in one part of your organisation affects the performance in another.

Using these evaluative and developmental processes we are able to identify many of the underlying causes contributing to the failures within current outsourcing contractual practices by examining the

Cornwall NHS out-of-hours GP service that had been contracted to a private company.

A prelude to this examination is provided by Margaret Hodge MP, chair of the Public Accounts Committee, who is reported to have said, "It is disgraceful that the public had to rely on whistle-blowers to find out that the out-of-hours GP services in Cornwall, provided by a private contractor Serco, was short-staffed and substandard, and that service data was being manipulated, making the company's performance look better than it was." "These large private providers are better at negotiating contracts than delivering a good, value for money service." "However, Serco appears to have a bullying culture and management style which inhibits whistle-blowers being open in the patients' interest. The company responded to stories reported by the press in a heavy-handed way, launching internal investigations and searching employees' lockers when issues were raised; staff were fearful of raising concerns." These observations were with regard to the introduction in May 2012, of the NHS Pathways new computer-based system for answering out-of-hours calls from patients. (We should reflect on the reported "bullying culture" and the management of vulnerable prisoners discussed above.)

The NHS Pathway system was introduced to overcome the problem of GPs not providing out-of-hours services, although historically that was part of their contracted service provision. The consequence of the GPs changing their service provision led to the inappropriate use of hospital A & E departments being substituted for a lack of GP out-of-hours services. The NHS Pathway service provision was a means for deflecting these created organisational problems rather than addressing them.

There are only two ways patients access NHS clinical services. The primary route is accessed through the GP after an initial diagnosis, treatment and/or referral. The second is through the trauma route, when a patient has to be taken directly to A & E for immediate clinical attention.

The failure to provide out-of-hours GP services is the core reason for alternative dysfunctional organisational practices being introduced. This has led to the abuse of hospital A & E services and the creation of computer based out-of-hours call centres as substitute for an individual having direct out-of-hours access to their registered GP's practice.

Patients are deferred to call centre operatives who are not medically trained and troll through uniformed computerised response listings to achieve a diagnosis. These computer operatives lack the appropriate medical and emotional competencies but are being asked to clinically triage patients. Highly trained medical staff in A & E, as well as GPs and Paramedics usually undertake triaging. Lack of appropriate professional medical cover has led to these operatives referring the patient to the ambulance services to protect themselves and their company from potential litigation, creating a further dysfunctional distortion of services within the ambulance services.

We can very quickly identify the spiral of dysfunctional decision-making practices emanating from the failure to address the core problem of GPs not providing out-of-hour services. This is a clear case of those responsible for the strategic and operational decision-making deflecting the problem by creating an alternative dysfunctional operational practice.

When we examine the initial decision-making we find that the inability to appropriately resolve the lack of GP out-of-hours services has spiralled into creating transferred dysfunctional practices and the spawning of out-of-hours services that is disassociated with a patient's personal needs. Patients have an identifiable relationship with the GP practice but not with a call centre. It is an android robotic detached service that fails to provide the assurance of being respected and understood.

These detached impersonal services have referred consequences that manifest themselves in other parts of the care service performance continuum. For example, the Care Quality Commission review into NHS and social care in England, up to April 2013, revealed that 530,000 over 75s – almost one in ten – had been admitted to hospital as emergency patients with avoidable conditions such as malnutrition and pressure sores. The commission reports an increase of 374,000 patients in 2007/8 and these increases are out-stripping the growth in the older population.

Attributed to these increased A & E activities is the fact that many elderly people do not have an easy accessible service to their GP's practice. This can be coupled to changes in the social care services that have introduced changes, and have prioritised and/or reduced their service provision. Whatever the reason, the net result is that the existing organisational decision-making practices in one part of the organisation are transferred to another part of the service provision. These failed basic strategic decision-making practices can only lead to flawed confused systems led processes when preparing and letting the contracts. Creating a *performance culture continuum* enables you to understand the potential consequential outcomes of your strategic decision-making.

For example, Margaret Hodge, chair of the Public Accounts Committee, discussed "the inability of government to contract-out in a way that protects taxpayer's interest." In the case of the Cornwall out-of-hours services she is reported to have said, "An absurd situation where a company was seemingly lying about what it was doing but there was nothing in the contract that allows you to terminate it – indeed they still appear to be eligible for their bonus payments. It's quite extraordinary." (Refer to Chapter Eleven, "Motivations and Remuneration" for possible answers to this question.)

By using an organisational approach the commissioning authority should have been able to design the organisation to identify the behaviour, the leadership style, and the nature of the professional interaction with the patient to assure their confidence in the service they received. We can proffer that the commissioning authority had little understanding as to what they were developing in service terms. Without this information you are ill informed as to how to design the systems and procedures that are needed to ensure the quality of this public service. (We, along with Margaret Hodge, should not be surprised that the contractor appears to be dictating the terms of the contract when you consider Harding's (1997) above observations on the provision of private prisons.)

Induced Contractual Behaviour

Without working through the preliminary evaluation, in organisational terms, this can lead to you simply displacing and compounding an existing dysfunctional practice. (For examples, refer to the above discussion on GP's failure to provide out of hours services and provision for private prisons.) When you enter into the contractual evaluation for managing the contract you will be transferring the existing *intent* of the dysfunctional systems practices on to your contractual arrangements. (Refer to Chapters Two, Three and Nine where we identify why organisations become dysfunctional.)

Inevitably, the inability to manage the contract effectively creates a situation where the blame game for failures will be displaced. The contractor, in this case can become, the "scapegoat" (Jaques, 1951) and Trist and Bamford (1951) or at the very least the relationships between the client and the vendor will progressively deteriorate. In the example of the out-of-hours services, the commissioning authority, influenced by a political imperative, created the situation and the contractor made the mistake of undertaking the contract. The mistake was the assumption the contractor could, by compromising the service delivery and managing the reported performance information, secure the bonus that formed part of the cost recovery strategy needed to make this 'loss-leader' contract profitable.

These developed relationships cause the service provider to develop defensive "tick box" records as a means for confirming that they are complying with the contractual arrangements. These "tick box" practices are also used to defend the contractor from potential litigation or loss. The clients' dependency on these systems creates a superficial sense of security, and displaced attachment. The client, as part of its regulatory management must, consistently but randomly, examine how these reports are recorded and developed to ensure the specified services are in fact being delivered.

This approach would have enabled an appropriate organisational service performance culture to be developed for bidding contractors to relate to. An appropriate cost model could also be developed that would satisfy these service requirements. Serco was one of the two bidders when the contract was let in 2011. Other potential bidders dropped out, as they could not stay within the cost ceiling set by the commissioning primary care trust. Serco informed the Public Accounts Committee that it was currently making a loss on the contract. Serco is a mammoth organisation and can initially afford to win loss-leader contracts with the expectation that they can recoup their losses. (Refer to case study nine, "Canary Wharf Technology and Change" for an example of how this type of contractor behaviour was successfully addressed.)

We must also accept that when a dysfunctional organisational practice is being developed, we all instinctively know that it is wrong, which influences the attitudes and behaviour of those developing the practices and the letting of the contract. This situation can introduce a response where those developing the services do what they have to do to satisfy their political masters and revert to what they are familiar with. With these political imperatives, are we surprised that the developed organisational practices are innately dysfunctional, poorly regulated and managed?

The lessons we can take from this brief example are that the commissioning authority did not have the organisational leadership skills or the ability to match the negotiating practices of the contractors. They failed to re-examine their cost model when other providers were dropping out. Having a competitive cost model would have enabled the Commissioning Authority to have an alternative contractor to be commissioned should the existing provider fail to meet the terms of the contract. This is all part of the tactical negotiating practice of letting contracts and the development of the regulatory management that should include operant conditioning and the ability to hold the contractor to account. The cost model had seriously reinforced the client's dependency on the service provider, and even if they had a termination clause, they were unable to quickly develop a substitute practice for continuing the services.

When you reflect on the above dysfunctional practices and the revelation that this contractor won the contract as a "loss-leader" you begin to ask the question about the contractor's conditions of payment. The primary question is why, when negotiating the contract, bonuses are negotiated to fulfil the contract. The contractor is contracted to meet the service standards of performance detailed in the contract. Bonuses can and do introduce undesirable practices that are identified above by Margaret Hodge MP in the interest of protecting these considerable bonuses. (Refer to Chapter Eleven, "Remuneration and Motivation" and the unwanted outcomes identified within developed "Bonus Cultures".)

Out-of-hours call centres bring to mind (Emery & Trist, 1973), observation that when there is confusion created by unresolved problems, this leads to acts of "superficiality", called "trivialisation" where anything is tried, which may effectively achieve a reduction in complexity. It appears that this maladaptive defensive behaviour is being used to defer the inevitable decision to renegotiate out-of-hours services and alternative working arrangements being provided by GPs. (For a further example of a failure to understand what is being led and managed, refer to case study "Transitional Nursing Care".)

Contractual Creep

An example of contractual creep introduced through these ill-conceived practices, can be explored by examining the privatisation of the pathological service in some of London's hospitals. GSTS Pathology is a joint venture between outsourcing's leading provider Serco and King's College Hospital Trust, Guy's Hospital and St Thomas' Hospital Trust. Corporate Watch produced information, obtained through the Freedom of Information Act, showing that the agreed 'turnaround times' were exceeded 46 times, with 'critical risk levels' breached 14 times. Over 400 'clinical incidents' that included losing or mislabelling patients' blood cell samples were flagged up over the same period. A review of the first year's performance indicates that there appears to be an increase in the number of these incidents since GSTS took over. In June 2011 the blood group analyser contracted a virus causing it to be shut down for four days, and compounded the continued poor service provision. In January 2012 a patient was given 'inappropriate blood' when their medical history was not flagged up. In May 2012 patients' kidney damage results were incorrectly calculated, after a 'software fault'. In September 2011 it was found that a preoperative blood transfusion interface failed at the same time every week.

GSTS had agreed to upgrade the IT systems, a crucial part of modern pathology, when it took over the contract. The annual accounts show that £2.7 million had been written off in 2011 due to 'potential uncertainty' caused by the new system. There are a number of other underlying concerns that have caused disconcerted scientists have left the organisation, as morale is poor and training inadequate. These failings and the lack of profit have seen many of the pathological provisions currently provided by St Thomas' laboratories being consolidated into King's College Hospital, which was given a £3 million renovation before GSTS managed the contract. St Thomas' Hospital has only an 'Essential Service Laboratory' creating 13 staff redundancies and only five staff being gained at King's College Hospital.

Essentially the failure to let and manage the contract, to let it be regulated, and controlled, to prevent contractual creep and incorporate effective sanctions has reduced and compromised the pathological service onto one site. The reduced costs are not through improved performance but through enforced cost recovery pressures. This is the contractor defining future performance expectation, not the service provider. This inverted process can be observed in many other outsourcing service practices.

Creating Systems Creep

We have explored, at length in other chapters why the current leadership and management practices create dysfunctional organisations and lack the capacity to identify and effectively address presented organisational problems. Those created problems often have a long history of solutions being unsuccessfully applied. These vexing problems are prime for outsourcing as it allows you to in effect, *transfer* the problem, for example the failure to resolve the out-of-hours GP services, or deflecting imposed employment regulations, discussed above, by changing the way individuals are contractually employed. Even though you have notionally transferred the problem you still have to manage the contractual arrangements. You simply displace the problem and create a further uncontrollable problem.

The Hatton Cross rail disaster (Chapter Three) could be cited in that they outsourced a provision that became unmanageable, leading to the accident, and resorted to taking that failed service provision back in-house. This may, on the surface, be considered to be a harsh observation. This is not unreasonable when you consider the original dysfunctional decision-making of separating dependency relationships, the dependant relationship of the rail stock and the track, and current management practices of finding panaceas, that the fad of outsourcing provides.

It should start to become obvious that these combined situations are an attractive way to rid your organisation of a problem. These forms of dysfunctional political decision-making are attractive to those who want to make a name for themselves and make short-term gains. (Refer to the privatisation of prison service above.)

We can begin to make connections with the discussion of "Remuneration and Motivation" in Chapter Eleven, where we identified that "Profit alone was not a reliable guide. It is fairly easy for short-sighted executives to show good profits – for a few years – by letting their own company's plant run down, or by gutting reserves of raw materials" (Drucker, 1977). We can translate these short-term profit driven activities into the desire to transfer problems that will provide short-term gains to improve the profit of an organisation. Drucker identified executive remuneration package ratios, indicating the *intent* and acting as an indicator for the potential management of these organisations to be poor. Even so, within the political arena, politicians defer problems for political capital. The consequential outcomes of these decisions do not often manifest themselves during the term of any government. It's the same kind of detached systems thinking.

Pursuing the above notion of political decision-making we find that the employment of new technologies (Chapter Nine), used to resolve current presented problems in the public services sector, are proven to not work, as the *intent* and the practice of decision-making is politicised. (Fig. 3, "Politics, Career and Overt Organisation".) This kind of thinking and decision-making allows those in power to defer the problems they create.

The *intent* to secure a *business advantage* by outsourcing often translates, within a political environment, into cost reduction, creating a potential for these systems to mutate into other forms. For example, "redesigning your business processes" (reengineering in another guise) encourages outsourcing as many of these "business processes" are redefined as "commodities" (Subramanian and Lacity, 1997). We are no longer outsourcing those activities that are not part of your core business. The GSTS Pathology services discussed above are primary

291

diagnostic core services that support the clinical performance of a hospital and GP practices. Again we find that it is the same kind of thinking, of panacea seeking, that leads managers down these divergent paths. (Reengineering and why it fails were discussed in Chapters One and Nine.)

Private Financial Initiatives

Examining the Private Financial Initiatives (PFI) provides an opportunity to explore contractual creep and dependency, and determines if a business advantage had been achieved. A government raises money from the private sector to fund the building of major capital projects. Projects using the PFI approach have been criticised for being a very poor deal for taxpayers through being too lenient with private contractors.

If we examine the recent past we can begin to identify how this practice has developed a high level of systems and contract creep and has become a highly profitable means for contractors to achieve inordinate profits. Examining the Private Financial Initiatives (PFI) provides an opportunity to explore contractual creep, dependency and determine if a business advantage had been achieved.

Recent History

PFI deals were invented in 1992 by the Conservative government led by Sir John Major that became widespread under the Labour government after 1997. The Treasury had previously funded these schemes that usually involve large-scale building projects such as schools, hospitals, prisons and infrastructure projects. These projects were put out to tender with bids invited from the building and construction industries. These industries would provide the investment to build new schools, hospitals and other schemes and then lease them back. Lease arrangements for PFI projects are long term, often twenty-five years or longer.

These costly programmes are funded and owned by the private contractor. To provide these public services, once the initial contract expires, the government has to begin from scratch or they have to enter into a new leasing contract, with limited public ownership.

Even though the evidence existed that these schemes were expensive and not value for money they were still popular with the government. From the 1990s, under the then chancellor Gordon Brown, ministers were allowed to secure large sums of investment in popular projects such as schools and hospitals, without paying the money up front. Repayment could be made over long time scales, usually between twenty five to thirty years, occasionally as long as sixty years, but at higher rates of interest. That meant that large debts were stored up for future taxpayers, which now have to be repaid. It also enabled the government to appear to be fiscally diligent, as these debts do not form part of the deficit balance sheet for the term of that government.

When did these PFI contractual arrangements begin to go wrong? Ten years previously, the trade unions were expressing dire warnings about the cost of the country's PFI schemes. In April 2011 a scathing report by the National Audit Office found that each household would be paying nearly £400 the following year to pay for hospitals, schools and motorways.

The above observations and examples are not an attack on the contractors; they have only been used to identify how systems and poor contract management emanate from initial *intent* of a strategic activity of outsourcing to private contractors. If the *intent* is to displace (dump) a problem, or if the *intent* is a cost led activity or there is *intent* to change and roll back the public sector, these influences will affect the way the strategic thinking is conducted. As a consequence these dysfunctional decision-making approaches to improve the affected organisation's performance will continue to fail.

The nature of the PFI contracts, because of their size, period of investment, and the structure of those investments, which required funding for the city's financial institutions, introduced another cost management dilemma. Many PFI contracts were signed on the basis of manipulative investment rates and indexation, causing the payment to rise annually. The NHS is generating huge profits and bonuses for the financial services industry under PFI contracts, while repayment terms for the debts are crippling the NHS.

For example, the South London Hospital Trust's debt payment of its PFI built hospitals is increasing at about £1 million a year partly because of a complex financial instrument known as derivatives that are based on the Libor rate. Meanwhile the total trust income has fallen in real terms in the past three years.

Creating Displaced Goals

These political activities have been identified to emphasise the consequential effects across an organisation's boundaries resulting in the health service managers being forced to service the fluctuating debt that is reducing the spending on direct care, education and/or other public services. These managers are also required to improve the quality and volume of services they provide. The problem is compounded by these additional and necessary costs, further increasing the various public services budgets, leading to the government attempting to bring some form of financial discipline by reducing the overall budget provision to these services. In organisational and even basic sustainable business modelling these arrangements are dysfunctional and in reality these public service organisations are bankrupt.

These managers are, in effect, being placed in a "bind" (Bateson, 1956), where the manager has to service the fluctuating budget demands and is required to improve the services with decreasing funds. They are criticised for poor service delivery and/or for poor financial management. These managers' careers are dependent on their ability to manage the budgetary constraints, and that has led to these organisations' goals being displaced.

An example of goal displacement can be identified in the following list extracted from the Executive Summary of the Report of the Mid Staffordshire NHS Foundation Trust, Public Inquiry: -

- A culture focused on doing the system's business – not that of the patients. An institutional culture which ascribed more weight to positive information about the service than to information capable of implying cause for concern.

- Standards and methods of measuring compliance, which did not focus on the effect of a service on patients.

- Too great a degree of tolerance of poor standards and of risk to patients.

- A failure of communication between the many agencies to share their knowledge or concerns.

- Assumptions that monitoring, performance management or intervention was the responsibility of someone else.

- A failure to tackle challenges to the building up of a positive culture, in nursing in particular but also within the medical profession.

- A failure to appreciate until recently the risk of disruptive loss of corporate memory and focus resulting from repeated, multi-level reorganisation.

The above practices clearly indicate that this organisation had a series of displaced goals. (Fig. 4) (Refer to the case study, "Transition Nursing Care".)

These created situations resonate with the Nimrod disaster, discussed earlier where the political influence of the UK government's identified *intent* created an 'overwhelming objective of finding savings' causing 'organisational trauma'. (Refer also to the case study, "NHS, Leading Transition for Change".)

These practices would not be considered in the private sector.
They would not enter into these forms of contracts, as they do not enable you to create a sustainable working business model. The desire of the different political factions, when examined, does provide some indicators as to why these unworkable business models have been allowed to proliferate. These political activities are not within the scope of this book; we are only examining, in organisational terms, the consequential effects.

This example has been used to indicate the devastating consequential effects of misplaced *intent* when making strategic and operational decisions. The use of a cost model to drive change invariably takes on the cloak of reengineering or in another guise: "redesigning your business process." This extreme example has been used to indicate the decision-making and implementation pitfalls that need to be considered when evaluating outsourcing opportunities. Although this example has identified the expressed ramifications, these same symptoms can be, although in different magnitude and guises, observed in other organisations. (You should be able to make some connections with the notions discussed in Chapter Two and in particular Chapter Three, "The Enemy Within and Why Change Fails".)

Decision-making to let and Manage the Contract

This is an opportunity to explore the processes and consequential effects of misplaced decision-making when contracting outsourced services. When considering contracting to a service provider it is essential that you understand what you require that contract to achieve in organisational terms. When, for example, project managing multiple contracts, it is crucial that you understand the needs of the end product not only in physical terms but also how the operating performance is required to behave in organisational terms. In other words, each project's delivery contracts have to be designed and managed to ensure that they collectively support the future operational performance of the receiving organisation. (Refer to case studies, "Greenfield Development Project" and "The Millennium Dome" contracting practices.)

The same kind of thinking also applies to the activity of letting a contract when outsourcing any of your business processes. Task group orientation (Fig. 33) is a notional example of these processes which implies that when outsourcing you are still required to manage these processes in terms of your overall organisation's *performance culture continuum*. These practices are designed to ensure that these contracted activities do not divert you from focusing on the essential continuous responsive development of your organisation's service delivery.

The cost of these essential regulatory management practices must be factored into the developed cost model for justifying the decision to outsource. You may also find that the level of regulatory management may prove that the practice of outsourcing can, in reality, be completed effectively in-house.

When considering outsourcing, as with any management technology, it is important to work through the *transition for change processes* to identify the dysfunctional practices that need to be addressed. When working through this process we often find that the need or the level of outsourcing will change as you have eliminated or restructured your needs for outsourcing. This prevents the transferring of the dysfunctional behaviour into the contracted practices that are only being used to push the problem away or to be dumped. Working through these processes will enable you to identify the consequential effects of your decision-making when outsourcing. This allows you to develop a contractual arrangement that supports your own organisation's future performance needs and limits the identified consequential outcomes. The proffered contractual practices are also designed to ensure that the contractor has the capacity to deliver the required services and protect them from entering into a contract they cannot effectively deliver.

The failure to manage the contract is not only costly but you may lose control of events leading to unwanted, even protracted consequences. Financial and contract creep discussed above may render a contract to be no longer value for money. Over time, when outsourcing you lose the comparative model to determine whether the developed contract remains value for money. As part of the decision-making process to outsource we must create an existing service cost profile model that becomes part of the process for *monitoring to manage*. This created monitoring cost profile model can easily be updated to test the on-going value of any outsourced provision. Keeping this cost model undated can, to a high degree, be automatically achieved and for a minimal time and cost input. This created comparator can provide you with the ability to monitor the cost, to test other performance indicators and act as an early indicator of any contractual creep. Within these regulatory management practices you have to ensure that the true *business advantage* is being consistently achieved.

CHAPTER ELEVEN

REMUNERATION AND MOTIVATION

This chapter is not intended to provide instructions for designing remuneration systems. It is an exploration of the motivation factors and the relationship of remuneration examined from an organisational and individual's perspective. Using an organisational approach enables us to explore leaders and managers' decision-making behaviour that has the capacity to introduce unwanted practices within their organisations.

Using an organisational approach provides an opportunity to begin to develop a theory or conceptual model that enables us to create a frame of reference to test any assumptions. (Refer to Chapters Four and Five, "Developing a Theory in Practice" parts one and two). Using an organisational approach allows you to examine the presented situational problem at the process level and to clearly define the task to work toward a sustainable and workable solution. (Fig. 40 "Decision Process Model".)

This allows us to manage the emotive issues, "...those socio-emotional components..." (Roberto, 2005) that have a tendency to cloud our decision-making, because leaders and managers are affected by the social, political, emotional and increased anxiety and stress caused by the potential discontinuity and disruption of power bases. Putting these issues into the context of your organisation enables these socio-emotional components to be simplified and understood, which in turn makes it easier to find appropriate solutions. (These notions are further developed in Chapter Twelve, "Development, Training and Recruitment" where we identify that we, as effective organisational leaders, have to use our developed *social emotional intelligence* to improve our own performance in social organisations.)

Herzberg's hygiene factors (Table 3) are used as the bedrock for good motivational practices and address those important extrinsic factors that need to exist to complement the use of an organisational approach. His research findings reveal that certain characteristics of a job are consistently related to job satisfaction, while different factors are associated with dissatisfaction. These are:

Factors for satisfaction	Factors for dissatisfaction
Achievement	Company policies
Recognition	Supervision
The work itself	Relationship with supervisor & peers
Responsibility	Work conditions
Advancement	Salary
Growth	Status
	Security
Table 3	

He concludes that job satisfaction and job dissatisfaction are not opposites. The opposite of satisfaction is no satisfaction and the opposite of dissatisfaction is no satisfaction. Therefore, remedying the causes of dissatisfaction will not create satisfaction. Nor will adding the factors of job satisfaction eliminate job dissatisfaction.

If you have a hostile working environment, giving someone a promotion will not satisfy that person. If you create a healthy working environment but do not provide members of your team with any of the satisfaction factors within the work they are doing, it will still not be satisfying.

According to Herzberg, the factors leading to job dissatisfaction are "separate and distinct from those that lead to job satisfaction." Therefore, if you set about eliminating dissatisfying job factors you may create peace but not necessary enhance performance. This placates your personnel instead of actually motivating them to improve their performance.

The use of an organisational approach is designed to address these hygiene issues through the development of the organisation (Fig. 20 "Leading Transition for Change") that satisfies a basic human need, "to understand what something means" (Phillips, 1973). The intention is to create an organisational environment that enables these issues to be reviewed, to correspond with the needs of your organisation, to respond to its environment, and to enable individuals' and workgroups extrinsic needs to be satisfied. Satisfying these extrinsic needs allows individuals' and workgroups intrinsic motivational drives to be expressed. (We can refer and make connections with the "Bonus Culture – Mismatch" discussed later in this chapter.)

These explorations are designed to provide you with a basic grounding in a few of the connected notions and theories that should influence the development of your *organisational thinking*, in relationship to motivation and remuneration. Herzberg's theory raises the issues of satisfaction and we can make the connection with fairness and Adam's equity theory that also plays its part in the behaviour that translates into being either satisfied or dissatisfied.

With Adams' (1963) equity theory on job motivation, his model extends beyond the individual and incorporates the comparative influence of others who are used as *reference points*. These *reference points* can be those *significant others* that are in comparative work, where they can make a comparison of their input/output ratios. This developed individual awareness of other *comparative situations* evokes a sense of fairness or unfairness, depending on the situation. This applies to your entire pay structure, from the CEO through to the lowest earner.

As with any systems theory we use the input and output model where the individual seeks to achieve a balance when trading; input is simply what we ascribe to our work and output what we take in return. Adam's equity theory suggests that when people feel they are treated fairly they are more likely to be motivated. Conversely when people feel they are being treated unfairly they will feel de-motivated. (Refer to "Bonus Culture" discussed later in this chapter and Chapter Twelve, "Development, Training and Recruitment".)

An example can be observed in local authorities at times of budgetary constraints. People with the experience and skills are made redundant or allowed to retire early, consequently leaving an experience and skills gap. Agency personnel are employed who lack the experience or the skills, which places the responsibility for completing the work onto the existing in-house staff. The ratio of fairness "equity" is destroyed as the in-house personnel are working harder to cover the inadequacies of the agency staff and at the same time are being relatively paid less. The reverse does not apply to the agency staff as they are paid relatively well, for less effort and reduced responsibility. A further example is observed within nursing provision when agency nurses in NHS hospitals are employed. Costs rise and the quality and standards of performance are compromised along with staff morale (refer to Deming's inverse ratio). (Refer also to the induced behavioural practices discussed in Chapter Ten and Chapter Five. Chapter Five considers the individual as a task system that has inputs, conversions and outputs you should be able to link these notions to Fig. 12, "Boundary Control for Task Systems".)

Inputs into Adam's model are effort, commitment, experience, skills, adaptability, enthusiasm, supportive attitudes, trust and importantly, personal sacrifices.

Equity requires that people can identify a fair trade-off between the inputs and the outputs. Once the issues of money have been equitably resolved, money is no longer a concern, allowing the individual to become fully engaged. This fairness ratio is achieved by comparing their trade-off ratio with *"referenced others" in comparative situations*. This includes outputs, pay/salary, expenses, bonuses, pensions, recognition, responsibility, training and development, a personal sense of achievement and prospects for promotion etc. These elements can be identified within the hygiene factors discussed above. (These issues are further explored in Chapter Twelve, "Development, Training and Recruitment".) (Refer to case studies, "Greenfield Development Project" and "Avonmouth".)

When the balance is perceived to be unfair they express themselves in different ways. They may become disgruntled, tardy, or begin to make demands for increased rewards or seek alternative employment. It is important that policy makers are aware of Adam's equity theory to ensure that the working environment and terms and conditions are appropriate.

This notion of the individual's expectation resonates with Maslow's theory of hierarchy of needs and self-actualisation (Fig. 36). He claims that every person has a strong desire to realise his full potential. These events described in the pyramid of needs are not distinct steps as they overlap and create intermediate stages. Also, individuals will, as their circumstances change revert, recover and continue to work towards that state of self-actualisation.

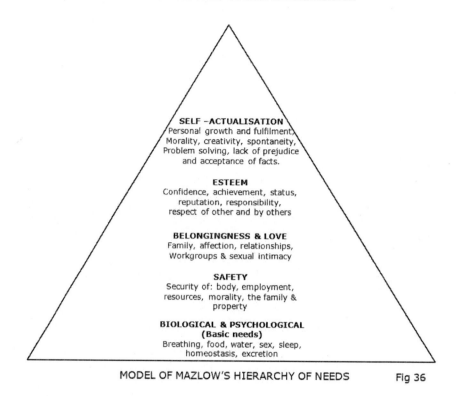

SELF –ACTUALISATION
Personal growth and fulfilment,
Morality, creativity, spontaneity,
Problem solving, lack of prejudice
and acceptance of facts.

ESTEEM
Confidence, achievement, status,
reputation, responsibility,
respect of other and by others

BELONGINGNESS & LOVE
Family, affection, relationships,
Workgroups & sexual intimacy

SAFETY
Security of: body, employment,
resources, morality, the family &
property

BIOLOGICAL & PSYCHOLOGICAL
(Basic needs)
Breathing, food, water, sex, sleep,
homeostasis, excretion

MODEL OF MAZLOW'S HIERARCHY OF NEEDS   Fig 36

Level 1   At the bottom of the pyramid is the basic survival needs.

Level 2   These two steps are important to the physical survival needs of the person.

Level 3   are psychological needs where individuals physically take care of themselves, *enabling themselves with others*, such as family and friends.

Level 4   is achieved when individuals are satisfied with what they have accomplished. The establishment of self-esteem is achieved through being competent and being recognised for their successes.

Level 5   is the cognitive level where individuals are intellectually stimulated and begin to explore.

Level 6   is the aesthetic level that requires the need for harmony, order and beauty.

Level 7   is the top of the pyramid, and is the need for self-actualisation when a person reaches a state of harmony as they have achieved their full potential. On reaching the state of self-actualisation a person may focus on building his or her own image.

The first four stages are known, as the *deficit needs*, sometimes referred to as the biological survival needs where we respond to hunger, thirst and sex. When you don't have enough of these four levels you retain a desire to gain them. When you have obtained them you feel content and these four levels are no longer motivating factors.

Interestingly money as a motivator is less important, as you progress beyond the first four levels of Maslow's hierarchy of needs. This observation may provide an indicator to the performance behaviour and the attached relative salaries that CEOs of organisations receive.

Reviewing CEOs Performance

Within Europe a discussion is taking place where the question being asked is – do CEOs work 200 times harder than anyone else and if not, why should they earn 200 times as much as the rest of us? The Swiss have rejected a referendum that would cap CEO's pay at twelve times the wages of the lowest-paid employee. These CEOs succeeded in part by threatening to move their companies abroad and because the capping ratio was too low. Germany has experienced over the past twenty-five years increases from 20:1 to 200:1 in CEO's remuneration. It is reported that in the 1990s, when CEOs routinely earned much less than a million euros a year, the top companies seemed to have no difficulties finding good candidates. Those same companies are now offering their CEOs tens of millions. The claim in this case is that it is not just market forces but also the cosy system of relationships with the supervisory boards. These events being played out in Europe and discussed in the United Kingdom support the enquiry as to whether these CEOs are value for money.

When you are at the lower levels of these hierarchies of needs, these sums paid to CEOs appear to be lottery money. This is an emotive observation and can cloud our decision-making until their situation is contextually understood. When we connect these notions to Adam's equity theory we can begin to understand why these payments to bankers and other senior executives can disturb a sense of fairness. There may be a connection with the needs of these executives to build their own image – level seven – and it would be interesting to test that assumption.

A perceptive curiosity that stems from making a connection with Maslow's "self-image", is the statement of John Sculley, CEO of Apple, where he referred to "Corporate America" and used those *"significant others"* as a reference point for making his decision to sack Steve Jobs, the founder of Apple. This indicates that these executives somehow become intellectually detached from their organisations. (Fig. 23, "Role Ambiguity and Confusion" positions C or even D.) The employed managed systems do not provide them with an answer; as with Sculley's "Corporate America", each has their own vicinage, which creates a sense of being in a rarefied corporate executive environment that services their personal decision-making. This situation implies that there is a misunderstanding of their roles. We have to understand that the organisation is not there for you; you are there for the organisation to act as its "agent."

An example, of the use of comparative information is generated when recruiting a CEO. External "significant others" are used as competitive and comparative benchmarks to achieve a notional sense of equity and fairness for the CEO. Other reference points are other organisations and shareholders of the organisation they are leading, where their additional benefits are derived.

The above observations of the CEO's own environment influencing their behaviour is not exclusive. These forms of referred behaviour can be observed at all levels within an organisation; every employee has a set of "significant others" that match their own roles and act as their fairness comparator. The difference between these two situations is that the consequential effects of the CEO's decision-making behaviour are far more significant in how they influence the overall organisation's performance.

We must not forget the type of leadership behaviour explored in Chapter Three, "The Enemy Within" that is often displayed by the type of personalities that seek to obtain these positions. We cannot apply a rational expectation as these traits can carry with them the desire to make the picture rosier than it really is, which leads them to take further risks, leading to cyclical escalation of risk taking. There is a limited vetting or audit trail of their decision-making, thus there are no penalties, no restrictions or discipline, and those that exist are retrospective and too late.

"When considering the reasons why leaders lead people astray, pride of place must surely be given to those personality factors, which through self-selection characterise the potential misleaders. The argument is simple; people are attracted to and prosper in vocations that suit their mental make-up. As a consequence it is not surprising to find amongst the ranks of leaders some who are power-hungry, manipulative, extrovert, sensation-seeking, theatrical, exhibitionistic, devious, pragmatic, prepared to take risks, and certainly not weighed down with moral scruples. For good or bad the natural characteristics of such people, encouraged by the job they are trying to do, will determine the decisions they make" (Dixon, 1989).

This suggested detachment from the operational side of the business and the main focus is to satisfy their environmental audience, which includes the shareholders, their "significant others" can reinforce these short-term gains and risk-taking cyclical behaviours. This is also to move into a personal competitive state with those "significant *others*" those being the other CEOs of comparative organisations. This is not about fairness; it's about status and creating their own self-image to position themselves within their rarefied CEO's vicinage.

Corporate Performance and CEOs' Compensation Packages

Testing these assumptions can, in part, be achieved by examining the following examples that may assist in identifying that sense of detached executive financial interest becoming differentiated from the needs of the organisations for which they are acting as the "agent."

Viacom's CEO Philip Dauman, in 2010 was reported to be the highest paid executive in corporate America, collecting a package valued at $84 million for nine months' work. In 2011, he received $43 million in salary stocks and other benefits. The 89 years old Executive chairman Sumner Redstone, in 2010, received $15 million in salary and bonuses. In 2011 his remuneration package increased to $21 million. Viacom's recent quarterly returns generated a net income of $534 million, compared with $574 million a year earlier.

A Viacom shareholder filed a suit, where he maintained that the Viacom board failed to comply with its own rules for calculating executives' pay. Within the case being pursued, included the demand that the law be changed to allow not only the Class A but also that Class B shareholders be given the right to vote on executive salaries. Currently only Viacom Class A shares have the right to vote and Redstone controls 80% of those shares.

Emerging issues that need to be addressed are the structure of organisations, and linked performance relationships of the CEO's remuneration packages and the need, particularly within banking and financial services, for the decision-making to be *consequentially tested*.

From the discussion above we can begin to identify flaws in the practice of inflated remuneration packages. This is further reinforced in the findings of Drucker (1977), where the relationship of the CEO's and the other senior executives' remuneration packages were disproportionate. We can also make the connection with Drucker's observation regarding the disparity between the CEO and other senior executives.

Drucker (1977) identifies one of the reasons for organisations succeeding or failing. He reports the following: "One of the country's smartest and most venerable banks recently sent a question to their research department. 'Are there any earmarks which will tell us the management of a corporation is good or bad?' They responded by saying that profit alone is not a reliable guide. It is fairly easy for short sighted executives to show good profits – for a few years – by letting their own company's plant run down, or by gutting reserves of raw materials. On the other hand, a firm which has never earned a penny may be on the door-sill of spectacular success, because years of development work and long-vision management are finally ready to pay off."

In the end – after studying hundreds of corporations – the researchers discovered just one clue. Here in effect, is what the researchers reported: If the top executive in a company receives a salary several times as large as the salaries paid to the number two, three and fourth executives in line, you can be pretty sure that firm is badly managed. But if the salary levels of the four or five men or women at the head of the ladder are close together, then the performance and morals of the entire management group is likely to be high.

'The size of the salaries doesn't seem to make much difference', the report continued; 'whether the president of the corporation gets $20,000 a year or $100,000 isn't important – so long as his vice president gets something like 75 to 90 per cent as much. But when the president pulls down $100,000 and his main subordinate get only $25,000 to $50,000, it's time to look for trouble.' (For examples refer to Chapter Ten, "Outsourcing Contractual Practice.)

These "equity" ratios also trickle down through the organisation, which infers that when designing the payment system for all employees, not excluding the CEO, there must be connectivity to retain a sense of proportionality, fairness and equity. (Refer to case study, "Greenfield Development Project".)

Recent History and Bonus Culture

Examining the recent history, using the banking environment, allows us to explore some of these notions of the developed bonus culture and the consequential effects of previous decision-making. In the UK the current banking culture began in 1986, when Margaret Thatcher's government introduced the "Big Bang" deregulation that ended an earlier, "clubby atmosphere" based on individual relationships that brought investment bankers to Britain with a culture of risk-taking, big bonuses and a focus on short-term returns.

Bank Scandals

The above exploration and in, particular, Drucker's, reported that banks' research findings that disproportionate pay structures are a clear indicator of an organisation being "badly managed." When we connect these findings with a brief examination of the history we find Margaret Thatcher's intent, to eliminate a 'clubby atmosphere' manifested itself in a different form; the CEO's' rarefied vicinage.

The consequential effects were expressed in the City of London, 2012 where a number of scandals, as one bank after another were facing allegations of massive misbehaviour. In organisational terms, this was a significant failure of organisational leadership through managing or in these cases manipulation of financial and regulatory systems.

Barclays Bank, its chief executive, Bob Diamond, reported to be the highest earner among the UK's corporate bosses, with a realisable pay of £20.97 million, was forced to step down, after British and American regulatory authorities fined the bank $453 million for manipulating the short-term interest rate; in question was the London Interbank Offering Rate (Libor).

Libor rates are calculated for ten different currencies and fifteen borrowing periods ranging from overnight to one year and are published daily at 11.30am. Many financial institutions, mortgage lenders and credit card agencies set their rates relative to it. At least $350 trillion in derivatives and other financial products are tied to the Libor (Thomson Reuters).

Barclays bank, in addition to the Libor scandal, is subject to a further probe into a £12 billion Gulf deal. The scandal that saw Barclays profit from mis-selling unnecessary loans to small businesses, it is reported, will cost the bank at least £450million. In addition, it is reported, that Barclays bank will have to put aside an estimated £300 million, which may rise even further, for compensation to cover the cost of mis-selling payment protection insurance (PPI), taking the total cost to £1.3 billion.

Barclays are subject to a further investigation by the Financial Services Authority over whether it disclosed in a comprehensive and timely fashion all the fees it paid to advisors when raising more than £5 billion of emergency capital from Middle Eastern investors at the end of 2008 (Peston, R., BBC business editor). This confirms that the FSA is working retrospectively and a good deal of time after the event.

Other banks are being investigated for their part in the Libor and PPI scandal. This is not surprising when these banks' CEOs belong to the same vicinage 'clubby atmosphere' and its developed detached competitive behaviour. The scandal that has engulfed Barclays has widened, both in London and elsewhere and includes HSBC and the Royal Bank of Scotland.

HSBC faces a fine of up to $1 billion after the US Senate issued a damning report in 2012 alleging it had failed to stop the laundering of Mexican drug money.

J. P. Morgan Chas & Co. disclosed a surprise $2 billion trading loss – later upgraded to $8 billion – created by its portfolio designed to hedge against risk. Standard Chartered bank has been accused by a regulator in New York of laundering Iranian oil money for years.

The US market is not devoid of these inappropriate risk-taking practices as it was the failure of the sub-prime market crisis that affected the whole of the international financial markets, which exposed the vulnerability and eventual collapse of the Northern Rock Bank in the United Kingdom.

Trends in CEOs' Compensation

The trend for excessive executive pay (compensation) can be traced to corporate America. It is reported that in the past decade executive pay in the United States has risen dramatically beyond what can be explained by changes in firm's size, performance and industry classification (Lucian & Yanis 2005). It is the highest in the world in both absolute terms relative to the median salary in the United States (Jacobs & Pierson 2010).

CEO compensation has outpaced corporate profits, economic growth and average worker's pay. Between 1996 and 2000, Forbes Magazine estimates total CEO compensation in the US grew 166% to an average of $7.43 million, whilst corporate profit grew by 16% and per capita incomes grew by 18%. CEOs made 400 times more than the average worker representing a gap twenty times bigger than it was in 1965.

The defenders of lucrative pay in America suggest that these compensation packages are necessary to attract the best talent. They claim executives earn their compensation packages because of the return they provide to the shareholders, which is somewhat contradictory when you consider the general relative and comparative performance trends.

Corporate CEO Failures

Examples of high-level corporate compensation among notable unsuccessful business that have filed for bankruptcy are:

In 1996 through to 2000, Enron paid its top five executives more than $500 million at a time when the company's accounts showed six fold revenue increases and the share prices steadily climbed. In reality, a study found there was systematic depredation of shareholder value, with its debts growing and margins eroding. Enron executives and directors sold $17.3 million shares of Enron stock from 1999 through to 2001 for a total of $1.1 billion. Towards the end of 2001 Enron's stocks were worthless (Jafee 2003).

Bernard Edders the CEO of the WorldCom telecommunication company was paid $45 million in salary and bonuses in the 1990s and enough of this company's stock option to own $1 million stocks by 2000 (Norris 2000). In 2000 he persuaded the board of directors to loan him or guarantee loans in excess of $400 million to cover margins on WorldCom that he bought with borrowed money (reported by the Investigation conducted by The Special Investigative Committee of the Board of Directors of WorldCom). Two years on, internal auditors unearthed $3.8 billion in fraud. By the end of 2003, it was estimated that the company's total assets had been inflated by around $11 billion. Edders is serving a 25-year prison term.

The founder of Global Crossing, Gary Winneck, earned $734 million from stock sales over the life of his telecommunications company that became bankrupt in 2002, not before devastating employee's retirement funds (Trigaux 2002).

As CEO of Countrywide, Angelo Mozelo made more than $520 million. Perks include subsidies for his wife's travel on the corporate jet and for associated taxes. In 2007 shareholders saw an 80% decline in share value, yet he was paid \$103 million. Countrywide ended up paying \$8.7 billion to settle predatory charges (Minow, 2012). Mozelo was given a lifetime ban from serving on the board of any public company (Morgenson, 2010).

In 2011, 97% of American companies paid their executives bonuses, including many whose performance was below the median level of their industrial peers (Minow, 2012). There is a myriad of departing CEOs who have received large severance pay for less than acceptable performances. An example, in 2009, Aubrey McClendon of Chesapeake Energy was among the highest paid CEOs in the USA, despite an almost 60% decline in stock price in 2008. He received more than \$114 million in total compensation including a bonus of \$75 million (Minow 2012).

We have focused on the behaviour of American companies within the above examples as these trends often find their way into corporate practices adopted in the United Kingdom. Shareholders in the UK are becoming increasingly disgruntled with well-known company executives' proposed compensation packages. They have voted against increased remuneration packages causing CEOs to resign. Reported compensation packages include considerable sums for the CEO's wife's travelling expenses. This arrangement could be compared to the compensation packages the CEO of Countrywide Angelo Mozelo, negotiated that included perks subsidising for his wife's travel on the corporate jet and for associated taxes.

The use of the term *compensation package* is interesting in that it normally relates to giving or receiving payment or reparation, for service or loss; the act or process of making amends for something given as reparation for loss, injury or indemnity. The use of this form of language implies that these *compensation packages* are designed to protect the executives from personal loss. This implies that these arrangements support potential and future incompetence. A trend that can be observed from the above is that as the corporation begins to get into trouble the CEOs find ways to improve their compensation package for their failures.

"When you support incompetence you invariably get more of it" (James Dale Davison). These practices of compensating an executive's failures set the standard for other corporate executives, "*significant others*" to expect the same levels of protection. There is a developing sense of the compensation systems design *intent* to protect the CEO, and no personal risk creates a culture where there is a permissive or excessive freedom of behaviour. Thinking organisationally you begin to develop a sense that these CEOs are consciously or unconsciously using their organisations as their personal "cash cow" (Bhattacharyah, 1981). The above example supports this notion, in that the only loss is executive status but they all gain financially. The existing compensation package is the vicinage that they operate within is a display of success to their *significant others* corporate executives.

These unrelated performance compensation practices, with the "Big Bang" deregulation in the UK, influenced the executive compensation packages within the financial sector.

Decisions and Consequential Organisational Behaviour

The consequential effects of the sub-prime market crisis caused Northern Rock to be the first company to be nationalised since Rolls Royce was taken under state control in the 1970s. Why did Northern Rock find itself in financial difficulties?

Banks and building societies use various methods to raise funds for mortgages. These include using the money held in deposit accounts, and borrowing from the wholesale market, where banks lend to each other and sell existing debts on to other institutions to raise funds for new home loans – this is a process known as securitisation. Northern Rock relied heavily on securitisation and buying funds from the wholesalers market, more than most of its UK counterparts, but this systems based strategy ran into catastrophic trouble.

Steep interest rates increased in the United States, led by a huge increase in the number of homeowners unable to meet their mortgage payments. The worst affected were the sub-prime borrowers – those on low income with poor credit ratings. The ramification of the US mortgage problem spread worldwide and created a credit crisis. The created level of uncertainty made the institutions nervous about lending, causing the wholesale credit market to virtually dry up. These institutions, not knowing which firms were directly affected by the American sub-prime crisis, exacerbated the reluctance to lend. The demand for mortgage-backed security also evaporated because they were worried that other borrowers, not just in America, would slip into arrears.

The consequences of these *environmental business threats* caused Northern Rock to borrow money from the Bank of England in order to meet its mortgage commitments. Customers lost confidence, withdrew their money and switched banks, causing a run on that bank, which had not occurred in Britain for more than a century. Since then the government and taxpayers have effectively been supporting Northern Rock to the value of £55 billion.

This developed taxpayer's relationship has and continues to highlight the lucrative remuneration packages and in particular the attributed bonuses that taxpayers are being asked to fund. The CEO of Northern Rock also exists within the same vicinage that the other banker's CEOs occupy and will want to follow the same benefits structure.

Throughout the development of this book on organisational leadership and problem solving we have advocated that these executives are responsible for continuously scanning their organisation's environment for opportunities and threats. The practise employed in the US was particularly at risk should the interest rates change as a good proportion of the loans were unsecured. Any financial analyst could have produced a risk evaluation model that asked "what if" questions, to determine any possible threat and its potential impact. This information was available but did not fit the desired personal drive, further fuelling executives' risk-taking culture within Northern Rock. Not heeding these warnings left them "unprepared" (Lagadec, 1993).

A further example is the near collapse of the Royal Bank of Scotland (RBS) in 2008 through the strategy of aggressive expansion, driven by the CEO, primarily through acquisitions that eventually proved be disastrous. The near collapse of RBS was caused by a liquidity crisis that emanated from the CEO's aggressive expansion strategy.

These situations provide examples of poor organisational leadership, where they failed to appropriately respond to the market's environmental scanning, leaving them unsighted and ill-prepared. These examples provide us with an opportunity to reflect on the consequential effects of the CEOs' compensation package.

The behaviour of the CEO led to the near collapse of this institution yet he was able, during the final period of his departure in 2009, to double his pension entitlement fund from £8 million to £16 million. This level of reward for failure caused condemnation from all quarters, including the treasury minister Lord Myners, who is reported to have said, "There should be no rewards for failure."

Bonus Culture – Mismatch

Bonuses are paid to employees as an incentive to increase their performance and output. There is an assumption that people will improve their performance when given performance contingent incentives. This assumption rests on two subsidiary assumptions: (1) that increasing performance-contingent incentives will increase motivation and effort and (2) you reward behaviour you seek, and punish behaviour you discourage, commonly known as the carrot and stick approach. This is based on an assumption that the main drive that motivates human behaviour is the drive to respond to the rewards and punishment in our society and places of work. However, psychologists experimentally identified that the reward punishment practices produced unexpected and unwanted performance outcomes.

Learning motivated by a manipulation drive was the subject of an experiment conducted by Harlow (1950). He used four rhesus monkeys that were given twelve days' experience in manipulating a mechanical puzzle whose solution did not lead to any special incentive such as food or water. He found that the experimental monkeys were more efficient than the control monkeys in solving the puzzle.

After a few days of being presented with various puzzles to solve they had become so adept that they were able to complete the tasks frequently and two thirds were completed in less than six seconds. They had progressively improved their performance with no previous experience or rewards. Harlow concluded that these observations were of *value to the theory of motivation that significant learning was achieved and efficient performance was consistently maintained without special or extrinsic incentives.*

Testing the assumption that rewarding these monkeys would further improve their performance produced interesting results. When the monkeys were rewarded with raisins for solving the puzzle they made more errors and their repetitive efficiency was lower, "it served to disrupt performance." The introduction of food tended to *disrupt, not facilitate,* the performance of the experimental subjects.

It was postulated that motivational drives of this class represented a form of motivation that may be as primary as other extrinsic drives, such as primary biological drives that powers human behaviour in response to hunger, thirst and sex and the second drive being the carrot and stick. Harlow concluded that the third drive, the performance of achieving the task provides the necessary intrinsic reward. The monkey solved the puzzles because they simply achieved gratification from completing the task by using intrinsic focused determination.

Edward Deci (1969) replicated these findings concluding that human beings have an "inherent tendency to seek out novelty and challenges, to extend and exercise their capabilities, to explore and learn." He also went on to define, which has become, the accepted Self-Determination Theory (SDT), where he proposed that human beings have an innate drive to be autonomous, self-determined and connected to one another. When that drive is liberated people achieve more and experience richer lives.

CEOs experience these same, "inherent tendencies to seek out novelty and challenges, to extend and exercise their capabilities" to satisfy their own character. "People are attracted to and prosper in vocations, which suit their mental make-up" (Dixon, 1989). (You may also be able to make the connection to why people when asked to operate as part of a machine model, which often introduces technological alienation, want to find ways to engage with this tendency towards *self-determination.*)

Research psychologists have documented situations in which increased motivation can result in a decrease in performance – a phenomena known as, "choking under pressure" (Baumeister, 1984). The idea that excessive incentives could undermine task performance is expressed in "Yerkes-Dodson Law." (Yerkes and Dodson, 1908), postulates that there is an optimal level of arousal for executing tasks and that departure from this level in either direction leads to a decrement in performance. They and other researchers found that since arousal is tightly linked to motivation and performance, these findings imply that increased motivation beyond the optimal level will tend to produce supra-optimal levels of arousal and decrements in performance.

Reality Check

Unlike the relationship between motivation, effort and pay, the relationship between motivation, effort and performance had not attracted much attention from economists, possibly through the deeply held belief that incentive induced motivation improves performance.

The studies set out in the working paper No 05-11 entitled, "Large Stakes and Big Mistakes" of the Federal Reserve Bank of Boston produced some very interesting comparative practices. This study is important as it directly relates to the research findings of Harlow (1948) and Deci (1969) on motivational behaviour. We can also make some connection with Maslow's hierarchy of needs (Fig. 36) where we interestingly discovered money as a motivator is less important, as you progress beyond the first four levels.

Economists were mostly interested in determinates of performance pressure as the level of performance-contingent monetary incentives and in particular, the effects of substantial incentives more common in workplaces. Their primary goal was to test effects of relatively large incentives, examining whether increased incentives beyond a certain point may result in lower performance. A secondary goal was to examine the generality of any detrimental effects of incentives.

The Massachusetts Institute of Technology (MIT) sponsored by the Federal Reserve Banks of America, were asked to test whether very high monetary rewards can decrease performance. Initially MIT students were subject to a battery of tests that required creativity, motor skills and concentration. They offered them three levels of reward; small, medium and large. "As long as the task involved only mechanical skills that were repetitive, analogical within the individual's control, incentives and bonuses worked as they would be expected: the higher the pay, the better the performance." Once the task called for "even rudimentary cognitive skills, "a larger reward "led to poorer performance" (Arriely et al, 2005).

These experiments were replicated by the University of Chicago and to test cultural bias, in rural Madurai, India. These experiments were designed to address the question of whether increased effort necessarily led to improved performance. The subjects in these experiments worked on different tasks and received performance-contingency payments that varied in amounts from small to large relative to their typical level of pay. The experimenters reported that with particular exceptions they observed that the higher rewards levels could have detrimental effects on performance.

"In eight of the nine tasks we examined across the three experiments, higher incentives led to worse performance." "People offered medium rewards did no better that those who received the lower rewards, and those that had the higher reward produced the worst performance" Arriely et al (2005).

Further experimental studies, conducted by the London School of Economics, analysed fifty-one separate financial incentives in employment and found overwhelming evidence that these incentives may reduce an employee's natural inclination to complete a task and derive pleasure from doing so. Importantly, "We find that financial incentives may indeed reduce intrinsic motivation and diminish ethical or other reasons for complying with workplace social norms such as fairness. As a consequence, the provision of incentives can result in negative impact on overall performance" (Irlenbusch, 2009). We, along with Daniel Pinks, have to ask the question, why have we not learned that these practices are unsatisfactory, particularly when we track the science-based research back over six decades?

A recent National Management Salary survey, conducted by XpertHR and the Chartered Management Institute, found that 30 per cent of UK managers whose performance was ranked as underperforming were paid bonuses in 2015. The survey took into account performance ratings alongside pay, and discovered that the payment for underperforming was rife in UK business. Almost 45 per cent of senior managers and directors, whose performances were rated as not meeting expectations, received financial bonuses.

A cursory examination will identify that many bonus payment are not designed to incentivise performance but to solve presented organisational and intractable systems problems. They are, for example, being used to either retain skilled personnel, to circumvent rigid pay structures, to encourage individuals to cross from the private sector into the public sector and simply to circumvent ingrained inflexible practices and systems. Of course these reported executives and managers receive these contracted bonuses as they are being misused, to, for example, only incentivise retention or to encourage compliance with a particular imposed doctrine. (Institutionalising compliance, for example, silencing whistle-blowers with ex gratia payments, etc., which is all part of the bonus culture.) Ann Francke, CEO of the Chartered Management Institute, when commenting on these bonus payment statistics is reported to have observed, "Too many managers are reaping rich rewards of their position despite being poor performers. Unfortunately, it seems to be a lot easier to reward poor performance than to face the awkwardness of having difficult conversations with underperforming staff." This may be one facet; the reality is that these are contractual commitments. These dysfunctional decision-making practices that are being use to resolve a presented problem create displaced goals (Fig. 4) and removes any possibility to effectively measure an individual's performance. (Refer to Chapter Twelve, "Development, Training and Recruitment" where we further discuss how to improve, measure and reward performance.)

Pink (2009) has studied these research findings regarding bonus payments and claims, "There is a mismatch between what science knows and what business does." His exploration into motivational drives has enabled him to reinforce the need for businesses to engage individual's intrinsic motivational drives. Pink claims that intrinsic motivation is derived from doing what matters, what they enjoy doing, what is interesting to them and doing something important. He refers to this as the new operating system that revolves around *autonomy, mastery and purpose*. He defines autonomy as the urge to direct our own lives, mastery as the desire to get better at something that matters and purpose as a yearning to do what we do in the service of something larger than ourselves.

Pink (2009) observes that with the complex and more creative style of 21st century jobs, traditional rewards can actually lead to less of what is wanted and more of what is not wanted. He provides evidence to suggest that the traditional approach can result in:

1. Diminished intrinsic motivation (The third drive)

2. Lower performance

3. Less creativity

4. "Crowding out" of good behaviour

5. Unethical behaviour

6. Short-term thinking

All of these listed results have been discussed and identified within this chapter and other examples throughout this book. It is for these reasons that leaders and managers are encouraged to adopt an organisational approach to enable them to design their organisations to enlist the intrinsic needs of their employees and to reduce the other created dysfunctional practices listed above.

The question for many executives is how to translate these findings into their organisation's environment and at the same time address their own remuneration package. These evoked issues can be successfully addressed by working through the proffered transition processes, as this will identify where the dysfunctional practices exist. The realignment of your organisation, armed with the above findings, will enable you to examine the payment practices that satisfy the new organisational arrangement that has been identified and applied. The examples cited by Pinks are exciting and interesting but cannot be simply applied to your organisation as we discovered in earlier chapters. Overlaying other reported successful practices from other organisational cultures, although motivational, could serve to simply reinforce any existing dysfunctional practices.

Regulatory Practices

Experience shows that often, monitoring and reporting practices fail to prevent unwanted practices. They are too late and acquire an unrelated and impotent retrospective capacity to be in any way truly effective. The developed deviant decision-making behaviour often becomes an ingrained accepted part of the performance culture of that organisation.

Using an organisational approach to design these monitoring arrangements would enable the systems to be simplified, and to remain timely and relevant for preventative action should there be inappropriate or even rogue behaviour on the part of an executive and/or other members of their organisation.

Not responding to scanned threats, in organisational terms, is not only a clear failure of organisational leadership to effectively act as an effective "agent", it also leads to a failure to honour the banks' fiduciary responsibility to their customers and other financial institutions. Fiduciary responsibility is a basic trust arrangement that has to be ingrained within the practices of these institutions. The failure to adopt these basic practices left them completely unprepared for any eventuality (Lagadec).

We could conclude that the RBS board failed to meet their fiduciary responsibility because they repressed the fact that the increase in pension for the departing CEO was discretionary and failed to use their discretion to not increase that CEO's pension fund. This is a rational conclusion but when you understand that many of these board members are aspirants for the lucrative vacant role they will want to enjoy the same benefits. They are part of this executive vicinage and it is the one they relate to and want to be a part of. Even so, their failure to service the organisation's needs was unacceptable, yet their behaviour was not in any way penalised, therefore reinforcing this permissive behaviour. (These personality driven activities and the desire to test regulatory systems have been discussed in Chapter Three, "The Enemy Within".)

The Barclays scandal, in particular, damaged the reputations of British regulators, the Financial Services Authority (FSA) and the Bank of England. One Barclay's executive said he had thought the Bank of England had ordered them to submit false data on those interest rates in order to appear financially healthier. The Bank of England refuted that claim, as did Barclays CEO, Bob Diamond, who neatly parried the suggestion by saying, "It was due to a miscommunication."

In organisational terms, we can begin to explore these reported 'miscommunications' by examining this failure to appropriately manage the various organisations' boundaries. The Bank of England has to remain completely detached to maintain its integrity. Yet, when examining the reported exchanges we find that the relationship between Barclays bank and the staff at the Bank of England was too cosy and possibly blurred the boundaries of responsibility. In other words the management of these boundaries was not regulated and managed appropriately, allowing these 'miscommunications'.

Having clearly defined these regulatory boundaries it is important to ensure that accusations can be confidently refuted, simply by instituting an audit trail for cross boundary decision-making and other management activities. When a critical market index influencer is involved, a decision-making audit trail is essential in that the practice reinforces the need for detachment by the Bank of England and forces the other banks to appropriately respond to this monitoring practice. These elementary practices introduce operant behaviour where the behaviour of the executive can be monitored to ensure compliance.

As we have tracked through these scandals where we have identified the failures to manage organisational boundaries and the developed permissive manipulation of systems, we find another examples where management systems are, at all levels in an organisation, susceptible to being manipulated through being inappropriately designed. This creates cultures where there could be an assumed permission to test the boundaries and viability of these regulatory practices. (Refer to Chapter Two where the anti-terrorist laws and surveillance powers have been used to monitor people that may be infringing minor local government regulations, which were not related to any terrorist activities.)

Banks and other financial institutions, by their very nature, demand that systems are employed to regulate, control and manage the business processes of these organisations. These systemised *management technologies* have to be specifically designed to ensure the business processes are effectively regulated to monitor to manage the business process. Within the design processes, the inculcation of the fiduciary governance and practices continuously reinforce the overall organisation's performance.

These systems, when designed using an organisational approach, personal and organisational value, efficacy and a defined fiduciary, supported by expressed performance feedback loops, would have assisted in significantly reducing these inappropriate practices and individuals' behaviour. (Refer to Chapter Six, "Leading Transition for Change" phase two, where philosophy and values are discussed.) It would have provided an early set of indicators that these systems were behaving inappropriately: in essence, the organisation's behaviour, when examined, does not match the needs of that organisation. An organisation has to be self-regulatory, not only in terms of the systems design but also the efficacy of the individuals within the defined fiduciary responsibilities.

The necessity for the systems to be designed appropriately to monitor excessive inappropriate executive and other behaviour also require personal applied sanctions to be in place. These systems should be designed to influence the behaviour of the CEOs, which raises the issues of *operant conditioning*.

Operant Behaviour

The design of regulatory practices must ensure that effective operant conditioning instils appropriate decision-making practices, to ensure the early identification of deviant systems and individual behaviour. To help service these developments it's important to have a well-developed organisational frame of reference to test all the decision-making and implementation practices.

Operant conditioning or instrumental conditioning is a form of learning, where an individual's behaviour is modified by its consequences. The behaviour may change in form, frequency and/or strength. Operant conditioning must not be confused with classical conditioning, Pavlovian conditioning or respondent conditioning. Operant conditioning is distinguished from classical conditioning in that the operant conditioning deals with the modification of *voluntary behaviour* or *operant behaviour*. Operant behaviour operates on the environment and is maintained by its consequences, whilst classical conditioning deals with the conditioning of reflex behaviour. A reflex action is an involuntary and nearly instantaneous movement in response to a stimulus. These types of behaviour for particular circumstances and for survival can be observed, at times, within military training.

Operant conditioning is where behaviour emitted by the organism is strengthened or weakened by its consequences e.g. rewards or punishment. These can be either positively delivered, following a response, or negative withdrawal following a response. A total of four basic consequences can be established, with the addition of a fifth practice known as extinction, i.e. no change in consequence following a response.

These are naturally occurring consequences, which can be said to reinforce, punish or extinguish behaviour that is not always delivered by people. It is important to note that the person being influenced is not spoken to in these terms of being reinforced, punished or extinguished.

The five procedures are:

1. **Positive reinforcement** (Reinforcement): occurs when behaviour (response), is followed by a stimulus that is appetitive or rewarding, increasing the frequency of the behaviour.

2. **Negative reinforcement** (Escape): occurs when behaviour (response) is followed by the removal of an aversive stimulus, thereby increasing that behavioural frequency.

3. **Positive punishment** (Punishment by contingent stimulation): occurs when behaviour is followed by a stimulus that results in decreasing that behaviour.

4. **Negative punishment** (Penalties): occurs when behaviour is followed by the removal of a stimulus. For example taking a toy away from a child following an undesirable behaviour.

5. **Extinction** is caused by the lack of any consequence following behaviour. When behaviour is inconsequential, producing either favourable or unfavourable consequences, it will occur less frequently. When

previously reinforced behaviour is no longer reinforced with either positive or negative reinforcement, it leads to a decline in that behaviour.

Thorndike's *law of effects* (Carlson, 1999) is operant conditioning, and therefore relates the enlisted voluntary behaviour identified above. The *law of effect* basically states that "responses that produce a satisfying effect in a particular situation become more likely to occur again in that situation, and responses that produce a discomforting effect becomes less likely to occur again in that situation." He suggests that response closely followed by satisfaction will become firmly attached to the situation and therefore more likely to reoccur when the situation is related. Conversely, if the situation is followed by discomfort, when connected to the situation it will become weaker and the behaviour of response is likely to occur when the situation is repeated. (Refer to Fig. 13, "Assumptions from Experience".)

Having clarified the nature of operant conditioning we can now begin to think of its application in modifying the excesses of executives. Financial penalties, although important, cannot be used alone to influence and improve these executives' decision-making. These penalties are often applied to the institution they lead and manage.

What Can We Learn?

The above examination of remuneration packages has identified some extraordinary practices in that they are not designed to improve and sustain the performance of the organisation. The CEO's manipulation of their compensation packages acts as an indicator that the design of these remuneration systems' permissive behaviour is a contributing factor and that Drucker's reported findings are a direct indicator to poorly managed organisations. If the government had examined, when outsourcing, the executives' disproportionate salary ratios of their main contractors it would have provided an early indicator that these companies were poorly managed.

We found that there is an extraordinary mismatch between the established behavioural incentive-based science and the practices business organisations continue to employ. We find that if there is a minimal cognitive requirement within the decision-making for providing solutions to presented problems; it produces a significant reduction in performance when incentives are introduced.

This is not suggesting that incentives schemes are not used but it does demand that they are far more effective when the task is mechanical, have obvious solutions and produce immediate feedback indicating effectiveness of performance, where they work very well.

Many roles in today's organisations do not have obvious solutions, as multiple-choice solutions need to be considered. Immediately this requires a degree of cognitive ability where incentives discussed above have the capacity to deplete decision-making and problem solving capability. Essentially we have to accept that these well-established replicated experiential findings do not work and are inappropriate for twenty first-century businesses. It appears that individuals perform better when they are paid more with an attached expectation that they perform effectively. Attached to this expectation is the need to ensure that the organisation is designed to enable individuals to perform effectively.

The tenet of this book is that we have to design and create appropriate working environments that enable and enlist those intrinsic motivational behavioural characteristics. This provides the opportunity to master the task, have the autonomy to do so and that they can relate these specific tasks to the whole of the organisation. The solution for enlisting these intrinsic motivational activities cannot be addressed by introducing a one off reported motivational method that works in another organisation's performance culture. Each situation has to be designed to fit the presented organisational problem within that organisation's specific performance culture. (These issues are further discussed in Chapter Twelve, "Development, Training and Recruitment".)

Accepting that the bonus culture is so well ingrained, yet the science-based evidence clearly demonstrates that they only work effectively within closely defined boundaries, you have to ask why decision-makers still persist in paying bonuses to employees and companies. Below are some possible scenarios that may assist us to develop and further our understanding.

- In the previous chapter we examined outsourcing and contractual practices where bonuses are paid to the contractor to complete the work they were contracted to undertake. The company receive the bonus, not the employees providing the service. This and other situations suggest that there are other reasons for employing bonuses.

- The outsourcing contractors negotiate these bonuses to protect and supplement their profits. This implies that the client has an ingrained belief that the contractor, by providing bonuses, will provide the incentives to ensure the contractor fills in the holes in the specification of the brief and expectations of the contracted provision.

- These incentives have numerous unwanted outcomes, six of which are identified in Pink's above listing. The fact that these companies are profit-based organisations means their centre of attention is about short-term gains that cause them to sacrifice the quality of service provision. (Refer to Chapter Ten, "Outsourcing Contractual Practices" that evidences why these practices manifest through the existing decision-making processes used to outsource.)

To achieve compliance within political institutions may indicate why civil servants, teachers and other public servants receive bonuses. These individuals are not in direct control of events and have to use a significant amount of cognitive and political skills. Often they achieve short-term goals and when they are not able to maintain these performance gains, they revert into short-term thinking, unethical behaviour, the crowding out of good behaviour, less creativity, lower performance and reduced intrinsic motivation (Pinks). A contributing factor for these decision-makers is that they exist in a political environment where they are not actually in control of the whole process of implementation. They operate within a decision-making environment represented by Fig. 3, "Political, Career and Overt Organisation" satisfying their masters rather than their organisation's needs.

The Millennium Dome case study identified that the adverse politically dominated environment directly affected the decision-making and management of this project. Not unsubstantial bonuses were provided for the executive and senior managers. These senior managers were also extolled to report any unwarranted and suspicious behaviour. These managers were on short-term contracts and needed to sell on to future employers. The person they may be reporting could be their direct line manager who controls the bonus payments. We shall never know what went unreported but many of the contracts when revisited were inadequately designed and managed.

When, for example, there is political or economic pressure to address by capping the salaries of senior civil servants, bonuses are a means for continuing the existing benefit culture in another guise. Capping bonuses within banking will encourage alternative practices to be developed that allows these benefits to be paid in other forms.

An important factor is to ensure these additional benefit structures are subject to long-term return on investment coupled with continued service performance delivery. To achieve these two expectations it is essential that the executives learn to lead and manage their organisation effectively by managing the systems in terms of the organisation's needs.

Review

This exploration is an attempt to demonstrate the value of using an organisational approach to begin to develop a theory or concept (Chapters Four and Five), of the induced behaviour that can occur when management technologies are inappropriately employed. This approach should enable you to compare the behaviour of your organisation and the unwanted behaviour of some executives. All assumptions have to be tested in reality for validity before sharing and assuming that is the case.

This form of evaluative *organisational thinking* provides you with a frame of reference, enabling you to develop your ideas in terms of the organisation's needs, and how to develop appropriate methodologies for improving the presented situation. Testing these assumptions with those who are the subject of exploration enables a dialogue about the organisation's behaviour to begin. Doing so in terms of the organisation does not place any assertion on these individuals, workgroups and or their organisation.

Operant conditioning, fiduciary and vicinage are incorporated in the notion corporate governance. There are many management technologies for monitoring and governing but once again if we become dependent on these systems we lose the all-important *intuitive feel* of our organisation and the consequential effects of the decision-making processes.

The consequential effect of the decision-making behaviour of these CEOs is felt by the organisation they represent through imposed fines. These CEOs may have to stand down and lose an element of their bonuses and maybe some of their benefits, but in the main they do not really feel the pinch. In essence they have nothing to lose other than their own reputation.

The design of their remuneration package is extremely protective with no real financial penalties that would act as moderators of their behaviour. This aspect is important particularly when what may be described as deviant behaviour is evident. The manipulation of the Libor rates, neatly attributed to "miscommunication" is a good example. Clarity of responsibility boundaries have to be identified and agreed to ensure that there is no confusion of authority or responsibility. Working across these boundaries should be treated as a *state of flux*, which demands that *regulatory management* be established.

For example, the Bank of England and the regulatory authorities have to have clear boundary management practices, which separate the Bank of England's responsibility for regulating banks to ensure that each organisation can be held accountable for its behaviour. For example, when there is manipulation of any of the rates, particularly if of a criminal nature, the miscreant should be clearly identified, held accountable and appropriately prosecuted. This practice would enable clear responsibility for decision-making, accountability and sanctioning.

These boundaries of performance have to be established for the protection of the institution and the profitability of the organisation, which must be considered when developing appropriate corporate governance. The regulating authorities should insist that the financial institutions are able to demonstrate that they have asked and acted upon "what if" questions to evaluate the environmental risks for all strategic and investment decisions. If this cannot be shown as an identifiable executive decision-making practice, further scrutiny will become necessary.

Although the centre of interest may appear to be with the banking community, these evaluative, organisational thinking and operant practices also apply to any organisation and firmly includes those executives within the public sector.

CHAPTER TWELVE

TRAINING, DEVELOPMENT AND RECRUITMENT

These three interdependent developmental *management technologies* have been selected to demonstrate that when you begin to develop your organisation's performance, it becomes essential that all the supporting management technologies be realigned to reinforce your organisation's overall performance. Often these management technologies are employed by other supporting professions and departments and become part of the contextual fabric of that organisation's environment. (Refer to Fig. 34, "Invasiveness of Technologies".)

These developmental *management technologies* are critical for the on-going development of your organisation's leadership and management competencies that are needed for the future development of your organisation. These competencies include the continued development of a candidate's *cognitive organisational awareness* that includes their *social emotional intelligence* within the context of that organisation. These three *management technologies* and their *intent* must be collectively designed to reinforce the overall and local performance needs of that organisation.

Accepting these assumptions and those responsible for these activities, you have to become completely responsive to the needs of the overall, sub-organisation's and individual's needs. To achieve this they must develop a shared *cognitive organisational awareness* of the whole; the sub-organisation's and individual's needs. They, with the respective line managers, need to develop a shared understanding of the development needs of that organisation, the created training needs, and development of individuals and workgroup's competency to service and reinforce the organisation's delivery performance. That in turn, supports the developed "maturity" (Hersey & Blanchard) and role positioning of the individual and the various workgroups.

These expectations are based on the following assumptions:

- That the line manager's integrity and responsibility is maintained in that they remain responsible for their specific organisation's overall delivery performance. This notion fits with the expectation that roles remain clearly defined, to avoid ambiguity and confusion of responsibility and accountability. It also supports the clear ability to evaluate an individual line manager's delivery performance. (Role confusion and ambiguity has been extensively addressed in Chapters Three, Six, Nine, Ten and Eleven.)

- This creates an expectation that these line managers remain responsible for directing their own development and performance. This fits with the notion that if the organisation has been designed to enable individuals to *motivate themselves* they may find areas of developmental deficit that they personally need to improve.

- People motivate themselves; you cannot motivate people. One of the basic tenets of this book is to clearly indicate that you, as the *organisational leader and "agent"* are expected to create the organisational environment where individuals enlist their intrinsic motivational drives and are enabled to direct their *motivational intent*. This fits the notion that individuals are always motivated; what we are attempting to achieve is to ensure that their *motivated intent* is employed to compliment and reinforce the organisation's overall performance. We have discussed the many forms of negative motivated behaviour that often stems from anxiety induced through the experience of working in a dysfunctional organisation.

- For example, the investment elements of the banks were motivated to beat the systems to maximise the perceived profits and their own bonuses.

- Or when an organisation, through poor design and increased dysfunctional behaviour has the effect of increasing individuals and/or workgroup's felt sense of anxiety they become defensive. They use their intrinsic motivational drive to create defensive avoidance mechanisms, which covertly and overtly influence the quality of decision-making that adversely affects the organisation's overall performance.

These assumptions indicate that there is a need for a change in the current mind-set with regard to the way development and training technologies are considered and employed. There is a requirement that they realign their own *directed intent* to ensure they reinforce the line manager's personal and organisational development needs.

Examples of where these areas of role confusion can begin to develop can be explored using the notions examined in Chapter Two ("Why Organisations Become Dysfunctional – A Systems Perspective"). These evolutionary processes can be observed when, for example, systems are being introduced to manage the expectation expressed above and the critical activity must be to maintain the *directed intent*. The *intent* must be to design your HR management systems to support and reinforce those differentiated organisations they service. This enables the line manager's role to be supported and not compromised.

The HR department's role has a primary function to advise and assist in reducing potential litigation. It is at these inter-departmental boundaries, where these *states of flux* are created, which requires that they are regulated and managed. For example, when considering the function and the design of the HR function, it is essential that it does not compromise the various sub-organisations' role through the introduction of one-size-fits-all systems. These homogenous systems, when introduced, have a tendency to become institutionalised and part of the control fabric rather than using them to develop a tailored response to specific individuals and departmental needs. The application of these one-size-fits-all systems creates role confusion and reduces the line manager's autonomy, in doing so we lose the ability to measure their true delivery performance.

These institutionalised systems are often developed to enable the HR provider to control the processes, rather than monitor to manage. These one-size-fits-all systems solutions can be observed precipitously introducing role ambiguity and confusion. For example, there is an implied notion that everyone has to run one hundred metres in a set time, when in a different part of the organisation the time frame may not apply and would act contra to that part of the organisation's performance management needs. (Refer to Fig. 41 & 42, "Clinical Service support Model" where response time differs for different parts of the organisation and to case study, "Transitional Nursing Care".) The behaviour of the creative research and development part of your organisation would be expected to behave and perform very differently to that of a predetermined production department. Therefore, the training and development practices need to be designed to accommodate the various individual and organisational needs.

These homogenous programmes are extremely difficult to evaluate. They do have the capacity to outsource the problem to an external agency or training provider to run and manage. When you outsource these training needs, the provider must be contracted to ensure that their activities continuously reinforce your organisation's developmental needs. (Refer to Chapter Ten, "Outsourcing and Contractual Practices".)

They also neglect to take into consideration the differences in learning styles and an individual's perceptive decision-making when considering their social and personal development. To compound the problem when evaluating a person's performance these detached processes are often used. (Reflect on Merton's (1940) observations, "Evaluation and promotion are relatively independent of an individual's achievement".)

Learning Styles

A brief examination of an individual's learning styles will provide an opportunity for you to develop an understanding, as to why these types of institutionalised systems do not enable you to identify those individuals who would match your organisation's future performance needs.

Kolb (1946) for example, introduced the notion of "Experiential Learning: experiences are the source of learning and development." He essentially identified the principle that a person would learn through discovery and experience. The theory is called "Experiential learning" to emphasise the central role that experience plays in an individual's learning process.

The Learning Process

This is an assumption that one cannot learn by simply watching or reading about a subject. To learn effectively, the individual, team or organisation must actually be involved in the process. (Refer to and keep in mind the processes used in Chapter Six, "Leading Transition for Change" as Kolb's theory supports the use and development of these transitional practices.)

Kolb's cycle of learning, Fig. 37, starts with a *concrete experience*, by beginning with doing something in which the individual, team or organisation work through a task where the central focus is learning through active involvement.

Kolb's Experiential Learning Cycle

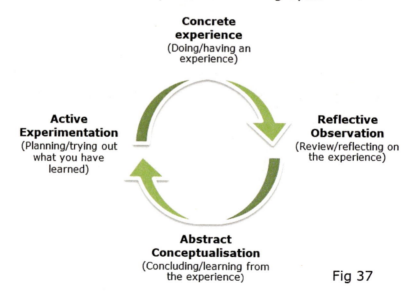

Concrete experience
(Doing/having an experience)

Active Experimentation
(Planning/trying out what you have learned)

Reflective Observation
(Review/reflecting on the experience)

Abstract Conceptualisation
(Concluding/learning from the experience)

Fig 37

The second stage is *reflective observation* where time is allowed to review the task and reflect on the experience. This process generates many questions and requires others to become involved to assist in resolving any emerging issues. Communication channels begin to open with other members, creating a need that a common language and subsequent dialogue be developed and understood. Working from an organisational perspective the shared dialogue must be within the context of the overall organisation's and workgroups (teams') perspective.

The third stage of *abstract conceptualisation* is the process of making sense of what has happened and involves interpreting the event to understand the relationships between them. At this stage the individual makes comparisons between what they have done, reflected upon and what they really know. They may draw on other experiences, theories, colleagues, previous observations and other knowledge they have gained.

The fourth and final stage is when the individual considers putting what they have learned into practice. They take this developed understanding and begin to translate expectations into an action plan for refining or revising the presented task that needs to be completed. For the learning to be useful most people need to place these processes into the context of their organisation that makes it relevant to them. If an individual is unable to find a useful purpose for what they have learned they will most likely forget what has been proffered. (We can make the connection with Chapter Five, "Developing a Theory in practice – part two" along with the processes used for "Leading Transition for Change" Chapter Six and, Fig. 13, "Assumptions from Experience".)

Kolb's developed learning cycle or spiral represents the individual progressing through *concrete experiences, reflecting, thinking and acting*. Immediate and concrete experiences lead to observations and reflections. These reflections are assimilated, absorbed and translated into abstract concepts with implications for action, allowing the individual to actively test and experiment with the developed concepts. The completion of this process enables the creation of new experiences. These notions fit the social expectation of an individual and/or workgroup when making a transition from one state to another. (Refer to Chapters Six, Seven, Eight and Eleven.)

Individual Learning Styles

Kolb's experiential learning theory is typically represented as a four-stage cycle of learning which immediate or *"concrete experiences"* provide a basis for *"observation and reflection."* These observations and reflections are assimilated and distilled into *"abstract concepts"* providing new understanding that needs to be acted upon where the person can engage in *"active experimentation"* creating new experiences for the individual. (Refer to Chapter Four, "Developing a Theory in practice – Part One" where it is suggested, "Everybody has theories": "They pass under other names, like myths or fantasies or proverbs or prescriptions or personal constructs, schemata, concepts or frames of reference".) (Refer also to the notions employed in Fig. 13, "Assumptions from Experience".)

Kolb identifies four types of learning styles that form a matrix that combines these four cycles of learning and learning styles. The four learning styles are: *Diverging, Assimilation, Convergence* and *Accommodation* that are represented in the diagram, Fig. 38. Kolb explains that different people naturally prefer a certain single learning style, which is affected by that person's personal social and institutionalised developmental life experiences all of which influence their preferred learning style. He defined three stages of a person's development where he suggests we have a propensity to reconcile and successfully integrate the four different learning styles. These improve as we mature through our development stages. He defines these as:

1. Acquisition from birth through to adolescence where we develop our basic abilities and cognitive structures.

2. Specialisation through schooling, early work and personal experiences of adulthood. These are further influenced by our development of a particular specialisation (professional) that has an attached learning style further shaped by social, educational, organisational experiences.

3. Integration developed through mid-career in later life that is expressed by a non-dominant learning style in our social and working lives.

These collective experiences directly influence our *perceptive decision-making* where we employ a quantitative or qualitative biased preference for decision-making.

Whatever influences our style of learning is the product of two pairs of variables causing us to make two separate choices, each with an attached conflicting activity. For example,

Concrete experience (Feeling) –V- **Abstract Conceptualisation** (Thinking).

Active Experimentation (Doing) – V – **Reflective Observation** (Watching).

Kolb's Developed Experiential Learning Cycle

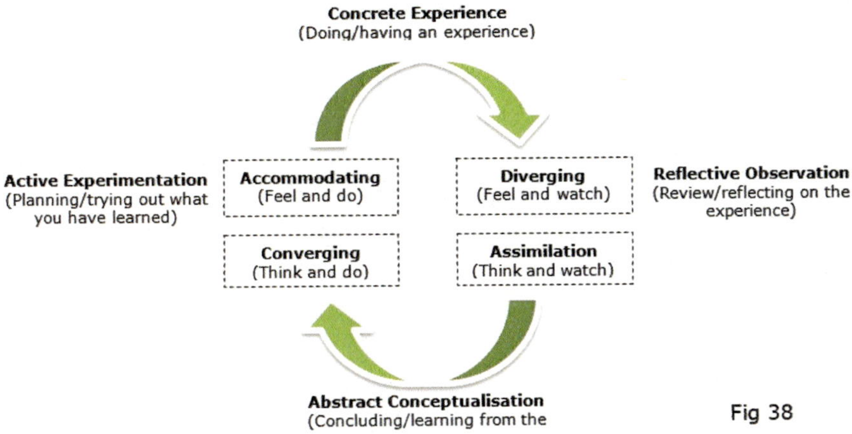

Fig 38

Other researchers, such as Peter Honey and Alan Mumford have developed their learning styles theories that are variations of Kolb's model. They suggest that "The similarities between Kolb **Fig 38** and ours are greater than the differences." These models can and do take on a proprietary role, creating a risk of identifying an individual with a specific learning style with an attached assumption that that is their only means of learning. When we are exposed to different situations we all adapt to that experience where we can observe various people dramatically changing their roles to effectively deal with the presented situation.

This brief overview and insight into the individual's development and acquired learning styles has been used to show that one-size-fits-all systems are likely to ignore, at the very least, 50 per cent of those employees you are attempting to influence and develop. It is important to note that Kolb realised that as we develop and have different successful experiences we do learn to become more accommodating, allowing us to develop and adapt ourselves to match the need of the presented situation.

The notion of *perceptive decision-making* (J. C. Kable, Queensland Institute of Technology, Australia) identifies how these individual differences affect students' dropout rates. He identified the conflict within an individual when studying a chosen subject that they are not suited to study that directly contributed to high dropout rates. We have identified that engineers and architects see solutions to problems differently because they employ either an intuitive qualitative or qualitative decision-making process. When not understood can lead to open conflict when particular design decisions have to be addressed.

Another area for conflict can arise between the individual and the job that they have to do. It was found that doctors were predominantly quantitative but the task, especially the role of being a GP, was predominantly qualitative. In effect, we are placing these doctors in an environment where they become neurotic and unhappy whose solutions to medical problems, like engineers, are mostly quantitative. In the United States, doctors are so unhappy and insecure that psychiatrists have the highest suicide rate of any profession and alcoholism is the most prevalent in the medical profession as a whole.

The above should have reaffirmed that the management systems and the management technology must be designed to enlist the individual's development to satisfy and enable them to compliment the overall organisation's performance. The above discussion indicates that in spite of all the training, we place the wrong people in the wrong jobs at the wrong time.

The HR function has been used as an example as they tend to be responsible for the three topics being discussed. These notions also apply to other service support department's roles. (Refer to Chapter Nine, "Technology Change and Managing the Consequences" to understand the invasiveness of other management technologies.)

Other Areas that Need Clarifying

It may be useful to begin to differentiate training, development and recruitment. A common denominator for all of these activities has to be attitude, which directs and focuses an individual's level and direction of their self-motivation. Recruitment needs to be addressed first as it has the capacity to recruit those that can *fit* the role and the organisation's needs best.

Experience of some of the recruitment practices and the filtering assessment practices should begin to raise issues regarding these systems targeting, consciously or unconsciously, people from certain educational backgrounds; or on the basis that individuals can pass examinations rather than on the potential for these people to gain some satisfaction from their work. The Civil Service chose candidates on the basis that administrators should be intelligent, well-educated amateurs. Lord Macaulay, who wrote in 1854, that civil servants should be men "who have been engaged ...in studies which have no immediate connection with the business of other professions." This spectre still pervades in some form or another in both the public and private sectors. These people may have the educated intellectual skills but may not have the "non-intellective" skills (Wechsler, 1958).

We find writers and psychologists, when they began to think and write about intelligence, they focused on cognitive aspects, such as memory and problem solving. These researchers recognised that the non-cognitive aspects were important, particularly in social organisations. For example, Wechsler (1940) referred to non-intellective, as well as intellective elements, by which he meant effective personal and social factors. In 1943 Wechsler was proposing that non-intelligence abilities were essential for predicting one's ability to succeed in life. He wrote, "I have tried to show that there are additional intellective and also defined non-intellective factors that determine *intelligent behaviour*. If the foregoing observations are correct, it follows that we cannot expect to measure total intelligence until our tests also include some measure of non-intellective factors." (We should be able to make the connection with "Adaptive Organisational Leadership" in Chapters Seven and Eight, "Leadership and Positioning in Groups" and the applied use of *"intelligent behaviour"*.)

Robert Thorndike was writing about "social intelligence" in the late thirties. Gardner (1983) proposed the "intra-personal" and "inter-personal" intelligence he referred to as "multiple intelligence." In the 1940s, under the direction of Hemphill (1959), the Ohio State leadership Studies suggested that this "consideration" is an important aspect of effective leadership. Specifically, this research suggested that leaders who are able to establish "mutual trust, respect and certain warmth and rapport" with members of their group would be more effective (Fleishman & Harris, 1962).

Leadership has been described as *social influence*, where you can enlist the aid and support of others to accomplish a common task, which these people seem to have accomplished. It could be useful to make the connection with the basic outcome of the Hawthorn experiment in 1923. The researchers expressed interest in these employees and their conditions of work. In doing so, they correspondingly found that productivity significantly increased. When the researchers completed their work and withdrew the productivity fell to original levels before the research began. The lesson was clear and impressive, yet we are still failing to learn this basic human need, that people respond to being valued through genuine "mutual trust, respect and certain warmth and rapport" (Fleishman & Harris, 1962). These abilities, strong leadership and team building skills, are the essential qualities of entrepreneurs and successful organisational leaders. The above resonates with Roberto's observations, "... cognitive decision-making tasks may prove challenging for many leaders, the *socio-emotional component* is often their Achilles heel."

The Office of Strategic Services (1948) developed a process of assessment based on the earlier studies of Murray (1938) that included the evaluation of non-cognitive as well as cognitive abilities. The "assessment centre", was first used in the private sector at AT&T in 1956 (Bray, 1976). The assessments centre included social and emotional competencies, such as communication, sensitivity, initiative and interpersonal skills (Thornton & Byham, 1982). By the early 1990s, there was a long tradition of research on the role of non-cognitive factors in helping people to succeed in both life and the workplace (Chemiss 2000).

When Salovey and Mayer coined the phrase 'cognitive intelligence', they were aware of the previous work on non-cognitive aspects of intelligence. They describe emotional intelligence as "a form of *social intelligence* that involves the ability to monitor one's own and others' feelings and emotions, to discriminate among them and to use this information to guide one's thinking and actions"

340

(Salovey and Mayer, 1990). We all have to have the ability to understand how we affect others and how others affect us.

In one study they found that when a group of people saw an upsetting film, those who scored high on emotional clarity (which is the ability to identify and give a name to a mood that is being experienced) recovered more quickly (Salovey, Mayer, Turvey and Palfai, 1995). In another study, individuals who scored higher in the ability to perceive accurate understanding and appraise others' emotions were better able to respond flexibly to changes in their social environment and build supportive social networks (Salovey, Bedell, Dettweiler and Mayer, 1999).

McClelland (1993) was among a growing number of researchers who were becoming concerned with how little traditional tests of cognitive intelligence told us about what it takes to be successful in life. (These notions have been contextually developed in Chapter Five, "Developing a Theory In Practice – Part Two – The Inter-Related Behaviour of the Individual, the Group, the Organisation and Environment" along with Chapter Seven, "Adaptive Organisational Leadership".)

An example is the study of eighty Ph.D. students who were subject to a battery of personality tests, IQ tests and interviews in the 1950s when they were graduate students at Berkeley University. Forty years later they were asked to produce a resume, allowing estimates to be made of their success, which were evaluated by experts in their own field and sources such as American Men and Women of Science. The results indicated that social and emotional abilities were four times more important than IQ in determining professional success and prestige (Feist and Barron, 1996). It is more important to be able to persist in the face of difficulties and to get along well with colleagues and subordinates than it is to have an extra 10 to 15 points of IQ. The same is true in most occupations.

This exploration has been used to identify that the old systems of assessment are inadequate to meet today's organisational leadership and management needs. We have confirmed that those that are most successful have that balance between the *technical and the social emotional skills*. This fits and underwrites the need of any social organisation that the technical and social are equally addressed, to ensure that important harmonisation is achieved within any organisation and also the individual. The harmonisation of these two attributes is harnessed to enable employees to relate and motivate themselves with the appropriate *directed motivational intent*.

When we extend this notion of harmonising the social and technical and consider these facets existing within the individual, we often find Roberto's observations coming into play, "…the socio-emotional component is often their Achilles heel." This infers that the necessary balance between the technical and the emotional are not in harmony within these individuals and as a consequence compromises their ability to lead and manage themselves, others and their organisation's effectiveness.

The Value of Emotional Intelligence at Work

Within this notion of having developed the appropriate directed motivational *intent* we need to consider Schulman's (1995) developed construct that he referred to as *learning optimism*. It refers to the causal attribution people make when confronted with failure or setbacks. Optimists tend to make specific, temporary, external causal attributions while pessimists tend to make global, permanent and internal attributions.

For example, at Met Life, Seligman found those new salesmen who were optimistic sold 37 per cent more insurance in their first two years than did pessimists. When the company hired a special group of individuals high on optimism but who failed the normal screening, they outsold the average agent by 27 per cent (Schulman, 1995).

Another study of *learned optimism* conducted by Seligman (1995), who tested 500 freshmen at the University of Pennsylvania, found that their scores on optimism were better predictors of actual grades during the freshman's year than Scholastic Assessment Test (SAT) scores or high school grades.

The attributes of "emotional intelligence" (Goleman, 1995) are as much to do with knowing when and how to express emotions as it does with controlling them. For example, in Seligman's research on limits of IQ as a predictor, we can refer to the Sommerville, Massachusetts's study of 450 boys, conducted over a period of forty years. Two thirds of the boys were from welfare families and one third had IQs below 90. However, IQ had little relation to how well they did at work or in the rest of their lives. What made the biggest difference was childhood abilities such as being able to handle frustration, control emotions and get along with other people (Snarey and Vaillaint, 1985).

Empathy is an important aspect of "emotional intelligence." Researchers have known for years that it contributes to occupational success. Rosenthal et al (1977) at Harvard University discovered over two decades ago that people who were best at identifying others', emotions were more successful in their work as well as their social lives. A more recent study of retail sales buyers found that apparel sales representatives were valued primarily for their empathy. The buyer reported they wanted representatives who could listen well and really understand what they wanted and what their concerns were (Pilling and Eroglu, 1994). (We can make the connection with the question that relates to nursing in the NHS, "Why do nurses have to have degrees?" When, in general nursing, competency and empathy are more related to the actual care needs of a patient.)

Golemen (1998) and Mayer, Salovey and Caruso (1998b) have argued that, by itself, emotional intelligence probably is not a strong predictor of job performance, rather it provides the bedrock for competences that are. Golemen (1998) has tried to represent this idea by making a distinction between emotional intelligence and emotional competence.

Emotional competence refers to the personal and social skills that lead to superior performances in the world of work. The emotional competencies are linked to and based on emotional intelligence. Essentially it is the ability to recognise accurately what other people are feeling, which enables us to empathise, relate and adjust our own behaviour to influence that individual to achieve the appropriate response to presented issues (Goleman, 1998). This is not in any way manipulation; it is your attributed behaviour that enables that individual to effectively evaluate their own response to the presented contextual situation. *It's all about being aware of the context of the situation and how others affect you and how you affect others.* It is a two-way emotional transaction that has to be understood and developed to become an effective *organisational leader.* (Refer to

Chapter Seven "Adaptive Organisational Leadership" and Chapter Eight, "Leadership and Positioning in Groups".)

The following adage can act as a shorthand reference that suggests, "Behaviour begets behaviour." If you are aggressive you will receive either an aggressive or submissive response. If you are insincere, that will be detected, as the respondent will not believe your intentions. If you put someone down they will resent you and may covertly make your life difficult. Carol Buchner offers the following thought, "They may forget what you said, but they will never forget how you made them feel." The lessons that we must all take from these examples, is that we need to examine and be aware of our own behaviour in different situations. Individually, we are responsible for the quality of our communicated message. To be effective we have to understand those behavioural aspects; for example, tone of voice and/or choice of language causing the receiver to reinterpret our message. (Refer to Fig. 29, "Communicated Message".)

As the demands and rate of change in organisations increase, the world of work will make ever-increasing demands on a person's cognitive, emotional and physical resources; these sets of adaptive abilities will become increasingly important.

The discussion above and supportive research should have further reinforced that a person's ability to perceive, identify and manage emotions provides the basis for developing these kinds of emotional competencies. The development of their *cognitive organisational awareness* provides a platform for understanding the organisational demands being placed upon them. The developed *cognitive organisational awareness* coupled with the individual's *emotional competencies* are the main planks for the development of successful *organisational leaders*. Having a well-developed *cognitive organisational awareness* allows the individual to employ and apply their competencies and skills within the contextual needs of their organisation.

The demands being placed on future leaders and managers are that they have to take responsibility for their continuous personal development. The Japanese call this daily quest for self-improvement, "Kaizen" and would suggest that if you are not striving for self-improvement you will end up going backwards.

This exploration raises other issues: what is the difference between training and development and, in particular, where do the personal development boundaries of responsibilities exist? If we identify a shortfall in our personal development it is our individual responsibility to address those issues. We may address these issues independently or if it is affecting your own and your organisation's performance you may enlist the support of the resources within the organisation. Whatever approach, you adopt the responsibility for addressing the identified concerns; they remain with the individual.

Career Development

"Organisations must make provision for its own survival and growth. To achieve this provision has to be made for the development for tomorrow's (*organisational leaders*) and managers" (Drucker, 1968). The future organisational leader, the "agent" must develop the capacity to demonstrate that they can contribute effectively to an organisation's overall performance and effectively resolve presented organisational problems. This will become a sought-after commodity, which in turn will enhance an individual's career. It is important to remember that the employing organisation want to engage people that resolve problems, not create them.

"The function of leadership is to produce more leaders, not more followers."
Ralph Nader

The benefit of developing this approach and its application is that it is transferable from one part of an organisation to another. The context will change but the nature of the process of *organisational thinking* and its application will be the same. The development of these competencies is all pervasive and needs to be designed into your organisation's leadership and management development programmes.

The advantage of adopting this form of leadership and management development programme is that it creates a common understanding and process for thinking through the issues and, importantly, a common dialogue. The development of a common leadership, management and problem solving language is that it enables an effective dialogue to ensure the collective ability to address presented organisational problems.

The expectation that you will have a job-for-life, in most fields of employment, has long gone. This means that we must have desirable transferable skills. This includes your existing organisation where other divisions, sections, and departments would benefit from the redeployment of individuals with these competencies. This approach also enables the organisation to begin to develop a culture of *knowledge sharing* that supports the notion of a responsive learning organisation. It can also serve to satisfy the "hygiene factors" to the benefit of both the employee and the organisation. For example, not everyone can occupy or even wants the top job. This approach for knowledge sharing can provide opportunities for individuals to still remain productively enthusiastic and continue to effectively contribute to the whole organisation's performance. This approach is designed to continuously engage an individual's intrinsic drive and their desire to do what they enjoy doing, what is interesting to them and to continue doing something important (Pink, 2009). (For a more detailed discussion refer to Chapter Eleven, "Remuneration and Motivation".) This, of course, requires a necessary change in mind-set to enable us to re-examine the way we currently employ our development, training and recruitment practices.

There must be an expectation that anyone that you employ must have the opportunity and develop their capacity to effectively contribute to your organisation's overall performance. If they are not readily available we must create the necessary in-house programmes to develop those skills and allow these individuals, from experience, to develop their competencies. Connected to these expectations for individual development must also be career opportunities that are not necessarily mapped out. We all change our assumption from our experience, as we realise that we could achieve more when opportunities arise. (Fig. 13. "Assumptions from Experience" and Kolb's Experiential Learning Cycle." Fig. 37 and 38.)

The employment of an organisational and personal development approach enables the identification of those with the potential to become effective *organisational leaders*. It also provides those opportunities for potential *organisational leaders* to make the transition from their professional bounded role to becoming an

346

effective *organisational leader.* (Fig. 24, "Mapping Career-Decisions".)

Performance Evaluation and Promotion

The above proffered approach will all come to nothing if the findings of Merton's (1940) studies are not reversed to allow genuine achievement to be recognised and appropriately rewarded. Reiterating his research finding, he identified that "competition within organisations occurs within closely defined limits. Evaluation and promotion are relatively independent of individual's achievement." Burns (1963) found that the consequential outcomes increased the political manoeuvring, causing the more ambitious people to become overtly ruthless, very often at the expense of others. That creates and adds to a climate of demoralising uncertainty. We should be able to make the connection with those executives who appear to receive disproportionate remuneration packages (Chapter Eleven, "Remuneration and Motivation") that can and does cause these executives to create inappropriate organisational leadership practices. This has to be reversed and be based on actual performance that is evaluated on their ability to improve their organisation's performance through the use of an *organisational leadership evaluation approach.*

Performance Evaluation

Argyris and Schön (1978) would encourage us to develop "learning organisations." Their philosophy supports the need for any organisation to continuously respond to its environment. We have to begin by focusing on these organisation's "agents" (Argyris), who need to constantly scan and interpret their organisation's environment. In turn, they interpret the various environmental forces, weigh them and manage their influences at the boundaries of their organisation. The generated information can be used to inform their strategic and operational decision-making, Fig. 10 ("Hourglass Strategic Thinking") and to develop the appropriate responsive organisational behaviour. This can be characterised as managing an organisation's business that appears to be an innate trait that entrepreneurs possess. They have that ability to retain the sense of what is needed to satisfy their organisation's delivery performance.

There is a developing level of confusion that we need to tease out regarding this notion of entrepreneurship as distinct from leading and managing. An early French definition of entrepreneurship was provided by Jean-Baptiste (1803) who describes entrepreneurship as an economic *agent* who unites all means of production; the land of one, the labour of another and the capital of yet another and thus produces a product. By selling the product in the market he pays to rent land, wages to labour, interest on capital and what remains is his profit. He shifts economic resources out of an area of lower and into an area of higher productivity and greater yield. It is this last statement that we need to focus on in that all leaders and managers are charged with, and what should be a basic innate responsibility.

Because of the confusion a new piece of language has been invented to describe this ability, which is intra-preneurship. This confusion stems from the fact that many leaders and managers have little understanding as to what they are leading and managing in organisational terms. This lack of understanding can be, to a high degree, attributed to the use of systems that detaches these leaders and managers from their organisational roots.

These leaders and managers are managing the systems and are bound by those systems' protocols. This induced ritualised decision-making behaviour slowly shortens their sight line, increasing myopia. Terms such as "intra-preneurship" come into existence as a reaction to these intellectual constraints. Extolling leaders and managers to "Think outside the box" implies that these constraints exist and that there is a need to change the existing systems decision-making processes.

When leaders and managers have a well-developed *cognitive organisational awareness*, the organisations being their product, they develop that ability to use the technical and the social emotional assets of their organisations to 'shift economic resources out of an area of lower and into an area of higher productivity and greater yield.' This is an elementary and basic expectation that all organisational leaders and managers must pursue; it is basic practice for the effective survival of any organisation. Drucker (1964) supports the above definitions and expectations. He writes, "Entrepreneurs search for change, respond to it and exploit opportunities. Innovation is a specific tool of an entrepreneur; hence an effective entrepreneur converts a source into resources."

To satisfy the above expectations and to make provisions for the future survival of your organisation, it is essential that the performance evaluation scheme be designed to evaluate an individual's capacity to act as an *organisational leader*. Working with the assumption that many organisations are dysfunctional we can reasonably assume that the existing development programmes must have a degree of dysfunctional, personality and political elements and as a consequence may not have an effective capacity to identify and support those people that have the potential to develop and apply their *organisational leadership* skills.

By inference this demands that the criteria for evaluating a person's performance must include the capacity to lead and manage an organisation and their ability to contribute effectively to the overall organisation's performance. The criteria that could be used are generally listed as follows:

- Has that person made the transition from their professional position to becoming "the agent" and leader of that organisation? (Fig. 24. "Mapping Career Decisions".)

- Are they able to develop, lead and maintain their workgroup's and team's contribution to the overall organisation's performance?

- Are they able to identify when workgroup teams have become ritualistic, less effective or even redundant, where they either refresh or close the activity to effectively reemploy the available resources?

- Can they design and manage that system that reinforces and complements their own and the overall organisation's performance?

- Are they able to design their systems to ensure that the systems effectively influence appropriate operant behaviour?

- Do they have the ability to effectively scan and manage their organisation's boundaries?

- Have they effectively developed cross boundary complementary working relationships? This must include the ability to evaluate the dependent and interdependent relationships and to have developed appropriate successful working arrangements.

- Has their organisation been designed where the *states of flux* occur and introduced appropriate regulatory management practices?

- Do they have the ability to successfully resolve conflict using their organisation as a *third party*?

- Do they have in place a development process for their staff? Where they enable their staff to, through experience, apply their skills under their tutelage? (Stretch development)

- Do they possess good influencing and negotiating processes that they tailor to best fit the situation where they are managing conflict, identification of the underlying problem and providing sustainable solutions?

- Can these people when applying these skills, be able to deliver measurable improved performances within the scope of their responsibility and authority?

These, in particular the last observation, have to be determined before any bonuses or other benefits are ascribed to an individual or workgroup. This also applies to any decisions to promote an individual.

These are some of the suggested areas where the evaluation of a person's application of their *organisational leadership* skills contribute to their organisation and the overall organisation's performance. Each person has to be evaluated within the context of the nature of that part of the organisation they are being asked to develop and effectively lead. These evaluation markers have to be agreed with the person involved to ensure that they have the ability to achieve them and that it is within their authority. Their ability may be affected by their organisation's dependent and interdependent relationships, which may demand that these cross boundary relationships require other parties' inputs. These collegiate arrangements have to be factored in. (Refer to case study, "Greenfield Development Project".)

There will be times when candidates will have to apply their *inverted organisational leadership* skills to influence the executive decision-makers to review their decision-making processes. Having a shared developed *cognitive organisational awareness* enables these influencing practices to be effectively employed through an appropriate *organisational dialogue.* This is an essential element that all leaders and managers at all levels within an organisation must employ. (Refer to the discussion on entrepreneurship above and "Adaptive Organisational Leadership", Chapter Seven.) This approach provides the information with regards to an individual's performance and identifies those agreed areas where an individual may need specific development. These may take the form of acquiring further management technologies, or personal adaptive skills and self-awareness may be a set. These sets of developmental elements will depend on the role that person is being required to fulfil.

Performance review feedback loops are an invaluable tool for aiding this evaluative process. Within this process the intent is to evaluate the individual's *cognitive organisational awareness* and their ability to influence effectively. They are aware that they are the organisation's "agent", which implies that you have to be constantly aware of the organisation and its environment to enable that individual to lead and manage effectively.

The importance of having well developed evaluative feedback loops, is that the evaluation is on going and not a one-off end of year event. Within the design of these evaluative feedback loops is the operant element, as this provides an opportunity for an individual to become aware of their behaviour and their contributing performance, providing them with an opportunity to learn from their experiences.

These developed practices service the Argyris notion of developing *learning organisations*.

Earlier we discovered that an organisation is unable to think for itself, it relies on its "agent" and that agent's ability to *think organisationally* using their well-developed *cognitive organisational awareness*. It is these people that must remain responsible for their own *adaptive developmental behaviour*, to service their organisation's responsive needs.

Any developmental evaluative process should not have any surprises when the two parties meet to discuss and record an individual's performance. All the issues to be discussed should have been highlighted at the time of observation, either in a shortfall in performance expectations, or work that was completed satisfactorily. This is a continuous process, not a one-off annual activity. These on-going practices are designed to enlist any shortfall that needs to be addressed and included as part of the continuous development process. We have discussed that the organisation is in a continuous state of responding to its environment. Naturally, if the organisation is developing to enable it to respond to its own survival needs, those employed within that organisation must, in parallel, continue to develop their own organisational and personal leadership skills.

Continuous Personal Development

It is the primary responsibility for a person's line manager to supervise their development whilst dealing with presented organisational issues. Delegated supervised exposure has proved to be extremely successful for accelerating an individual's leadership and management development whilst simultaneously improving the organisation's performance.

This technique, sometimes referred to the *stretch development*, is useful, for quickly providing accelerated development through direct and supported experiences. We must keep in mind that the rate and nature of organisational change is accelerating and will not wait for these competencies to be developed over a protracted period of time. The other reason for employing this approach is the identified difficulty of well-developed external training programmes not transferring into your organisation's performance culture. We identified that often, the transfer of the acquired knowledge is resisted by the existing organisation's performance culture.

The *stretch developmental* approach consists of delegating responsibility to an individual along with the appropriate degree of authority to complete a specific task (Kolb's *concrete experiences*). The best tasks are the ones that are outside their notional comfort zone and have an organisational issue to be resolved. In essence, they are thrown into the deep end but with a proviso that if they are struggling they confer with their line manager and if necessary redefine the areas of responsibility.

The outcome of these developmental experiences' success or failure remains with the supervising line manager. These processes identify an individual's ability to improve their organisation's performance. It provides an opportunity to identify those areas where an individual needs either more support through coaching, the development of specific management technologies, or areas where their *socio-emotional competencies* need further attention.

The *socio-emotional component* has to remain the responsibility of the individual, as these possible personal change issues have to remain within that individual's control. We are not working to change personalities; it is for the individual to identify their own personal development needs. The individuals can only motivate themselves to make any personal changes when they recognise, understand and accept the need for them to personally make changes.

The experience of being exposed and stretched in a controlled and managed way ensures the individual learns from those experiences. This form of exposure is testing and the candidate should be provided with the opportunity to decide what their capabilities are and whether they want to develop their skills even further. These developmental notions stem from people learning from their experiences. (Refer to Fig. 13, "Assumptions from Experience" and Kolb's "Experiential Learning Cycle" Fig. 37 and 38 discussed above.) These exposed developmental experiences help an individual to understand themselves and how they react and affect the working environment they are being made responsible for.

The benefit of this approach is that an individual's efforts, if structured and managed appropriately, will directly transfer into the organisation's performance. The individual is made responsible for their own development and contracts with their line managers to be prepared to step outside their own comfort zone.

Critically these processes prepare an individual to make the personal transition from their bounded professional role to becoming a successful organisational leader. Fig. 24 ("Mapping Career Decisions") enables you to consider an individual's maturity and role positioning. The Hersey, & Blanchard Model provide an opportunity to develop a sense of your workgroup's maturity, which can also notionally be used at the individual level. Should any weakness exist that prevents them doing the assigned task, it allows you to take remedial action. The need to step in and work in parallel with the candidate enables you to complete the task and for the individual to learn and develop. Essentially, the line manager still provides the necessary support to enable that person to reduce their anxiety and direct their effort into the learning process and opportunity.

The capacity of line managers to develop and provide these developmental support practices becomes available through the employment of the line manager's *freed intellectual space*. We have previously discussed that when you employ your *cognitive organisational awareness* and as a consequence develop the necessary maturity of your workgroup's and individuals' competencies, the created *redundant intellectual space* can be redeployed for the purpose of developing individuals, workgroups, interdepartmental work and the overall organisation's performance.

"As we look ahead in to the next century, leaders will be those that empower others."
Bill Gates

354

Self-Motivational Development

The majority of these skills are developed through *inquisitive enquiry* and *learned optimism* (Seligman, 1995), and from taking opportunities to learn from developed experiences. This accelerating process works with an assumption that although we can learn from our experiences, it takes a good deal of time. Supervised exposure provides the opportunity for the individual to learn from those who have the experience and skills to successfully lead and manage their organisations.

A benefit derived from this approach is that it keeps your line managers inquisitive, excited and wanting to develop further their organisational leadership skills from experience. It prevents what Kets de Vries emphasises in Struggling with the Demon, where executives he has known are stuck, "governed by the past" and locked in a "psychic prison." Today's organisations cannot afford this depleting practice, not if they want to survive and flourish.

This discussion and the following, Fig. 20 ("Leading Transition for Change Processes"), Fig. 24 ("Mapping Career Decisions") and Fig. 39 ("Evaluation Model") all imply that we need to re-examine our practices by continuously evaluating and developing an individual's *organisational leadership* performance. The essence of this model is that it is focused on the needs of the organisation and to ensure that the incumbent and new recruits contribute effectively. The proffered model is being used to indicate the evaluation and decision-making process for recruiting individuals into roles where organisational leadership skills are required. The range of people likely to be included are all those that have the responsibility for supervising others. These parameters will be influenced by the nature of the organisation and the roles that need to be completed in the future state.

Recruitment and Retention

In today's organisations it is essential that we have the ability to adapt to match the demands of the responding organisation and those of the individual's needs and expectations. We have identified that if we fail to do so, we shall all be redundant if we have yesterday's skills. It is counter-productive not to match the individual's developmental expectations. The new recruit will soon become part of the furniture and sit back and not challenge as they feel they are unable to effectively contribute to their organisation's performance. The consequences are that a significant part of your *organisation's collective intelligence* is not being utilised.

This raises the issues of the *psychological contract* between the individual and the organisation, discussed earlier. (Refer to Fig. 18, Common Regions for the Individual and Enterprise".) Fig. 39 is a notional process model that has *intent,* in that it is designed to enlist the *best fit* for the organisation and the individual. The organisation's needs must take priority and may not fit the needs of an individual.

EVALAUTION MODEL

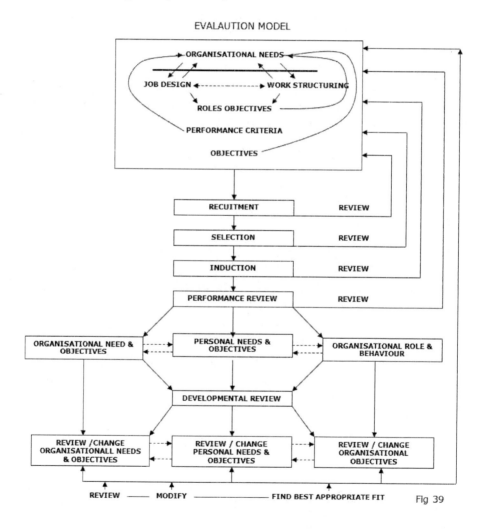

Fig 39

The British Intelligence and Security Community's headquarters, GCHQ Cheltenham, have begun to recruit individuals that are dyslexic because they have a particular ability to think and perceive events differently. They have the ability to make connections with what may be considered as abstract disconnected events that may prove to be critically important for the evaluation of collected security intelligence.

The need to achieve the desired match is important in that the term 'retention' does not only apply to keeping an individual within your organisation. It also applies to the active retention of those individuals' desire to continuously contribute to your organisation's overall performance. "There are a number of people in this organisation that are already retired" is an expression that identifies the opposite unwanted behaviour.

To maintain the vigour in an organisation the employment of management technologies have to be continuously challenged and re-examined to ensure that they are appropriate. This applies particularly to the leadership and management of workgroups' development. As an organisation changes the various workgroup boundaries will also have to be re-examined and redrawn.

Working from an organisation's environmental perspective it is important to examine the environment of those training and development providers. Universities, management institutions and other providers' funding are based on number of students passing examinations and/or acquiring a qualification. A brief examination of these organisations will find that many (as they are operating within a cost driven funding system) follow the trends of the existing dysfunctional business development, rather than creating and leading the necessary developmental educational processes. As a consequence, we are creating followers of these trends rather than influencing the reversal of these developed dysfunctional practices.

Coaching and Mentoring

The identified created organisational and personal expectations expressed above introduce the need for leaders and managers to have well developed *mentoring and organisational coaching skills*. Those that provide the development of these mentoring and coaching skills have to have an understanding of organisational leadership and management development skills that are tailored to fit the "contextual" and respective organisational development needs.

This form of developed organisational leadership and management coaching must be the basis for an individual's leadership and management development. Using an organisational approach enables the coach to identify within the individual the issues that need to be addressed in terms of their organisation. They must have the ability to help that individual to resolve internal conflict and confusion that may stem from their own personality or confused historic development. Once the individual has developed an understanding and taken ownership of these issues they are responsible for working through and resolving these areas of personal conflict.

We have explored how you may design and develop these systems to reinforce and continually develop those people with the potential to use their *organisational leadership* skills to the future benefit of your organisation. It is also a process that enables you to tap into the *collective intelligence* of your whole organisation. If the developers and users of these management technologies do not have a well-developed *cognitive organisational awareness* they will develop systems that do not fit your changing organisation's performance needs. They, along with your organisation, will become stuck and create or reinforce existing dysfunctional practices.

The Way Forward

If we start with this basic assumption that we are constantly required to 'shift economic resources out of an area of lower and into an area of higher productivity and greater yield,' we have to remove all those blocks that prevent a leader's ability to improve their organisation's performance. Whatever technical skills they may bring to an organisation they must rapidly gain an understanding of their organisation. This is achieved through their developed *cognitive organisational awareness*. Technical skills such as finance, engineering, information technology, and regulations surrounding Health and Safety and employment legislation, for example, can be developed off site. These programmes can be generally categorised as training.

Training, by definition, becomes a measurable product that you can demonstrably complete. You can either calculate the development of budgets or the design of structures. How you translate and employ these skills and use them to reinforce the continued development of your organisations becomes a developmental issue.

The development element is when the individual is able to employ those skills within the contextual environment of their organisation. Those developed *"social and emotional intelligences"* are components that enable them to successfully apply these competencies. Researchers have known for years that it contributes to *occupational success,* Rosenthal et al (1977). These *cognitive organisational awareness* skills have to be developed within the context of your organisation's needs; the *"social and emotional intelligence"* factors are part of that individual's personality and social development.

Many coaching programmes are in the form of personal development and may make the individual feel good through the attention provided (Hawthorne effect, 1923). We discovered earlier that our ability to transfer what we have learned becomes difficult and at times even impossible because of ingrained organisational performance cultural differences. (Refer to Chapters Two and Three, "Why organisations Become Dysfunctional" and "The Enemy within and why Change Fails".) These coaches must put these personal development programmes into the context of the employees' organisation, which requires that they, the coaches, have a well-developed *cognitive organisational awareness* of the organisation where candidates are employed. This developed competency ensures that the individual's development is within the context of his or her own organisation.

PART FIVE

Case Studies

Goals and Introduction

CASE STUDY ONE
Brewing Industry – Industrial Transition

CASE STUDY TWO
Avonmouth

CASE STUDY THREE
Greenfield Development Project

CASE STUDY FOUR
Ullage, CO_2 and 'as if' Organisations

NATIONAL HEALTH SERVICE

CASE STUDY FIVE
Leading Transition for Change – District works

CASE STUDY SIX
Operating Theatres Resolution of Conflict – Brook Hospital

CASE STUDY SEVEN
Greenwich District Hospital

CASE STUDY EIGHT
Transitional Nursing Care- Solution Equals the Problem

APPENDIX TO NHS CASE STUDIES

TECHNOLOGY & CHANGE

CASE STUDY NINE
Financial Sector

CASE STUDY TEN
Millennium Dome – Organisational Leadership

CASE STUDY ELEVEN
Canary Wharf – Technology and change

GOALS

To demonstrate:

- That this is not a quick-fix technique; it is a process for identifying organisational problems and sustainable solutions that can successfully be applied in all forms of organisations.

- The application of these evaluative and analytical processes can be used for resolving complex organisational problems.

- How these organisational processes inform the design, development and management of your organisation.

- How these practices can resolve multiple problems simultaneously.

- How these processes support and improve decision-making through to successful implementation.

- The use of an organisational approach as a third-party for conflict resolution.

- How this approach can be used for conflict resolution, improve workgroups, teams, interpersonal and individual performance.

- How all of these practices are set and developed within the contextual demands of the organisation's responsive needs.

- These processes have a capacity to enable you to audit the current performance of your organisation.

Introduction

These case studies have been placed in order of experience to demonstrate that the proposed organisational approach is durable over time with the capacity to successfully address presented issues within different organisational environments. It is not a fad, quick fix or a one-off panacea; it is an organisational process that once understood and applied provides sustainable supportive solutions that directly benefit the individual, workgroups, teams and the organisation, creating an opportunity to resolve multiple problems simultaneously. An important outcome of using an organisational approach improves the credibility of the leadership and management.

These case studies are working models of the application of the developed ideas and practices discussed earlier, enabling the presented problems to be effectively identified through the use of these supportive evaluative methods: *performance culture continuum, variation analysis, socio-technical systems* and understanding *the consequential effects* of introducing *new technologies*. They also improve your ability to regulate your organisation, workgroups, systems, procedures, practices and your own personal boundaries. That translates into improving your organisation and your own performance by significantly reducing goal displacement, role conflict and dysfunctional personal and organisational behaviour.

We explore the consequences of socio-economic and technological transference across organisational boundaries and the imposed responsive needs of the organisation. During the implementation process we identify how the Hawthorne effect and transferred behavioural consequences cross social systems, management systems and departments. We explore how changing one social system affects others. For example, causing a spiralling resistance to change being identified within the ranks of senior and middle management and by being aware of this phenomenon you can successfully work to alleviate these overt and covert trends.

These explorations are being examined to enable you to make the connections between the various academic concepts and research findings, enabling you to relate and incorporate these developed ideas into your *organisational thinking* and your own personal development. Nothing is sacred, except the primary task; everything else has to be under constant review to ensure that the organisation is enabled to respond effectively.

These case studies can only be snapshots of some of the processes that have been used to improve various organisations' performances. They are extracts from more extensive complex programmes of successfully leading and managing transition for change. The dynamics are complicated and have been described in broad terms to ensure the general application of this approach is understood. Even so, you will find that although these experiences are in different organisations there will be a degree of repetitive behavioural and decision-making practices that stem from the behaviour of those affected by the situation they are experiencing.

BREWING INDUSTRY

Introduction

The first four case studies are within the brewing industry and are being used to demonstrate the internal behaviour of an organisation when experiencing major external boundary influences; particularly brewing process technologies, new markets, and social, political and economic activities. The brewing industry creates an insight into the enormity and the relative rapidity of change experienced causing the confused decision-making that ensued.

When exploring the relative change experienced within the brewing industry they cannot be compared with a Google type of emergent computer based company, it would be unrealistic to do so. Yet the transitions for change experienced by this very traditional, stable industry through the introduction of advanced brewing process technologies were enormous. With the introduction of new invasive technologies into your organisation, you could experience similar confused strategic and operational decision-making behaviour.

This induced confused decision-making behaviour should enable us to make connections with previous developmental chapters, where we discussed dysfunctional organisational behaviour, the application of the organisational theories and in particular the effects of the social expectations, changing markets, competition and the development of new technologies and their consequential effects.

Markets and the employed technologies determine the primary task and the scope of the design. The developments of the regulatory management practices are defined by identifying the *states of flux*. It also identifies the systems design, procedures and practices servicing the decision-making and the development of the operational organisation to ensure the service delivery of that business.

This exploration provides an opportunity to understand the effects of market influences and the introduction of new technologies and their consequential effects, and how these influences created differentiated product process boundaries, confusing decision-making and organisations' behaviour that affected the leadership and management styles and developing performance cultures. It provides a valuable insight into individuals' and the organisation's responsive behaviour during the transition for change processes.

We also explore the developed decision-making processes for leading and managing a major project for developing a centralised national brewing, processing and distribution complex, along with the need to develop satellite wet-production sites, and consequential outcome of market expansion and the centralisation of production.

CASE STUDY ONE

INDUSTRIAL TRANSITION

Influencing Strategic Decision-Making

It is essential to understand the recent history to gain an understanding of the *here and now*. Essentially traditional breweries had a geographical localised territory that was determined by the production of cask-conditioned beers and its vulnerable short shelf life. These limitations were originally of no consequence as the product was distributed by horse drawn drays and/or canal barges.

The first significant technological change that affected the organisation was the introduction of motor driven transport. This change in technology meant that the product could be transported further, in an acceptable time, and without reducing the storage and shelf life. The centres of production could be further apart.

More ambitious brewing companies built new breweries but the preferred solution was to purchase an established brewery along with their trade outlets. The industry entered into a process of acquisition and mergers to improve their market share and reduce competition. The process of continued acquisition created regional brewing companies. These regional organisations initially had their own management structures that were a carryover from the negotiated mergers. Often protective brewing families' interests drove these negotiated mergers, influencing the design of the organisation reflecting the various factions' interests.

Determining the Brewing Process Boundaries

The basic brewing process had changed little over the past century, although the supporting technology had taken advantage of modern materials and process control systems. The major technological changes that have taken place in the brewing industry have been in the techniques for processing and sterilising the beers and the types of packaging used to increase the range for distribution. These technological changes have, at one level, been market driven and has created new market sectors at another.

The brewing process includes the conditioning process, to the stage where the product is rendered stable. For the purpose of clarification the following definition is proffered. If a beer is in any way still fermenting, whether in the first or second stages of fermentation, the brewing process is in effect continuing. In other words, the product is still maturing and progressing towards a condition where it is free of protein in suspension. The beer becomes stable and clear at this stage, and providing the product is maintained in the right conditions and not disturbed, the brewing process can be deemed to be complete.

The breweries selected their publicans primarily on their ability to manage beer cellars and interface with the customer. The cellar management skills, which are part of the regulatory management, were necessary to ensure the secondary fermentation process was completed successfully. Product quality and presentation were paramount. The expression "He keeps a good cellar" or "He Looks after his beer" or "He serves a good pint" was often heard. All these comments are statements about the landlord's ability in cellar management and husbandry towards the product. The beer cellar and the maintenance of suitable conditions for the beer to "drop bright" can be seen to be an extension of the brewery process being managed in numerous satellite retail outlets. The product's development and its boundary ended in the cellar of the public house. The technology of these products and their processing requirements imposed geographical constraints, creating localised breweries, localised product identification and customer bases.

Market Share

The drive to acquire market share came through changes in customer mobility and expectations for new products such as lager-based beers. To satisfy this demand other brewing technologies were introduced to enable the production of what may have been described at that time as continental style beers. The other customer expectation was the predictable pallet and presentation of their preferred beers, even when it was not served within the geography of their preferred brewery.

The local breweries attempted to compete by expanding the geographical scope of their product but inevitably they began to lose control of the all-important product quality. (We can relate this situation to the Toyota rapid expansion and product safety becoming the victim.) To overcome these constraints they introduced "brewery conditioned bright beer." This was a major technological shift and directly affected the ability of the breweries to compete not only at the regional level but also nationally.

The need to satisfy the market demands led to the introduction of new brewing and processing technologies that retained the control within the breweries' physical boundaries and removed the dependency on the skills of the publican or other trade outlets. Being able to produce a stable longer life product, which was no longer geographically dependent, changed the way breweries could be operated and compete in the market place. The critical changes were those that enabled convenient packaging of these products into bottles, cans and pressurised stainless steel kegs. The pressurised kegs were necessary to retain the CO_2 within the product.

The availability of these new packaging technologies enabled new markets to be created. The convenient product, bottled and canned beers, could be sold through off-licensed premises, off-sale from public houses, and in supermarkets and clubs. Social habits changed as customers could drink at home and in the streets so they had no need to visit a trade-dispensing outlet, such as a public house. These changes in brewing process technologies serviced and created alternative markets. All of which had a huge influence on the way these brewing companies needed to be led, managed and operated. (Refer to Fig. 34 "Invasiveness of Technologies")

Differentiated markets create internal competition between the traditional public house sales and the free trade open market sales approach. This internal marketing dilemma had to be managed without compromising one or the other markets being serviced.

Differentiated Product Boundaries

For the brewers, they were able to define the product's process boundaries. The traditional product is "cask conditioned beers" where the product is still in a state of secondary fermentation as it leaves the breweries' physical boundaries. The regulatory management boundaries are, for this type of product, extended to the trade outlet. The brewers manage and regulate the licensee of the trade outlet to ensure they ensure the product's management during the final stages. Two other regulatory management practices have to be completed, one being that the cask, once stillaged and settled, is not in any way disturbed. The other is that the product's shelf life is twenty-eight days and must be sold within that period or it would be returned as ullage as it had passed its shelf life.

The second product, bright beer, is filtered and sterilised within the physical boundaries of the brewery. Therefore, the product's regulatory management boundaries are within the breweries' physical boundaries. The fundamental difference is that brewery conditioned bright beers are filtered, conditioned and pasteurised, producing a sterile and inert stable product. These kegs of bright beer could be safely distributed over greater distances and on arrival, be dispensed almost immediately. The risk of infection was minimal.

On the other hand, cask conditioned beers are still fermenting when delivered into the trade outlet. It cannot be dispensed immediately and the relative shelf life is limited; reduced even further in hot weather. The need to be within the product's regulating management boundary limited it to a defined geographical location.

The brewers, with the cask-conditioned beer, still retained a relationship with the product once it left the physical boundaries of the brewery. Conversely the sterile inert bright beer sealed in a stainless steel keg required no further regulatory management once packaged. This had the effect of further removing the brewers from the product's life cycle and customers (Fig. 2 "Evolutionary Growth of an Organisation" and Chapter Nine, "Technology Change and Managing the Consequences" where we discovered that new technologies have the capacity to detach leaders and managers from the business of their organisation.)

Managing Differentiated Product Technologies

These changes in technology presented different critical organisational issues, in that these two products have two distinct process boundaries. The brewers were being forced to make an important market positioning strategic decision to embrace the bright beer technology and abandon the traditional brewing practices, or remain as a traditional local brewery. (Refer to case study, "Transitional Nursing Care" and the differentiated service boundaries model that can facilitate your decision-making.)

When examining and comparing the production of cask conditioned beers and brewery conditioned beers, the "territory" and "technology" boundaries no longer matched (Miller, 1959). The development in the brewery conditioned beer technology had, what Miller (1959) would refer to as the characteristic of the operating system as being "differentiated by territory." He wrote, "Characteristic of operating systems differentiated from one another, only along the territorial dimension that the output of the total system to which they belong is the added sum of the outputs of the constituent systems. Output from one system can be high or low, or even absent without directly affecting output from the others. In other words, where differentiation is only territorial, inter-dependence is minimal." But cask conditioned beers are not independent territorially and are inter-dependent technologically. Although the "sub-systems" are not inter-dependent on one another, the dependency on the brewery is reinforced not only by the "technology", but by a "time factor" which is introduced through the 28 day shelf life of the product.

The outcome of these alternative decisions shall be discussed and developed in more detail at a later stage. These differences in the use of technologies, would in turn, separately affect the organisation's behaviour and structure and the customer bases they would eventually serve. Woodward's (1965) studies of industrial organisations noted that there seemed to be a pattern of organisational appropriateness to the technology employed. Whatever technologies are employed, they will, without exception, directly affect the regulatory management within your organisation's performance culture, the styles of leadership and the management hierarchical structure. (Refer to Chapter Nine, "Technology Change and Managing the Consequences".)

The term 'technology' has been used only in reference to the *employed product technologies* not *management technologies*. We shall further develop this notion of differentiated technologies to identify how and to what extent it directly affects the decision-making behaviour, leadership and operational management of an organisation.

Vulnerability

The process of acquisitions and the need to develop market share created regional brewing companies. The drive and focus was to continue to grow and become national breweries and to position themselves to compete effectively. The growth and development of these brewing companies and their profitability made them prime subjects for acquisition by other non-brewing organisations. Courage breweries were absorbed into the Imperial Tobacco Group of companies and became a "cash cow" (Bhattacharyah, 1981).

The small traditional brewing companies retained their relationship with the product and their customer base. The product was alive in an organic sense and it could be inferred that the organisation had a more tactile relationship with its product, and therefore customers, the traditional drinking public. Those companies that became regional/national were trading in sterile products and the organisational and management development began to be more 'sterile.' There was disengagement with the 'new' remote customer base being created by the employed processing technology for producing "bright beer." (Refer to Chapter Nine and make the connection with the introduction of IT and the sterilisation of the developing data processes and production *machine model* for operatives.)

Fig. 2 ("Evolutionary Growth of an Organisation") identifies this condition when the organisations make the transition through the systems to the operational stage and in turn become further removed from their customer base. To encourage customers, often referred to as "punters" to drink in public houses where sterile products were served, the customer relationship with the establishment had changed to what we may refer to as being sterile. The ambience of the establishment reflected the product's sterile lifeless behaviour. This led to the trend of "theme pubs" to reintroduce the attachment of the drinking public with an establishment; not necessarily the product but its alcoholic consumption and social attractions.

Strategic Decision-Making Process

These brewers were responding to their organisation's need to incorporate these new technologies, to service these emerging markets, and to compete and maintain their market share. Within the brewing industry they were experiencing unprecedented turbulence and change.

This is an area where decision-making can become confused, irrational and dysfunctional. Warren Bennis (1997) writes, "Our mythology refuses to catch up with us" referring to the need to adopt appropriate leadership and decision-making practices that relate to the changing needs of the organisation. This leads to the use of outmoded leadership and management techniques; the skills redundancy factor. The confusion and apparent complexity is further exacerbated by the fact that an alternative viable organisational arrangement has not been identified and agreed. Therefore preventing the identification of leadership and management styles, decision-making processes and implementation practices, the systems behaviours and the processes that needed to be adopted. Historic practices and myths gain strong attachment to an individual, particularly when no viable organisational alternative is available; it's what they, the brewers and brewing families, understood. They fell into the trap of "trying to use out-of-date organisational systems for coping with entirely new situations" (Burns, 1963).

Shock Wave

Being absorbed into the Imperial Tobacco Groups of companies began to challenge some of the existing power based assumptions. The breweries each had their own hierarchy of brewers who were defensively passionate about running their own brewery, a legacy from the old localised brewing practices and attached mythologies. These influential factions were able to encourage the localised development of the different breweries to service the increasing market demands. As the brewing industry was extremely profitable the influence of the brewers and other power based interest groups was tolerated.

Johnson (1983) wrote: "It is interesting that the Head Brewer would take great care to produce a product, which matched the local drinking man's palate. The brewer was directly influencing and actively involved in the purchasing of the ingredients and in marketing decisions. With the size of the organisation ever increasing, it was seen fit to differentiate functionally. This caused the Head Brewer to be further removed from the purchasing of the basic ingredients, which was undertaken by individuals who specialised in these activities. The Head Brewer was progressively being removed from the basic procurement and marketing decisions. Their role was gradually reduced to becoming production process managers."

These role changes were being determined by the changes in technologies and their need to be regulated and managed. These technological changes to meet the market needs saw the nature of the product change from organic to sterile and innate, which in turn changed the emotional relationship with the product and processing practices.

"These changes were transmitted throughout the whole of the company. Changes in the brewing technologies' subsystems affected the ability to communicate meaningfully with the other brewing personnel. So it can be said that the functional differentiation within the territorial units had a detrimental effect on the management and maintenance and quality of the product" (Johnson, 1983).

The failure to understand the influence of the markets, the consequences of an acquisition strategy and the changing technologies of the organisation's behaviour led to the executives managing the created dysfunctional practices and not the overt organisation. The inability to understand what was being led and managed, in organisational terms, led to strategic decision-making being compromised. Profitability caused complacency to set-in, further compromising the strategic decision-making, leading to an inability to make the hard, but necessary, strategic decisions. The existing mind-set was being heavily influenced by their emotional experience of managing a traditional brewing process, the texture of the product and markets along with their customer base relationships. They had experienced the direct line from the product development through to reinforcing the satisfaction of the customers.

Profit complacency is extremely dangerous as organisations develop a comfort zone that insulates them from the market and technological trends that are influencing their organisation's developmental needs. This can be described as the internalising myopic politicking that affected the decision-making and losing sight of the customer needs (Fig. 3) where decisions are based on politics, careers and then the overt organisation. This can lead to a short-sighted perception of the organisation and dysfunctional strategic and operational decision-making.

The executive was informed that this behaviour was destructive, that internalised politicking was taking their eye off the organisation's needs and doing so would not only affect the organisation but also their careers. Their own levels of anxiety unfortunately prevented them accepting these unwanted observations. It meant that they would have to collectively accept what may be deemed a failure. An example could be in the failure of Courage Limited's Board's ability to defend itself from the interests of the predatory Imperial Group of Companies. (We can make the connection with the example of American Express internalising its behaviour when introducing reengineering practices, in Chapter One.)

"Professional Management"

Being absorbed into the Imperial Group of Companies saw the introduction of a rigorous professional accountancy styled management. This cost based management technology and those who employed them had no attachment to the history and culture of the brewing industry. They were focused and determined to further improve the overall profitability of their new brewing division. These cost based practices began to challenge the assumptions regarding the further development of the existing breweries, not before attempts were made to improve the capacity of the traditional breweries by re-examining the existing brewing practices with a view to speeding up the processes. This confusion led to acts of "superficiality", which Emery & Trist (1973) called "trivialisation" where anything is tried, which may effectively achieve a reduction in complexity. This maladaptive defensive behaviour was being used to defer the inevitable decision to centralise production.

The existing breweries were on prime real estate sites that were unable to physically expand as they were limited by other properties. The breweries owned many of the public houses and naturally these real estate values were factored into the profitability equation. A legitimate consideration, as the market of the product was no longer dependent on the control of the product in the trade outlet. The packaging enabled wider, more varied, markets to be exploited. The cost modelling and the factoring of the physical constraints identified the need to rationalise the brewing, processing, and packaging and distribution activities onto one major production site.

The next question was the funding of this major capital project. The feasibility studies identified the overall capital cost. Within the feasibility studies they had identified that the sale of the prime real estate of the old brewery sites would provide a major contribution to the capital cost of the new centralised brewing complex. With an almost self-funding cost model the decision was made to create a national brewing complex on a prime distribution site. The chosen site provided direct access to the M4 and therefore, the national motorway network.

Further Technological Innovation

Coincidentally another brewing process technology had been developed, that of high gravity brewing. This influenced the decision-making for rationalising all the brewing capacity onto one major site.

Traditionally the fermentation process was completed on open relatively shallow rectangular copper lined vessels. The innovation that changed this was the introduction of high gravity brewing, which meant that sixty five-foot tall cylindrical enclosed vessels were to be used to manage the fermentation processes. The advantage was the improved control of the fermentation process and the reduction in the physical area needed for fermentation. The introduction of this innovative approach had huge beneficial cost implications that reinforced the need to develop and centralise the brewing, processing, production plant and distribution. The decision to rationalise the production process, packaging and distribution onto a single site had major organisational implications.

An interesting decision that became attached to the development of a major centralised-brewing complex, on a Greenfield site, was the abandonment of the production of cask condition beers. The management of the bright beer fitted with the newly imported, what may be classified as clinical, analytical management style of decision-making. The cask-conditioned beer did not fit a controlled predictable model that brewery conditioned bright beer provided. We can now begin to observe how the product's behaviour was affecting the decision-making. This developed mind-set that stemmed from a strict cost modelling approach had the effect of losing sight of the various customer needs. The focus was on bulk brewing and the reduction of unit costs to further improve profitability.

Economic and Social Market influences

The created range of products, each differentiated by their distinct behaviours, were required to satisfy specific market sectors. Each product's technology required its own organisational performance culture and it attached *performance culture continuum*. The intuitive leadership and management styles were being determined by the behaviour of the products. This incompatibility, in organisational terms, required that the organisation be differentiated at the product management levels.

Schon (1965) writes "New products create new markets, new processes reduce the cost of existing products, or permit improved products to be produced without increases in cost, thereby extending markets." This is true, but the "changes in the organisation that result, must be managed to reflect those changes" (Woodward, 1965); an example of these influences on an individual's role, which has significantly changed the ability to influence markets and other strategic decisions, are those of the head brewer discussed earlier.

The market forces drove the decision-making, in that the decision to abandon the cask-conditioned beer in favour of bright beers was vigorously contested by a coordinated campaign group, the Campaign for Real Ale, to preserve cask-conditioned beers. This campaign for real ale, and pubs and drinkers' rights was extremely successful in that Courage had to retain one brewery to specifically brew cask condition beers. It also enabled other traditional breweries to survive the onslaught of the larger brewing organisations trying to rationalise the market by only producing bright beers. This trend initially caused many small breweries to close and has subsequently experienced a revival of microbreweries to meet localised geographically identified market demands. Those small traditional breweries that did not follow the bright beer trend have survived and are reported to be extremely profitable.

Economic Influences

The decision had been made for Imperial Tobacco to pump-prime the capital project to the new and centralised production and distribution site. The time it took to make the strategic decisions to centralise and to develop the project along with the implementation programme exposed the organisation to further market influences. Paradoxically the brewing division was being squeezed by further demands for increased profitability. At the same time the national beer sales were declining dramatically. Within this recession the value of real estate plummeted directly affecting the justification cost model. The ability to produce more beer than the market required saw the accelerated closure of other brewing production centres to satisfy the economic production performance of the new brewing complex. These factors exacerbated the capital cost recovery model causing further pressure to increase profitability.

Having set out some of the external and internal influences it would be useful to examine the consequential effects on how the organisation, the executive and employees were affected.

Consequential Effects and Analysis

The term 'traditional' has been appropriately used, as the rate of change in the industry had been relatively stable over a considerable period of time. It is important that when we talk about rate of change and change accelerating it has to be viewed in terms of that particular organisation's *employed technology and the market's behaviour*. For the brewers the accelerated rate of change was inordinate and extremely difficult for the affected individuals to comprehend the consequential effects on the developing organisation.

The decision to centralise brewing and production created pressure to develop a more appropriate organisation to accommodate the new technologies (Woodward 1965, Burns & Stalker 1961 & Lawrence & Lorsch 1967A). The failure, through the lack of understanding of the changing organisation's behavioural expectations and substitution of a political decision-making power base, caused the organisation to compromise its ability to satisfy its markets.

This confused internal politicking within the organisation caused personnel to suffer from role conflict, confusion and anxiety. These internal organisational problems, which stem from the change in technologies and market demands, were increasingly exacerbated by the desire for increased profitability. The Imperial Group's Board requirement for greater profitability along with the instability of the market place created a turbulent confused existence within the organisation.

Connections can be made to open systems theory, in that when a traditional organisation is required to adopt new technologies to meet the market needs, and should it fail to do so, it tends to become a "closed system" (Katz & Kahn, 1978); in this discussion we are identifying that the executives had internalised their behaviour, as a defence against anxiety, which meant they lost contact with their market environment. This can become dangerous as it can lead to the final demise of any organisation. The concept of any organisation tending towards "dynamic homeostasis" is appealing, particularly when an organisation has to cope with a "turbulent environment" (Emery & Trist, 1973). Emery & Trist said, "That to cope with a turbulent environment, men will try to make the environment less complex and in doing so, will adopt what they have identified as maladaptive defensive behaviour, "superficiality, segmentation and dissociation."

All responses are forms of passive adaptation and the environment can trigger them off. They are essentially defensive mechanisms in that they seek to negate and downgrade the environmental texturing with which they are confronted. The effects of the environment on the company were considerable and a lack of understanding of the phenomena that this created led to acts of "superficiality" and "trivialisation." "When a situation becomes too complex for organised, meaningful learning, an organisation regresses to various trial and error behavioural responses, firstly to this and then to that, in a way which is unrelated to the structure of the environment, but it may be highly correlated with its prejudices." The result is that the anxiety driven decision-making causes the organisation to become dysfunctional in that, in this case, the executives internalised their focus and lost sight of the market needs and the ability of their organisation to deliver. We can connect these practices to Argyris' (1986) observations regarding management practices, which he entitled "Skilled Incompetence."

The consequential failure to meet the profit performance saw the replacement of the Chairman and Chief Executive. It was not a surprise as the Chief Executive had summoned the leader of the operational management development group for, what was described as, a quiet discussion. He was politely asked about the development programmes, only to be informed that, "I hear you are doing magnificent things but I do want to ask you to ensure that these developments do not cross the threshold of this office." These comments confirmed that he and other executives had little comprehension of the consequential effects of developing a new centralised brewing complex on his and others' existing roles.

It does serve as an indicator of how people who are confused by the rate of change and lack the understanding, in organisational terms, to manage their anxiety by defensive behaviour: "... superficiality, segmentation and dissociation." He was caught up in the mythology of the old brewing culture and had failed to move with events and could be described by Kets de Vries as, stuck, "governed by their past" and locked in a psychic prison. It is worth taking note of Toffler's comments: "We are all redundant if we have yesterday's skills."

Wagman et al. (2008) writes, "The difficulty is not always a factor of size and scale. Even leading small organisations has become more complex and challenging than it was a decade ago." "It is no wonder that, despite the lure of the executive suite, a growing number of senior leaders are declining the top job or choosing to drop out. As one executive told us after talking himself out of consideration to head the conglomerate's fastest growing division, 'I know this job. It consumes your life. It's not what I want for me and my family.'" Even if you do take up the senior position, Wagman et al. (2008) suggest that, "many chief executives find tenure elusive." 'Perform or perish' has become the rule." They also identified that, "Study after study shows how tough and tenuous the top job is: in 1995, 72 per cent of departing U.S. and U.K. CEOs either retired or died in office. By 2001 that group dropped to 47 per cent. During that same period, CEO turnover went up 53 per cent." They also write that, "Such studies do not show the struggles these executives go through long before they exit. They continue to soldier on, realizing all the while that despite their best efforts, they are not achieving the results they need." (We can make connections with the compensation culture discussed in Chapter Eleven for CEOs and the manipulation of their benefits packages being increased even though their organisations were failing to perform effectively.)

The Missing Piece of the Puzzle

From an experience of successfully leading and managing major organisational *transition for change*, it would not be unreasonable to conclude that these executives may have many good executive qualities, the *missing piece of their development puzzle* had been the failure to understand what they are leading and managing, in organisational terms. They had not developed their *cognitive organisational awareness*, which would have significantly improved their organisational decision-making. They had not made the transition from their professional role to becoming organisational leaders. (Fig. 24 "Mapping Career Decisions".)

The above exploration of the extraordinary transition the brewers were experiencing was all being influenced by their organisation's need to respond to its environment. In particular, the changing technology and market forces were acting as the primary influential forces. (Fig. 11, "Managing Organisational Boundaries".) These experiences were further complicated by the dramatic changes in the economic market and property values.

The problem with these situations is that these acts of "superficiality" and "trivialisation" contribute and increase the dysfunctional decision-making and personal and organisational behaviour. The concern is that this practice can only translate and further compound the developed dysfunctional practices at all levels within your organisation. With these levels of anxiety people begin to only hear those suggestions that do not compound the levels of anxiety being experienced.

This practice of containing anxiety can be expressed through controlling the nature and way information is presented. For example, a review was commissioned to identify the real and potential losses in the "brewing trade." The identified losses were considerable and had attached a set of strategic proposals that would easily and quickly reduce these losses. At an early stage in the development of the report, the identified losses were embarrassingly considerable and proposed an initial intervention strategy that would begin a process of recovery.

It was felt that to make this information public in the form of a formal report, the nature and extent of the losses were shared with selected executives who refused to engage and continued to insist on a full and published report. The result was that the contents of the report, even though the research could not be faulted, were rejected. This report had served to compound the anxiety and, in effect, paralysed the executive's ability to act effectively. The group board was under pressure to improve profits, and ordered a similar review, using the content of this report, and lost patience with the regional board, with serious consequences. (We can make the connection with the repressed extensive list of complaints discussed in the case study, "Transitional Nursing Care".)

The effects of these changes caused a number of people to leave the company and many new people being recruited who had little experience and knowledge of the brewing industry. Many of these people had been recruited from industries where they produced non-perishable products. We established earlier that technology and the market serve to directly influence the culture and style of management of any organisation. This influx of "professional managers" created a series of conflicting relationships.

It destroyed the accepted career structure, which had undesirable effects. Merton's (1940) studies identified that "competition within organisations occurs within closely defined limits. Evaluation and promotion are relatively independent of individual's achievement." This increased the political manoeuvring (Burns, 1963), causing the more ambitious people to become overtly ruthless, very often at the expense of others.

The breakdown of the career structure and the attendant behaviour introduced a great deal of neurosis. The climate over the period of this experience had changed from a caring, paternalistic, almost "indulgent pattern of management" to "a punishment centred bureaucracy" (Gouldner, 1955A). People were promoted who were distinctly out of their comfort zone.

One sales director was asked to oversee the Technical Services Department of which he had no experience or interest. The organisation's environment and internal behaviour was in a state of "turbulence." The created insecurity and uncertainty were two of the factors that served to compound the confusion, along with the feeling of being under attack, further increasing his anxiety and feeling of being isolated. This prevented him being able to trust those responsible to him, even though they had a successful track record of managing the technical services department.

The sales director's coping strategy was to become unnecessarily aggressive using tactics such as asking a senior manager to bring "all the files" relating to potential industrial action. On arrival the manager would be kept waiting whilst the director, with his feet on the desk, conversed on the telephone with his mother, real or otherwise. Having carried all the files the director discussed everything but the subject contained in the files. This practice continued on numerous occasions. He would not accept a brief on how to address the industrial relation's issue and was deliberately rude and dismissive of the senior manager.

Realising the industrial situation was degenerating the manager took appropriate action with the collaboration of the HR Director and achieved a satisfactory resolution with the employees. The sales director attempted, unsuccessfully, to bring a disciplinary action against the manager in question. This failure only served to compound the deterioration of the relationship, and the senior manager finally resigned from the company. Further industrial relations issues needed to be resolved, adding to the sales director's anxieties, which led to strike action through the failure to take appropriate action. There was a suggestion that the technical service staff took retaliatory action for what they saw as the "sacking of our manager." (We can make the connection in the previous chapter, where Elton Mayo said, "Further research revealed the existence of informal groups or "cliques" within the formal groups. These cliques developed informal rules of behaviour as well as mechanisms to reinforce them. The cliques served to control group members and to manage the bosses".)

The neurosis caused by the fear of dismissal or at the very least the loss of career prospects had a marked effect on people's behaviour. With the increase in insecurity and sectional loyalty, and as people consider their careers as important as the needs of the organisation, clear conflict of interests do arise (Burns, 1963). (Refer to Fig. 4, "AS IF Displaced Organisational Goals", Chapter Three, "The Enemy Within", and denial of CO_2 in beer.) When we experience these levels of confused thinking, confused assumptions will exist. We can make the connection with the lack of understanding of these organisational phenomena, creating acts of "superficiality" and "trivialisation" in an attempt to be seen to be doing something. These induced behavioural practices are often designed to relieve anxiety rather than solve the organisation's presented problems. This can lead to, for example, inappropriate decisions to outsource to relieve the induced organisational anxiety. (Refer to Chapter Ten, "Outsourcing and Contractual Practices".)

Bulk Distribution and Wet Sites

The cost modelling had identified the advantages of rationalising and centralising production and distribution. It also became evident that the distribution costs would increase as the various products had to be moved over considerable distances. Moving small units of packaging such as cans, bottles and even kegs proved costly. The solution was to introduce satellite "wet processing and packaging units" supplied by bulk tankers.

Large bulk tankers would supply these satellite "wet processing" sites, decanting their load into cold storage vessels. These storage vessels formed part of the product's processing plant that would be used to supply the various bottling, canning and keg racking lines. The introduction, development and location all combined to create significant production problems. These difficulties are discussed in the following Avonmouth case study, which explores the consequential effects of developing this particular site.

CASE STUDY TWO

AVONMOUTH

Wet Processing, Packaging and Distribution Site

The Task

The task was to provide sustainable solutions to presented problems that consisted of: low productivity, unions and management entrenched conflict, high labour sickness and absence (ranging from 35% to 40%) and inherent design faults within the technical operation of the production plant. These problems had compounded over a period of two years since the commissioning of the plant. A great deal of time and expense had been employed attempting to provide solutions, all of which had failed to provide sustainability.

The approach to providing solutions had followed the traditional format of using a series of single systems initiatives. This included the "panacea approach", that is, the adoption and applications of solutions that had been reported to work in other organisations. They were in that cycle that many busy managers create, which is, "today's problems come from yesterday's "solutions" (Senge, 1993).

Having successfully worked through the necessary transition for change processes, the sickness and absence was reduced to three per cent. With confidence in the developed working arrangements and the increased production productivity, the site's future was secured by further expansion of the production plant.

Recent History

With the changing fortunes of traditional industries, the nature of the product and service management changed dramatically from labour intensive to mechanisation. Two drivers for change were the availability of new technologies and the desire of managers of those industries to be rid of the union controlled demarcated work, commonly referred to as "Spanish practices." The history of demarcation can be traced to the Trade Unions using these practices to initially protect existing employment.

In Chapter Nine ("Technology Change and Managing the Consequences") we discussed the development of the transportable sealed shipping container, a "just in time" innovation, which led to the demise of the traditional dock labour dependent practices. The consequential effect of these large industrial changes was the wholesale loss of jobs creating "black spots" of high unemployment. (Refer to Chapter Nine and Bent Flyvbjerg's observations regarding the effects of introducing new management technologies and their social consequences. "IT projects are so big and touch so many aspects of business, government, and citizens' lives that they pose a singular new challenge for top management" and to Fig. 34, "Invasiveness of Technologies".)

These redundant dock industry employees had well developed normative ingrained practices from years of union militancy. To compound these problems, many of the industries that were originally dependent and located near the docks had become permeated with very similar sets of normative behaviours that were directly influencing attitudes and practices. In this particular area, the numerous unions were culturally militant, underwritten by a complete mistrust of managers.

The Government solution to reducing these employment 'black spots' was to encourage businesses, through subsidies, to open new industries in these areas to reduce the local unemployment figures. Many companies took advantage of these incentives, building new plants to satisfy their own distribution, market and expansion needs.

Executive managers of the established industries, this brewery's counterparts, worked with the assumption that the unions were untrustworthy and militant. The local managers were instructed to be on their guard against any local militancy. To reinforce this instruction the executive managers withdrew the authority of the plant managers to negotiate with the various union representatives.

Within the Avonmouth process and packaging plant, conditions of employment were extremely competitive, in an attempt to compensate for the unwanted unionised normative behaviour. The working conditions were far better than many of the employees had previously experienced in both the docking and ancillary industries. (Refer also to case study, "NHS Greenwich District Hospital", where these normative behaviours were also transferred by association.)

This accounted for a 'them-and-us' standoff attitude expressed by both the management and the union shop stewards and supported by the full time officials representing the numerous unions. These hostile entrenched positions engendered further mistrust and the inevitable conflict often spiralled into threats of and/or going on strike. They retained links with the local activist, which meant they would respond to collective industrial action, if asked. It was known as "sympathy strike action", in support of their colleagues.

The management of the processing and packaging site were dealing not only with the immediate site closure, but the knock-on effects of bulk beer delivered from other production sites and also the pressure to reduce the loss of sales. The political implications were considerable from remotely placed executives who had little understanding of what was happening on the ground. These difficulties were further exacerbated, as local managers were unable to negotiate with the union representatives without referring up the command chain. These executives had also developed tacit agreements with the management of local established industries to prevent benefits spiralling, creating their own localised executive vicinage.

The various union factions, in different companies, would use one another to improve benefits, causing other local companies to be compared with their "significant *others* that are in comparative work" and used for negotiating purposes. The imported unionised normative behaviour had created hyper defensive practices to be introduced to combat the outcomes. The Personnel Director had become the power broker; it was his area of expertise causing others to defer to this techno-manager. (Refer to Chapter Eleven, "Remuneration and Motivation" and Twelve, "Development Training and Recruitment".) The dynamics, when negotiating, were impeded and tortuously slow, created by the defensive actions of both the unions and the senior executive management.

With this background, it was little wonder that even with very minor changes in work practices, there would be lengthy competitive negotiations. These negotiations were often conducted with a number of unions that represented the craft unions and general workers' unions. One of the transferred practices was the deliberate demarcation of work. Agreement with one union would create further difficulties, and other unions would want to maintain any differentials they had previously negotiated and established between different work practices. This practice of spiralling led to confused compromised management decision-making. The uncertainty attached to these situations created a fire-fighting mentality rather than a developed and agreed on-going working practice. This behaviour affected the mind-set of managers, which became inculcated into the management attitudes, practices and defensive negotiating styles with the unions.

Within the employment community, where most of the employees lived, the normative behaviour was an ingrained collective need to defend themselves against historically unscrupulous employers, namely the dock owners. This was an archaic behavioural legacy as the radical Labour government, between 1945-1951, had nationalised many industries, including the docking industry. With the traditional docks virtually closed with the loss of employment through the introduction of new technologies, these inculcated feelings were further reinforced.

Using an Organisational Evaluative Process

A quick overview of the production process took the form of a simply sketched variation analysis flow chart. This practice enables the identification of the *states of flux* that exist within the total production and delivery process. These *states of flux* exist where the product or process changes from one condition to another. The importance of identifying these critical *states of flux* is that there is often a *state of transition* that requires *regulatory management*. That, in turn, will directly influence the structural development of managing, supervision, monitoring to manage and the developed organisational design. (You can relate the situations in Fig. 2, used to demonstrate transition points, *states of flux* and the need for regulatory management.) The consequences of failing to identify, regulate and manage these *states of flux* led to this organisation becoming increasingly dysfunctional.

This process of using *variation analysis* provides you with an insight into the compounded effects of a decision or error in the process where consequential outcomes are enacted further and even remotely within the overall processes. An error that can occur at a very early stage in the process can compound things and eventually the ramifications can be experienced remotely in the trade outlets. These compounded consequential effects and their detached relationship is expressed in the following, "Cause and effect are not closely related in time and space" (Senge, 1993). Miller's concept of "technology, territory and time" should also be used within your developed organisational thinking.

For example, within this process was the delivery of the beer from a remote production centre, the filtration and carbonation, sterilising and filling, sealing and labelling of the bottles. Packaging, for example, should involve the transfer of the finished product without damage or delay being made for distribution. The delivery of the product by road tanker from another production site became the primary management focus. The reason being that if the product was in any way contaminated, or had high or low CO_2 readings, the consequential effects on bottling and eventual dispensing would be unacceptable. Beer could not be bottled with high or low levels of CO_2 as the final product, once in the trade, would be unacceptable when dispensed.

Should any of these products arrive in the trade they would be returned. These "returns" created a costly practice of decanting the unwanted beer, the need for what is referred to as "ullage" to be processed in separate facilities. There was also the costly and time-consuming process of recovering the Customs and Excise Duty that had been paid earlier in the process.

Benefits of Using an Organisational Approach

This process of determining the variation and consequential compounded outcomes can be quickly completed. The value of this process, even when no more than a mental process, provides you with an understanding of the critical focuses for regulatory management attention, the divisions of responsibilities, and the interdependent and dependant relationship between individuals and inter-departmental activities. It assists you to obtain a clear understanding of those activities that must take priority and be ranked against other demands that also need attention. When collectively working through this process you begin to develop a common language and dialogue as to "what matters" at the process and task levels (Fig. 40).

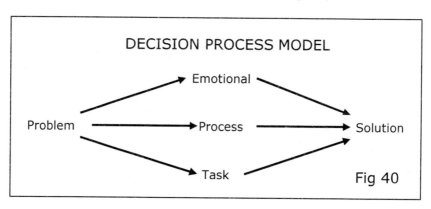

In this case it enables the clear differentiation of the engineering department's responsibilities and those of the production department. For example, being able to differentiate between the "twiddling" of settings and controls by the production operatives and genuine technical problems. It also provides an opportunity to evaluate why the production operatives are given to "twiddling." "Twiddling" refers to an expression of technological alienations causing operatives wanting to in some way regain control over their work practices. (Refer to Chapter Nine, "Technology Change and Managing the Consequences" Chapter Twelve, "Development, Training and Recruitment" and case study "Greenfield Development Project" to further develop an understanding of these induced practices.)

All the accusations and blame along with not taking responsibility for the initial problem had become buried under "yesterday's solutions." It focused each party on what had to be collectively achieved to improve the prevailing production failures. It enabled the limited engineering resources to be focused on those areas that had the maximum affect in assuring the constant supply of quality products across departments and to the customers. It identified, in the case of this particular business, the centre of the public house bar, was the point at which the trading transaction took place. In other words the centre of the bar was where the whole process was completed in exchange for money. It became known as the 'profit line', as failure to successfully complete these transactions, increased cost and reduced margins of profit.

Behavioural Activities

There was a need to constantly reaffirm that the initial brief was to examine the failings within the engineering department and the effects on productivity. The first task was to put this into the context of the organisational processes and the role of the engineering department. The value of using this approach was that it prevents you from working at the assumption level. (Fig. 40, "Decision Process Model".)

This is particularly important when attempting to evaluate any presented problem that has a developed history created within a dysfunctional organisation. It allowed, for example, the failures attributed to the engineering department to be rejected or owned. It is an enabling process that provides an opportunity to constantly test assumptions, with the specific intent to clarify the presented situation, within the context of the organisation's needs.

This developed approach was used, as the credibility of the management was virtually non-existent. Before breaking down these non-productive normative practices the credibility of both the management and unions had to be addressed. It is essential that when making interventions you develop and maintain a *detached engaged* role. (Refer to Chapter Seven "Adaptive Organisational Leadership" and Chapter Eight, "Workgroups – Leadership and Positioning in Groups")

A *detached engaged role* requires that you do not become involved in the normative reactive problem solving cycle of the existing site management. This detached role positioning enables you to complete the evaluative process of notionally unpeeling the onion to get to the core of the problem. The process of constantly *working for clarity,* in terms of the organisational process needs (Fig. 40) enables you, along with those affected, to identify and agree associated problems and to prioritise them in terms of "what matters" (Mant).

Prioritisation has to be set in terms of those issues that are affecting those *states of flux* within the overall process, as these solutions will, in turn, reduce or eliminate other consequential compounded problems. A significant benefit of this process is that when resolving one problem, particularly one that has compounded consequences, it automatically provides obvious solutions to many other associated presented problems.

Even though you may have clearly identified the problem, it is extremely important to work through the process with those affected, to jointly identify the presented problem. The purpose is to develop not only their understanding but also to develop their sense of ownership. They often produce improved workable solutions and in doing so develop a higher level of motivated ownership.

The purpose of working through the processes of the organisation's needs has a clear intent, which can be defined as developing a focused dialogue about the organisation's needs. It cuts across the blame game by using *the organisation to act as a third party*, enabling issues and accusations to be evaluated in terms of the organisation's needs. It avoids the situation becoming personal and individuals becoming evasively defensive.

This process included the affected engineering staff, production management and supervision along with the respective union shop floor representatives. It quickly became evident that the local management and supervision were far less cooperative and quickly slipped back into their entrenched negative posturing. To retain the union representatives' engaged interest, it was essential to develop shared credibility by jointly providing an appropriate solution to a presented problem. The selected problem would have to be chosen from one directly affecting the managements of the organisation and having a consequential impact on productivity. The chosen problem was the demarcation practices employed by the Boiler men. Although this was not a technical issue it was a management issue that was directly and significantly reducing production.

Demarcation – Boiler Men

The Boiler men were a workgroup of shift operatives, who were responsible for the generation of steam, refrigeration and compressed air. These services were provided on site but detached from the main production facilities. The steam was being used for heating the machines for washing and sterilising the bottles. It was also used for cleaning and sterilising the process plant, not an uncommon practice that many other diverse processing and production industries employ.

The recent history confirmed that there was an accepted demarcation practice between the trade unions and the general workers' unions. In essence, an unqualified person could not undertake the qualified tradespeople's work.

The steam was remotely supplied to the sterilising machines and for safety and good operating practices had stop-valves fitted to the steam main at a point where the steam mains connected to the sterilising machines. The Boiler men decreed that because the steam main was transferring generated steam, the stop-valve was part of their responsibility to operate. The production operatives were not allowed to operate these valves, the valves had to be opened and closed only by the Boiler men.

They refused to open the valves to preheat the plant until the production operatives came on shift. The Boiler men were part of the engineering staff and would not "operate" the plant, as that was the responsibility of the production operatives. This demarcated transferred practice was instituted during the period the plant was being commissioned and put into operation. The warm up period for the plant was approximately one hour and in the winter, even longer. This was a huge loss of production capacity, as production could not commence until the full sterilising temperatures were achieved.

An obvious question was – why not simply fit an automatic valve? In response to this question the tradesmen declared that it was still their responsibility to operate the safety stop valve. An automatic valve would still require a stop closure valve to enable the automatic device to be maintained. The valve had to be closed and locked off when the operatives were cleaning the machines. These claims were supported by their full time union officials and coupled with the threat that if any changes were imposed the collective union response would be considered. History showed that any attempt to force the situation would lead to strike action by the engineering staff. The process, production and distribution staff would collude with the engineers in supporting strike action.

Negotiating a Solution

An initial felt sense was that the Boiler men's behaviour was petty and without foundation, which is an initial emotional response (Fig. 40) that needed to be suspended. The operation of a simple steam valve did not need engineering training. They were using the technology and the dependency of the production process to create the negotiating currency for the Boiler men. On the surface it is petty, which raises the question – why did they put so much effort into defending this demarcation practice? In search for an answer it became evident that it was not a technical or competency problem but a social and status issue.

The nature of the social and status issue became evident when speaking directly to the Boiler men, collectively and individually. It is important, when engaging in these discussions, that you suspend any preconceived assumptions (Fig. 40) or possible solutions, as this enables you to engage in the dialogue. When you have preconceived assumptions or ready-made solutions (task level Fig. 40) rather than the process level, these will play in your mind and consciously or unconsciously encourage you to move the conversation towards your preconceived solution. This practice is part of the *detached engaged process* that will become evident as we work through this case study.

The discussion revealed that the current shift patterns, in simple terms, were affecting their families' social lives. They referred to the current shift practices as a "social affliction." They were making no demands for any financial rewards or changes in responsibilities. They had previously expressed a desire to change their shift patterns and had been informed by the Chief Engineer with the support of the Director of Personnel that this would not be possible.

Testing these assumptions with the Chief Engineer and the Director of Personnel, it became evident that they were not willing to disrupt the "existing stability." The "existing stability" referred not only to the current arrangement within this plant, it also included those other industries that were part of these executives' vicinage. They stated that they would vehemently resist any changes. They held these views even though the production time losses were considerable which on the face of it was completely irrational. They held the view that any changes in the Boiler men's shift patterns would involve additional cost and other unions wanting to change their work patterns. In essence, it was too risky and could create a spiral of uncontrolled events and, in particular, benefit spiralling. They also intimated that that it would affect the stability of other local industries.

This discussion confirmed that they had little idea of the demands and needs of the organisation at the local level. The notion of being between a rock and a hard place comes to mind. Even so, it was essential to address this problem irrespective of all the constraints. These situations demand the employment of *inverted organisational leadership skills*.

Sharing the concerns of the Chief Engineer and the Director of Personnel with the Boiler men and their representatives brought an interesting result. They offered, if we were able to find a working solution, to personally talk to the other union representatives and make their case.

The parameters for the discussion were that there would be no further expense incurred by the company. The Boiler men agreed that they would turn the steam valve on prior to production to warm the plant through ready for production. They were asked to define in clear workable terms exactly what they were attempting to achieve that would satisfy their expressed social needs.

They produced collectively agreed sets of issues, which centred on the unsocial shift patterns, which directly affected their families and their social lives. The main requirement was to develop a shift pattern that would provide them with one full weekend in four enabling them to engage in normal family social activities. These demands appeared to be reasonable. The task was to identify a shift pattern that would provide a seven-day week and twenty-four hour cover that could be simply regulated and managed. Within this design was the need to reduce the current levels of sickness and absence. (Some of which was to compensate for working with unsocial shift patterns.) The other requirement was that there would be no increases in remuneration.

Being unfamiliar with the various forms of shift patterns required further research. The existing negotiating practices could take a good deal of time and engender a cycle of making an offer and rejection, which would be disheartening for both parties. Information on various shift patterns was obtained along with biorhythms and information on health related issues attached to shift working. Each of the Boiler men was provided with the information and asked to read it in preparation for further discussions.

In a very short time they asked for a meeting to discuss the information provided. They wished to know if they could use the information to design their own shift patterns to achieve their expressed aims. It made sense and their request was agreed. In less than two weeks they had designed an alternative shift pattern that met all their needs. It also included health considerations, which pointed them to designing a notional reverse continental shift. They realised that by reversing the patterns they reduced the health risks and could simply achieve the one in four weekends off with their families. They had kept the other union representatives informed as to the content and nature of the on-going discussion. The Boiler men were extremely motivated to produce a shift pattern that satisfied their demands. They considered it their problem and not the company's.

During the ensuing discussion it became evident that as they were hourly paid they would experience significant changes in their weekly take home pay. This occurred through the different hours worked attracting a higher or lower hourly rate of pay. The variation in weekly pay was unacceptable and needed a method of smoothing their pay packets. The presented solution was for them to be salaried. Now we had moved into realms of possible conflict and resistance, not from other unions, but from the remote-overseeing executives and, in particular the Director of Personnel.

The Boiler men's representatives discussed with the other union representatives that making them salaried would not see their hourly rates enhanced. That it was, in reality, an appropriate method of convenience.

Persuading the remote executive to adopt this approach, even though they had assurance from the other union representatives, they still blocked the process. Having made many attempts to persuade them to directly negotiate and gain a sense of the Boiler men's integrity, their remote stonewalling required a collective assault. Collective pressure was put onto the Personnel Director, from the site managers, supervisors, distribution manager, and now the Chief Engineer along with the numerous unions' representatives. This was also supported with a cost model on the benefits for improved productivity. The real issue was that should the Personnel Director refuse to cooperate, the existing compounded entrenched union versus management practices would dramatically worsen and isolate the Personnel Director.

The problem of the low productivity would now become the sole responsibility of the Personnel Director. His stance of becoming the sole arbiter moved him from an advisory role into a line role causing a high degree of role confusion and the creation of displaced goals. (Refer to the discussion regarding target setting and ownership. Along with Chapter Twelve, "Development, Training and Recruitment" where management technologies, in this case HR, create role conflict.) The ground swell was being used to persuade the Personnel Director to attend the site and work through the process described above. The intention was not to corral him but to directly engage him in the reality of the issues being discussed and for him to develop a level of ownership.

The historic ritualistic collaborative practice of Personnel Directors within other local industries had caused him to relate and collegially work to protect the collective notional stability of these industries. They had created, over time, an alternative vicinage that he appeared to be locked into and unable to disengage for the sake of his own organisation. Obholzer (1989) observed there is a sense of self, derived from belonging to a group and an institution that wore a layer of "psychological skin" to foster a sense of identity and security of belonging. Unfortunately this created, within the Personnel Director, displaced goals that had serious unwanted consequences, isolating him from his own organisation.

Breaking through the Blockage

Working with this information we now turned to how the new management arrangements "if salaries could be agreed" would work. They were prepared, as they were actually working the shift that they should organise and manage the new shift arrangement. This included managing the sickness and absence cover. They were very aware they had to control the management of the shift work to ensure they all equally benefitted from the new shift patterns. With freedom comes responsibility, which meant that any arrangement they made had to be recorded and reported for information and obtain agreement with the line manager.

Essentially we were developing semi-autonomous workgroups that had the capacity to create strong self-regulating norms. The shop floor workers all knew who was "swinging a leg" and not pulling their weight. Supervisors often know but do not have evidence or authority to act. Membership of these workgroups introduces a strong sense of belonging and self-discipline that centres on not wanting to violate the established group's regulating norms. They also know that the penalties of being caught out can be severe.

The accumulative pressure from the ground swell and the opportunity to work through the process and task levels (Fig. 40) persuaded the Director of Personnel to reconsider and agree, although reluctantly, along with attached blame codicils to agreeing the proposed terms. The new working arrangements were instituted without any negative repercussions. They self-managed the shift patterns and cover for sickness and absence. The sickness and absence rate significantly reduced to a level that it no longer became an issue.

The motivation and willingness to engage was palpable. They became willing agents for supporting appropriate changes in other areas of the plant. At the very least they were a working example of how trust and collective focused intent can achieve the necessary desired results. The success of these changes that took less than two months to complete had a knock on effect that reverberated throughout the plant.

Transference and the Hawthorne Effect

This responsive transference can be compared with having created what can be referred to as a "Hawthorne effect." Landsberger, when analysing the original 1924-1932 experiments at the Western Electrics factory, the Hawthorne Works, situated outside Chicago, coined the term 'Hawthorne effect' in 1950. The Hawthorne Works had commissioned a study to determine if its employees would become more productive in higher or lower levels of lighting. During the experiment the workers' productivity improved when changes were made and slumped when the study was concluded. The conclusion drawn from these changes were that productivity was due to *the motivation effects of the interest being shown in them* during this experiment. The other factor that is being added to this conclusion is: that even though the lighting experiment was conducted in one shed another remote shed recorded improved productivity even though it was not under observation.

Within the Avonmouth transition for change programme the Hawthorne effect could be observed to be working when engaging with the Boiler men. The second element was the transference from one area to another and in this case from the Boiler men to the production, warehousing and distribution. The levels of mistrust had been significantly reduced, the willingness to engage and encompass changes significantly improved. The other and most important experience was the fact that the improved productivity was sustainable and not short lived. (Refer to Fig. 1, "Sustainable Comparative Performance Chart" and Fig. 17, "Product life cycle".)

Production Shortfall

The resolution of attributed engineering problems exposed the many shortfalls within the production operations. The blame game was exposed, leaving the production management to own and begin to address underlying issues. These issues were to develop an understanding as to why they were experiencing high rates of sickness and absence, and low morale and productivity. The production managers were encouraged to examine the consequential effects of any shortfalls and identify those that had the highest compounding outcomes. A good deal of this had been completed for the engineering department.

It was essential to develop ownership of the presented problems for the production staff to work through the process, focusing on the production issues. The first issue was to understand what the underlying causes contributing to high levels of sickness and absence were. In parallel the engineers wanted to know why operatives found it necessary to "twiddle" the regulators and control mechanisms.

Much of the servicing of the large cleaning and sterilising machines was extremely repetitive and required a good deal of physical work. The operatives of the plant were mainly women supervised by men. The discussions regarding the working conditions were conducted initially on the shop floor.

Further discussions were held with the occupational nurse to discover if there were any medical trends that contributed to the current levels of sickness and absenteeism. The main ones were the natural menstrual cycle, normal cuts and bruises, back pain but not injuries, headaches, and listlessness. The occupational nurse was asked to establish if there were any particular trends within specific work activities, sectors or in general. It did establish that age was not a factor except in reliability, in time keeping and quality of work. Initially the occupational nurse trawled through all her existing records to establish any existing trends. This information was to be used as comparative data, to monitor and compare the outcomes of any of the changes within the work practices, without identifying any of the individual operatives.

Operative Work Practices

The bottle loading into the cleaning and sterilising plants was by hand. Cases, of twenty-four bottles, were mechanically brought to the rear of the machine where the women would remove the bottles by hand from the case and place them on a moving table. The bottles would be transferred onto the mechanical carriages that transported the bottle through the machine to be cleaned and sterilised. On completion of the cleaning and sterilising cycle, the bottles were discharged onto conveyers and transferred to high speed-bottling machines, where they were filled and crowned with a sealing cap.

The beer supplying these machines was pumped from the processing plant to a rotating, header storage tank within the bottle-filling machine. The bottles were rapidly conveyed to a labelling machine, before being conveyed to case packaging machines. They were automatically repacked into the cases that were decanted at the beginning of the process. The replenished cases were transferred to pallet machines ready for storage and distribution. Male operatives invariably operated these machines. Men were used at this point as these machines had design faults that caused the machines to jam and trap the cases. Releasing the cases required a considerable amount of physical effort.

There were a number of processing and packaging lines that all completed the same task. The operatives tended to have fixed stations with little movement between activities. The speed of the machines had to be moderated to accommodate the physical capacity of the women feeding the cleaning and sterilising machines.

The resolution of many of the engineering faults that caused parts or all of the processing and packaging plant to come to a standstill had masked the fatigue experienced by female operatives. The numerous breakdowns acted as respite periods for the operatives. With progress reliability of the operating plant the period of continuous work for the production operative increased.

To gain relief the operative would "twiddle" with the equipment to either slow it down or create incidents that caused temporary failures to the machine or conveyer systems. With the improved engineering response providing reliable solutions these covert activities became evident. It also became evident that with the improved reliability the sickness and absence began to increase. This information clearly indicated that the work practices had to be reviewed and new routines introduced.

Production Processes Review

It was evident, from the earlier discussion with the operatives and line supervision that the work these operatives had to undertake needed to be examined and improved. Even though this was obvious from the outset, it could not be developed at that stage in the review process. The production management would be resistant, as they had developed a fixed mind-set, which was directed at improving production by introducing further draconian controls.

The independent respected views of the occupational nurse and the evidence of the covert activities of stalling the production lines provided the production management with an initial insight into some of the operatives' concerns. This opening of the production managements' minds enabled the process of evaluation to begin. This removal of the blinkers helped the managers to begin to accept that they did not have all the solutions.

Working with the premise that management and supervision were not actually performing these daily operative tasks, it was agreed that the operative should contribute and determine the new working practices. The production managers were asked to define the brief that the union representatives and operatives had to keep in mind. They identified that there should be no demands for additional remuneration, that there would be no further increase in the number of production operatives and that any changes in working arrangements had to be reported to the supervision for sanctioning.

The process was to share the generated information from variation analysis to develop an understanding of the consequences of their actions. The occupational nurse was also asked to provide them with the hard general information of the sickness and absence records. This was strongly resisted by the management who had, over a number of years, developed a deep mistrust of the employees and their union representatives. They were concerned that they would use the information to increase their subversive activities.

Even though the production management had raised their objections, progress had to be made. Meetings were arranged with the union representatives and a selection of the operatives, to test and gain support for the review process. They were made aware of the parameters of the discussions. They were provided with an opportunity to define their views and expectations from the review process. After they had time to consider the proposals they accepted the expressed requirements and added their needs for the process to work effectively. The structure of the review process would be led from the shop floor and they had to eventually undertake the developed work practices. Not too big a demand, although when reported to the production managers and supervision, this increased their anxiety as they felt they were losing control.

The resistance of the supervisory management tended to negate their contribution, which created a need to hold separate meetings. The risk of bringing the two parties together at that stage in the process would have been counter-productive. The underlying behavioural dynamic that these supervisors and managers were expressing was the *felt sense of redundancy*. They had, for a number of years, been fire fighting and these changes in practices created by the removal of dysfunctional practices no longer required them to fire fight. They were being asked to make the transition from fire fighting to responding to the needs of the production processes and enabling the operatives to contribute to improvements of their own working conditions.

To assist with these managers' concerns they were asked to work through the transition for change processes to enable them to "let go" of past practices and to adopt the roles identified from this process. With the experience of working "as if" they were experiencing the future state, they slowly began to accept the relative changes to their roles. (Refer to Chapter Six, "Leading Transition for Change".)

Giving people an opportunity to be innovative when developing their work practices and roles always generates a good deal of enthusiasm and focused intent. The example of the Boiler men introduced extremely innovative sustainable practices. These may never have become evident if management had only generated the ideas. Using the *collective intelligence* was the purpose of both of these review activities. (Refer to Pink's observations he calls "the new operating system" that revolves around *autonomy, mastery and purpose*. He defines autonomy as "the urge to direct our own lives, mastery as the desire to get better at something that matters and purpose as a yearning to do what we do in the service of something larger then ourselves".)

Acting as a go-between the two factions worked well as it enabled a *detached engaged* negotiating mediating role to be accepted by both parties. This process introduced a shared negotiating platform that persuaded the production management to enter into a joint review and negotiating arrangements. The discussions with the production operatives and the unions were developing to a stage where they wanted layouts to support and enable the on-going discussions. They had identified all the areas where they experienced difficulties coping with the work. They openly discussed why they "twiddle" with the plant settings and introduced short-term stoppages, all related to the desire to gain some control over their work and how it was to be achieved. They reported, "Management didn't listen so we used our own initiative." These observations were reported back to the production and supervisory management to test their reactions. Prior to disclosing this information agreement was obtained that they would not take any retaliatory action.

The role of acting as a mediator was devised to create a bridging process that would eventually bring the two parties together. This was being accelerated by the positive progress of the operatives in developing alternative work arrangements. This had been partly fed by the provision of information on alternative work practices including semi-autonomous workgroups. Each party was supplied with the same supporting information. The intent was to open people's horizons and to begin to develop a common language that would enable the two parties to generate a dialogue about improving their collective performance. Performance referred to production tasks, communications, respect for each other, supporting each other and the ability to have an on-going dialogue about motivational performance.

The excitement for the production operatives was palpable as they had all to gain. The production management began to see the benefits for improving productivity and their working relationships, but were still reticent. They felt they had more to lose and felt threatened by the development. (Refer to Chapter Seven and "felt sense of redundancy" when different working arrangements are introduced.)

Issues were raised that centred around losing control, loss of authority, divisions of responsibilities, accountability, future employment and their careers. Written confirmation on the supervisor's futures was obtained but the other issues would have to be worked through and determined from the agreed working arrangements.

A leap of faith was required. Being aware of the operatives' progress and proposed arrangements, the supervisors' anxiety regarding loss of control and authority was being amplified. This desire to engage in the discussion had to be handled carefully. One of the constraints placed on the production management was that they were not allowed to reject or veto any proposal. The managers were asked before the joint meeting to accept the proposals as a given and identify any role changes they may have to adopt to enable the process to work.

The first meeting was brief and deliberately informal. It was an information meeting where both parties were briefed on the proposal and counter proposals. They were instructed to evaluate both proposals and come back to the table when they had identified common areas of agreement. The areas of non-agreement would be simply identified and recorded. Both parties came together to discuss only the common areas of agreement. This was designed to quickly identify where and why areas of agreement existed and to begin to generate a dialogue about the way forward. This process is used to enable all parties to experience a small win, which is designed to enable each party to experience success. The intent was to change perceptions and assumptions through experience. (Fig. 13, "Assumptions from Experience" and therefore, attitudes.)

After a reasonably successful meeting the two parties were asked to now, independently, discuss the reasons why those areas of non-agreement existed. They were asked to examine these areas of concern to find alternative solutions that could be discussed at the next meeting. Complete agreement was not achieved but it was agreed that those areas of agreement could be introduced. They all realised that they had little experience of working with these processes and felt better, as they put it, "learning on the job". (Refer to Kolb's Experiential Learning Cycle, figures 37 and 38.)

They all understood the need to provide regulatory management for those areas identified as *states of flux*. They jointly agreed and identified who had responsibility for standards of work, monitoring and reporting, along with the development of an individual's specific role. The operative roles and those of the supervisors were all jointly discussed.

Focusing on the bottling process, the operatives developed and agreed the process, which they managed by job rotation. The way they were to manage this was important in that each rotation had to be with the flow of production. This is important, as the person moving with the flow would have to rectify any faults or failings generated from their own work. This introduced a strong sense of duty to one another. It soon became evident that if someone had to unscramble anybody's shoddy work, the workgroup would collectively find a solution. (Refer to operant conditioning, Chapter Eleven, "Remuneration and Motivation" which was designed into the operatives' work practices.) The cohesion within the workgroups was strong and, as with the Boiler men, they knew who was "swinging a leg" and soon acted to bring the culprits into line.

The productivity increased consistently and dramatically. Sickness and absenteeism fell, on average, to three per cent. Labour turnover was reduced to acceptable standards, which also meant that recruitment and retention dramatically improved. In fact the improvement in the working relationships within the plant introduced the need to produce a waiting list for applicants.

These improvements identified further weakness in the design of the mechanical handling plant that needed to be rapidly addressed to support the new working arrangements.

Confidence in the management and workforce along with their ability to sustain improved performance attracted further investment in a new production plant to increase capacity. The new plant that was to be installed was a high-speed keg racking plant.

Review

This early case study can only provide a general overview of the issues and processes employed to resolve the presented problems. Even so, we can extract a number of lessons.

This case study found that Deming claimed, "The workers are not the problem. The problem is with top Management." And his further claims that workforces who are only responsible for 15% of mistakes where the system is designed by management are responsible for 85% of the unintended consequences, was clearly observed throughout this organisation.

The expression that managers get the unions they deserve strongly resonated throughout this plant. The lesson is that people respond to how others behave toward them: "Behaviour begets behaviour."

In this case, the use of an organisational approach enabled the discussion and eventual dialogue to be centred on the organisation's process and not the personalities. This is referred to as using the organisation as the third party when negotiating. The value of this approach is that any observation is reflected onto the organisation and not the personalities. It avoids confrontation and the need for the various parties to save face. It proved to be an excellent way to resolve even deep-seated resentment and areas of conflict.

It also refocused everyone's *intent*, which in turn influences attitudes and individuals directed motivation. At the beginning of this case study the levels of active motivation was high but were of a negative negating nature. The *intent* was to compete and not lose face. We have to remember these union representatives have an audience that they represent. At the end of this case study the *intent* was firmly focused on jointly resolving presented organisational issues. That meant that the representatives and the workforce's positive motivation reflected in directed contributions to the plant's overall performance.

The Hawthorn transference effect, the transference of goodwill throughout the developed organisational practices spread into other parts of the plant. The satisfactory resolution of an intransigent problem, using an organisational approach to find sustainable solutions to the Boiler men's issues, transferred across the boundaries of other departments. This led to their representatives being prepared to discuss alternative work patterns and practices to reduce sickness and absence and improving the quality of their Working Lives (QWL).

Making connections, which we have to do all the time, between different social systems is important as this is also expressed and observed above. Senge (1993) when referring to compensation feedback, examines the consequential effects of one social system being modified, having transferred, in his examples, created unwanted outcomes. For example, "…Compensatory feedback processes have operated to thwart food and agricultural assistance to developing countries. More food availability has been 'compensated for' by reducing deaths due to malnutrition, higher net population growth and eventually more malnutrition." Within the context of an organisation the term *consequential effect* has been used, but *compensation feedback* is useful when examining the wider social system that maybe your organisation is influencing.

You can adopt this notion to create *learning organisations* (Argyris) by designing feedback loops that keep you informed of the consequential outcomes, both negative and positive. These feedback loops provide you with information, early in the process, to allow you to respond to these consequential outcomes. The working arrangements of the plant operatives and Boiler men had feedback loops that each group used to regulate the behaviour of one another. Each of these arrangements had operant conditioning to ensure individuals and workgroups learned from their work practices.

These experiences contributed to the development of a theory of organisational problem solving. The type of process was used to clarify the real situation that had to be addressed and to generate the appropriate information to make informed decisions. The use of an overall organisational process enabled the identification of specific causes and effects, referred to as the compounded and *consequential effects.* These were all used to move the discussion away from vitriolic blaming to centring individuals' minds on the real issue of solving identified organisational process problems.

The use of an organisational approach includes the use of socio-technical systems as these provide you with the insight into the systems requirements and the social impact that they pose. Hence the identification of the *states of flux* that required regulatory practices to be employed. This in turn, influences the management and supervision of the processes and the organisation of work. Another important issue is that when using an organisational approach the model (Fig. 13) ("Assumption from Experience") is employed. You are able to experience alternative (future state) practices, test assumptions and modify the experience and begin to change attitudes. Changes in attitude have to be achieved before you can begin to redirect and improve levels of personal motivation.

The other aspect of using this approach is that it automatically addresses issues such as the Quality of Working Life (QWL). It also has the capacity to resolve multiple problems simultaneously. This stems from the fact that many of the problems, estimated to be almost 90 per cent, are generated from the dysfunctional practices within organisations. Therefore, the employment of an organisational approach naturally attempts to address these multiple dysfunctional organisational practices.

The outcomes of using this approach brings to mind the Pareto Principle, often called the 80/20 rule, which states that, for many events, roughly 80 per cent of the effects come from 20 per cent of the causes. It therefore, proves to be extremely cost effective to employ an organisational approach as it provides sustainable solutions when working with the 20 per cent made available for you to influence. (Refer to Fig. 19, "Organisational Behavioural iceberg and Chapter Eleven, "Remuneration and Motivation".)

Improved work practices and management enabled the reduction, from 35 to 40 per cent sickness and absence on average, to 3 per cent. Self-management workgroups exacted levels of discipline within the workgroups that direct line supervisory management could only wish for, as the workgroups owned the task. (NOTE: Lessons can be learned from these production processes when introducing new management technologies that introduce data productions processes. These potential issues were identified in Chapter Nine, "Technology Change and Managing the Consequences".)

The final observations were that the organisational processes that were being used enabled the critical organisational leadership practice to be expressed, to influence the situation and the whole organisation's behaviour. In this case study we can observe an *inversion of leadership* being practiced. This would not have worked at all if a systems approach had been employed. Using the organisation as a "third party" for resolving conflict is a very persuasive non-confrontational process.

CASE STUDY THREE

GREENFIELD BREWING DEVELOPMENT PROJECT

This case study discusses the development of a centralised national brewing, processing, packaging and distribution Greenfield development site, which was an outcome discussed earlier in the introduction to "Overview of the Brewing Industry." This provides an opportunity to demonstrate the capacity of the employment of an organisational approach to improve the design, the introduction of new technologies, development, project management, developing and maintaining the decision-making communication processes, the application and development of socio-technical working arrangements and negotiating changes. This was particularly important when there is a turbulent environment created by the economic situation and the cost driven influence of the holding company.

To support the future development and operating needs of the major brewing and distribution site, a range of research programmes were instituted. This included research into internationally based comparable organisations' practices, current leadership practices, technical and building design, and visiting those academic centres where research programmes were being undertaken. The management and the operations of large production installations were undertaken to facilitate these developing practices.

To support the decision-making and implementation processes, an organisational approach was employed, which was supported through the use of socio-technical systems that included the Quality of Working Life (QWL) programmes that naturally included *variation analysis*, the development of the *performance culture continuum* and a well-developed *organisational awareness*. These processes were used to initially identify the critical decision-making workgroups and their dependent and interdependent relationships.

These processes provided a developed understanding of the dependent and interdependent relationships of the employed technologies. This practice was initially developed to improve the communication and decision-making for the effective development of the site and project management. This shared understanding enabled the identification of each workgroup's role and responsibilities, and their terms of reference, accountability and their dependent and interdependent relationships.

It, in turn, provided a working arrangement where the full-time union officials, the shop stewards and the respective employees collectively worked together for the identification of workgroups and the operating practices. These development and communication practices, supported by extensive research, identified that the brewing process control systems were over complicated and would only serve to alienate the operatives. It provided the ability for all parties to continuously work for clarity in terms of the organisations' needs; in this case, the executive organisation, the project delivery, the operational delivery and those ad hoc development workgroups.

When dealing with Trade Union's full-time officers we must remember that they are not part of the organisation, they have to be seen to deliver by protecting the company's employees' interests whatever form that takes. To that end, it is important to enable their visible inclusion, to enable them to contribute responsibly and support the collectively agreed decision and implementation practices. They have their own experiences of other organisations; either negotiating within change programmes or being involved with other major capital projects; you can view them as a valuable resource. We should underwrite this expression of engagement with the union's representatives by stating that the best cooperation stems from the felt sense and expressed *intent* of the changes being made.

The union representatives will soon pick up on whether *the underlying intent* expressed or acted out is appropriate to the organisation and its employees' needs, and they respond accordingly. It is a similar process to *leader's intent* and behaviour being interpreted and translated by the receiver of the communicated information. (Refer to Chapter Seven, "Adaptive Organisational Leadership".) These collective developmental and negotiating practices soon identify whether there is an external political agenda influencing the union's activities at a national or local level. (Refer to the international, national and local environmental influence experienced in the "Avonmouth" case study.)

Working with a Greenfield site enables you to develop the design of the physical arrangements to reinforce the desired social and behavioural needs for the successful operation of the site. At the early project development stage of a Greenfield site there is a sense that there are no historic barriers that cannot be managed and changed. The other powerful feeling is the sense that, at the design stage, you can move large physical structures and introduce changes by redrawing a pencil line. This also applies to our ability to intellectually reframe our current leadership and organisational development practices to *"fit"* the identified needs of the developing organisational arrangements. This must include the harmonisation of the social and the technical needs of that organisation.

The Decision-Making Arrangements

Predating all the physical design, an essential *transition for change process* had to be worked through to identify the successful future operating performance culture. Those who are going to finally operate the plant should have worked through these processes to establish and own the future operating and performance culture. Working through these processes will identify the necessary socio-technical design that, in turn, should directly influence the physical design of the buildings, plant design and layout, the use of new technologies and the way the whole site is to be led and managed.

To manage these various processes it became essential that appropriate workgroups be identified, their roles and responsibilities defined, along with their accountability to those with overall authority. For the purpose of this discussion the relevant groups will be identified. They were the Courage Ltd main board, which included the representatives of the Imperial Tobacco Group's main board. There was the project team that was responsible for the design and delivery of the overall project. They were responsible for the letting and management of contracts.

In parallel with the project delivery team were the site operations development team who were to be the senior managers responsible for the operation and delivery performance of the whole production and delivery site. The programming of all the activities of these triadic workgroups was carefully choreographed to ensure the decision-making processes were coordinated and clear. (Fig. 33, "Task Group Orientation".) Although authority was sought from the main board, the decision-making process was, as near as possible, a collective representation, which all parties owned and signed up to. This orientation process of all the task workgroups, was designed to support the decision-making process, and to evaluate and identify the consequential performance outcomes applied throughout. In other words, it was all embracing. The service delivery and operation workgroups provided a valuable form of feedback regarding the proposed development and changes.

Working from the perspective of the operation's development workgroup, we can briefly examine how their crucial role affected the overall physical design and operational performance. They were charged with getting rid of unwanted historic practices but to retain what was good. With this all embracing brief, the workgroup, who were still responsible for the operational line roles, began to examine and identify those activities that were dysfunctional, non-productive and needed to be realigned.

Some of the issues identified were, for example, the remuneration structure that prevented capable hourly paid staff from transferring into salary based supervisory management roles. The disparity in earnings prevented them from making the transition. Management and union relationships, the division of facilities such as differentiated dining facilities, car parking, the receipt of a free alcohol allowance, disciplinary procedures etc., all supported and reinforced the style of leadership and management that needed to be developed for the future operation of the site.

These decisions directly affected the leadership and management style, employment practices and the way management technologies were employed. To address these developments it is necessary to work along the brewing, fermenting, processing, packaging and service delivery *performance culture continuum*. In other words, how the

413

performance culture continuum worked as each of these activities and employed technologies affected their *primary tasks* and performance culture. All of these practices were specifically designed to ensure that all the activities along the *performance culture continuum* enabled each department to complement the *service delivery continuum* focusing collectively on the final customer service and their repeated satisfaction.

Brewing Hall Design

The brewery hall was commonly known as the "cathedral" as the style seemed to imply that sense. It contained all of the brewing vessels and looked clinical and extremely impressive. The physical designers had begun to develop the design of the brewing hall and the control technology and as usual followed a practice that was prevalent at the time. The technologies were available to automate and control the whole process. The process would be represented on a mimic-panel with various lights indicating the status of the brewing process. The operators would be housed in a sterile sound proofed room, with air-conditioning, which at first sight, to the uninitiated, was considered to be reasonable practice.

Experience and extended research in the USA, Europe and the United Kingdom, included the physical examination of these processes and ancillary process plants, clearly indicated that isolating the operator from the plant introduced sub-optimal performance. The sub-optimal behaviour stemmed from the operatives' felt sense of isolation and lack of control, although held responsible, only having the ability to act once a defect had been registered. At the time the mimic–panel would indicate the status of the process yet the actual process was in default and not registering. The consequential effects of recovering from these failures was hugely significant and extremely time consuming and costly.

Interestingly when these incidents occurred, although rare, the operators would be required to leave their observation box to physically assist the technicians in locating the various instruments; this they enjoyed as they had the opportunity to engage with the plant in a tangible form. These operators were openly expressing their frustration as they felt they could eliminate or at the very least reduce the consequential effects. They agreed that often boredom had distracted them as they occupied their time in other ways but were not always attending to the performance of the plant. This detached behaviour is often found where technologies have been inappropriately employed. The physical cocooned detached environment prevented the operative having a tangible relationship with the operation of the plant, leading to technological alienation. (We can make a connection with the intensive care nursing situation discussed in Chapter Nine, "Technology Change and Managing the Consequences".) This detachment from physical activities is similar to the leaders and managers becoming detached from their organisation and servicing displaced goals.

Raising these issues with the design team initially produced further recommendations for additional technologies to be introduced to compensate for these potential failings. The identification of these consequential outcomes serviced a cost management approach being used to justify the introduction of further control instrumentation and computer supported systems. Yet, neither the first nor the second proposal was satisfactory and they were both extremely expensive.

The final agreed design using a socio-technical approach enabled the physical design team and the main board to be persuaded that an alternative approach should be adopted. The alternative was to remove a good deal of what may be referred to as the secondary control computation and instrumentation, allowing the operators to have a higher degree of direct control. This meant, for example, that the large mimic control panel was placed in the middle the brewing hall. Objection from the physical design team regarding noise and heat were simply overcome by introducing attenuation. The reason for the operators being exposed to the operating sound of the brewing plant was to provide them with a sensory feedback from the plant that a plant valve had opened/closed, confirming the activities of the warning lights on the mimic-panel.

The background to these changes was the need to enable the individual operator to retain their human contact with the plant, which provided a sense of personally being in control and actively operating large elements of the process. The intention was that these operators were not just responding to retrospective information but to live, sensed information that they could act upon. It provided sensory responsive feedback.

This enabled the consequential effects to be either eliminated or be significantly reduced. The approach was preferred by the operators and significantly reduced the potential for *technological alienation*. Subsequently we find that the Japanese use a term 'Jidoka', which loosely translates as automation with a human touch, which matches this earlier developed socio-technical approach. The results were that the cost of the technology was significantly reduced, the control and operation of the quality of the brewing process retained its integrity and subsequent reviews indicated that the operators were not feeling any sense of *technological alienation*.

Packaging "Shed" Design

When retaining a human dimension, 'Jidoka' is important. If you fail to do so, the physical design of the building can and will alienate those who work there. For example, if you were to imagine yourself standing in an empty hangar that normally housed a Boeing 747 you would find that there is a limited human dimension. In other words, you cannot relate to the space, other than be amazed and maybe intimidated. Put a Boeing 747 into that space and immediately you will begin to develop a spatial sense and relationship with the building and its contents.

Imperial Tobacco designed a building that one could simply call a hangar, it was huge and employees had to walk considerable distances within the corridors of this building before being able to break out onto the production floor. The employees, when interviewed, all declared that they disliked the distance they had to travel to begin and to leave work. They also complained about the building being "lifeless and having no atmosphere." They were paid well and the conditions of employment were recognised as good and the only reason for staying. Underlying these observations there were a number of festering issues that the management had to continually counter when dealing with their local union representatives that often stemmed from the induced alienation from the building's design. (We can make the connection with the notion of Herzberg's hygiene factors, of satisfaction and dissatisfaction, discussed in Chapter Eleven, "Remuneration and Motivation".)

The machines producing cigarettes without the feeders can be physically compared to a large saloon car but no more. The other ancillary equipment that fed, for example, the loose tobacco, was not in any way large. The packaging of the rolled cigarettes was once again similar to the actual cigarette-rolling machine. There were many production lines housed in the hangar shaped building, which was bright and airy.

Essentially the building design did not fit the employed production technology. When the machines and production lines were viewed in the space, they were insignificant. The building was a design suitable for an aircraft but not cigarette production; it simply lacked a human dimension relative to the production technology employed. This insight along with other evidence-based practices confirmed that these large impressive structures were not the answer.

The packing and racking plant size was massive but in relative terms had a human dimension. The unscientific measurement was that all columns supporting the roof would be no more than two bus lengths. It was felt that people were familiar with the size and proportions of red Double Decker buses. The plant would be placed in the space created by the columns and the mechanical handling would be simply designed if necessary to weave their way around the columns. The roof space would be roughly the height of a Double Decker bus. The design and the development of this shed shaped building provided the flexibility should the plant need to be redesigned or replaced. These unscientific proportions provided the human dimension to avoid the technological alienation created by the building experienced within the tobacco-manufacturing example.

Persuading the physical design team was not difficult as the design and the layout of the plant complemented the development of the semi-autonomous workgroups. These operator workgroups had been identified and developed by development workgroups, which included those to be employed on the lines, the union representatives and the packaging production management. These workgroups were set up to deal with the different elements of production, processing, brewing and distribution. Where dependent or interdependence was identified, the workgroups were merged to develop and manage the identified boundary arrangements and *states of flux*. They were introduced to socio-technical systems and job design, which enable the *states of flux* to be identified and the necessary regulatory management arrangement to be designed and agreed. Many of these design considerations and their generation were deliberately worked through to reduce the kind of organisational and work alienation (discussed in Chapter Nine, "Technology Change and Managing the Consequences").

Fermentation Vessels

The developing brewing process technology was high gravity brewing, which reduced the volumetric space needed for high volume production output. Conventional production processes for low gravity fermentation would require significantly more production space.

Traditional breweries would use flat horizontal rectangular vessels for fermenting the product, which required a considerable amount of space to accommodate these large and quite deep vessels. The new approach was to ferment the products in vertical fermenting vessels. These vessels were stacked like grain silos on the outside of the building with only the access door available with a specially constructed corridor building. From the outside these vessels were nicknamed "Cape Canaveral" as they looked like rocket silos. These innovations to the brewing process were, in terms of the brewing industry, extremely radical ground-breaking advances.

As with any advances in development they were likely to introduce unexpected consequences. In this case the brewers and the designers of the vessels had not anticipated that the CO_2 would stratify with these very tall fermenting vessels. Stratification is the building up of layers; in this case when the head of fluid is such that if the pressure of the fluid above is in excess of the force created by the precipitating gases, the gases will stratify. In other words the CO_2 gases would be trapped and settle at specific but different levels within the vessel. The consequences are that when the product was packaged the quantity of CO_2 varied throughout the product.

Some of the packaged cask beers would have a high CO_2 and others normal level of CO_2 contents. When dispensing in the trade, the keg with the high CO_2 content would create a creamy gaseous product that needed time to settle before it could be consumed. This inability to dispense the product consistently and present the product to the customer was totally unacceptable. It also created a great deal of waste and the product would be returned to the brewery as ullage. Not only was it an unwanted activity, it also affected future sales. A solution to the problem had to be quickly identified. (The organisational issues that stemmed from this are discussed in the case study entitled "Ullage, CO_2 and "As IF" Organisations".)

These examples have been picked to specifically raise the issue of introducing new technologies and are intended to provide you with an insight into some of the processes and issues that you will need to consider. It is accepted that there are still many questions that need to be answered. This book is about the way we *think organisationally* and the processes we use to complement and reinforce the overall organisational delivery performance, and although briefly, some of the issues have been addressed.

Review

The processes briefly described above, of the integrated teams and the responsibility of the operation's development teams attempting to clearly define and design the organisation that led to the physical design, significantly improved the decision-making and implementation progress of the project.

- The project was completed three months earlier than programmed and on budget.

- Contributing factors were the operation's development team who were able to develop and clearly define the brief for the project team, avoiding unwanted changes to the briefs, delays and increased costs.

- The relationship between the various teams had to be managed, which had the benefit of the normally detached executives being physically and mentally attached to the decision-making processes. This also prevented 'whimsical nice' aberrations suddenly being introduced and preventing *acts of "superficiality"* and *"trivialisation."*

- Ownership of the processes and the decisions were inculcated throughout the triadic team practices. The physical design and delivery team published their programmes and asked that all the other programmes match with the set planning time line, preventing unscheduled cost overruns.

- The operation delivery team were responsible for working for clarity and to provide the scope of any brief to the design delivery project team.

- Any unresolved issues between these two teams were referred to the executive team. Each party would put their case and the three parties would be required to adopt the appropriate solution. The appropriate solution being the interest of the organisation's needs and the decision-making and implementation processes.

CASE STUDY FOUR

ULLAGE, CO_2 AND "AS IF" ORGANISATIONS

We identified in the "Overview of the Brewing Industry" and the previous case studies that when new technologies are employed, unforeseen events will disturb the existing organisational power cabals and can introduce unexpected consequential outcomes. In this case the stratification of CO_2 in the fermentation vessels. This case study is the process of using an "as if" organisation to identify the centre of the technical problem disguised by the generated conflict and organisational problems.

The brewers were confident that the process for monitoring the CO_2 contents during the fermentation, processing and racking of the product into kegs was accurate and satisfactory. As owners of the new brewing and fermenting technology, they developed a siege lock-down mentality, projecting all the failures onto the two disparate communities, the Free Trade and Tied Trade outlets.

Free traders are independent retailers and can freely purchase products from different breweries. They used their strategic purchasing capacity to bring pressure onto the brewers by refusing to sell these poorly dispensing products. The tied trade, as implied, is tied and could not, at that time, acquire products from other suppliers. They are tied to the brewery and often the brewery owns the public house. These properties are managed outlets and had to endure the complaints of their clients. These two communities did not have a common voice and were being ignored by the brewer's systems driven certainties.

The sales and marketing functions were becoming increasingly frustrated with the loss of free sales and the complaints of the tied outlet managers. The brewers had systems-developed repetitive evidence that they used to defend the monitoring practices. The assumptions regarding the managed and free trade outlets' behaviour were based on historic redundant myths that no longer applied. That caused them to automatically respond by accusing the trade outlets of tampering with the products. Even though the new sealed packaging technology made this extremely difficult, as any attempts to tamper could easily be identified. The entire production on this site was bright beer. The protraction of this entrenched attitude caused the loss of further free trade sales. Also, the managers of the tied outlets were becoming more militant and threatened collective action.

Historic Trade Outlet Practices

The brewers historically were aware that tampering in the trade outlets where cask conditioned beers were on sale did occur. The Customs and Excise Authorities were not always convinced and would refuse to refund the excise duty. The loss of sales and the increasing cost of handling the high volumes of ullage were not only exacerbating the sales and marketing departments, but also the main board. The brewers initially had the ear of the main board but that was beginning to wane and a solution needed to be provided to this on-going problem.

The brewers were entrenched and resistant to external examination and the trade outlets were unable to collectively develop a persuasive case for the brewers to take heed. The solution was to set up a quality audit trail that tracked the product from its source to each trade outlet. The information was available as each batch had a gyle number that enabled the product to be tracked throughout its entire journey.

Introduction of a New Management Technology

The introduction of a quality audit tracking system was seen as introducing a new *management technology*. By its very nature it would cross all those organisational and departmental boundaries that were responsible for the production and delivery of the product. The new management technology would automatically have to have the authority to cross departmental boundaries. It also had to be autonomous and independent of the authority of each of those departments. The management of this "as if" organisation had to be sensitive and aware of the organisational cultural differences that

422

would exist within each of these departmental functions. This examination of the cultural differences was expressed along a *performance culture continuum* that assisted the "as if" organisation to identify the pitfalls and the necessary approach that would be designed to engage these different disparate organisational cultures.

Here we are bringing to the forefront the notion of *cognitive organisational awareness* where leaders are required to modify their behaviour to satisfy the organisation, workgroups and individuals presented with situational behaviours. This well-developed ability to competently use your *cognitive organisational awareness* is absolutely essential as you are working across many departmental and organisational cultural boundaries. It required the development of an organisation that has the ability to work across these various departmental functions and not in any way usurp their authority. The intent of these developed management practices and the design of the management technology was to generate information to track the behaviour of the product through its life cycle. (Refer to and compare this situation with the techno-managers discussed in Chapter Nine, "Technology Change and Managing the Consequences".) The notion of *performance culture continuum* (Chapter Four, "Developing a Theory in Practice") comes to mind, where each function is employing different technologies and has other service delivery needs than that of other functions within the continuum, which influence and create different organisational performance cultures.

The organisational solution was a temporary "as if" bridging organisation that had the authority, through developed credibility, to identify the source of the problem. The design of this "as if" organisation was critical, as it had to be credible to all of those affected. It had to be independent and only accountable to the main board.

Setting up and introducing an "as if" organisation required that all parties had to sign up to the authority and responsibility of this auditing process, whilst also being aware of the potential influence it would have on the various constituent parts of the whole organisation and in particular how the decision-making would directly influence their performance culture and behaviour. Because of its invasiveness, even though a very small organisation, it was being designed by using an organisational approach.

The primary task was identified and agreed with all parties. From this process the boundaries of authority, responsibility, sanctioning and implementation of any changes were defined and agreed. The values and the behaviour of the organisation were defined which, in turn, determined the leadership and management style that was to be employed. "All parties" refers to all the departments that were being scrutinised within the product's quality audit trail scheme. This included the supplies of raw materials, brewing, fermentation, processing, distribution, technical services, the Tied Trade Outlets and the Free Sales activities. The Free Trade were not in the negotiating cycle because they were not bound by the brewery to sell their product and operated in a free market and had no interest in working to solve someone else's problem.

The geographical area was large which made it impossible to individually visit every outlet when a complaint was raised. Imposing sanctions on the various trade outlets had to be handled delicately. A system of evidence-based warnings was introduced to ensure that each outlet understood not only the gravity of their behaviour but also that hard information was being generated and shared. The nature of the sanction was also defined for each part of the organisation to individually manage. The militancy of the trade outlets had to be managed.

A three warning system, using operant conditioning, was introduced to ensure fairness, which meant that at the first identification of any variation they were made aware of the issues, a second variation meant they received a written notice and on the third they were disciplined. This could range from, in the case of the tied trade managers, being sacked and/or as with the free trade the refusal to trade or even prosecution, as Customs and Excise Duties were involved. This approach had the full cooperation with all the trade outlets.

Creating feedback loops that serviced the overall systems process automatically informed the individual, within the trade outlets, of any variations. The design of these feedback loops created a direct responsive action, which created an *operant condition* to deliberately achieve a responsible change in behaviour within the trade outlets. These operant practices were designed into the systems feedback to encourage all parties to learn from their experiences and change their behaviour.

Introducing New Computerised Technology

It required a computer system to be rapidly developed to capture the data and to produce credible information for tracking events. The quality of the information and the identification of the source of the problem would have to be completely credible to persuade, for example, the entrenched brewers should the problem be within the breweries' boundaries.

This "as if" bridging organisation had to be designed to satisfy its *primary task* and its behavioural *intent*. To achieve this systems and procedures had to be specifically designed to reinforce these required performance outcomes. It also provided a clear systems design brief for the computer systems designer. Within the design specification the behaviour and intent of the system were also specified.

The initial behaviour of the computer systems designer was to begin by telling the host organisation what he was going to design. He was clearly instructed as to what was expected from the design of the computer system and that he had to satisfy the prepared brief. Experience of other clients abrogating responsibility through deskilling relied on the systems designer to interpret their needs that, he declared, often took the form of "What do you think?" This abrogation of responsibility is totally unacceptable as you are the "agent" of your organisation.

This form of deskilling is not unusual, particularly when we are presented with a new situation and we are outside our own comfort zone. The introduction of new technologies can have this effect particularly when the recipients are outside their existing intellectual skills and experience. This condition is exacerbated when we are intimidated by the size of the presented computer technology that is to be installed, as we have a developed sense of introducing significant change for which we have no control. Not having a developed perspective of the consequential effects of introducing these management technologies leads to these forms of abrogation. Are we surprised that those charged with these projects deskill and become unacceptably dependent on the techno-manager?

425

Once briefed and provided with an explanation of the intent of the organisation a working system was quickly produced. Even though this is a small system compared with others, the same experiences of deskilling can be acted out when the situation is unfamiliar and outside your normal experiences. The all-invasive nature of the introduction of this IT system and the attached protocols can also be intimidating when the consequential outcomes are not understood in organisational terms.

This practice is further compounded when dealing with large systems as a sense of being overwhelmed can ensue. A dependency begins to develop on the IT techno-manager, who becomes the source for relieving and even unloading induced anxieties. (These difficulties are discussed in depth in Chapter Nine, "Technology Change and Managing the Consequences".)

The design of the quality audit tracking system was specifically developed to track the product's journey through the brewing, fermentation, processing and packaging processes, through the distribution systems, and identified by each trade outlet. It also included the sales profile for each of these outlets to determine if they were unnecessarily over ordering, particularly cask conditioned products.

Creating this tracking system and the development of the body of evidence forced the brewers to re-examine their practices. They were supported by the "as if" group to specifically work through and test the assumption of the auditing processes throughout the brewery site. This continuous testing and evaluating of the progress of the product as it moved through the various processes identified that the inconsistencies existed within the breweries' boundaries.

Tracking back along and thinking through the *variation analysis* and the results recorded began to focus everyone's interest on the fermenting vessels. The samples were being taken from the bottom of the vessel. Continuous sampling throughout the vessel clearly identified the inconsistencies and posed the question – why? Addressing this question led to the identification of the stratification of the CO_2 in the fermenting vessels. Having identified the focus of the problem a satisfactory solution was quickly introduced.

Resolving this problem at its source enabled a number of other practices to be reviewed and discontinued. The majority were, as a consequence, introduced to compensate for the effects of inconsistent CO_2 content. When organisations are dysfunctional you often discover a myriad of practices, systems and procedures that are only there to compensate for the existing dysfunctional organisational behaviour.

Understanding the Notion of Consequential Effects

It may appear to be incredible that an "as if" organisation had to be set up to deal with this issue. When you considered that the brewers were always product assured and historically the problems were invariably in the trade, adopting this entrenched stance can be understood. We must also remember that there was a great deal of pressure being applied by the main boards of both Courage and Imperial Tobacco Ltd. They were also subject to the increasing pressure of the sales and marketing departments.

Their reputations were on the line and that affected their behaviour. Their influential and powerful intransigence was further increased by the fact that they were the owners of this new brewing technology and they were totally convinced of its invincibility. All of which added to their anxiety and the need to displace and transfer the problem on to someone else. (These anxieties have been discussed in detail in Chapter Three, "The Enemy Within", where the brewers even denied that CO_2 was a by-product of fermentation.) They were also subject to what can only be described as a "power raid" by the now displaced main board executives. These on site operational executives were being directly influenced by the anxieties being felt and expressed by these notionally displaced main board executives.

The use of an "as if" organisation is valuable as it enables you to develop a credible temporary organisation to evaluate, as in this case an unexpected technical problem, to work across boundaries to explore alternative ways of developing your various organisation and work practices. It provides the opportunities to legitimately work across multiple boundaries and provide what may be suppressed by the existing organisation's cultures within different functions.

The remoteness of the consequential outcomes of one's decision-making and actions can create a state of detachment, particularly when there is no feedback as to the nature of these consequential outcomes. In this case feedback existed as the product was being returned and sales were being directly affected but the evidence was not being heeded. "Cause and effect are not closely related in time and space" which can"...keep people from seeing important interactions" (Senge, 1993).

Closure

The completion of the "as if "organisation's analytical work normally requires that it be shut down. In this case the systems for auditing the product were transferred to service the marketing and sales distribution and technical services department. Its ability to audit trail the various products and how they were performing in the trades proved to be extremely useful for managing the various products' reordering, delivery and any other issues surrounding the delivered product and their containers.

Review

- The cost of the computer system was recovered within three months.

- The credibility of the brewers and the Trade outlets was restored. Importantly, the two parties were able, through the development of this audit tracking system, to discuss any product quality issue on a process and task basis. (Fig. 40)

- Once the seat of the problem was identified the "as if" organisation's role changed, which meant that the "as if" organisation had to be restructured and the system devolved.

- The other valuable result of this approach was that nobody would lose face, as the brewers, once faced with the identified problem, were able to quickly provide a working solution. All parties were relieved that the problem had not escalated.

THE NATIONAL HEALTH SERVICE

CASE STUDY FIVE

DISTRICT WORKS

LEADING TRANSITION FOR CHANGE

Recent History

This is an exploration of the systems behavioural dynamics of a dysfunctional organisation that was inherited when charged with the responsibility for transforming the failing Greenwich District Works Department. This department was responsible for the effective management of the entire estate and all the utility services.

The realignment of the dysfunctional District Works Department had consequential outcomes that directly affected other departments, functions and power cabals. This usually occurs – when you remove one dysfunctional practice, it unveils another, which may be directly related and/or completely unrelated.

This District consisted of eight hospitals historically distributed throughout the London Borough of Greenwich. The District executive administration was responsible for the performance of the whole District, consisting of the Chief Executive Administrative Officer and a number of other senior executives that could be described as working towards retirement. This created a climate of maintaining the status quo, causing these executives to take the expedient route of avoiding any unwanted conflict leading to ineffectual decision-making and a power vacuum. This power vacuum was filled by the Treasurers department, which had young enthusiastic leaders.

This power base was further enhanced by poor financial management, which needed to be addressed throughout the various hospitals. The Treasury were intent on improving the financial and cost control but they had little experience of line management within a direct dependent service delivery function. These Treasurers had also formed political cabals with senior clinical consultants who collectively wielded a considerable degree of political influence. It takes little imagination to realise that these cabals created *displaced organisational goals.*

The incumbent District Works Officer was over promoted and unsuited to occupy this senior district leadership role. His professional bias was toward capital projects and had little capacity for the leadership and day-to-day running of the revenue based operational service delivery activities. This bias in interest towards capital project management caused him to lose track, over a number of years, of the revenue expenditure leading to consistent budget overruns. This failure to attend to the revenue expenditure caused a power vacuum, providing an opportunity for the Treasurers to begin to over exert their influence. They had virtually taken control of the operational activities of the District Works Department.

Another factor, which reinforced the disengagement of the District Works Officer, was the geographical positioning of the Works Department's offices. They were situated on a remote rundown mental care site that was located on the extreme periphery of that District's responsibility. This isolated remote geographical location had the effect of detaching this service from the day-to-day activities of all the hospital services. There was no engagement or sense of belonging to the District or various hospital services. The location of these services is important if you wanted to retain any sense of the urgency and needs of the various hospital services.

This satisfied the temperament of the incumbent District Works Officer as it enabled the reduction and control of any direct contact with those who wanted to influence his practices. He was able to use this situation to not only physically withdraw, but also psychologically. It provided a means for managing his increasing induced anxiety caused by his inability to address the considerable cost overruns.

The Treasurers, not having the skills to run a District Works operation, in organisational terms, made a number of major errors. They directly influenced the decision to devolve the local on-site operational works activities to each hospital's executive administrators. The hospital-based administrations, along with the Treasurers, were unable to effectively lead these various Works Department's services. Neither had the *cognitive organisational awareness* skills or the technical skills to lead and support the local onsite Works staff.

These failures to understand the nature of the organisational problems caused them to resort to what they knew best. The individual hospital executive administration simply accepted that they were their responsibility and this amounted to no change in their attitudes or management of the Works service activities. They only responded when other clinical disciplines or the Treasurers began to insist that action be taken.

Treasurers were frustrated and far more aggressive in their intent to effect changes in the District Works Department's performance. Their frustration, with little progress over a number of years, extended to the possibility of fraudulent behaviour. Whether this was devised as a means for unseating the District Works Officer or to establish why the costs were increasing was never really established.

These aggressive practices by the Treasurers were designed to fail. Their attention was on the capital control and looking for fraudulent practices. Yet, the revenue costs were not being managed on any of the hospital sites and the problem worsened further, fuelling the Treasurers frustration. They had resorted to having treasury personnel hiding behind trees to discover fraudulent practices. They instituted investigations into the various senior District Works Officers' personal accounts without any evidence that fraudulent practices existed.

Creating a debilitating "Double Bind"

Works staff had resigned to simply respond to the reactive frustrated behaviour of the actions taken by the Treasurers and the individual hospital executive administrators. They used the expression of keeping their heads below the parapets, which simply means they were regulating their activities to keep out of trouble and not attract attention. The behaviour of the different factions, the Treasurers, the

Administrators and the clinical staff created a situation where the Works staff were experiencing the effects of being in a *double bind*.

A *double bind* is an emotionally distressing dilemma in communications in which an individual or workgroup receives two or more conflicting messages in which one message negates the other. This creates a situation in which a successful response to one message results in a failed response to the other, or vice versa. They are wrong, regardless of the response. The preferred focused activity that the Works staff understood was to respond to clinical support needs and when doing so, they were countermanded by other confusing instructions. The instructions from the on-site administration usually had a political bias unrelated to the prioritised clinical services support needs. The other unrelated but simultaneously introduced instruction could be the control of expenditure disenabling the Works staff from completing the necessary work.

Bateson and his colleagues first described the double bind theory in 1956. Leaders and managers who are incompetent develop a tendency for bullying and often resort to this sort of behaviour. It is utilised as a form of control without open coercion, which makes it difficult to effectively respond to or to resist. The double bind is often misunderstood as being trapped by two contradictory demands. A double bind is subject to these two contradictory demands; the differences lie in how they are imposed, how the victims interpret the situation and who or what imposes these demands upon the "victim." The "victim" has difficulty defining the exact nature of the paradoxical situation in which they find themselves.

Typically someone they respect or who is in authority imposes a demand upon the "victim", but the demand is inherently impossible to fulfil because some broader context forbids it. An example could exist when a person in authority issues two contradictory conditions and there is an unspoken rule that you do not ever question their authority. These injunctions need never be expressed but the victim understands them. (We can notionally connect this situation to the observations of Agyris (1986) in his article "Skilled Incompetence" which identifies how managers who are skilled communicators but want to manage the potential risk employ the use of ambiguous communication. The receiver of the communication clearly understands the ambiguity and responds accordingly. This ritualistic behaviour is also part of the developed corporate working environment that we all, over time, fit into and do not challenge. See the extract from Chapter Five.) In essence a double bind is two conflicting demands, each of which is on a different logical level, neither of which can be ignored or escaped.

Treasurers controlled their budgets, regulated the expenditure and prevented the staff from completing tasks effectively. The administrators were pressing for work to be completed but had no power to agree expenditure. This placed the Works staff in a position that meant that the executive administrators' demands could not be met. There was regulatory work that had to be completed but funds were withheld; yet they would be asked to prioritise their work to meet those activities that interrupted the clinical services. This left them with a dilemma of not meeting the regulatory demands, which had severe penalties, or concede, to the clinical service needs to prevent the clinician from harassing executive administrators. "I must do it, but can't do it" is a typical double bind response. Not surprisingly the levels of sickness and absence increased servicing to further exacerbate this stressful unworkable situation. (We are able to make the connection with the Enquiry 2010 into the Nimrod disaster where the political environment had created an, 'overwhelming objective of finding savings' causing 'organisational trauma' and displaced organisational goals. The behaviour within the Nimrod example had become normative and accepted.)

Leading Transition for Change

Reviewing the recent history enabled a picture to evolve of the unhealthy behavioural dynamics that had developed over a number of years. The first thing that needed to be addressed was the need to define the role of the District Works Officer and define the boundaries of responsibility for leading the necessary *transition for change*. These activities were designed to position the District Works Officer so that everyone understood his role, intent, responsibility, accountability and authority to act. The boundaries were defined and managed to ensure that any unwarranted influences of the Treasurers, the executive Administrators and the clinicians were manageable. Managing these political situations cannot be ignored: they have to be managed in terms of the organisation's needs (Johnson, 1983).

434

This can only be effectively achieved by the adoption of an organisational approach. In this case it became an essential process as the Works function and anyone associated with it was tainted with the history of incompetent unprofessional leadership practices. Any opinion expressed was discounted in preference to the prevailing political protagonists who, of course, knew. This had to change and fast.

Using the notion of boundary management they were persuaded that either they or the District Works Officer was responsible for transforming the performance of the Work's Department. One requirement was all the Works personnel would be directly responsible to the District Works Officer both technically and for day-to-day operational activities. It would be impossible to lead a transition for change programme having to work through the various hospital sites' executives and/or the Treasurers. Reluctantly these expectations were accepted after a good deal of persistent and forthright discussion.

Even though the agreement had been reached as to who was responsible and where the boundaries were, the Treasurers who had tasted unbridled influence and power found it difficult to "let go." For example, they had subsequently met with a company who claimed to significantly reduce the energy consumption by renegotiating the utility supplier's tariffs. They, the Treasurers became agitated when they were informed that they were wasting revenue funds signing this contract and that the District Works Officer would not in any way cooperate.

They had not realised that the Works staff would complete all the work and this company would receive ten per cent of the revenue savings over a period of ten years. They were not aware of the fact that the way heat was being supplied to two of the hospitals was being completely reconfigured. The capital budget that was funded by the Regional Health Authority had been reduced through these changes by £1.5 million. In line with these physical heat generation changes the tariffs had all been renegotiated. They had not become aware that the reduction in oil consumption would be a direct function of changing over to gas.

This confused thinking existed because they were unaware that one of the first things a Works Officer should address is the energy cost which must include the renegotiation of tariffs. They were entering into a ten-year contract where ten per cent of any saving would be credited. They were outsourcing (displacing the problem) the management of the energy budget yet the contractors, other than renegotiating the energy tariff, were unable to influence any other direct activity. Yet the contractor would consume a good deal of the Works staffs' effort either defending their cost claims and/or the servicing of the information they required.

The alternative and valued use of these contractors was to employ them to examine the existing tariffs and make the necessary recommendations to beneficially change them. They would receive a fee for the analysis and recommendations but no on-going commitment. The responsibility for accepting and implementation would remain with the District Works Officer. In either scenario the Works staff were responsible for negotiating the tariffs and reducing the overall energy budget. The treasurers were unwittingly creating displaced goals and using the existing Works staff to do the work for the contractor.

From the treasurers' perspective they assumed they were breaking new boundaries. They were, in fact, outsourcing an activity that was the direct responsibility of the District Works Officer. They were creating displaced organisational goals by placing the District Works Department into a subordinate role servicing the contractor's demands. (Refer to the muddled thinking that can surround outsourcing decisions, Chapter Ten, "Outsourcing and Contractual Practices".)

This desire to outsource simply confirmed that they had not yet accepted the authority of the District Works Officer, indicating more work had to be done to influence their current thinking. (Refer to "Role Ambiguity and Confusion" (Fig. 23), where we discuss the role of others who transgress the line manager's role and cause confusion and the unwarranted need to defer to these non-line support functions.) This is a classic situation that can be observed in many organisations.

It also demonstrates the reluctance of those who assume power, through any vacuum, to resist when the power structure is, by necessity, being realigned. Their assumed power was only obtained through the dysfunctional behaviour of the District Works Department and the consequential affects within other departments.

The focus had to be on improving the overall performance of the Works department, not being distracted by other non-line activities to ensure it complemented the needs of the clinical staff. The distraction of this energy saving system was interesting in that the Treasurers felt that the District Works Officer should report directly to them regarding any changes being made. They were reminded that the accountability for any activity was the two District Executives, and that they would be notified only of any projected overruns of expenditure. As a courtesy it was agreed they would be briefly informed of any projected changes but not to obtain permission.

They had been previously asked to draw up a profile of cost expenditure for the whole District Works. That was to be differentiated by each hospital, which would provide them with the ability to monitor the changes in the cost profile. If they had completed this task they would have seen the cost profile and energy costs being significantly reduced. Access to the cost profile would also enable the District Works Officer to prioritise the necessary activities that needed to be completed. When completing this comparative cost profile they could monitor and support any changes that needed to be undertaken. Eventually they created the required cost profile. It was a long process persuading them to "let go."

The clinicians also felt that they had an input into the decisions relating to the operational performance of the Works Department. They convened a meeting and demanded that the District Works Officer attend. Most of the consultant clinicians were in attendance, plus the hospital's Executive Administrator and other interested parties. This meeting took the form of instructive requirements to prevent particular actions, for example, the testing of the backup generators at Greenwich District Hospital (GDH). Or even to countermand an instruction to move, on a temporary basis, one of the senior Works Officers from one hospital site to another.

On each occasion, they were gently reminded that they were not responsible for either of these decisions. Historically when the collective might of the clinicians was brought to bear, they always got their way, under the previous District Works Officer, but on these occasions they were politely refused. This was enabled through the use of an organisational approach where the organisation acted as the "third party" for any conflict resolution.

These incidents indicated that more work had to be completed on the transition process. This could only be successfully achieved department by department to ensure the transition process translated into tangible successful outcomes. (Refer to Fig. 13, "Assumptions from Experience".) They were informed that should their department be affected they would personally be involved to ensure the changes met with their clinical service needs. This was a process for progressively building confidence and the ability of the Works department's capacity and competency to consistently deliver agreed standards of service performance. A "Clinical Service Support Model" (Fig. 41) was used to prioritise and agree the work that needed to be addressed by the Works department. This approach enabled the management of the various clinical political cabals to allow the Works department to focus on "what mattered."

Management Development

All of the Works department's managerial staff were required to attend a four-day residential workshop to learn to *lead and manage transition for change*. These workshops were designed and led by the District Works Officer with the valuable support of the Deputy Personnel Officer. It provided an opportunity for all the Works managers to work together and understand each of their problems. They were able to develop a shared language and dialogue about their own and the overall organisation's performance. They were enabled to collectively understand what was expected of them and how to continuously develop their organisational leadership and management skills. These workshops were extremely successful. The Works managers at the Greenwich District Hospital (GDH) no longer felt isolated, as they now understood whom they were working for and to what end. Their own hospital Works department's environment had changed and they understood how that would affect their current management practices.

438

In parallel with these workshops, the immediate presented problem was the operating theatres at The Brook Hospital and that was where the initial attention was placed. The reason this was chosen as the first issue to be addressed was determined by this department's position on the "Clinical Support Service Model" response time continuum (Fig. 41).

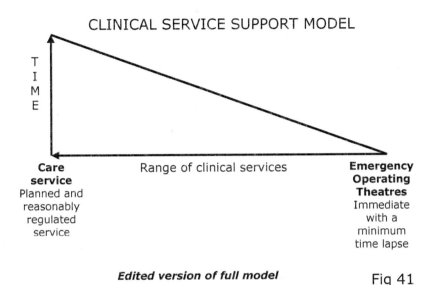

CLINICAL SERVICE SUPPORT MODEL

T
I
M
E

Care service
Planned and reasonably regulated service

Range of clinical services

Emergency Operating Theatres
Immediate with a minimum time lapse

Edited version of full model

Fig 41

Problem Solving and Thinking Organisationally

To service the thinking and understanding of the problem it was essential to gain an understanding of what was being serviced, in organisational terms. This required a developed understanding of that organisation's services' role within the operational service performance of the hospital's and other clinical service provisions. It was necessary to develop a clear and shared understanding of the primary task of the District Works in terms of each clinical services provision. One of the main issues this process identified was a need to prioritise and differentiate services delivered across a range of geographically displaced, clinical practices.

The primary task was defined as *to provide and maintain a physical envelope that supported the clinical staff in the delivery of their services.* The prioritising of these disparate services was developed through the creation of a notional Clinical Service Support

Model (Fig. 41). The purpose was to take what appeared to be a complex organisational problem and simplify it into a process model that could be used to communicate and find agreement with all affected parties.

This model was developed by the use of the concept of "territory, technology and time" Miller (1959), that enabled the analysis of the response *time variations* of each of the disparate services. Working through and positioning each department respectively along a developing *performance culture continuum,* all the services were placed and ranked by the response time they needed to achieve when required to deliver their particular patient delivery services. In the development of this notional model, consideration for the *employed technology* and that department's organisational environment, which included its *notional* market response, were taken into account as these elements directly affected the response time that service commanded.

The clinical service support model (Fig. 41) indicates that the minimum response time would normally be reserved for the Accident and Emergency (A & E) at one end of the continuum. When you move along the continuum, for example, to the recovery ward, the response time will marginally increase. Should the patient relapse the response time would be changed and the patient would quickly shift towards the emergency and trauma end of the continuum.

The model may appear to be over-simplified but it is important to remember that you are looking at the organisational processes and not the specific clinical practices. The model, although simple, allows the various clinical practices to contribute to the development of the model. They are the practitioners and you are attempting to relate your services to complement their clinical service needs. They are the clients; you are, in the case of the Works Department, the support services provider to enable the clinicians to perform safely and effectively.

The process of developing this notional model assists in defining roles, and the ownership of presented problems and tasks that needed to be completed, along with the different clinical service cultures and responsive behaviours. It enables, when working through this process, to identify and agree the dependent and interdependent relationships of each of these activities. Those *states of flux* that need to be regulated and managed can be identified, and appropriately designed changes can be incorporated into these necessary agreed practices.

Even so, you would often find the different services would be particularly precious as to the reaction time, which was being influenced by their recent experience of the Works Department's poor performance. Attitudes begin to change when those affected have small wins that, in this case, the agreed services were delivered on time and consistently. (Refer to Fig. 13, "Assumptions from Experience", discussed in Chapter Five, "Developing a Theory in Practice, Part two".)

Coupled with this service performance change was the important change in the ward sisters and other clinical personnel developing a felt sense of being in control of how these services were delivered. Within a brief period of time the various clinical services became more accommodating and were prepared to agree when Works personnel were to complete a piece of work. (The only exception was the Greenwich District Hospital (GDH) the reasons are discussed in the case study, "Greenwich District Hospital".)

As you begin to achieve a degree of clarity in the organisation, deep-seated interdepartmental conflicts begin to surface. Some of these are repressed and accommodated by developing what may be referred to as unofficial practices. The repressed frustration, when finally released, can be very forceful, accusative and highly defensive.

Using an organisational approach enabled this pent-up frustration to be harnessed and redirected away from the personalisation and towards the more tangible organisational issues. You are able to move the conversation away from a "punishment centred bureaucracy" (Gouldner, 1955A), where confrontational historic blaming and "scapegoating" is ascribed to a person or department and begin the process of jointly resolving the presented problems. These frustrations develop from apparent intractable situations; the wrong solution being developed to solve the wrong problem and the gradual development of dysfunctional accommodating practices.

When dealing with these emerging situations that have been unearthed, through the employed organisational processes, the secret is to not be tempted to own any of the projected accusations. This venting of their frustration is part of the process individuals need to exercise to allow them to be free to address the real issues and make their own personal transition for change and "letting go." (Refer to Chapter Six, "Leading Transition for Change".) Invariably these people quietly, once the process and conflict has been satisfactorily resolved, apologise for what they now perceive to be their unwarranted behaviour.

The value of this theoretical approach (Refer to Developing a Theory in Practice) is that it is relatively quick and has the added value that you develop a common language enabling a dialogue to develop in relation to their own organisation and the development of their clinical services. It allows the two parties to begin the development of an agreed decision-making and implementation process that is designed to improve the service and complement the recipient organisation's own performance. The developed understanding of the interdepartmental complementary relationships improves collaboration and operational decision-making.

You can also plot the changes in your own organisation's operating and service cultures, adaptive leadership styles and role relationships. (The use of this approach and modelling can be further explored by referring to the case studies "Operating Theatre Conflict", "Transitional Nursing Care Services" and "Greenwich District Hospital".)

Servicing the Organisation's Needs

The process for developing this model can be adapted and used for other service departments by adding in the responsive nature of that particular clinical service influenced by the need to respond to market forces. For example the emergency end of the service continuum where A & E is positioned is market driven; they respond immediately to whatever emergency presents itself.

Further along the *service performance continuum* the clinical services are more predictable and allow a higher degree of planning; for example, elective day surgery, where a surgical procedure is performed, that allows either the patient to leave that day or after a further day's observation on a ward. This means that, for example, the

Treasurers can adapt this model and use it to formulate the budgeting and cost management practices being designed and employed to reinforce that clinical service delivery performance.

This approach can be employed not only for the service support departments, but also in those departments where dependent and interdependent relationships have been identified. For example, an x-ray department needs to tailor their responsive behaviour to complement the diagnostic processes of a patient's condition for the A & E department. This is a multi-response time diagnostic service that once again has to be able to evaluate and prioritise its activities.

They need to be able to directly and rapidly complement the emergency demands of the A & E department, which move the x-ray service towards the immediate response time identified on the Clinical Service Support Model (Fig. 41). At the same time they have to service other clinical departments that require their diagnostic service, within a differing time frame, which moves those services further towards the planned events end of the continuum.

It enables not only the dependent and interdependent relationships to be identified but also it specifies the various roles these service organisations have to manage. It enables the identification and agreed service levels to be specified and agreed. It provides a non-emotional evaluative development process for these practices. The identification of the agreed service performance enables the work structuring and the *states of flux* to be regulated and managed, allowing the work practice to be developed that enables these services to be cost-effectively delivered. Using an organisational approach identifies and provides a common organisational language that enables an on-going effective dialogue regarding clinical service delivery.

This developmental organisational approach has the added value of effectively justifying the service delivery performance standards that the Treasurers could apply to departmental budgets. Should they refuse to support these services at a cost, level two actions are triggered. The first action is to address an imposed requirement that the service delivery be contracted to fit these budgeted constraints. The second action is to address the volume of the service being delivered but not by reducing the quality of services, to ensure the appropriate patient care is maintained. By using this approach the various respondents within the negotiating practices have to take responsibility for their decision-making. If reduced budgets are imposed the responsibility of the consequential outcomes must remain with the one imposing the changes, in this example the Treasurers.

These evaluative and diagnostic activities enable the appropriate organisational design to be adopted, to enlist the operant service performance behaviour. It prevents *acts of* "superficiality." These acts of "superficiality" over a period of time can introduce imperceptible changes from a caring, paternalistic, almost "indulgent pattern of management" to becoming "punishment centred bureaucracies" (Gouldner, 1955A); this condition can always be tracked back to the style and systems led monitoring practices that has detached leadership and managers from the management of the organisation. (For an example, refer to the "Transitional Nursing Care" case study.)

CASE STUDY SIX

OPERATING THEATRE RESOLUTION OF CONFLICT

Brook Hospital

Background

The manifestation of this problem can be traced to the previous political dysfunctional behaviour of the whole organisation discussed in the previous case study, "Leading Transition for Change." The behaviour of the Treasurers brings to mind Deming's cost/quality ratio, where he argues that if you use a cost driven approach quality will suffer and cost will subsequently increase. It also displaces organisational goals and the consequences manifest in other dysfunctional activities, one of these being the ensuing conflict between the operating Theatre Sisters and Works personnel. These unresolved issues created other dysfunctional compensatory practices, each adding to the cost model.

Within this organisational environment, interdepartmental and interpersonal relationships had become fractious, progressing to open conflict and verbal attacks, causing the Works staff to avoid, in particular, interaction with the Theatre Sisters. Having become aware of the conflict it was evident that the two parties should meet to resolve the presenting issues. The anger and despair felt by the senior Theatre Sisters was powerfully expressed and often spilt over into quite aggressive challenges and disparaging remarks about the Works staff.

The Underlying Issues

Historically the Works staff had a good working relationship. With the progressive deterioration of the Works department's performance and experiencing a sense of being in a "double bind" they were unable to defend themselves. They were unable to defend their failures to maintain the theatre to the necessary standards. Secondly, they felt that the constant sheer aggressive attitudes of the Theatre Sisters left them feeling castrated and powerless. They dealt with the conflict by avoiding theatre suites and the staff. The Theatre Sisters, by the very nature of their roles, were very determined strong willed and extremely protective of their patients' safety and care.

The Process

The conflict was satisfactorily resolved within less than a month by addressing the issues through the use of an organisational approach. A tenet, developed from experience of managing many conflicts within organisational social structures is, never to judge or apportion blame but to gain an understanding of the recent history in terms of the organisational practices.

The value of using an organisational approach enables the development of a cognitive shared understanding of the underlying organisational issues. You are able to put these developed issues into the context of the consequential outcomes of the overall organisation's created political environment. This, in turn, enables the developed organisational understanding to be used as the *third party for conflict resolution*. It critically provides a common organisational language that all parties understand and can use. This approach also clarifies boundaries, the roles for all parties, their authority, responsibility, and accountability.

When using an organisational approach you displace the search for a resolution on to the organisation and not the individuals. It is non-threatening and enables each party, in terms of the organisation, to be asked to review their observations. The capacity to displace is extremely important for a number of reasons, in particular, that all the interpersonal cankers are healed, to prevent on-going unresolved conflicts, which only serves to dissipate one's energy. It is all part of the process of an individual making the transition from one state to another and being enabled to "let go." (Refer to Chapter Six, "Leading Transition for Change".)

When challenging an individual's contribution that is inappropriate or critical of another person you can ask, "How does this contribute to the identified organisational problem?" This displacement prevents you from directly challenging that individual with the risk of them taking exception. Some leaders, senior surgeons and other influential individuals find being directly challenged very difficult, causing them at times, to display unreasonably aggressive behaviour in response. Using an organisational approach enables you to displace these reactions on to the issues of organisational problem solving, causing their observations to be re-evaluated in terms of the organisation's needs.

Each party was interviewed separately to gain an understanding of their concerns and expectations in terms of their organisation. Because of the recent history the Theatre Sisters were initially resistant to yet another meeting. Once they were engaged in explaining, to a declared complete novice, what they do in patient process terms they would talk forever. The value of this was that we were able to agree and identify the *primary task* of the theatre provision and importantly their ultimate responsibilities and accountability.

The Theatre Sisters were responsible for the safety of the patient. They clearly understood their role of managing the safety process to *protect the patient* and to them that was their *primary task*. They managed the supervised preparation of the theatres, the sterility of all the equipment to be used, the management of the staff and the recovery of the patient once the surgeon had completed their procedures.

In theatrical terms the Sisters were the stage managers and set the stage for the surgeon to undertake their role without concern, to enable them to effectively perform their surgical procedures. To complement the Sisters' stage management they were heavily dependent on the sterility and functioning of the air conditioning equipment. They were also responsible for other theatre equipment in support of the theatre staff carrying out their individual duties. The sterilising equipment for the instruments had to function effectively and without failure. The safety factoring could be compared with aviation zero failures.

This requirement introduced the notion of a revolving door were the Theatre Sister never had to interact with the Works maintenance staff. This implied that the maintenance activities were planned and the operating outcomes were never impeded. This interdependency was the critical cross-functional activity, the *state of flux* that required regulatory management. Identifying and agreeing these necessary procedures and regulatory practices at the boundary laid the foundation for a developed understanding, and clarification of role expectation, authority, accountability and responsibility.

Members of the affected Works staff were interviewed in an attempt, in organisational terms, to determine the difficulties they were facing. They openly declared that the forcefulness of the Theatre Sisters was very difficult to deal with for a number of reasons. They were dealing with women, for whom they had a great deal of respect. They desperately wanted to resolve the problems. They were disempowered by their own lack of authority and being deskilled when managing the contract, to act using their own discretion without unwarranted budgetary constraints. The lack of leadership and management skills within their own department was compounded with an inability to find a working solution. They were, in fact, being placed in a "double bind"; if they acted they were incurring costs, if they failed to act they were incompetent and attacked.

The Works staff had to work through the needs of the Theatre Sisters to enable them to understand why they were so defensively aggressive. Another misconception that Works staff played out was the belief that they were responsible in some way for the care of the patients. The Works functional role was to "provide an environment where the clinical staff can safely practice" and provide patient care.

The Works personnel were also preoccupied with all the other failures that were being reported in other clinical services. These other clinical difficulties were of no interest to the Theatre Sisters. To assist with the decision-making with regards to how to prioritise the Works department, the notional timeline model and clinical service response model was employed (Fig. 41). This reaction time-line notional model helped to clarify the critical nature of the theatres' clinical service provision and serviced the decision to priorities this particular conflict.

The next stage was to bring the two parties together to share their concerns in terms of their organisations' needs, with no reference to the history. They were armed with the information that the requirement was for each party only to discuss what needed to be undertaken. Using an organisational approach enabled an adult-to-adult discussion to take place and in a very short space of time agreement along with an action plan was identified. This process was worked through to ensure that both parties owned the outcomes and worked collectively to achieve it.

The *primary task* of the Theatre Sisters was the safety of the patient and the procedures were not the responsibility of the Works staff. The Works department were responsible for providing a safe working environment for the theatre staff. These two clearly understood focused intentions provided a clear understanding of each party's boundaries of responsibility. It also identified the shared value that each party would apply to their particular activity. This shared information provided not only an action plan that each party would enact, it provided a common language that enabled each party to effectively communicate and maintain an on-going dialogue about improving the theatres' support services.

Review

An organisational approach enabled the understanding of the political activities. It enables you to manage the political game-playing of the Treasurers' department, the clinical consultants and the hospital's Executive Administrators. This form of conflict resolution is part of the process of inverted organisational leadership, which is identified and discussed in Chapter Seven ("Adaptive Organisational Leadership").

The quick resolution to the Theatre Sisters' dilemma provides a degree of credibility when addressing other service issues. This Hawthorn transferred effect, discussed in the Avonmouth case study, and influenced discussions when finding resolutions to problems in other clinical service areas.

CASE STUDY SEVEN

GREENWICH DISTRICT HOSPITAL

This case study provides a number of opportunities to identify significant differences in the various hospital organisations within the same District Health Authority. It is necessary when examining this case study to keep in mind the political decision-making organisational environment discussed in previous case studies and in Chapter Six, "Leading Transition for Change."

This case study examines the developed inverse relationship of this hospital's Works Department's management and the onsite Trade Unions shop stewards. We shall discuss the analytical process used to determine why this unmanageable situation had developed along with the processes used to solve the presented organisational and managerial problems.

The dysfunctional organisational behaviour discussed in this case study has to be placed within the reluctant leadership of Greenwich District Health Authority. This reluctance to provide direction and to resolve presented problems created an undesirable permissive organisational environment, coupled with the developed, relatively recent depletion of the District Works Department's own leadership performance. We need to keep in mind the other environmental issues, that of the depletion of the London Docks and the consequential outcomes of employing those redundant maintenance dock employees. (There is a direct correlation with the normative behaviour discussed in the case study, "Avonmouth." And that of the militant redundant London Dock's employees.)

It provides an opportunity to compare the performance cultures of the different hospitals that came under the umbrella of the operational control of the Greenwich District Health Authority. Viewed from the

Works Department's perspective, we shall find that in the onsite Works Departments, organisational performance cultures were all different. In the case of Greenwich District Hospital (GDH) it provides an opportunity to explore the effects of this hospital's location and how the building design affected that hospital's Works Department's performance culture.

Recent History

Greenwich District Hospital was built on a restricted site and required a building designed to accommodate these physical limitations. The developed design earned a number of awards. The building can be described as rectangular and deep planned; the only natural light serviced the wards that were situated on the external perimeter walls of the building. All other facilities such as operating theatres, x-rays, the pharmacy and other clinical services, along with the maintenance workshops were buried within the depths of the building with limited access to natural light. The enclosed corridors created problems with orientation; they were soulless and lacked any relatable social features.

The maintenance of the service and access for the Work's Department's staff were what could be referred to as subterranean. The service, air conditioning, water, medical gases and electricity were accommodated within voids above the wards and other clinical practices. The voids were serviced and accessed by secured vertical shafts, which fed and distributed the services. The height of the voids would prevent an adult standing fully erect. The voids were hot, dirty and both the steel structure of the building and many of the services were clad in asbestos.

The relative location of this hospital to the River Thames and its associated industrial docking activities coupled with major social changes within the demise of the London Docks had a direct impact on this public service. Public services were politically expected to employ some of the redundant dock employees, who imported their normative unionised behaviour. (Refer to the "Avonmouth "case study.) The NHS, represented in the form of the Greenwich District Health Authority, was unprepared to manage the expressed levels of union militancy and its attendant unpredictable behaviour. Rather than address the presented issues they withdrew and hoped that it would be managed locally.

Increased Dependency

This deep-plan design of the hospital building had inadvertently designed in an increased dependency relationship, of the medical staff and others, with that of the Works Department. For example, should there be a power cut the whole hospital would be plunged, at whatever time of the day, into total darkness. All the staff occupying the building, medical or otherwise were dependent on the emergency power generators to service the emergency lighting and other facilities, for example, operating theatres and incubators in the maternity wards. This was a good example of systems dependency being designed into the building's design and in some form almost inverted the normal relationship of the clinical staff and the Works Department.

This created a higher dependency on the Work Department's service provisions, which should have demanded stringent testing and maintenance of the back-up emergency facilities. All hospitals, particularly if they have operating theatres, are protected by standby generators to supply electricity; an absolute essential provision for protection of the patient during an operation.

Reviewing the practices of the Works Department on this hospital site revealed that the emergency generator tests were inappropriate. A planned periodic full-load test of the emergency generators would, in any hospital, be a standard procedure.

For the development and use of an organisational approach, it is useful to become *detached engaged* when attempting to make the connections with the various organisational issues being addressed. When leading and managing transition for change it is good practice to notionally withdraw all authority until those responsible to you demonstrate they are competent.

It is also good practice to periodically test the assumption that those reports you receive are, in fact, reporting the reality of the situation. You should also use your *cognitive organisational awareness* antenna to feel whether what is being reported somehow does not fit or instinctively feels not quite right. This may be derived from the way the information is given or other factors that somehow do not stack up and fit your developed *organisational cognitive awareness*.

In this hospital it was at the early stages of assumed responsibility. This should be standard practice particularly when you are about to engage in a programme of leading and managing *transition for change,* that the acute nature of the dependency relationship instituted an examination of all the maintenance and emergency back-up procedures.

The staff had, for a period of twenty-one years, dutifully run and recorded the testing of the emergency generators. When examining the procedures it became evident that they had never put these generators on full-load. To overcome this problem and ensure the system could work fully loaded required that the whole system be tested. The dependency on these reporting procedures prevented the operatives from challenging the assumption, as they had ritualistically been accepting it over a considerable period of time. It is not uncommon to observe these and other systems dependency failures in other organisations. (Refer to case study "Transitional Nursing Care".)

In other hospitals these tests could be achieved by using selected suites of theatres that were being serviced by a dedicated emergency generator. In the deep-plan design all the theatres were affected along with many other administrative and other clinical services. The clinical consultants refused to comply with the requirement to allow these full-load tests, to be conducted. The historic political defensive decision-making behaviour of the clinicians caused them to lose sight of the life-threatening, consequential effects of the generators failing to function effectively.

The clinicians and the hospital management demanded that the District Works Officer attend a meeting to hear their objections. They were used to getting their own way and were highly intelligent politicised professionals. In this situation they had failed to grasp the consequences of their refusal to allow a full-load generator test, as it would disrupt all their theatre lists. They had disconnected the fact that in other hospitals that work within in this District, all had periodic generator tests that required their surgical lists to be accommodated.

There were a number of distinct behavioural dynamics influencing the clinicians' attitudes, behaviour and consequently their decision-making. In other hospitals they often have specific standby generators to service suites of theatres. In this hospital all the theatres were simultaneously affected. This politicised clinicians' behaviour was influenced by poor strategic and operational decision-making practices within this hospital and within the District Authority, causing them to become politically protective of their specialist clinical services.

The clinicians did not regard the Works Department to be competently managed and when you examined the recent history, this was not an unreasonable assumption. They were misinformed that the generators were regularly satisfactorily tested. They had not understood the change in the dependant relationship, created by the design of the building. Many of these clinicians had private practices and any change in the theatre list would have a direct impact.

They were made aware of the increased dependent relationships and the fact that the generators had not been tested when fully loaded. By connecting these changes to their patients' safety, caused by the building design and historic practices, they grudgingly agreed to examine their surgical list to determine a suitable date.

The generators' switching mechanism, when subject to a full load test, failed to engage. An investigation and the involvement of the manufacturers revealed that there was a design fault within the switching mechanism that proved it was not fit for purpose. These emergency services had not been fully commissioned and/or appropriately tested for a period in excess of twenty years. The manufacturers provided a solution enabling the generators to be satisfactorily tested.

There were combinations of organisational behavioural elements that were being used that enabled this and other practices to be uncovered. A well-developed *cognitive organisational awareness* enables you to intuitively examine the relationship and deployment of all these technologies and the behavioural practices attached to them, which must include the building's design, as discussed in the case study "Greenfield Site Development." The design of this building and the maintenance of the service facilities had distinct implications for the management of the Works Department within this hospital.

Industrial Relations

Greenwich is historically and therefore inextricably connected to the industrial working activities of the River Thames. The demise of the traditional docking activities associated with the River Thames saw many of the now redundant employees finding work in other industries and institutions. Unfortunately, the militant unionised practices that were inculcated in these ex-employees were transferred into, in this case, Greenwich District Hospital.

The style of the NHS' Works management and the Executive Administrators were not prepared for this level of militancy and were ineffectual in dealing with a new influx of a hardened unionised militant workforce. They were used to the political decision-making practices (Fig. 3), where they would find a compromise and fail to address the real problem. This decision-making practice was further underwritten by the politicised collective action of the clinicians who filled the missing leadership void.

These collusive sets of relationships can be better understood when we understand Menzies' (1970) observations, "A social defence system develops over time as the results of collusive interaction and agreement, often unconscious, between members of the organisation as to what form it will take." These mental cooperatives take the form of ideologies and schools of thought, and enlist compliance within the group, which directly affects the direction of decision-making and when challenged they can be aggressively resisted (Obholzer, 1989). (Refer to Chapters Three, "The Enemy Within" and Chapter Five, "Developing a Theory in Practice -- Part Two".)

These new Works Department employees, the ex-dock maintenance personnel, brought with them what is referred to as "Spanish Practices" that meant that much of the work was demarcated and controlled by the nominated committee of Union Stewards. The purpose of these "Spanish Practices, in this situation, was to regulate the work flow and enhance potential earnings. No-go areas for managers, such as the voids and service shafts, were created. Rather than deal with the direct challenge to their authority, the managers would retreat and allow the shop stewards to manage the situation. These managers, through experience, understood that the hospital administrative executive and the Districts executives would not support any works manager's initiative to combat the collective Trade Union's power base.

The failure of the District Works Officer to support the onsite Works managers reinforced the felt sense of isolation that was experienced by the on-site Works managers. They had no form of appeal for help or support, which left them increasingly isolated. They were also subject to creating 'mental cooperatives' to defend themselves against the induced anxiety. This situation was further compounded, as they were also subject to the cost savings initiatives that were being aggressively employed throughout the District.

Should there be a threat of industrial action by the Trade Unions, the District and hospital-based management along with local Works managers sought ways to ameliorate rather than address the presented issues. These financial cost saving initiatives were, by their very nature, disrupting the existing inverse power relationship. The on-site Works managers were being placed in a "double bind", discussed earlier. These Works managers' situation was further exacerbated by the dysfunctional, corrupt inversion of the union power base and on-site Works management working relationships.

These created forms of defence mechanisms make change in organisations difficult "because change threatens existing social defences against anxiety" (Jaques, 1955). Menzies (1970) also found that this occurred "when social defence systems are dominated by primitive psychic defence mechanisms." These behavioural dynamics could be observed in the behaviour of the executive and line management and in particular the GDH Shop Stewards, whose power base would automatically be challenged. (Refer to Chapter Five, "Developing a Theory in Practice – part two".)

Newly recruited Works managers soon adapted to these concessionary deference practices and accepted the created Trade Union-led organisational performance culture. If they attempted to change the existing arrangements they were discouraged from disrupting the current accepted inverted power attributed to the Trade Union's Shop Stewards. The behaviour of these new recruits soon emulated the behaviour displayed within the experiment discussed in Chapter One, "Monkey See and Monkey Do" (Paler Louis, 1999). This form of acceptance of the existing performance culture and the new recruit even becoming complicit can be observed in many organisations.

These infectious dysfunctional cultures become part of the "corporate performance culture" that old and new members learn to live with and not challenge. They become risk adverse and career orientated (Nyquist, 2009). (The "Transitional Nursing Care" case study is a good example of this form of depleting complicit behaviour.) This ever-increasing level of abrogation by the onsite Works managers created a situation where the managers were unable to differentiate between their authority and that of the senior shop steward.

When the new District Works Officer began to examine and question existing work practices, this was interpreted as a challenge and a threat to the sovereignty of the Shop Stewards. They actively and aggressively resisted any perceived form of challenge to their power base. Historically, all they had to do was to threaten to resist any initiative, and this achieved the desired result of that initiative being totally watered down and/or negated, allowing the shop stewards to maintain the status quo. Employing an organisational approach for *leading and managing transition for change* had revealed these dysfunctional practices and would forewarn you of those potential power cabals that may be disrupted by any intervention.

The response to this apparent challenge to the Trade Union's power base exposed the inverse relationship of the Trade Unions and the Works management. This became absolutely clear, with the hospital's Works management colluding with the Trade Union's Shop Stewards, by blocking initiatives to improve the management of the services. The introduction of what was considered to be standard practices led to the senior Shop Steward writing a letter to the District Works Officer, threatening strike action should any changes to the existing practices be introduced. The Shop Stewards had persuaded the onsite Works managers to all countersign this document.

There are echoes of the same generated social dynamics "…suspicious bargaining over which both management and the men are in collusion" (Trist & Bamford, 1951). These managers had to be made aware, along with their respective union full time officers, that this letter was unacceptable. All of the managers involved were made aware that they had made themselves unemployable unless they withdrew their signatures and confirmed their intent in writing.

The stark realisation enabled them to realise how serious the situation had become. This development and working the issues through with the respective Trade Union's full-time Officers developed into good working relationships, except for one. He was of the old school that was locked in the psychological prison of a previous union power base. His ritualistic combative threatening behaviour prevented any appeal to rational discussion and created a requirement for a regional full-time union officer to intervene. Experience of working with regional officers introduced improved working relationships, particularly if they understand that the *intent* of your actions is appropriate and clearly expressed.

The precipitous behaviour of the senior Shop Steward accelerated the process, unfortunately creating a toxic combative relationship. They were used to threatening behaviour and historically the management would simply concede to their demands. The situation the senior Shop Steward had created made the inverse union Works management practices explicit, in turn creating demands for the onsite Works managers' roles to be clearly defined and the need for their authority to be re-established. The Shop Stewards had created a forced choice situation that needed to be addressed even if it meant dealing with any threat of industrial strike action.

Leading and Managing the Transition for Change

It is necessary to keep in mind that the developed behavioural dynamics had been acceptable through the permissive behaviour of the District and local hospital executives' complicit failure to appropriately take responsibility. The District and the hospital management, in the eyes of the Shop Stewards, were complicit in turning a blind eye, disempowering the onsite Works management; they were, in effect, giving permission for these Shop Stewards to take control.

The new District Works Officer had a good deal of experience of dealing with militant union activities that had often been created by defensive intransigent management. Even with this information it is important not to engage in the *blame game* but to remain *detached engaged* and to only use an organisational perspective, as this allows you to position yourself to negotiate the necessary transition for change.

Acknowledging the historically created situation was shared and discussed with the full-time Union Officers and the Shop Stewards. The agreement with the full-time Union Officers was that attempts would be resolved locally and with the onsite shop stewards, and that they would be kept informed.

Analysis of the *cost profiles* that had been developed alongside the *transition for change processes* indicated that the GDH Works staff wage costs were significantly higher than comparative Works staff on other hospital sites. Even with the complexity of the building design, these could not be justified. This information was shared with the local and full time trade union officers along with other information to indicate why changes to the current situation were necessary.

These cost disparities indicated, when tested against existing work practices, that there was a possibility that members of the night shift were sleeping in the voids. Works staff working in the other hospitals had become aware of these practices and wondered why no action was taken. The local and senior managers were aware that this practice may be true, but never tested the assumption.

These assumptions were not tested at the beginning of the transition for change process, to prevent an uncontrolled escalation of potential industrial action. It was better to monitor to manage, at this stage of events, rather than impose one's authority. The intransient aggressive behaviour of the Shop Stewards coupled with their historic industrial history required some preparatory work to manage any industrial and/or strike action. Imposing one's authority could create the "chaos" you were attempting to avoid. Lagadec's (1993) observations come to mind, "Our ability to deal with chaos depends on structures that have been developed before the chaos arrives."

Due to the absolute need to protect the clinical services and safety of the patients from any threat of industrial strike action, the providers of utilities such as electricity, water, oil, gas, the fire service, sewage and waste disposal, and suppliers of clinical and other services were all contacted. They were informed of the potential threat of strike action and to determine whether they would cross any picket lines. The general agreement was that they would cross the picket lines because it was a hospital. They were sympathetic as the ethos of hospital care was shared, felt and understood by these service providers. The full time officers of the respective onsite Works department unions were also kept within the information loop.

It was important to engage the executives, to ensure that agreement had been achieved, to support the strategy for dealing with the consequential effects of any industrial action. They were provided with an opportunity to work through the processes and the evidenced based cost information, provided by the Treasurers, to ensure they were fully aware of the consequences of not addressing the presented issues.

Alliances were formed with the Deputy Treasurer and the Deputy Personnel Director to keep their respective executives informed. They each had acquired implicit authority to support the District Works Officer's *transition for change* processes. These developed relationships are critical at a number of levels, in particular, to create the developed authority to act. The Deputy Director of Personnel's understanding of the contractual employment regulations and other regulatory requirements was particularly useful.

These developed relationships created what may be described as an umbrella management system that had implicit permission to act providing it did not affect those in power. These developed processes were all part of the practice of *inverted organisational leadership*. It is important to ensure that those within the created political umbrella understood the boundaries of responsibility and who was accountable for particular decisions and their deliverable activities. The focus, when employing an organisational approach, is not to block the political influence but to persuade them to engage and use their skills to reinforce the necessary *transitional change process*.

The developed relationships with the utilities services were shared with the District and local hospitals' executives so they were clear about the *intent* and strategy. The intent was shared with all the hospitals to ensure they were aware that these activities on the GDH site might permeate to their own hospital boundaries through sympathetic industrial action.

The onsite Works managers were collectively working through the *transition for change process* to ensure they understood their developed future roles, along with their responsibilities, authority and accountability. They were also made aware of their legal responsibility as their existing management practices would not be acceptable should a situation be subject to litigation. They needed to personally work through the transition for change process to enable them to make their own transition to manage and change the existing dysfunctional managerial practices. They were relieved that they were able to use their professional skills and to manage effectively in the interest of the whole hospital.

Social Dynamics

When working in hospitals the *intent* is clinical and social, care and recovery, which induces an ethos that stems from the fact that these institutions are there to provide these services for humankind. This service is not dealing with a commodity: it is a life support institution, where, on the other hand, the production of inanimate objects such as tin cans, for example, does not induce that same sense of emotional concern and responsibility. For example, from experience of working in other hospitals you could observe the practice of managers and other administrative staff delegating upwards to the onsite executive. In the same way, nurses would delegate upwards to defend themselves against anxiety (Menzies, 1970).

These are reasonable expectations that need to be set in the historic social dynamics created by the absence of directed leadership from the top of the organisation as well as locally. The consequential outcomes over many years had allowed the earning capacity for the Works employees and in particular, the Senior Shop Steward, to become the norm. Their earning potential governed their living standards and financial commitments. Any changes in their earnings, however justified, would be resisted to protect their ability to service their financial commitments. They, naturally, would resist losing these privileges as they had enjoyed them over a considerable number of years. At the same time their power base was being challenged, which meant that they had to make a personal transition from being an unauthorised leader to taking supervisory instructions. The realignment of the organisation created a demand that they make the necessary transition. The difficulty would be with them making a personal transition. These Shop Stewards found themselves unfortunately between a rock and a hard place, which meant that they would be expected to aggressively resist the changes.

An organisational approach was used and designed to identify the potential areas of possible resistance to change. It enabled preparation for projected eventualities and to develop means for managing these areas of resistance to change. These areas of resistance are not confined to the shop floor workers; senior and middle management often express them overtly and even covertly. (Refer to the case study, "Avonmouth" and the 'felt sense of redundancy.')

Changes in the Negotiating Position

When addressing the issue of strike action with the on-site Shop Stewards they were informed that the threat was being taken seriously and all necessary steps to protect the hospital's services would be put in place. They were made aware that under their contracts of employment all the Works staff could be sacked if they took unauthorised action. This apparent confrontational approach was not preferred. The issuing of a threat of strike action had forced the need to act to ensure the hospital's clinical services were protected.

The Works managers and the Shop Stewards were reminded that the union were not the paymasters and had no authority to manage or regulate the workflow or any other activity. They were also reminded that all the Shop Stewards along with all the other Works personnel were employees of the Health Authority and that was their first priority, not their union activities. For example, if the Shop Stewards wanted a meeting they were required to seek permission, if in working hours, which is standard practice, which was seen as a direct challenge to the Shop Stewards' historic power base.

This created a significant and threatening set of dynamics that had the effect of corralling the Shop Stewards. They did not have the full support of their own full time Union Officials; the utility services would cross any picket line, the support of the clinical and nursing staff had evaporated, the other Works staff on other hospital sites were not prepared to support any industrial action by the GDH Shop Stewards and importantly many of the onsite Works staff wanted change.

They realised that strike action was no longer an option and chose to impose a work to rule, i.e. the full imposition of work demarcation. This was a preferred option as this could be managed. They were asked specifically, in writing, to identify what they considered to be demarcated work practices. This created an opportunity to continue to discuss and negotiate the activities of the Works department, even though it was from the Shop Stewards' perspective.

The identification of the areas of demarcation could not be simply accepted, as they could and would not fit the needs of the Works department to provide quality services to the clinical practitioners. Agreeing to the Shop Stewards' areas of demarcation would implicitly agree that they were legitimate. All demarcation activities that were determined by the Shop Stewards' would, by implication, impose the maximum disruption. Therefore the management would decide the areas of demarcation in the pursuance of service quality and to ensure safe practices.

The processes for determining where demarcation legitimately existed were identified by working through a *process of variation analysis and identifying the performance culture continuum* to find the created *states of flux*. These *states of flux* needed to be regulated and managed, which determined the nature and style of regulatory management that needed to be employed.

No matter how the discussion was framed they had put themselves in a bind or, as some would say, they had painted themselves into a corner. This further alienation of the Shop Stewards was not a desirable negotiating climate. This frustrated alienated positioning of the Shop Stewards created some expected and unexpected *consequential outcomes,* particularly when you consider this was within a hospital environment.

Sabotage and "Scapegoating"

The realignment of the onsite management's authority brought further intransigence from the union representatives, who engaged in the kind of behaviour that alienated workers often resort to. Walton (1972) writes, "In some cases, alienation is expressed by withdrawal, tardiness, absenteeism and high labour turnover, and inattention on the job. In other cases, it is expressed by active attacks, pilferage, sabotage, deliberate waste, assaults, and other disruptions of work routines." All were prevalent when dealing with the increased intransigence of the local Shop Stewards.

These activities were expressed through such activities as sabotage of services to the wards, further demarcation of work by introducing additional unofficial locks on access areas. Withdrawal, tardiness and absenteeism increased, along with covertly blocking supervised instructions. Sabotage by switching off medical gases to selected wards and applying sticky tape to the District Works Officer's car when parked in the hospital's car park, forcing him to park off site.

The Shop Stewards projected all the blame onto the District Works Officer and made him the "scapegoat." When people in a group are being persecuted they develop a precise and equally strong dislike of their persecutors. During the time the internal problem, in particular with the group of Shop Stewards, was unresolved, the process of projection acts to relieve the group's anxiety and this can be achieved by finding a "scapegoat." That took the form of other departments and, in particular, the District Works Officer.

The whole of the Works department staff were informed that if any other form of sabotage was perpetrated the police would be contacted, as these activities were potentially putting patients' lives at risk. The location of the sabotage could be traceable to an individual or group and disciplinary and police involvement would be instituted. The frustrated Senior Shop Steward, who was a big man, and he made his physicality clear and threatening, without making a direct threat. The implication was that he was prepared to take it further. He was warned that his behaviour was becoming unacceptable and he was put on notice to that effect.

During a meeting with all the Union Shop Stewards to discuss the unauthorised interference with the medical gases that had affected the maternity wards, one of the union representatives informed the meeting, "The patients would have to wait." Even the other union representatives quaffed with laughter. It had the effect of the union representatives realising that they had lost sight of the reason for them working in a hospital, and some of the Shop Stewards became aware that although they needed to change their behaviour, they didn't know how to bring about these changes.

Unfortunately not all the Shop Stewards understood this and still carried on as usual. A change in the onsite Works manager's attitudes was expressed by one of the Shop Stewards being identified drinking alcohol, although off site. Consuming alcoholic beverages during working hours was a direct violation of his contracts of employment.

This situation required that he be disciplined and put on notice. As a Shop Steward he would be very much aware of these regulatory practices. The Health Authority had practiced an overly conciliatory approach when dealing with disciplinary action, to avoid conflict. The history indicated that if you demanded, for example, a written warning, the practice would be reduced to a verbal warning. The instruction was, for this person to be sacked, knowing that this would be reduced to a final warning. The intention was to ensure that the Shop Steward took note of the severity and consequences of his own behaviour. Unfortunately, even with these operant practices, he transgressed a second time and was sacked. A lesson we can all take from this example is that you do not sack employees, they sack themselves, or they move on.

Review

The final outcome was that the authority was restored to the managers who relished the possibilities of being in control and leading the service provision. The other Works employees were also relieved by not having to work under the union's political control. They also indicated that they realised that the existing situation, even though it had been practiced for many years, had to come to an end at some time. Even though they were losing a level of stable income they accepted it had been good whilst it lasted.

The cost recovery was regulated, managed and brought back under control. The practice of sleeping in the voids was satisfactorily resolved as this was adding to the costs and reduced quality of service delivery. The service quality and the same respective practice introduced into the other hospitals were provided to the clinical staff within the GDH setting. The interdepartmental response and supportive behaviour improved significantly, earning the respect of those accessing these support services.

The one person that had to be specifically monitored and managed was the senior Shop Steward, who was unable to accept the changes even though he acknowledged that it was necessary.

CASE STUDY EIGHT

TRANSITIONAL NURSING CARE

The Solution Equals the Problem

Overview

Using an organisational approach enables the examination of a transitional nursing care facility's insidious depletion of care, which led to a patient being institutionally abused. Examining the causal effects we find that the outsourcing practices were flawed, and that the basic practices for developing, letting and managing the outsourced contract were not in place. This led to the patient being transferred as a "bed-blocking problem" and not as a person in need of reparation and therapeutic transitional clinical care. The failed contractual practice enabled a patient to be transferred into a care institution that was already dysfunctional, and that had a developed management and nursing culture that was not fit for purpose. The failure to apply basic outsourcing contractual practices prevented any individual being held accountable for tracking the quality of this patient's reparative care.

There was a total lack of any tracking of this patient's care provision, as no specific care plan existed. The lack of any elementary monitoring to manage practices caused this patient to be dumped out of a hospital into an unsuitable care provision. These nursing care practices caused the patient's health to deteriorate requiring her to be transferred to the original outsourcing hospital. When returned to the same care facility the care staff were not prepared for the specific needs of this patient. She was finally placed in another hospital where she died, leaving a sense that her death was accelerated by the lack of compassionate nursing care or any professional accountability.

To compound the frustrated difficulties experienced when attempting to encourage the nursing staff, their managers and executive to appropriately respond, the difficulty was further reinforced by the designed attrition and application of the complaints procedure.

The findings throughout this case study are not confined to this nursing care service; it appears to be prevalent in other parts of the NHS. The value of working through this process, using an organisational approach, clearly demonstrates that this applied evaluative process would prove to be of immense value in improving problem-solving capacity, decision-making and leadership. There would be considerable cost savings and critically, a significant improvement in the quality of patient care.

Recent History

This case study is situated in an NHS nursing care facility that was established to cater for people, referred to as *clients*, who were unable to live independently and who required supportive care. This provision had been established in a BUPA private care home. NHS staff provided the care; the contracted connection with BUPA was the use of the accommodation facilities and the provision of food from their kitchens. The nursing and clinical care was provided by the Oxlease Foundation Trust NHS staff.

This nursing care provision had, when anecdotally compared with other nursing care sites within the responsibility of this NHS Foundation Trust providing nursing care, was perceived to be the best option. This anecdotal information influenced the family to allow their elderly relative to be transferred from Lewisham District Hospital to receive transitional nursing care in the NHS Oxlease Foundation Trust's Bevan Care Unit. There was an implied assumption that this nursing care facility would have the experience or, at the very least, the developed capacity to provide transitional therapeutic, nursing and clinical *patient* care, which was not the case.

A national problem of 'bed blocking' is experienced in many NHS hospitals. "Bed blocking" is a situation where, normally a person, often elderly, receives emergency or elective treatment, which also requires a longer reparative period that includes therapeutic rehabilitation and nursing care to ensure effective recovery. This reparative rehabilitation therapeutic practice should be the remit and responsibility of the hospital providing that patient's clinical care. The intent, of this practice, was to ensure that the individual was enabled to return to an independent life style.

South East London Healthcare Trust was reported to be losing £1 million a week and by the end of 2013 would have accumulated debts of more than £200 million. These deficits are putting pressure on other health care trusts to supplement these deficits. As a consequence the Secretary of State placed the South East London Healthcare Trust in administration. (Refer to the political outsourcing practices, discussed in Chapter Ten: "Outsourcing Contractual Practice" that identified a huge burden of cost being placed on the NHS, creating displaced organisational goals.) (We can make the connection with the Nimrod enquiry where "political influence, of the UK government's identified intent created an 'overwhelming objective of finding savings, causing organisational trauma".)

The administrator, Matthew Kershaw, is reported to have said, "The Lewisham Healthcare Trust (Lewisham Hospital) would have financial challenges of its own, adding to South East London's financial problems." The objective of "finding savings" permeated across the boundaries of social services and affected the level of care provision they were able to provide. These consequential cost transferences further exacerbated the 'bed blocking' problem. Many of these transferred problems could have been identified through the use of an organisational approach, and the components of variation analysis and a developed *performance culture continuum*, when combined, would have identified the consequential effects and provided an effective sustainable alternative solution.

The Solution Becoming the Problem

To provide a solution to the bed blocking problem Lewisham Hospital had arranged with the Oxlease NHS Foundation Trust's nursing care services to provide transitional care for a period of two to three weeks. Transitional care is required when a patient that has lived an independent life receives clinical reparative rehabilitative therapeutic care to facilitate their return to self-sufficiency and living independently.

The notional model (Fig. 42) is being used to identify the created organisational issues that emanated from the outsourcing of a core care service from one care institution to another. Fig. 42 is a modified version of Fig. 41 used for prioritising service provisions for hospital clinical services to demonstrate the organisational service boundary management that needed to be addressed. The boundaries of responsibility for the patient's care from the hospital have extended beyond that of the hospital's physical boundary. As part of the duty of care the hospital staff should have, at the very least, inspected and assured that the facilities they were commissioning were capable of satisfactorily providing the prescribed therapeutic clinical transition care. When outsourcing, the responsibility and accountability remains with the commissioning organisation. The contractor is accountable to the commissioning organisation for the provision of, in this case, transitional nursing care

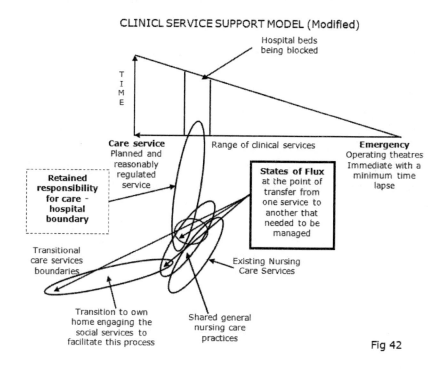

Fig 42

Within this evaluative process the competencies of the existing executive, site management, nursing and therapeutic staff needed to be determined. In essence the hospital, in discharging its duty of care, must ensure that when the patient is transferred they are safe and able to receive the same standard of rehabilitated care they would receive within the hospital's physical boundaries.

Had a basic contractual management approach been used to develop, define, let and regulate to manage, the nursing home would have been found to be inappropriate. It would have, at the very least, exposed the current failings and forced the executive to make the necessary changes in the existing nursing care provision. Critically the patient would have been protected from an already dysfunctional inappropriate care institution.

This contracted duty of care, which has to be matched by receiving transitional nursing care services, requires that the quality of care provision must travel with the patient, not just the budget. In turn the receiving transitional care services have to ensure that they have the facilities, equipment and the quality of qualified nursing and therapeutic staff within their services before accepting the contract. This is all part of the management and continued development of the *performance culture continuum* that identifies accountability and the necessary regulatory management to ensure transference of the quality of a patient's care.

(In the earlier brewing case study we discussed the products differentiated boundaries of management transferring across the physical brewery boundaries into the public house. This patient's duty of care and the attached *performance culture continuum* extends into the outsourced care facility. Management practices are the same the only difference is the product that requires the necessary specific developmental care.)

A jointly developed continuum of care is best developed through the creation of an "as if" jointly staffed development organisation. This may only consists of those who will lead the transition and those who will manage the receiving care organisation. There are, as indicated (Fig. 42), a number of *transitions* creating *states of flux*, which need to be regulated and managed over the entire *performance culture continuum* that the patient is expected to consistently experience.

The *performance culture continuum* would be from the GPs intervention and contracting the hospital services, through the referral experience of the hospital contracted to provide the clinical reparative care services, and into any therapeutic care facility that may have been contracted by the hospital, then finally returning to the GP to ensure that the care had been appropriately provided. The GPs are the gatekeepers for patients being referred into NHS hospitals; as a consequence, they have to remain responsible for the monitoring of the total care service provision. It would be irresponsible for any GP to refer (a contract with a clinical provision) a patient to an inadequate contracted clinical service provision. The GP becomes the person who has to monitor and ensure the referred patient's clinical and reparative care, completing the care assurance loop.

In practice, the patient's reparative care standards and expectations should have been defined and contracted with the new service provider. Within the contractual arrangement the specific provisions must be identified and specified, which all form the patient's care plan. The above notions support the process of organisational thinking and allow you to create the appropriate care plan that follows the patient. It also provides the opportunity to put in place the monitoring to manage practices to ensure the patient's needs are fully met. Any weakness in the planning and practices can be monitored, corrected and the organisation has the ability to learn from the quality of the patient's service delivery practices, creating a continuous learning organisation (Argyris and Schön, 1978).

It is important to emphasise that this practice of managing and monitoring (tracking) the patient's care provision is critical. All patients should have an individual care plan attached to any contracted activity to ensure that the receiving service understands that patient's specific care needs. The responsibility for the patient's care has to remain with the hospital in this case. In essence it requires someone to retain the responsibility for the patient's care as they move across the various care service boundaries.

The patient's own General Practitioner (GP) was not made available, even though that GP's practice was within the same Greenwich Healthcare Authority, further disconnecting this patient. Other locum GPs were employed who were not familiar with that particular patient's medical history. These GPs were further ill-informed, as the patient's care plan and not been determined and related to their medical history. GPs have a responsibility to ensure that those services they contract on behalf of the patient can be monitored and regulated. They must have a duty of care by ensuring they do not transfer a patient's care to an inappropriate clinical service provider. In essence, they must retain an overall responsibility to monitor the quality of their patient's care when they contract any clinical support services.

Employing this process of developing a *performance culture continuum*, you automatically identify and place the presented situation within the total context of the patient's clinical and care provision. You identify those *states of flux* and where the necessary regulatory management, the nature of the organisation, and the way it is led and managed are identified. These are the identifiable organisational issues that have not been understood that led to the patient being disenfranchised and processed as a commodity.

111-Call Centres

For all parties not to develop these practices to improve the diagnostic decision-making implies that the activities were functional. We should be able to make a connection with the consequential dysfunctional, displaced 111-call centre; a reaction to GPs no longer providing out of hours services, further disconnecting the patient from their GP who should remain responsible for the total care provision that has now been further displaced. (We can make a connection with the developing defensive practice of "tick box" mentality that develops detached defensive ritualistic behavioural practices.) That further reinforces the displacement of other care activities, creating a care culture of indifference.

The Executive Summary of the Report of the Mid Staffordshire NHS Foundation Trust Public Inquiry identified a series of organisational and management failings. The first three items immediately resonate with this case, which are:

- A culture focused on doing the system's business – not that of the patients'. An institutional culture which ascribed more weight to positive information about the service than to information capable of implying cause for concern.

- Standards and methods of measuring compliance, which did not focus on the effect of a service on patients.

- Too great a degree of tolerance of poor standards and of risk to patients.

- Within the receiving transitional nursing care services this was blatantly obvious to any casual nursing professional visitor.

Organisational Arrangement

The failure to understand that a two-tier nursing care service was required compounded these unwanted consequential outcomes. One service tier was to provide supportive care for the existing clients, which had its own *primary task and intent*. The second tier service was to provide a transitional therapeutic led service to support patients making the transition from the hospital to their own homes, which had another *primary task* and a different *intent*.

Fig. 42 demonstrates these two-tier services, their boundary relationships and the overlapping boundary arrangement of continuing care. It could be said, the existing facilities were 'by maintenance' by nature and the transitional care was reparative and transitional. The technologies employed would be different and therefore the nature of each organisation's clinical and nursing service cultures would be different. It takes little in organisational terms to understand that each organisation, even though they share common nursing care practices, is distinctly different.

Placing these services on a time-based continuum (Fig. 42) the transitional patient care response time would have been placed closer to the immediate end of the time related continuum, where the client based care would have been a good deal further away from the immediate end of the response time continuum. The failure of the discharging hospital to ensure that the outsourced services were adequate served to further compound the dysfunctional care culture of the nursing care provision.

Testing these Assumptions

A comparative examination of the practice of outsourcing within the manufacturing industry has developed contracted management outsourcing practices to assure the product and attached service provision. With products being manufactured by another company you would, at the very least, ensure that the provider of that service was able to meet the required quality and service standards. The manufacture of these commodities are monitored and managed to assure the service standards are met.

Parcels are tracked; and items purchased are tracked, which leaves the question that even though the product is inanimate in nature the monitoring of the service and the tracking attributed to these products are specific to ensure the quality of the service delivered.

The question that has to be asked is that why these elementary standard practices were not understood and rigorously employed within these healthcare provisions? Each of these services discussed above have attached and specific identification registration numbers that allow them to be tracked from source through to delivery. Within the NHS all patients have a National Insurance number that could simply be used to track the quality of care of individual patients.

When outsourcing a service, a manager would be deemed incompetent, if they did not, at the very least, ensure the following: That the services to be outsourced are specified in terms of service provision, quantity, quality, timeliness, responsibility and accountability for the various elements of the service provision and the contracted unit costs. All of these activities are simply tracked and monitored to ensure that the appropriate service quality is constantly achieved. If we translate and compare these elementary practices into the above findings you cannot fail to conclude that the nature and culture of this NHS care service had become dramatically dysfunctional and was working with displaced goals.

The failure to employ these elementary basic practices leaves the hospital open to the accusation of 'dumping the problem.' 'Dumping the problem' is a way of relieving the induced organisational anxiety created through the need to compensate for the consequential effects and imperative to "make savings." This brings to mind Deming's inversion equation being played out through the management servicing the created displaced goals. (Fig. 4) The focus on cost has reduced the quality of care services with increases in cost being experienced through significantly increased levels of litigation. The threat of litigation created a high degree of anxiety that reflected in the hyper defensive design and implementation of the complaints procedures.

This case study could have easily degenerated into charges of abuse and neglect being brought against the Oxlease NHS Foundation Trust had the complaint not been vigorously pursued by the relatives. An important point to note is that the primary *intent* of the family was to protect their relative and secondly to ensure other patients were not subject to this level of abuse.

The Symptoms of Organisational Decay

Not understanding what was being led and managed, in organisational terms, prevented the existing management of both institutions identifying the appropriate organisational service delivery requirements. This missing piece of their development puzzle compounded the existing organisational malaise in both institutions and the absence of care normally associated with the nursing care profession. Had the executive put in place an appropriate monitoring review process within their nursing care facilities, these failings would have been identified and provided an opportunity to rectify any existing and future failures. The lack of adequate monitoring to manage processes, created over time, and the precipitous consequential decay and depletion of the nursing care services became the performance norm that was accepted and not challenged. This led to "Too great a degree of tolerance of poor standards and of risk to patients." (Mid Staffordshire NHS Foundation Trust, Enquiry.) The application of an organisational approach to evaluate your existing organisational performance enables these insidious depletions and decay to be identified and rectified.

Reluctance to Complain

Within these care services these elderly clients are reluctant to complain as they develop a dependent relationship on the care service being provided. Many clients are without relatives and feel that retaliatory action would be taken if they complain. This developed culture of not complaining and not having an adequate voice for their complaints to be addressed creates a climate of management immunity.

This immunity was further reinforced through the developed leadership style of onsite line management, which lacked any form of *operant conditioning* or instrumental conditioning in the form of learning from testing or feedback. The onsite manager violated the existing reporting procedures by simply filing the extensive list of complaints. This failure to adequately test and review, by the executive directors, prevented any modification of individual or workgroup's behaviour. (Refer to Fig. 20, "Leading Transition for Change Processes." And Chapter Eleven, "Remuneration and Motivation".)

These defensive practices create a political environment that further compromises decision-making, notionally giving permission for the misuse of systems. These defensive practices stifle the individuals and the organisations from learning from their mistakes. "This places an inordinate emphasis on the appearance of success rather than the reality." The developed "appearance of success" feeds into the political decision-making model (Fig. 3) where the prioritising practice develops to service the politics, career and then the overt organisation. (Refer to Chapters Two and Three, "Why Organisations Become Dysfunctional" and "The Enemy within and Why Change Fails".)

An examination of this organisation's depletion found that the diaries of the director of nursing and the operational director confirmed that they had regularly visited the site under discussion. Yet, even the untrained eye could readily identify a number of activities that were inappropriate and would have contravened basic health and safety practices. For example, the carers and/or the client had removed cushions from other seats to increase the height of their seated position. Normally patient or client's chairs are elevated through the use of specifically designed and tailored frames that are fitted to the legs of the chairs. The need for elevation of the chair is to assist the individuals to stand without assistance. If these obvious practices could be easily observed, why had these two directors not taken remedial action and begun to ask further questions about the service being provided?

Further exploration started to identify an unhealthy colleagueship that had a sense of managing the status quo that placed an "inordinate emphasis on the appearance of success rather than the reality." The need to protect the created organisational climate led to a Pavlovian response procedure being introduced into the complaints procedure where the trigger word for action was "abuse" creating a practice where complaints were not acted upon unless the complaint contained the trigger word "abuse." Yet the six-page complaint listed numerous failures in care practice that collectively constituted institutional neglect and abuse. A further letter was passed to the authority with the word abuse, in bold upper case, to trigger some response to this long list of complaints. All the time these exchanges were being executed the patient was still enduring the abusive neglect.

The introduction of these Pavlovian conditioned response triggers had the effect of obfuscating the fact that these care services were declining and needed attention. This nursing care service had not suddenly depleted, it had been in the making for a number of years. It also had the effect of those operating within these systems to feel comfortable with their existing practices. Unfortunately they stopped using their nursing care antenna, even though all of the senior and executive staff had nursing backgrounds. (We can make some connections with the organisational environment created for the onsite Works managers at the Greenwich District Hospital, discussed earlier.)

Once the complaint had become formal both the Chairman and the CEO became involved and Lagadec's observations came to mind. "Our ability to deal with chaos depends on structures that have been developed before the chaos arrives." What became evident was that the "appearance of success" rather than the reality came to the fore. The Director of Nursing and Directors of Operations had not satisfactorily instituted effective regulatory monitoring practices. Neither had made the transition from their professional nursing roles to becoming organisational leaders and proved to have very little knowledge of what they were leading and managing, in organisational terms.

The failure of the director of nursing to develop structures and management regulatory practices affected her ability to deal with chaos when the "chaos" arrived. When attempting to discuss the background and asking why this situation had developed, the Director of Nursing was reduced to reciting a defensive mantra. She repetitively recited a list of numerous actions that were being put in place to rectify the created "careless" nursing environment, most of which were to do with basic nursing and therapeutic care management that she should have ensured before the "chaos arrived." She was absolutely distraught at being found wanting but her failure and playing the systems put people at risk. All that should have been part and parcel of the general management of these nursing care facilities and maintained by these executive directors.

The colleagueship arrangements were too comfortable where the participants had not developed the practice of being *detached engaged*, which ensures that those working for you were competent and remain focused on the quality of the care services being delivered. (Refer to Chapters Seven and Eight, "Adaptive Organisational leadership" and "Workgroups".) Understanding these variable role relationships would have created the working climate, enabling those responsible to the CEO and any other person in authority, to be aware of the depleting situation and have the authority to take remedial action. This is a comparable state to the Mid Staffordshire NHS Foundation Trust, Public Inquiry. "A culture focused on doing the system's business – not that of the patients'; an institutional culture which ascribed more weight to positive information about the service than to information capable of implying cause for concern."

The CEO should also have randomly tested the performance reports; a brief unannounced visit to this site and other sites would have provided an opportunity to test the existing reports. The CEO set the climate and people infer and tailor reports to what they consider the CEO wants to hear. The CEO had created a myopic understanding of what was really going on in this organisation. This detached hands off reporting systems approach invariably leaves the executive being isolated and ill informed. The dependency on these systems creates a superficial sense of security that reinforced the required "appearance of success", even though there are major service delivery failures being ignored.

The Existing Nursing Practices

It is important to tease this depletion of nursing care practices a little further to determine what other lessons we can take from this experience. An examination of Fig. 42 ("Clinical Service Support Model") enables us to notionally place the reactive time demands this service needs to provide. They would be operating this service at the planned, regulated and low response time of the care support continuum.

Normally there is a reasonable degree of attachment between the client and the carers but this was not evident in this institution. The time frame can become ritualistic and with the lack of engagement with the client group, the carers become more detached from the service being provided in terms of the clients' service needs. This led to the staff doing only the basics to get through the day. This state of disengagement further increased the functional relationship with the existing clients. The clients had become commodities that had to be ritualistically managed with the least inconvenience.

An example of their behaviour would be the use of the phrase "just a minute" which was used to defer and often meant that they would not return to assist a client/patient. The client may be forced to remind the nurse or care assistant that they need to be assisted to the toilet. When suffering a degree of incontinence this can cause the client/patient to have to sit with the discomfort of wetting themselves. This neglect creates a spiralling deterioration of, in this case, the patient's general condition. This was avoidable for this patient as she was used, when at home, to elevating herself out of her raised chair to attend the ablutions. The nurses' refusal to raise the patient's chair created an unnecessary dependency on the nursing and care staff.

This patient's discomfort was further increased by the sores that emanated from sitting in wet underwear that was normally treated with medicated cream. The nurse chose to use the patient's own un-medicated face cream to treat the chapped and sore areas.

These practices were distressing and led to loss of weight, which for this patient was important, as she was already frail. When reported to the senior nurse that she had lost 7lbs she dismissed the claim and saw no reason to act. Further insistent pressure forced the nurse to arrange for the dietician to attend. The weight loss exposed her skeletal frame creating pressure points where she was being forced to sit all day. The request for an inflated seat ring to relieve the pressure was constantly ignored, with the patient's relative being told they did not have one, which was an unbelievable claim. One of the resident clients, after four days, informed the relatives that a ring was on the open shelf opposite, in full view of the nurses' station and had been there from the time of the initial request.

The "appearance of success" was played out in the form of a cleaner constantly cleaning the corridors that radiated from the central point. Individual wards were not cleaned and sterilised to an acceptable standard for this form of institution, it was proved that these areas had not been cleaned for some time.

On the occasion of the patient returning from a hospital it would be a reasonable assumption to expect the patient's needs to be clearly recognised. Yet, her room had not been cleared, cleaned and sterilised before she was admitted.

The previous occupant had passed away but their own belongings had not been cleared from the room. The bed had not been prepared for the returning patient who now needed a special mattress to relieve the pain of the pressure sores. All of these issues had to be arranged by the patient's relatives whilst the patient sat in the corridor in a wheelchair.

The floor of the unprepared room was sticky underfoot and required another request to the line manager to arrange for the floor to be cleaned. This finally amounted to no more than a cleaner asking an attending GP and the patient's relatives to lift their feet whilst the cleaner generally mopped under their feet. This *superficial* cleaning was a clear indicator that sterility was not a priority. It also indicated that this floor had not been cleaned regularly for a considerable time, which must have included the time of the previous patient's occupancy. Attending nurses must have experienced their shoes sticking and should have taken appropriate action to remedy the situation.

Compromised Reporting Systems

The failure to have any form of operant regulatory practices created this inevitable downward spiral of inappropriate practices. The nurses had forgotten they were nurses first. If they introduced any initiative the on-site line manager treated them the same way as she did with the filing of the extensive complaints reports. The nurses simply stopped trying and settled into the current poor practice, which was considered acceptable. This is reminiscent of the behaviour demonstrated in the experiment, "Monkeys see Monkeys do" even though it was alien to the ethos of their basic nursing training.

These spiralling incidents have been used to indicate the nature and attitude of the management, the nursing staff and naturally the care assistants. Whilst all these exchanges were taking place, the patient was still being neglected and "abused", as the existing attitudes and care culture was still in place. The lack of comprehension and instinctive reaction was completely nullified by the existing ingrained institutional practices. The sense of detachment was palpable. The patient's health deteriorated to such an extent that she was transferred back into another hospital where she died.

The onsite line manager and the nursing staff's behaviour clearly demonstrated that they were locked in their own historical psychic organisation's behavioural practice. They were unable to respond to the numerous charges of dereliction of duty even when this was physically demonstrated to them.

For example, when the six-page list of complaints was physically handed to the line manager for discussion she was unable to comprehend the serious consequences of the failed management practices. She knew it was wrong but she was culturally conditioned to report what she felt the executive wanted to hear rather than report the facts that these failures existed. The list of complaints had the effect of increasing her levels of confusion and when these feelings exist within the leader, the organisation's "agent" those factors that influence why leaders mislead come to the fore. Should there be a failure to develop their *cognitive organisational awareness* to fit their new role, symptoms of "Why Leaders Mislead" (Chapter Five) will begin to emerge as their levels of anxiety increase.

As a consequence she became what could be described as "stuck, governed by their past" and locked in a psychic prison (Kets de Vries). The line manager's response was not to respond or begin to take appropriate action but to file the unwanted information. The repression of the information was a way that the line manager was able to relieve her own anxiety. Any action, particularly considering the nature and severity of the demonstrated situation, did not fit the "appearance of success" that was being politically managed (Fig. 3, "Politic, Career and Overt Organisation").

The above situation should encourage you to ask what is or has happened to these clinical/nursing care services when a patient's basic care needs are no longer a priority. Unfortunately there are other care institutions that also fail to provide appropriate care, damaging patients' confidence and encouraging further disruptive interventions by the Government.

Argyris and Schön (1978) would agree that it is the wrong sort of learning; they are not learning about the improvement of the organisation, it's more to do with how to play the political and career game, at the same time as losing sight of why the organisation exists and creating further displaced goals (Fig. 4, "AS IF Displaced Organisational Goals"). The visiting director of nursing, failing to *monitor to manage,* further compounded this situation where her neglect had created an accepted climate where the failures in care became acceptable. That, in turn, fed the cycle of precipitous depleting displaced nursing care.

Complaints Procedures

The complaints procedure is being specifically discussed because it is a *management technology.* It should be used as an opportunity to learn and improve your own and your organisation's service performance delivery. Or it can, in this case, be designed as a defensive shield to hide the failures and repress the opportunity for other parts of your organisation to learn and improve their performance. Earlier we discussed that management technologies and the systems they deploy do not think for themselves. They have to have an "agent" who designs and develops the employment of these *management technologies.*

483

When designing these systems we have to consider the *intent* that will be influenced by the external and internal environmental factors of the organisation where they are to be employed. Mr Haddon-Cave QC, chairman of the Nimrod enquiry said, "A sacred and unbreakable duty of care owed to the men and women of the Armed Forces." The professionals providing clinical and nursing supportive care, along with their respective managers all share that "sacred and unbreakable duty of *(patient)* care." If this does not ring bells for those managing within the NHS and the failure of care for this patient, it ought to. Yet, we find that repressive anxiety driven systems are developed to contain the individual and institutional anxiety.

This situation is further compounded by Deming's quality cost inversion equation, which indicates that when initiatives are cost driven they are short term and the quality of the service is reduced. This is reflected in the increase in the number of complaints and the forms of costly litigation that is reported to take place within the NHS. If you reverse this equation and use quality as a driver the cost, over time, is reduced.

This created political conundrum is expressed within the service and the design of the complaints procedures, which were identified as defensive and damaged the confidence of patients and the general public. The main elements that contribute to the defensive anxieties are primarily careers connected to the threat of litigation. When we examine the decision-making model that appears to be prevalent in many organisations (Fig. 3, "Politic, Career and Overt Organisation"), the politics are defensively influencing attitudes to careers. The Nimrod Enquiry identified displaced goals where cost savings were determinates of career, which had the consequential effects of displacing the primary organisational purpose, in this case, the quality of patient care.

In this case study it was the career-orientated leadership style and management that created displaced organisational goals. The "appearance of success" created an illusion that all was well when all was not well. In fact, the cycle of events could have led to litigation if the relatives had not addressed it. Although the overall NHS environment was cost driven, this organisation was well funded, and the precipitous depletion of care could be directly attributed to the leadership style, systems design and the inappropriate collegiate management culture.

The need to maintain and to defend the institution of the NHS against anxiety led to the complaints procedure being extremely defensive and challenging for the plaintiff and had the designed *intent* to repress any complaints. The complaints procedure was used to induce a high degree of attrition to prevent any issue being discussed or made public. The patient's relatives had to agree to a non-disclosure clause. A conciliator was engaged, employed by the health authority to facilitate the meeting, who further reinforced the need for non-disclosure. Without the agreement to the non-disclosure clause, the CEO and the other executives refused to meet the patient's family.

What the designer of the complaints procedures had not understood was that most people are not seeking compensation; they simply want someone to positively respond to their desire to ensure their relative receives appropriate clinical and nursing care. This also requires that the responses to any complaint be effectively addressed within an appropriate time frame. The time frame must include the *immediate* relief of that patient's discomfort.

Unfortunately the defensive behaviour of the designed complaints procedure prevented any appropriate early response to the presented situation. If they had acted with appropriate skills and compassion the complaint would possibly have never been made. When the complaint was formally made it was met by a system of attrition that appeared to be designed to break the plaintiff's "will" and to prevent them pursuing the complaint. This implies that the whole management function was dysfunctional and not designed to ensure patient care.

These examples have been used to demonstrate the shift in the notion of *intent* applied to these service care provisions. The publicity surrounding the *intent* was to improve the service and bring those who had failed in their duty of care to account. In reality the system was designed to defend and preserve, by repression and containment, the good name of any service under scrutiny. Argyris and Schön (1978) would not have described this organisation as a learning organisation as there is no opportunity to learn from these mistakes. It is a hyper-defensive organisation that is too anxious to learn from its failings.

Not one item on the list of complaints was ever challenged or refuted; it was dated 6th December 2006 and the procedure was unsatisfactorily concluded in 2008. A year earlier the patient had died. We are not dealing with a commodity but with human emotion and the need to desperately defend and protect their own family member, yet the process could have been dealt with at source satisfactorily. At the end of this process the patient's family did not achieve closure.

As a result of persisting with this complaint, initially to achieve relief for the relative without success, this transformed into a need to prevent others from being subject to the same form of institutional abuse.

Appendix to NHS Case Studies

The NHS is mammoth and complicated: when you use an organisational decision-making approach it significantly reduces the complexity.

An examination of the general references and the case studies clearly identifies that many of the presented problems are as a consequence of political decision-making. This causes those who are required to implement those decisions to reinterpret them within the context of their own situation.

Two forms of conflict ensue – that of satisfying the political masters (career motives) and the other stems from the needs of the organisations and the tension created by the unwanted behavioural consequences of these politically driven single initiatives. These confused sets of arrangements fit the dysfunctional decision-making model represented in Fig. 3, "Politics, Career and Overt Organisation." (Refer to the created (P) political influence identified in the "Dome" case study and Nimrod enquiry.) (Reflect on the misuse of bonuses and the potential consequential outcomes. Pay particular attention to Chapter Eleven, "Remuneration and Motivation" where we discuss "Bonus Culture – Mismatch." This has the capacity to create displaced goals and misdirect the intentionality (refer to Fig. 3 and Fig. 4) of those charged with leading and managing these politicised organisations.)

Politicians' perceptions that they can manipulate and change this and other mammoth institutions', organisational performance cultures, within one term in office are ill founded. It only serves to create a climate of instability and the need "to play the political game" to satisfy these (capital P) political whims, causing those attempting to lead and manage to lurch from one political doctrine to another.

These politicised organisational environments consciously or unconsciously recruit those that are compliant, further reinforcing the created ingrained leadership style of management. This leads to "the appearance of success" and induces the manic and at the same time aggressive desire to silence whistle-blowers, even if it means putting patients/clients at risk. (Refer to "Transitional Nursing Care" case study and Mid-Staffordshire enquiry. Couple these with Merton's (1940) studies that "competition within organisations occurs within closely defined limits. Evaluation and promotion are relatively independent of an individual's achievement." This increased political manoeuvring causes the more ambitious people to become overtly ruthless, very often at the expense of others. Which can and does translate into those dependent and vulnerable users of these services becoming the victims, whilst these games are being played out.

Experience of working nationally and in a variety of NHS services confirms that NHS leaders and managers are good at restructuring to meet the political demands but not good at leading transition for change. This practice needs to change, along with rewarding failure. "When you support incompetence and poverty you invariably get more of it" (James Dale Davison). In this case poverty refers to the lack of *cognitive organisational awareness and organisational leadership skills*.

Making Transition for Change within the NHS

Leaders and managers, in parallel with their organisation, need to make the transition from the politically led to an organisational led decision-making practice. This would require that the central and local executives have the understanding and ability to enable their organisations to respond effectively to local demographically defined social and clinical service needs. To ensure the continued high performance of their hospital's services they need to be able to understand and interpret the wider social, clinical, economic and technological environment. (Local Services provide direction for those national based organisations to effectively support the identified local needs, not the other way around.)

The value of using an organisational approach is that you develop a common organisationally focused language and *intent* that would allow an appropriate dialogue to be conducted about the creation of achievable consistent quality service delivery. The translation of the overall strategic *intent* could be consistently applied throughout the whole organisation.

It would enable the identification of an appropriate *performance culture continuum,* both vertically and along the service delivery track that everyone understands, owns and can measure their own and others' overall performance against. It would provide that all-important consistent continuity of care that travels with the patient/client when referred via their GP or through the trauma route into the NHS.

Having identified and developed a responsive service delivery organisation, using an organisational approach would enable the different political doctrines to engage with the organisation's needs and become part of the appropriate responsive development of the NHS, preventing the costly and unproductive practice of lurching from one political doctrine's motive to another. This requires the organisational decision-making to change; from Fig. 3, "Politics, Career and Overt Organisation" to Fig. 5, "Overt Organisation, Career and Politics."

Cost models can be designed to monitor the proffered organisational service delivery performance. It can also be designed to monitor the changes in the cost profiling as the dysfunctional practices are eliminated, enabling informal cost management practices to redirect funding on a rational supportive basis. The alternative is unrelated reactive cost control practices with attached unsupported target setting, coupled with a continuing depletion in the quality of care. (Deming's cost vs. quality inversion equation.)

This process could be employed to identify those areas that are contributing to the enormous litigation costs. It would also provide an opportunity to identify those organisational decision-making practices that are contributing to these clinical failures. Having removed the dysfunctional decision-making along with the dysfunctional organisational practices the created intellectual space could be used to concentrate on improving those clinical practices that have been identified as contributing to cases of costly litigation. The real value of this employed process is that it not only saves lives it saves time, money and significantly improves the quality of services delivery.

Supported aims should be introduced to replace the current disastrous use of the management technology "performance targets." Whenever these are employed in any organisation the intrinsic skills of individuals are not employed to improve the organisation's performance. They are used to service defensive displaced goals and the "appearance of success."

Even those with limited organisational knowledge understand that the current inconsistent operational service delivery must change. Using an organisational approach is a viable alternative. The very brief overview of the change in mind-set outlined above would provide the opportunity for those benefits to be effectively derived. Importantly, the local service delivery would reflect the social, economic and technological environment of the hospitals, community care and social services. These connected services would provide consistent continuity of care for the patient/client as they move through the various reparative and therapeutic care provisions.

A tenet that would need to be established is that the NHS is not responsible for your health; individuals are responsible for their own health. The NHS is there to provide reparative supportive care. Changing the mind-set of the general public is the combined responsibility of the various political parties as they belong to the Parliamentary institution that has contributed to the current misunderstanding.

A further major challenging problem to be resolved is the issue of persuading the existing leaders and managers to "let go" of the mechanisms they use to defend themselves from the existing induced organisational anxiety and responsive dysfunctional practices. The institutionalised decision-making behavioural practices are so engrained they would take a while to enable an organisational led decision-making practice to become the norm. Even so it is achievable using an organisational led approach.

The assumption and proffered organisational leadership and management approach can resolve many of the presented problems. For this to be successfully achieved, a frame of reference has to be established, that in practice, can operate without the direct and conflicting political dogmas. A political overview on performance is inevitable and appropriate; using an organisational approach enables this to be effectively achieved without compromising the organisation's delivery performance. Critically you reduce the potential for creating ineffective and even dangerous dysfunctional organisations where vulnerable dependent individual patients and clients require reparative support. (Refer to Nimrod enquiry and Chapter Ten, "Outsourcing and Contractual Practices" where we discuss the government's responsibility for the leadership and management of UK limited, and where we identify the unwanted consequences of direct (P) political influences.)

TECHNOLOGY & CHANGE

CASE STUDY NINE

FINANCIAL SECTOR

ASSURANCE

Background

A successful Marketing and Sales Director's reward was to be promoted to become the Chief Executive. The presented problem for this company (name withheld for commercial reasons) had, over a short period of time, experienced a drastic reduction in sales and market shares. The loss of sales was attributed to the inability to retain existing customers, creating a high turnover of sales personnel. These events coincided with the introduction of a new mainframe computer.

The Presented Problem

The presented sales problems were seen through the marketing and sales perspective. This led to extensive training and retraining of the new and existing sales personnel. After a failure to improve the loss of sales, further training was introduced along with improved incentives to retain sales staff. To complement this drive the Actuaries were required to design new, more attractive products. The Actuaries, when interviewed, revealed that the existing products were satisfactory and should be attractive for existing and new customers.

Senge (1990) writes, "The cure can be worse than the disease." In this case this held true. The creation of new products created a product redundancy cycle. The existing customers, who were being sold new products to replace their existing products, were unhappy and wanted to retain their old agreements, creating a negative cycle of events. This took the form of customer alienation in that they were losing confidence in their current product portfolio and the sales personnel. The consequential outcome was that these customers moved to other providers.

The existing customers became increasingly resistant to further sales interventions. These difficulties were further compounded when the salesperson was unable to quickly and confidently track the performance of existing and new products. Another factor that reduced customer confidence was the high turnover of sales staff.

A fundamental expectation of an assurance sales person is that they have readily available valid updated performance information relating to their customers' investments. It is all part of the assurance process, which is to retain customers' confidence in the safe provision for the inevitable. The persistent loss of sales and haemorrhaging of existing customers began to seriously damage the performance of the company and its credit rating.

It was evident that to retain customers, the sales personnel had a dependent need, on the provided data, to effectively track the respective products' performance. They were totally dependent on the centralised mainframe computer to readily monitor the performance of each customer's product portfolio and make that information readily available to the sales personnel.

The rapid loss of customers was directly influenced by the fact that the majority of new customers came through satisfied customer referrals. The role, therefore, of the sales personnel could be identified as generating new sales through networking, managing referrals, and critically maintaining the existing customers' portfolios.

Analysis

Working through the sales personnel experiences and role expectations assisted in identifying the real problem. This was not with the sales force but with the head office staff not providing accurate, timely and valid customer information.

The developed *time line* used for tracking the *recent history* indicated that the presented sales difficulties began with the installation of a new mainframe computer. The introduction of this critical and invasive *management technology,* along with the magnitude of this type of event, as in many cases, was challenging and outside the experience of the executive.

Experience indicates that executives tend to abrogate the responsibility for managing the introduction of their mainframe computer systems, to the preferred supply contractor. The practice of abrogation and deskilling can be observed in many organisations that engage in the introduction of new *management technologies,* particularly IT computer-based systems.

The skills these executives have are an understanding of the needs of the business and the regulatory authorities. They can, at the very least, apply these business interest skills to ensure that the techno-managers are designing the systems to reinforce the organisation's overall performance. They can further improve the quality of the brief to the contractor when they attach their business understanding to an identified future state organisation. This can be effectively achieved by working through the *transition for change* process before designing the new computer systems. Without these inputs the techno-managers will interpret what they, from experience, consider to be best for your organisation.

When reviewing the recent history you were left with the sense that those with the skills of leading and managing this organisation had deskilled in deference to the techno-manager, who understood the systems but not the business and its developing performance culture. The production of a *performance culture continuum* would have facilitated the cognitive organisational awareness of the executive. From this position they would have been able to direct and control the activities of the supplier of this *management technology.* (Refer to Chapter Nine, "Technology Change and Managing the Consequences" its invasiveness, and ability to displace organisational goals and detach the leader, causing them to manage the systems rather than the organisation.)

The business of assurance is framed in the title of the business. The difference between insurance and assurance are that with insurance, there is a level of probability that it may happen but with assurance, it will happen. With the latter *intent* in mind the customers make the necessary financial provisions. This is a simplification but catches the essence of the *intent* of this institution and the assurance industry.

Working with this notion it became essential to rewind and test these assumptions from a customer's perspective. (The service delivery end of the *culture performance continuum* that we are all working to satisfy.) The requirement from the customer's perspective was for them to be, as and when required, assured that their product portfolio was performing as well as projected. For the sales person, to retain an on-going satisfactory working relationship, they have to have readily to hand their customer's portfolio performance details. In essence the information has to be up to date, accurate, timely, and unambiguous and presented in a form that the customer can simply understand.

The data collection has to be such that each product, at source, has to be monitored by tracking its performance. The data has to be stored and configured to enable each customer's portfolio to be updated when required. It has also to be readily accessible to each sales person. The same process of monitoring all the product performance also provides the executive and Actuaries with the performance trends for each product. This generated product monitoring information provides opportunities to improve the product performance or develop another one to replace it in the interest of anticipating and maintaining customer satisfaction.

This process is simply working back from the customer's satisfaction needs and ensuring the management systems are designed to *reinforce the identified individual's service delivery*. This is represented in Fig. 10 ("Representation Hourglass Strategic Thinking") where you scan the service delivery environment to ensure the service delivery performance is appropriate. It also introduces the notion that you have to scan the product's environment to ensure that any market changes can be detected early and factored into any future strategic and product decision-making. The top of the hourglass notional model represents that part of the process where you scan your business environment. This scanning process allows the executive and Actuaries to develop products that compensate for any shortfall in performance providing an opportunity for the sales person to discuss the changes, in the interest of their respective customers. In other words, assuring the customer's interest by protecting the investments.

These scanning and conversion processes have to be designed into the practice and performance of the computer systems design. At the one end to service the strategic decision-making, enabling the interpretation and conversion processes to ensure the customer's needs are constantly being assured. At the other end this process also provides an opportunity for the sales personnel to service feedback processes regarding presented concerns or trends.

This is an important process in that the customers' needs are leading the intent of the initiative, not the displaced intent to generate sales. Sales generally are, in this particular industry, generated from referrals; therefore, the complete satisfaction of existing customers is paramount, and not the continuous reinventing of products that need to be sold, even though many of the existing product's life cycles had not peaked (Fig. 17, "Product Cycle"). The *displaced goals* created by the inadequate performance of the new mainframe computer caused the inversion of the process that led to the alienation of existing customers.

This process of examining the recent history and the development of a timeline in the form of a *performance culture continuum* enables you to quickly identify various process boundaries. This enables you to identify the *areas of transition* from one process to another, the associated *states of flux* and the need to create the necessary *regulatory management* practices. It also enables the design and development of appropriate feedback loops that enable you to monitor to manage and control the direction and operating delivery performance of your business organisation (Fig. 20, "Leading Transition for Change").

When tracking back through the recent history and the displayed processes, the dysfunctional behaviour took the form of the systems being managed and the customer apparently being neglected by the head office administration. Their working environment was that of dealing with the political consequences of the dysfunctional displaced behaviour of the systems, the organisation and the leadership. They were reduced to employing the *politically dysfunctional decision-making model* (Fig. 3, "Politics, Career, and Overt Organisation").

This overview of the process has been simplified for this discussion but it should provide the general essence of the computerised *management technologies* role. The process of introducing and installing the new computer had become the focus of the administration to service the systems rather than the system being there to service the organisation's strategic needs, sales and their customer's assured satisfaction. This created displaced systems goals (Fig. 4, "As if displaced Organisational Goals").

The Consequential Outcomes

The computer personnel exposed another cyclical induced problem, that of other non-computing employees designing and using unauthorised alternative programmes. It was important to gain an understanding as to what and why these practices existed. The use of these unauthorised programmes was a source of expressed envy, irritation and "scapegoating" to those unauthorised personnel that were writing computer programmes. There were high levels of interdepartmental conflict and this was exacerbated by the refusal to stop using the unauthorised systems. The unauthorised programmers had more confidence in their created micro IT systems than that of the mainframe services.

Research revealed that many of those involved were Actuaries who were primarily employed to design products and protect the company from losses. These are extremely intelligent, capable people who felt that the existing mainframe computer support was totally inadequate. The Actuaries' programmes experienced a high degree of ownership for their developed products, which generated a strong vested interest in "their" product performing well. They sympathised, in a detached way, with the sales personnel's dilemma, as they were passionate that their products performed well.

The inability, at a rational level, to discuss the mainframe's inadequacies created unresolved dissipating conflict between the Actuaries and the computer operation staff. The activities of the Actuaries were not in any way malevolent in all cases; they were genuinely trying to provide a working solution to the problems they were experiencing. A degree of competition had begun to surface as to who could write better computer programmes.

We have discussed in previous chapters the political ownership of particular strategic initiatives that executives adopt for specific projects. The inability to communicate what needed to be done was further exacerbated by the Chief Executive experiencing a great deal of anxiety in his new role. He had expressed that it felt it was like a house of cards. The anxiety he was experiencing was expressed by removing himself from the day-to-day incidental meeting of other employees. This was his way of preventing alternative views being expressed that may challenge his frame of reference, as with presented problems with his sales personnel. His physical and mental withdrawal was making it difficult to address the underlying problems created by the failure of the mainframe computer's performance.

It is not difficult to imagine the degree of frustration when confronted by this situation that was being generated within the organisation. Often others were withdrawing their services, which was expressed by resigning and seeking other employment, resulting in a high turnover of staff, particularly in the sales department.

Providing the evidence and tracking the problem enabled the identification that the operating procedures of the mainframe computer was the culprit, and agreement was eventually achieved for the operating systems to be redesigned. Importantly, the brief for the redesign had to be specific and with a focused intent. This meant that the tracking of a product's performance was accurate and timely. Satisfied customers equal more referrals, which was one of the primary means for increasing sales. Critically, it provided the service needs that would satisfy the regulatory authorities.

Summary

We can learn from this case study a number of lessons. Often the presented problem is not the actual problem. The consequential effects of a failure in one part of the decision implementation process can manifest itself, in another guise, within the practices of another dependent part of the organisation. Everybody was aware that the company was under performing and why, which is often the case.

Another lesson we can take from this case study is the need to have a clear understanding of the recent history to understand the here and now. To introduce any new *management technology* you have to have a clear understanding of the needs of the organisation before introducing any new technology. This is important, as any new technology will disturb the existing power base and political arrangements. The design of the computer systems, therefore, has to have a clearly expressed *intent* in terms of the expected organisation's regulatory and service delivery performance. (Refer to Chapter Nine, "Technology Change and Managing the Consequences".)

Without this *directed intent* and *expressed scope of the brief*, developed from working through the *transition for change processes,* the techno-managers will introduce what they feel the computer can deliver. This creates further dysfunctional practices such as the Actuaries acting as computer technicians and the sales personnel not being able to maintain and create new business. Therefore the interface between the technology providers and the company, the owner of the new system, has to clearly be defined in terms of the organisation's service delivery needs.

The other critical practice that can make or break the introduction of new technology is the design and management and the letting of the contract. Retaining the ability to manage the contract from the client side is absolutely critical. Experience of managing major contracts often demands that the contract manager has to reposition themselves relative to the client and the provider, the *detached/engaged* placement, being on the boundary between both these organisations. In essence, they have to be able to identify and design the contract so that it can be managed in terms of the clients' needs. This can only be achieved when you work with the provider to ensure they understand their role in the process of complying with the *scope of the brief* and contracted practice needs. It is "as if" you are independent to both the client and the contractor with the sole intent of ensuring the *contract is managed effectively*. (Refer to Chapters Nine and Ten, along with the "Millennium Dome" case study.)

CASE STUDY TEN

THE MILLENNIUM DOME

This case study enables us, within a unique organisational environment, to examine the transitional life cycle of an organisation from development through to its completion and closure. We can briefly explore the transition processes of clearing a contaminated brown-field site, the construction programme, the creative development and the transition from a capital funded project to an operational, revenue-generating business, through to the decommissioning, liquidating and eventual closure of an exhibition site.

The opportunity to live through the life cycle of an organisation is a once in a lifetime experience. It provided an opportunity to experience the transitional behaviour and the influence of its politically charged environment on the decision-making and responsive practices within this organisation.

Recent Developmental History

The following background information is a general overview to provide you with a sense of the organisation's decision-making environment. The Millennium Dome in London was a purpose built temporary structure created to house a year-long "Millennium Experience" visitor attraction to celebrate the year 2000 milestone of the third millennium. The Millennium Experience exhibition, featuring interactive exhibits, shows and other entertainment, was built around three primary themes: "who we are", "what we do" and "where we live." The event was designed to draw tourists into London during the Millennium year and was intended to be a celebration of mankind's achievements. What we need to keep in mind is that this was designed, as a "Once in a Lifetime Visitor Attraction"; the slogan was "One Amazing Day."

Construction of the Dome

The Millennium Dome (Fig. 43) is a dome-shaped building, used to house the Millennium Experience. The Dome was the centrepiece of the visitor attraction to be held in Greenwich and was strategically built on the site of the Meridian Line, symbolising time.

At that time, the Dome was the largest single construction project in Europe, and the largest dynamic building structure of its type. It was the biggest dome in the world. The construction site occupied 300 acres of a formerly derelict site of a gasworks, a steel stockyard and a munitions factory. This site had been derelict for more than two decades and was the largest undeveloped site on the River Thames.

Design Concepts

Mike Davies, Project Director, and Gary Withers of 'Imagination' developed the design concept. Together they plotted the projection of the comets and stars, dawn to dusk, onto the Dome's surface prior to its detailed structural rationalisation, and the twelve hours, the twelve months, and the twelve constellations of the sky which measure time were all integral to the original concept. The twelve towers are intended as great arms, outstretched in celebration. In plan view it is circular, 365 metres in diameter, which incorporated into the design one metre for each day of the year.

The Millennium Dome was intended as a celebratory, iconic, non-hierarchical structure offering a vast, flexible space, providing 100,000m² of enclosed space (2.2 million cubic metres), with a circumference of one kilometre and a maximum height of 50 m. The Dome is suspended from a series of twelve 100m steel masts, held in place by more than 70km of high-strength steel cable which in turn supported the Teflon-coated glass fibre roof (Fig. 43).

Fig 43

Externally, it appears as a large white marquee with twelve 100m-high yellow support towers, one for each month of the year, or each hour of the clock face, representing the role-played by Greenwich Mean Time. It has subsequently become one of the United Kingdom's most recognisable landmarks.

This element of the design and construction of the "Dome" was a resounding success and the building itself was relatively inexpensive; £43 million for ground works, the perimeter wall, masts, cable net structure and the roof fabric. The design and development practices devised a non-adversarial procurement route involving standardised components that delivered the building within fifteen months and under budget. The construction and design received many major awards.

Millennium Experience Exhibition

The interior space was subdivided into fourteen major interactive experiential entertainment zones that circled a central arena where 'The Central Aerial Show' was successfully performed 999 times with an artistic cast of 160 acrobatic performers.

The list of surrounding zones and exhibits were:

Who we are:

Body, Mind, and Faith comprised five sections: History of Christianity, Making of Key Life Experiences, How Shall I Live? Night Rain (a contemplation and Faith Festivals Calendar), and Self Portrait.

What we do:

Work, Learning, Rest, Play, Talk, Money and Journey.

Where we live, shared ground:

Living Island and Home Planet.

This combination of exhibits and events was designed to provide for the visitor that "Wow Effect" and to create that "One Amazing Day".

Political History

On the Greenwich Peninsula, where the Dome was sited, the Deputy Conservative Prime Minister Michael Heseltine originally saw the clean-up operation as an investment that would add a large area of useful land to the crowded capital. This was part of a plan to regenerate a large, sparsely populated area to the east of London and south of the River Thames, which included the reclamation of the entire Greenwich Peninsula.

Originally proposed by the ruling Conservative government, the project concept was expanded and championed by the Labour Party Prime Minister Tony Blair when he took office in 1997. Political issues related to the Dome influenced Peter Mandelson's and John Prescott's political careers. Another historically associated fact was that Herbert Morrison (Peter Mandelson's grandfather) had been involved with the Festival of Britain in 1951, of which negative comparisons were often made. This exhibition had the "Dome of

Discovery" resembling a flying saucer, creating an exciting futuristic impression.

It has been reported that the Millennium Dome attracted intense media coverage and generated more political and public debate than any other British building of the last 100 years. When the Millennium Experience opened on 31st Dec 1999, initial reaction from the press was poor. Lack of content, lack of clear themes and lack of creativity were common criticisms. The press reported a lack of vision, poor execution, and lacklustre content resulting in negative experiences for visitors. The resulting negative PR, stemming from those reported experiences, contributed to the failure to generate the expected visitor numbers.

The Millennium Dome project was one of the most controversial public works projects ever undertaken, for a large number of reasons:

- The reputation of the leading politicians of the day was vested in the success of this project. Consequently their influence created confusion and misdirection of *intent*. An example was the reported direct intervention of the Prime Minister, who intervened to reverse the decision on the grade and life cycle of the Dome's fabric. The Dome fabric's life cycle was increased to twenty years, which created a different perspective for the Dome's future.

- The whole project was to be a temporary structure and the original fabric choice was made to meet that requirement. The sudden extension of the life span of the fabric introduced the notion that this project had an attached future development plan, which proved not to be the case. If the Dome structure were to be developed into a more permanent events venue the internal design philosophy would have been directly affected.

- This visitor attraction was to run for one year, be sold on, or decommissioned and demolished. There was a failure to plan properly for the post event disposal of the venue. When the Dome exhibition finally closed the Government struggled for years to find a buyer. For many years the venue remained empty and as a result, remained a liability. Eventually ministers in 2002 handed the site over to developers. It finally re-opened, housing the successful 20,000-seat O2 concert and sporting arena.

- From the start the Dome's content was criticised as bland and vacuous. Ticket receipts were dismal which the constant poor press affected. A number of senior executives were sacked, and the financial failures turned this ambitious scheme into a politically divisive one.

- The political decision-making process reduced the development time for these types of project. The time frame for the development was considerably less than what most development organisations would normally experience when managing these kinds of projects. This meant that the time frame for clearing the site, completing the construction, design and development of the exhibits and making the transition to an effective revenue operational organisation had become compressed.

- Being part of a millennium celebration, the opening date was fixed and could not, under any circumstances, be moved. This meant that this exhibition opened at the end of December in the middle of winter.

- Finally, the project was financially mismanaged. A 2000 National Audit Office report declared that the NMEC grossly over-estimated the number of visitors likely to attend (this figure was scaled down from twelve million to seven million in May 2000, and the final figure was 6.5 million). The failure to attract the public could be attributed to the failure to effectively market it and manage the political influences and the created negative response of the press.

- Information released by the National Archives show that the Dome's operating company struggled to pay its bills from the start and ran out of cash completely by January 28, 2000 – just four weeks after the attraction's notoriously chaotic opening night – and was forced to apply to the Millennium Commission for more Lottery money to stay afloat. Throughout the year the operating company, NMEC, struggled to pay its bills. Records revealed that in July alone the company had thirty four County Court judgements issued against it for non-payment.

- A contributing factor was the financial predictions being based on an unrealistically high forecast of visitor numbers at twelve million. During the twelve months it was open there were approximately 6.5 million visitors — significantly fewer than the ten million paying visitors that attended the 1951 Festival of Britain, which only ran from May to September. The Empire Exhibition, in Scotland 1938, held in Glasgow, attracted more than twelve million visitors and was open through May to October.

The press still savaged the project even though the visitor feedback was extremely positive and ranked as the most popular tourist attraction in the year 2000.

Political and Management Issues

The project was largely reported by the press to have been a flop: badly thought-out, poorly executed, and leaving the government with the question of what to do with this vacant exhibition site. During the year 2000 the organisers repeatedly asked for, and received, more funding from the Millennium Commission, the Lottery body that supported it. Numerous changes of management at Board level, before and during the exhibition, were disruptive and had compromised the transitional development from a capital to a revenue generating operation.

The Chief executive of the New Millennium Experience Company (NMEC) was sacked one month after the dome's opening. The Millennium Central Ltd, latterly the New Millennium Experience Company Ltd (NMEC), was set up to administer the project, and ministerial accountability for the project was assured initially through Peter Mandelson, as Minister without portfolio.

January 1998: Creative director Stephen Bayley resigned from the project. He is reported to have been at "loggerheads" with Peter Mandelson as to who was in charge of the project.

December 1998: Peter Mandelson resigns from government after a financial scandal.

January 1999: Lord Falconer of Thoroton replaces Peter Mandelson. The Director of Operations had cause to resign six months prior to the project becoming a revenue generation business. The Operations Director's resignation was at a time when the organisation was beginning to make the critical transition from a capital funded organisation to a revenue generating operation.

This left the organisation without an effectively developed management organisation to regulate the *states of flux* that needed to be managed from one state to another. This vacuum in the operational organisational regulatory management fed in to the many operational failures. These failures drew less attention than the chaotic opening arrangement for managing the attending selected audience, in particular the press. The Millennium Dome officially re-opened as the O2, on 24 June 2007, on the day that Tony Blair resigned as Labour Party leader and John Prescott resigned as Deputy Leader.

Thinking Organisationally

The created political environment was not conducive to clear directed developmental decision-making. Even so we have to develop strategies that enable you to remain focused on successfully achieving the necessary delivery service performance outcomes. One of the issues that you must address is to ensure that the political influencers understand the boundaries of responsibility and who is accountable for particular decisions and deliverable activities. The critical focus, when employing an organisational approach, is not to block the political influence but to persuade them to engage and use their political skills. Those political skills need to be used to influence the political environment outside the boundaries of the organisation.

Using an organisational approach is a process that provides a platform and language that enables engagement through dialogue, without confrontation, between those of different skills, developmental experiences and/or political persuasions.

A critical lesson we can take from this project is whatever the quality of your strategic decision-making; the test of your leadership is the ability to translate that into a viable service delivery performance. Leadership is about influencing and the persuasion of others to appropriately follow the service performance delivery path.

The decision-making process must always include the successful implementation, as this is the area where we are all finally judged. It is this issue that will be explored in organisational terms to demonstrate the difference between an ad-hoc systems approach, compared with an organisationally led approach.

Contract Management

Comparing contract management practices provides an insight into the different leadership styles, and project and contract management activities employed for two main delivery organisations. The image of The Dome is that of a circus tent. Within that tent the Central Show and the numerous exhibits discussed earlier contextually fit. The Central Show could be considered to be one circus ring and each exhibit to be independent circus rings. The Central Show could be led and managed independently. The numerous exhibits can be considered as independent circus rings that required an umbrella organisation to regulate and manage each exhibit's development. The style and leadership for each of these organisations is distinctly different and needed to be understood as they directly affected the performance delivery outcomes of each organisation. Making a comparative examination, we find that they were not, and this created unwanted consequential outcomes.

The Central Show could be considered to stand alone, with management arrangements structured to enable this to operate independently with one ringmaster. Each of these exhibits generated their own organisational culture that would have been affected by the employed technologies, which, in turn, influenced the leadership style and management of that specific project. The ringmasters responsible for leading and managing these differentiated organisational cultures needed to develop their competencies to understand and complement these created organisational cultures.

Even so, the procurement for all the contracts that included the central show and the exhibits could employ standard regulated procurement practices. The difference in practice is that the letting and the management of each contract had to be developed, led and managed for each circus ring's created organisational service performance culture.

Contracts that serviced the dependent and interdependent relationship of all these events were the responsibility of the Central Show's contract manager. This arrangement was to ensure that these contracts were centrally managed, regulated and controlled. Some of these contracts were supporting the national information and communication facilities for the regulation and management of revenue generated funds. The individual contracts for the exhibits were the responsibility of another contract manager. Both these contract managers were responsible to a senior overall contract manager.

Applying this concept to the central show will allow us to make the necessary connections to the leadership and management of the other notional circus rings, formed by the other events. There were 120 contracts to be let; some had multi-million pound budgets, which were dedicated to support the central show. Others were servicing contracts, such as lighting, sound, communications and networking, and were considered in the context of the various elements, locally and nationally, that needed to be serviced.

Contractual Development Practices

The central show was conceptually considered in isolation with the entire set of contracts being designed to ensure that each one complemented the other, in terms, of the interrelationship and interdependent relationship, and the consequential effects one had on each other. This allowed the *states of flux* to be identified along with the boundaries of responsibilities and authority of each contract to be clearly defined and expressed in the design and development of the contract before it was let. This practice is based on the following tenet: the way you develop and let a contract enables you to effectively monitor and manage that contract. Within that tenet there is an agreed and contracted expectation that each dependent contractor takes responsibility for any areas of possible inter-contractual conflict.

During these contractual developments, the operating procedures are agreed to enable those *states of flux* that are automatically created between various contracts are effectively regulated and managed. This is an example of developing decision-making processes, in organisational terms, that support the processes for designing and developing this *management technology*. Contract management practices must be designed and developed, to reinforce the overall organisation's service performance delivery culture.

The process adopted begins once you have decided on the preferred contractor. It is at this stage that you begin to further develop the organisational approach. This enables you to examine the dependent and interdependent relationships and identify each *state of flux*. Engaging the contractors in this process ensures the contractors understand their regulatory and management responsibilities, that is, in terms of one another and particularly the collective delivery of the service performance outcomes.

Contractors, from experience, all demonstrate that they want to succeed and to that end they welcome the expressed *intent* of this approach. This approach automatically identifies the positive and negative consequential outcomes. It is at this early stage that the working relationships between the various contractors and the client are clearly established, in terms of the directed decision-making processes, responsibility, authority and accountability. (Refer to the notional model Fig. 33, "Task Group Orientation" Chapter Eight.)

Other benefits of this negotiated contractual arrangement are that the operating performance of the various contracts can be identified, clarified and agreed. This also allows the separate development of the contract for maintaining the equipment and that equipment's performance expectation, which will identify the response time relative to the other activities it may be supporting.

When working through these negotiations it is essential that you intellectually position yourself at the boundary between the client and the potential contractor. It allows you to work with the contractor to enable them to develop their contractual practices to ensure that they collectively meet the expectation of the client's service delivery. Using an organisational approach simplifies the process for both the multiple dependent and interdependent contractors and the client organisation. The created dialogue is, in terms of the future organisation's performance needs and the development of the working relationship, between the various contractors and the client.

The purpose of orientating and linking these activities is to ensure that all the workgroups and, in this case, the contractors are servicing the overall *organisation's developing performance culture*. (We can make a connection with the notion of "Task Group Orientation" (Fig. 33). Having a well-developed *cognitive organisational awareness* enables you to develop and retain a mental image (Fig. 8, "Internalised Thinking Processes (COA) and Fig. 31, "Group's Cognitive Organisational Awareness") of how these activities fit on the *performance culture continuum*. (It is the same kind of intellectual organisational practice you would employ for contracting regulating and controlling outsourced services.)

A precursor to these discussions, which becomes the entry point with the contractor, is to determine whether they have the capacity and ability to deliver the contract, on budget, on time and to the required performance standards. This requires that you determine their viability, their capacity to produce and deliver the goods on time, and that they have the management capabilities to deliver the contract in terms of the client's needs. These contractual practices were rigorously applied to all the above contracts for the central show and those dependent and interdependent contracts.

These rigorous practices were not applied to the development and management of the various exhibits' contracts. The leadership and the contractual practice were inappropriately developed to fit the management of the multiple circus rings. The leadership style that needed to be developed was to satisfy the performance culture, at the service delivery end, where the visitor interacted with each exhibit, creating a need for each circus ring to be managed to satisfy these factors influencing each organisation's performance culture. The overall ringmaster for all of these exhibits needed to have a clear understanding of the different performance cultures for each of these organisations. This meant that the leader of each of these exhibit circus ringmasters had to be supported to enable them to develop the necessary and specific organisational performance culture.

To achieve this, the holding organisation's ringmaster needed to have a well-developed cognitive organisational awareness that enabled the collective intent of these combined sets of exhibits needed to deliver. The practice implicit in the notional model Fig. 33 ("Task Group Orientation") would have ensured that all the binding practices were designed to ensure each exhibit achieved the same quality of interactive service delivery. The binding of this notional holding group organisation was the designed, developed and managed practices and procedures that each exhibit ringmaster needed to practice. The failure, in organisational terms, to understand these organisational differences directly affected the servicing and delivery performance of the various contractual arrangements.

Differences in the employed technologies do affect the design and development of any organisation. For example, with The Central Show the high wire aerial performers were dependent on the structure and equipment. It is similar to a pilot who is dependent on the systems functioning correctly. The exhibits that employed technology did not have this level of safety dependency. The dependency factor meant that the contracts had to have a comprehensive maintenance schedule that needed to be managed to ensure the high wire performers were safe throughout the 999 performances. The Central Show was considered to be a resounding success from a visitor's perspective. It was delivered on time, on budget, to specified performance standards and without any contractual conflict.

The contractual behaviour within the exhibits' letting and management had not used the same rigorous letting procedures and had failed to factor in adequate on-going operational maintenance activities. If this had been factored into the letting of the contracts, some of the interactive exhibits would have designed equipment that could endure the interactive activities of the visitors. As a consequence, equipment failures would have not compromised visitors' experiences or fed the critical press with unwanted negative stories.

Consequential Outcomes

The invested political and intensive media interest coupled with the consequential costly overruns of some of the exhibits created a siege mentality for those attempting to retrospectively recover from those issues that had not been addressed at the contract letting stages. The raised anxiety became evident when the "chaos arrived, it served as an abrupt and brutal audit: at a moment's notice, everything that was left unprepared became a complex problem and every weakness comes rushing to the forefront."

This left individuals having to resolve complex problems that should have been resolved prior to the letting of these exhibit contracts and other service contracts, and before becoming a revenue generating organisation. They were not experienced and their first impulse was to grasp for some explanation, any old explanation. These retrospective recovery activities were a distraction and fed into the political, press and cost management of this visitor attraction; the anxiety was palpable.

The combination of the financial difficulties, the reduction of visitor numbers, the footfall, and the constant bad press compounded the sensed experience of being under siege. They were very aware of any failures finding their way into the public domain. The siege mentality was further put under pressure through the need to meet these essential demands that emanated internally from the dysfunctional operational organisation.

They were, after the event, attempting to develop the revenue control procedures and tighten all the processes for controlling the cash flow. There was a fixation with the need to meet the fixed deadline, which led to a sense of 'put the show on, and worry about the operating activities when they occur'. This, in turn, created unregulated management practices that had serious consequential, cost and service delivery outcomes at the visitor interface.

For example, the clearing and decontaminating of the site, from the start through to the completion of the construction of the Dome and its surrounding facilities was a standard capital regulated construction programme. In parallel the internal creative design would be developed in preparation for the next set of construction programmes and the introduction of the access facilities and the utilities support services. These developments would have been well defined to enable the support facilities to be incorporated into the Dome's construction. These programmes would be for the other exhibits, the central show and other facilities such as shops, restaurants and other small ad-hoc events along with all the service support facilities.

The next phase would broadly be the developed exhibits being designed ready for construction. This required that the contract being let for each of these programmes had to be designed to enable the capital construction, commissioning and maintenance programmes. It also required that these contracts be collectively designed to satisfy the future management of the operating facilities, which must include the operating revenue costs for managing each exhibit, which should also include the cost of the on-going maintenance programmes, and notionally having cost centres.

Reviewing many of the contracts for the exhibits, they nearly all failed to ensure that the capital costs were monitored to manage and controlled the programmes. They also failed to include operating monitoring to manage and control the revenue expenditure. The entire central show contracts were designed to enable the capital elements and the operational contractual arrangements to be successfully monitored to manage and be controlled over the life of the service delivery performance.

The reality of the financial situation became starkly evident when the managers were required to now change their management style from that required of managing a capital funded project to one of leading and managing a revenue generating operation. The manifest confusion produced the predictable reactions where the ... "the first impulse is to grasp for some explanation, any old explanation."

Approaches to Cost Recovery

In response to the created dilemmas, a new CEO was recruited and charged with virtually rescuing the organisation, and containing and recovering expenditure. A financial modelling systems approach to solving the problem and to establish where cost savings could be identified was being developed. This is a top down centralist approach where blanket instructions are formulated and introduced. Another person whose background was from the construction industry, not maintenance, was redeployed to develop and manage a planned maintenance system. All of these events were at the time when the operation had become a revenue-generating organisation. These activities were retrospective responses to the created financial crisis partly created through the failure to understand and manage the transitional organisational stages.

A lack of understanding, in organisational terms, of these phenomena that these changes created, had led to these acts of "superficiality" and "trivialisation" (Emery) where "anything is tried, which may effectively achieve a reduction in complexity." The problem with these situations is that these actions contribute and increase the dysfunctional decision-making, and personal and organisational behaviour. "When a situation becomes too complex for organised, meaningful learning, an organisation regresses to various trial and error behavioural responses, firstly to this and then to that, in a way which is unrelated to the structure of the environment, but it may be highly correlated with its prejudices." The result is that the anxiety driven decision-making causes the organisation to become dysfunctional, in that the managers internalise their focus and lose sight of the service delivery needs. We can connect these observations to management practices, which Argyris (1986) entitled "Skilled Incompetence." It neatly creates myths that we were 'doing something'.

It is essential that the costs are examined and where possible costs be reduced or at the very least brought into a manageable state. The conventional response to this type of crisis, the use of a cash driven single systems approach, is employed as described above. Usually there is a declaration that the service provision must not be affected. This conventional systems monitoring approach identified that circa two million pounds could be recovered by simply culling various budgets. This had the effect of increasing the line manager's frustration through the demand to bring the various exhibits up to the appropriate operating standard.

When compared with the employment of an organisational approach, identified further savings could be recovered along with a direct and significant improvement in the overall management of the service delivery functions. The important differences between the systems and organisational approaches were that the systems approach was retrospective, as it used information relating to events that had already taken place. Using an organisational approach caused you to work directly with the actual activities under examination to ensure it complied with the organisation's ethos, which allowed changes to existing practices to be immediately enacted. It directly generated cost savings from the realignment of the dysfunctional organisation. The value of the systems monitoring approach allows you to track the changes in the cost performance of the directly transferable organisational led approach.

An example of this direct approach was the examination of one contract that had been let to provide a chemical infusion into the open water systems to prevent Legionella, a life threatening airborne respiratory infection. Legionella is the collective name given to the pneumonia-like illness caused by legionella bacteria. Outbreaks of the illness occur from exposure to legionella growing in purpose-built systems where water is maintained at a temperature high enough to encourage growth, e.g. cooling towers, evaporative condensers, spa pools, and hot water systems used in all sorts of premises, business and domestic.

When physically inspecting all the systems listed for treatment, thirty percent were found to be closed systems and did not require treatment. The contractors agreed that the existing contract was indefensible and as a consequence agreed to reduce the contract to service only the open systems. To recover the cost each treatment was revised downward until the over expenditure had been recovered. To ensure they completed the agreed contractual treatment they were required to register their presence on site and sign off each treatment.

A person without any engineering background had organised this contract and the contractors simply took advantage. When the management systems are inappropriate they allow these variations to take place and they become accepted and become part of the institution's practices. The systems spreadsheet approach is unable, as the information is generated in isolation, to identify these contractual errors. That contract was operating within the agreed contractual parameters and would not be flagged up, as there were no expressed variations.

The important lessons we can learn from these two approaches is that they are interdependent. The cost generated profile can be effectively used to monitor the outcomes from the changes in organisational behaviour. The benefit of using an organisational approach is that the dysfunctional activities are addressed and rectified, with these changes being directly transferred into the organisation's improved performance. When you adopt a systems approach you identify the cost imperatives, and you then have to implement the changes that are necessary for recovering those retrospective costs.

The comparison has been used to demonstrate that these two approaches have an interdependent relationship. The centralised systems approach is useful for identifying the cost deviation and should be an on-going monitoring process. When managing transitional change it is useful for monitoring the changes in the generated cost profile during the management of the *transition for change processes*. The systems approach does not identify the root cause of the costs; it only identifies the retrospective elements of the generated costs.

Often, many of the unexplained costs are due to the accepted ingrained practices that have been generated by the dysfunctional organisational behaviour. Changing these dysfunctional practices and realigning the organisation has the effect of automatically identifying the dysfunctional elements and the consequential costs within the existing cost model.

This takes the form of exploring whether a cost profile from external sources had been produced, with each of these being specified against a service performance profile necessary to satisfy each activity. This would enable the service and cost profile to be clearly matched. The development of this information would enable any decisions to be compared against the created and contracted benchmarks, and then validated. The decision process could also be defended and as the process would have an effective audit trail within the accountability and political environment of this organisation, this would have been an essential practice.

The above process was not followed and contributed to this organisation becoming retrospectively managed. The cost profile produced in the conventional form only highlighted the consequential cost created by these dysfunctional organisational practices. An organisational leadership approach would test that the initial design was correct and test the kind of organisational and management decision-making. In parallel, the design of the organisation and its cost management practices would be completed to service the operational decision-making. An example would be that an examination of the technology would enable the areas of technological and skills demarcation to be appropriately determined. These areas of demarcation would each require a different type of organisation that would be driven by the technology and skills required and the responsive performance demands to maintain the visitor experience.

NMEC appointed a new chief executive, David Jones, on 5th of September 2000. He was a financial trouble-shooter brought in to help rescue the Dome and declining visitor numbers. He was not only required to rescue the current financial situation but also to manage the liquidation of the Dome's assets.

Dome Fraud

It was at the initial process stage for developing the contractual practices that the lighting contractor failed to comply with the scrutinising process of their organisation. They consistently prevaricated and refused to agree to their company's directors (responsible for the contract's delivery), to be identified and interviewed. These failures to comply and further prevarication caused concerns, which were flagged up. The lighting contractor prevaricated and complained about The Central Show's contract manager's (the client's agent) demands for compliance. The concern stemmed from the realisation that the lighting contractors were writing their own contracts.

These obvious and natural concerns increased the level of attention by the responsible contract manager for ensuring compliance. This resulted in complaints being levelled against the interference of The Central Show's contract manager responsible for the lighting contract. They structured the complaint to evoke the anxiety associated with the need to meet the fixed deadline. This was all designed to raise the senior contract manager's anxiety by coupling further complaints with a threat of a possible delay in the lighting contract's delivery. The increased anxiety had the effect of encouraging the head of contract management to take over the responsibility and the overseeing and letting of the lighting contract.

We should be able to make the connection with Argyris (1986) "Skilled Incompetence" as it neatly creates a myth that we were doing something, that is, in reality, is an act of "superficiality" and "trivialisation" (Emery). Unfortunately it was the wrong thing, the contractor should have been forced to comply and expose any potential fraudulent intent.

It was obvious that the behaviour was inappropriate when all other contractors were cooperating without question. These concerns were clearly expressed; even so, the senior contracts manager accepted full responsibility for any possible outcomes. The allegations relating to a lighting contract's mismanagement was the same kind of practice that occurs when systems are inappropriately designed and or applied.

The Central Show's contract manager was asked to examine those contracts that were 'haemorrhaging monies.' Within this brief the lighting contract was identified as needing immediate attention. It soon became obvious that the structure of the contract was inappropriate and invited fraudulent practices, which were part of the intent of the contractor who refused to work through the compliance process.

We have discussed in earlier chapters that when a system, the process and the regulatory management are not designed with appropriate intent it will provide opportunities for those practices to be mismanaged. The failure to heed the early warning signs that were identified at the letting and development stage of the lighting contract, allowed the creation of a poorly designed contractual practice. This meant that the earlier intent to defraud was missed and allowed circa £3 million to be fraudulently removed.

These failings were exposed when the lighting contract's operating practices for managing and controlling the work and cost of the contract were put under scrutiny. Further investigation of the paper trail, the decision trail and ordering practices soon began to expose inappropriate practices. When compared with the design and development of the contracts for the management of the Central Aerial Show they would have failed at the first hurdle. The existing practices were changed to ensure appropriate monitoring, regulating, cost management, commissioning of work and confirmation that those contractors employed actually attended site and completed the specified work. Instituting these standard regulatory controls practices began to expose that the orders were being funnelled through "phantom" business addresses. All of these observations were presented to the internal auditor.

Eventually four people were arrested over allegations of contract fraud at the Millennium Dome. Police allege that the New Millennium Experience Company (NMEC) may have unfairly awarded a lighting contract. The police claimed there was an, 'inappropriate relationship' between the lighting contractors and the NMEC. Scotland Yard's Serious Fraud Squad SO6 made the arrests as part of an on-going investigation. These people were finally convicted and imprisoned for defrauding circa £3 million from the NMEC. The Judge, when summing up, observed that the Central Show's contract manager's expressed concerns should have been acted upon, preventing this case coming to court.

Systems myths were also used to mask these fraudulent activities. They took the form of elaborate planning systems that were designed to create an air of being in control. For example, Planned Preventive Maintenance (PPM) and the productivity of those involved. The reality was that these various systems were not PPM systems; they were only reactive maintenance that gave a sense of critically high activity working and being in control. Even though some of these systems were very sophisticated and used electronic monitoring devices they failed to effectively monitor the employment of labour and costs. They were designed to appear effective but were acts of "superficiality" to mask the fraudulent practices. These activities also had the effect of appearing to be in control when in fact they were not. It was not until an applied organisational approach was used that the exposure of these fraudulent activities became evident and acted upon.

CASE STUDY ELEVEN

CANARY WHARF

TECHNOLOGY AND CHANGE

An installation contractor was losing money on the contracted work for Canary Wharf Limited. The subsequent recovery programme clearly demonstrated the failure to understand and fully engage with the new practices that provided this insight. They had failed to understand and engage with the rigorous regulatory management practices of Canary Wharf Limited and had failed to develop their own practices to complement the developed regulatory performance culture. Millions of pounds of justifiable variations were recovered, making the contract viable, with a distinct improvement in the practice of avoiding unnecessary variations. This was achieved through improved focused project management along with the development of inter-contractual working relationships.

To learn from any situation it is important to appreciate the *recent history* to understand the here and now. This will provide an insight into the reasons for the changes in the regulation of this contractual management technology.

In 1802 the West India Docks, London, opened and were considered to be the country's greatest civil engineering structure of the day. These docklands became the world's largest manmade inland waterways. The docks grew and developed over 200 years, with growth particularly fast in the 19th century. By the 1930's the Port of London carried 35 million tons of cargo, worth approximately £700m carried by 55,000 ship movements. 1961 saw the peak years for the docks when over 60 million tons of cargo was handled. Over 150,000

Dockers and ancillary workers were dependent on the Port of London Authority (PLA) for employment.

New technology, in the form of shipping containerisation, meant that London Docklands became uncompetitive and by early 1970's the docks had closed – West India dock, London, closed in 1980. Between 1966 and 1976 there were progressive disinvestments as the business of closing the five London Dockland boroughs created 150,000 job losses. This represented 20% of the jobs in the area. This can be compared to 2% for the whole of Great Britain. By 1981 the whole of the traditional docking industry had ceased to trade. (Refer to Chapter Nine, "Technology Change and Managing the Consequences" and the influence of containerisation on the docking industry.)

The London Dockland Development Corporation (LDDC) was created, its role was to secure regeneration by bringing land into use, to encourage industry and commerce and assist in providing housing along with social facilities. This became an Enterprise Zone that offered tax allowances for both investors and developers.

In 1985, G. Ware Travel Stead, proposed a 10 million sq. ft. office complex on the Canary Wharf site. They were unable to fund this scheme allowing it to be taken over by the North American developer, Olympia & York. In 1987 the master building agreement was signed between Olympia & York and the LDDC for a 12.2 million sq. ft. development at Canary Wharf. In 1988 construction began at Canary Wharf. In 1992 Olympia & York Canary Wharf Ltd went into administration. In 1993 Olympia & York Canary Wharf Ltd came out of administration, renamed Canary Wharf Limited.

Canary Wharf Limited, when it became responsible for the management of this massive project for the second time, learned from their experiences. The cause of Olympia & York going into administration was when the world property market collapsed in the 1990s. Tenant demands evaporated and the project was further hampered by failure of the development of the Jubilee Underground train services to be completed on time. These accumulative circumstances forced Olympia & York into administration. Their recovery was probably bolstered by the impending Millennium celebrations, which demanded that the Jubilee Underground train services be made ready. There was, as with any failure of a major event of this nature, a good deal of anxiety felt by commerce and the Government of the day, which all in turn influenced commercial decision-making and the need, with this new opportunity, to learn from the experience and getting it right.

Historically contractors had to win contracts, often making bids that could be described as 'loss leaders.' Within this practice of using a 'loss leader' approach to winning a contract, it encouraged a process of claiming inflated variations to offset any potential losses. With some contractors, this was their profit margin.

Canary Wharf Ltd, having been through this experience, must have been very aware of the need to make sure they could regulate, manage and control these various contractors to regulate and control their cash flow. They, for example, developed a process where contractors could bid for contracts and instituted a control process to prevent unwarranted variation claims. The market was extremely competitive and obtaining a contract carried a good deal of prestige. Some may have seen it, from a historical perspective, as an opportunity to make a good deal of money.

To complement these changes it was essential to move away from the construction industry's culture of profiting from variation, with its unpredictable financial outcomes, to one where these uncertainties were removed. To change the prevalent construction industry's culture and the critical need to manage cash flow effectively, they developed the necessary *management technologies* to control the contractors' responsibilities, accountability, authority and behaviour.

They appropriately shifted the responsibility for the delivery and coordination, for example, the multiple trades involved in any fit-out programme, to collectively take responsibility for avoiding situations where variations could be encountered. This is a form of using the systems management to monitor, regulate and control, which also introduces the necessary operant behaviour of the contractors. These variations to the contract could occur, for example, through delays of material being transported when on site, to other contractor's installation blocking, for example, a piping installation, or contractors not completing their programmed work on time. This all translated into delays and accumulated cost expressed as variations.

To change their behaviour, the contractors at the stage of tendering, were contracted to the defined boundaries of responsibility. An example, and it is a critical one, is the shift of responsibility for the management of variations. Historically, the main contractor would become involved in every dispute and be required to provide a solution. The changes made were that this responsibility became the collective responsibility of all the associated dependent fit-out contractors. They were charged with firstly, avoiding any disputes and secondly, to provide solutions in advance. If they failed and it caused a variation, they would collectively bear any generated variation cost. The fit-out contractors involved would determine, through discussion, calculate as to what proportion of the cost, they each would take responsibility for. The *management technologies* were all designed to ensure that this culture shift was achieved to ensure a controlled cash flow and the delivery performance of each contractor.

The *management technologies* were redesigned, for example, designing and letting of contract practice to reinforce the desired cooperative delivery performance culture. This enabled the contracts to be managed to defined boundaries of responsibility, authority and accountability through the appropriate development of policies, practices and procedures. Also the developing of the procedures for managing variations were all designed to reinforce the desired performance delivery culture. The employment of IT technology was extensive, successfully designed to support and reinforce the collective performance outcomes through the use of this *management technology*.

Learning from their experience and clearly defining what performance outcomes they required, the executives designed all their subsystems and supporting management technologies to ensure that this was consistently and effectively achieved. Borrowing a saying from quality management, "If you start right you will stay right." Some of the contractors did not survive the rigors of the new culture and lost money when they failed to make the transition from the old practice to the new performance culture. It was one of these companies that required an intervention to ensure it developed its own practices to successfully work within the created performance culture of Canary Wharf Ltd.

References

Adams. J. S. (1965) *Inequity and Social Exchange*. Adv. Exp. Psychology. 62.335-343.

Argyle. M. et al. (1970*) Extract from The British Journal of Social and Psychology*. Vol. 9, pp 222-31.

Argyle. M (1978) *the Psychology of Interpersonal Behaviour*. Penguin Books Ltd, England.

Argyris. C. (1999). *On Organizational Learning*. 2ed Blackwell publishing, England.

Argyris, C., & Schön, D. (1978) *Organizational learning: A theory of action perspective,* Reading, Mass: Addison Wesley.

Armstrong. D. 1995. Paper on *Groups Relations and Organisational Behaviour*. New Bulgarian University, Tavistock Centre Consultancy Services, London UK.

Arriely. D, Gneezy. U, Loweinstien. G, and Maxar. N. (2005) *Large Stakes and Big Mistakes,* Federal Reserve Bank of Boston working paper No 05-11.

Bale. R. F. (1950) *Interactive Process Analysis*. Cambridge, MA: Addison Wesley.

Baumeister, R. F. (1984) *Choking Under Pressure: Self-Consciousness and Paradox Effect of Incentives on Skills Performance,* Journal of Personality and Social Psychology, XLVI 361-383.

Bertalanffy, von, L. (1968). *General Systems Theory*. New York: Braziller.

Bennis, W. (1997). *The secrets of great groups, Leaders to Leaders.* (Winters).

Bhattacharyak, K. (1981). *How Companies Can Escape Degeneration and death.* The Boston Group of Consultancies.

Bion. W. (1967) *Experiences in Groups*. Tavistock Publication Ltd, London.

Blandford, A. & Wong, W. (2004). *Situation awareness in emergency medical dispatch*. International Journal of Human–Computer Studies, 61, 421–452... Arlington, VA: National Training Systems Association.

Brown. T (1994). *De-engineering the corporation*, Industrial Weekly, April 18. p. 18.

Bruce. A. L. (1965) *Systematic Methods of Design*. London Council of Industrial design. OCLC 2108433.

Burns, T., Stalker, G.W. (1961). *The Management of Innovation*. Tavistock, London.

Burns. T. (1963). Industry in a New Age. New society. In Pugh. D. S. (1971). *Organizational Theory*. Penguin Books, England.

Burn, T. (1963). *Mechanistic and Organistic Structures in Pugh*, G. H. (Ed) (1978), Organizational Theory, Penguin Books Ld., England.

Bateson. G., Jackson. G. D., Haley. J and Weakland. J. (1956). *Towards a Theory of Schizophrenia*. In Behavioural Sciences, Vol. 1, 251-264.

Carlson. N. R. Et al. (1999). *Psychology: The Science of Behaviour. Prentice Hall*.

Carlson. N. R. et al (2003). *Psychology the Science of behaviour. Pearson's, Canada,* United States of America.

Chemiss. C. (2000). *Emotional Intelligence: What it is and why it Matters. Paper presented at the Annual meeting of the Society for Industrial and organizational Psychology*, New Orleans, and LA.

Cialdini. R. B. (2007). Influence: the Psychology of Persuasion. Harper and Collins Pub. New York.

Cox. C, J. & Cooper. G. L. (1988). High Flyers – *An Anatomy of Managerial success.*

Davenport. T & Short. J. (1990), *the New Industrial Engineering: Information Technology and Business Process Redesign,* in: Sloan Management Review, summer 1990, pp 11–27.

527

Davenport, Thomas (1995), *Reengineering – The Fad That Forgot People, Fast Company*, November 1995.

Deming. W. E (1986) *Out of the crisis*. MIT Press.

Dewey, J (1981) *The Philosophy of John Dewey*, Edited by J, McDermott.

Dewey. J. (1998) *the Essential Dewey: Volumes 1 & 2* Edited by L Hickman and Thomas Alexander. Indiana University Press.

Dixon. N. F. (1976). *On the Psychology of Military Incompetence*. Pimlico, London.

Dixon. N. F. (1989). *Why do leaders Mislead?* In The Nuclear Mentality. A Psychological Analysis of the Arms Race. Ed. Barnett. L. & Lee. I. Pluto Press, London.

Drucker. P. (1964) *Managing for Results*. New York Harper & Row.

Emery, F.E., Trist, E.L. (1973). *Towards a Social Ecology*. Contextual Appreciations of the Future in the Present. Plenum Press, London.

Endsley, M. R. (1995b). *Toward a theory of situation awareness in dynamic systems*. Human Factors 37(1), 32-64.

Endsley, M. R., & Jones, W. M. (2001). *A model of inter- and intra-team*.

Endsley. M. R., McNeese. M., & Salas. E. (Eds.) (2001). *New trends in cooperative activities: Understanding system dynamics in complex environments*. Santa Monica, CA: Human Factors and Ergonomics Society

Flin, R. & O'Connor, P. (2001). *Applying crew resource management in offshore oil platforms*. In E. Salas, C.A. Bowers, & E. Edens (Eds.), Improving.

Gray. P. (2010). Psychology. Worth. NY. 6th Ed pp108-109. *Situation awareness: Implications for design, training and measurement*.

Greenbaum. J. (1995). *Windows on the workplace*. Cornerstone.

Goffman, E. (1974) *Frame Analysis*, publisher, Harvard University Press.

Gouldner, A. W. (1955A). *Patterns of Industrial Bureaucracy*. Routledge & Kegan Paul.

Gouldner, A. W. (1955B). *Wildcat Strikes*, Routledge & Kegan Paul.

Hacker, J. S. Pierson. P. (2010). *Winneners Take-All Politics*. Simon & Schuster.

Hammer, M. (1993) *Reengineering the Corporation. A Manifestation for Business Revolution*. Nicolas Beasley Ltd, London.

Harlow, H. F.Kuenne., M. and Donald. M. R. (1950), *Learning Motivated by a Manipulation Drive* Journal of Experimental Psychology, Vol. 40(2), 228-234.

Henslin, J. (2008). *Sociology: a down to earth approach* (9th Ed). Person education.

Hersey. & Blanchard (1969). *Life Cycle Theory of leadership*. Training and Development Journal.
Hersey, P. & Blanchard, K. H. (1969). *Management of Organizational Behavior – Utilizing Human Resources*. New Jersey/Prentice Hall.
Herzberg. F. (1959). *The Motivation to Work. New York*, John Wiley and Sons

Hutton, G. (1962). *Management in a Changing Mental Hospital*. Human Relations **15,** 283–310. *Managing Systems in Hospitals*. Human Relations **15.** 311-33.

Hutton, G. (1972) *Thinking about Organisation*. Second Edition. Tavistock Publication in association with Bath University Press.

Irlenbusch. B. (2009). *When performance-related pay backfires, London School of Economics.*

Jaffee. A. L. (2003) *Wheels of Justice Turn Slowly*. Netwmd.com.

Jaques. E. (1955). *Social Systems as a Defence against Persecutory and Depressive Anxiety*. In New directions in psychoanalysis. London. Tavistock publication; New York: basic Book.

Johnson, A. (1983) *Technology, Change & Managing the Consequences*. M.Sc. Thesis, University of Bath School of Management

Kable. J. C. *Analysing Decision Preference – People and Jobs*. Queensland Institute of Technology, Australia.

Kolb (D. A. (1946) *Experiential Learning: experiences the source of learning and development.* Englewood Cliffs, Prentice Hall.

Kuhn. T. (1962). *The structure of Scientific Revolution.* 1st ed., Pub, Chicago: University of Chicago.

Katz, D., Kahn. (1978). *the Social Psychology or Organisations.* John Whiley and Sons, New York.

Kotter. J. P. (2008) *A Sense of Urgency.* Harvard Business Review Press

Kübler-Ross E. (1969) *On Death & Dying.*

Lagadec, P. (1993) *Preventing Chaos in a Crisis,* publisher, McGraw & Hill.

Landsberger. H. A. (1958) *Hawthorne Revisited.* Ithaca.

Lawrence, P. R., Lorsch, J. W. (1967). *Organisational Environment.* Harvard University Press

Leth, S. A. (1994) *Critical Success Factors for reengineering Business Processes. National productivity Review,* September 22 P. 557

Lewin. K. (1947) *Frontiers in group dynamics.* University of Chicago Press.

Lewin, K. (1963) *Field Theory in Social Science.* N.Y.: Harper, and London Tavistock.

Likert. R. (1961). *New Patterns of Management.* McGraw-Hill, London.

Lucian. B. Yaniv. G. (2005). *The Growth of Executive Pay. Harvard University: John. M. Olin Centre for Law, Economic and Business.*

Mayo. E. (1949) *Hawthorne and the Western Electric Company, the Social Problems of an Industrial Civilisation.* Routledge.

Maslow. A. H. (1943) *A Theory of Human Motivation,* Psychology Review 50, 370-96.

Maslow, A. H. (1943) *Motivation and Personality.* Harper & Row, New York.

Menzies, I. E. P. (1970). *The function of Social systems as a defence Against Anxiety.* Tavistock Pamphlet No. 3.

Miller. E. J. (1959) *Technology, Territory and Time*: the internal differentiation of complex production systems, Human Relations 12, 143-72.

Miller, E. J. (1959). *Technology Territory & Time*. Human Relations, Vol. 12, pp. 243-272.

Miller, E.J. & Rice, A.K. (1967). Systems *of Organisations, the Control of Task & Sentient Boundaries.* Tavistock Publications, London.

Minow. N. (2012). *Executive Decisions.* Tnr.com

Mintzberg. H. (1973) *the Nature of Management at Work.* New York: harper and Row.

McCormack. M. H. (1984*) what they don't teach you at the Harvard business School.* Pub: William Collins, United Kingdom.

Merton, R. K. (1940). *Bureaucratic Structure and Personality Social* No. 18, pp. 650-568. In Pugh, D. S. (Ed) (1971) Organisation Theory Penguin Book Ltd., England.

Morgenson. G. (2010). *Angelo Mozilo of Countrywide Settles Fraud Case for $65 Million.* New York Times.

Morris. F. (2000). *WorldCom Scramble to Raise Cash.* Nyt.com.

Nyquist. J.R. (2009). White Paper on Strategic Crisis 2009
The Decline of American Power, Military Decrepitude and CIA Incompetence.

Obholzer. A. (1989). *The Comfort in Groups.* In The Nuclear Mentality. A Psychological Analysis of the Arms Race. Ed. Barnett. L. & Lee. I. Pluto Press, London.

Patler. L, *Tilt! Irreverent lessons for leading innovations in the new economy.* 1999. Pub Capstone Publishing Limited, Oxford, United Kingdom P. 11.

Peter. T. & Waterman. (1982). In *search of Excellence.*

Phillips, D. L. (1973) *Abandoning Method.* Jossey-Bass, London

Pink D.H. (2005), Drive, *The Surprising Truth about What Motivates Us,* first Pub, Riverhead Books, imprint of penguin Group (USA) Inc.

Porter. M. (1980) *Competitive Strategy*. Free Press. New York

Porter. M. (1985) *Competitive Advantage*. Free Press. New York

Pugh. D. S. (1971). Senge. P. M. (1993) *The Fifth Discipline, The Art and practice of the learning Organization*. Century Business. London, *Organizational Theory*. Penguin Books, England

Rice, A. K. (1958). *Productivity and Social Organisations: The Ahmedabad Experiment*. Tavistock Publications. London.

Rice, A. K. (1963). *The Enterprise and its Environment*. Tavistock Publications. London.

Schon, D. A. (1965). *Technology and Change*. Pergamon Press, London.

Senge. P. M. (1993) *The Fifth Discipline, The Art and practice of the learning Organization*. Century Business. London.

Stanley, M. (1974). *"The Perils of Obedience."* Harper's *Magazine*. Archived from the original on 2011-05-14.Abridged and adapted from *Obedience to Authority*.

Tapscott. D. & Williams. A. D. (2006) *Wikinomics – How Mass Collaboration Changes Everything*. Atlantic Books Ltd, London, England.

Trist. E. A. and Bamford. K. W. (1951) *Some Social and Psychological Consequences of the Long wall Method of Coal Getting*. Human Relations Vol. 4. 1951.

Trist et al. (1963) *the Social Psychology of Organisations 2nd*. Katz. & Kahn. L. (1978) John Wiley & Sons, Inc.

Trigaux. R. (2002). *Corporate Scandal Same Story Different Company*. sptimes.com.

Wageman, R., Nunes, D. A., Burruss, J. A. & Hackman, J. R. (2008) Senior Leadership Teams. Harvard Business School Press, Boston.

Walton. R. E. (1972) *How to Counter Alienation in the Plant*. Harvard Business review.

Woodward, J. (1965). *The Theory of Social and Economic Organisations* Free Press, New York.

Woodward. J. (1965) *Industrial Organisations: Theory and Practice*. Oxford University Press Business Library.

Woolf, H.K. and Tumins, S. (1991) *Prison Disturbances*, April 1990: Report of an Inquiry by Rt. Hon. Lord Justice Woolf (Parts 1 and 2 and his Honour Judge Stephen Tumim (Part 2), Cm. 1454. London HMSO.

Yerkes, R. M., Dodson, J. D. (1908) *the Relationship of Strength of Stimulation to Rapidity of Habit-Formation*, Journal of Comparative Neurology of Psychology XVIII 459-482.